Late Victorian
Literary Collaboration

LIVERPOOL ENGLISH TEXTS AND STUDIES 102

LATE VICTORIAN LITERARY COLLABORATION

Authorship, Co-Authorship, and Popular Fiction

ANNACHIARA COZZI

LIVERPOOL UNIVERSITY PRESS

First published 2024 by
Liverpool University Press
4 Cambridge Street
Liverpool
L69 7ZU

Copyright © 2024 Annachiara Cozzi

Annachiara Cozzi has asserted the right to be identified as the author of this book in accordance with the Copyright, Designs and Patents Act 1988.

All rights reserved. No part of this book may be reproduced, stored in a retrieval system, or transmitted, in any form or by any means, electronic, mechanical, photocopying, recording, or otherwise, without the prior written permission of the publisher.

British Library Cataloguing-in-Publication data
A British Library CIP record is available

ISBN 978-1-83553-686-5

Typeset by Carnegie Book Production, Lancaster

For Lia Guerra, inspiring scholar, teacher, and friend

Contents

Acknowledgements	ix
Abbreviations	xi
List of Illustrations	xii
Introduction	1
1 Walter Besant and James Rice	25
2 E. Œ. Somerville and Martin Ross	95
3 Fashionable Collaborations	161
4 Literary Collaboration and the Late Victorian Imagination	201
5 Literary Collaboration and the Figure of the Author	233
Appendix: A selection of co-authored novels, c. 1860–1920	267
Bibliography	273
Index	289

Acknowledgements

This project started even before my academic career did. It was 2016: I was twenty-four, just graduated, and working as a teacher at Trinity College Dublin. One day my boss, Cormac Ó Cuilleanáin, hosted a dinner where I met a young researcher, Francesca Medaglia. She was going to give a lecture the following day. I didn't feel inclined to attend, but politeness made me go. There were very few people at the conference. My expectations were low. Then Dr Medaglia started to speak: she talked of a novel written collaboratively by F. T. Marinetti and Enif Robert. It was the first time I had heard of literary collaboration: I had always thought of creative writing as a solitary activity – indeed, *the* most solitary activity. I could not visualize it as something to be shared. I was captivated.

I started to wonder if some cases of collaboration could be found in English literature. I expected few. I was so wrong: just by surfing the net, I found so many. And I discovered that literary collaboration had in fact been common in the last part of the Victorian era. Now, I interpreted this as a sign: I had always found the Victorians fascinating.

In the early summer of that year I came back home, to Pavia, and went to the professor of my MA thesis, Lia Guerra. She immediately encouraged me to pursue the project. So, I plunged into research. I remember bringing her, some time later, a ridiculously long list of collaborations, which included poetry, drama, and fiction from various geographical areas. I also remember how she remarked that the project lacked focus, and that it was unrealistic. I walked out of her office into the hot summer streets, feeling dispirited. But – as always – she was right. I pulled myself together, and with her help I outlined a PhD project on Victorian co-authored novels. That project became my full-time job for three years. After discussing my dissertation in 2020, I kept working on the subject for another three years as a post-doctoral researcher. *Late Victorian Literary Collaboration* is the outcome of it all.

My first, most heartfelt thanks must go to Professor Guerra. Long before supporting my PhD project she inspired and sustained my passion for English literature. I will always remember her reading *Frankenstein* in class and how we, sophomore students, all listened enthralled. When I graduated, she encouraged me to go to Dublin. When I worked with her during my PhD and post-doc years, day after day she offered not only invaluable scholarly insights but also unfailing generosity and kindness. She remains the model to aspire to.

My dearest thanks go to Silvia Granata, who brilliantly stepped into the role of my tutor in these last years. I own a huge debt to her for her support and patience during my weekly airing of problems connected with this work. Her advice and her countless readings of the book through its various stages provided enormous help; her acute intelligence and eagle eye are matched by thoughtfulness, sympathy and a brilliant sense of fun.

I want to sincerely thank Elena Cotta Ramusino, who read my drafts with patience and generously commented on them. She provided me with precious feedback and many helpful suggestions. Her great expertise on Irish literature and history helped me approach the partnership of Edith Somerville and Martin Ross from the period of the writing of my thesis.

I remain deeply indebted to my editor, Christabel Scaife, for believing in this book and giving me the opportunity to publish with Liverpool University Press. I hope to express here some fraction of my sincere thanks. I am grateful to the readers of my book manuscript, who provided thoughtful and engaged readings: I have benefited greatly from them.

My thanks and esteem go to Mariaconcetta Costantini for the interest she has always shown in my work: her encouragement kept me motivated. For many years now I have been presenting portions of my research at national and international conferences, and am especially grateful to *Victorian Popular Fiction Association* and *British Women Writers Association* for their encouragement. Kirsty Bunting, host of my very first conference back in 2017, deserves special notice for showing so much enthusiasm about my project, thus reassuring me that I was going in the right direction.

These years have put me in touch with wonderful people – above all Serena Codena, remarkable scholar, even more remarkable friend. Thanks to Dario Russotti, brilliant artist, for giving visible form to my thoughts in the illustration for the cover of this book. Last but not least, big thanks go to Chicco, who brightens my days without even realizing it.

Abbreviations

Autobiography   Walter Besant. 1902. *Autobiography of Sir Walter Besant*. London: Hutchinson & Co.

CA   Walter Besant and James Rice. 1878a. *By Celia's Arbour*. London: Sampson Low & Co.

IM   Edith Œ. Somerville and Martin Ross. 1917. *Irish Memories*. London: Longmans, Green & Co.

Letters   Gifford Lewis, ed. 1989. *The Selected Letters of Somerville and Ross*. London: Faber & Faber.

"Lit. Coll."   Walter Besant. 1892c. "On Literary Collaboration." *The New Review* 6.33: 200–09.

MFB   Walter Besant. [1894] 1897. "Ready-Money Mortiboy." In *My First Book*, edited by Jerome K. Jerome, 2–14. London: Chatto & Windus.

PB   Walter Besant. 1899a. *The Pen and the Book*. London: Thomas Burleigh.

RMM   Walter Besant. 1887. Preface to *Ready-Money Mortiboy: A Matter-of-Fact Story*, by Walter Besant and James Rice. London: Chatto & Windus.

"Two"   Edith Œ. Somerville and Martin Ross. [1946] 1952. "Two of a Trade." In *Dr. E. Œ. Somerville: A Biography*, by Geraldine Cummins, 180–86. London: Andrew Dakers.

Illustrations

1	Title page of *Ready-Money Mortiboy*, by Walter Besant and James Rice	38
2	Portrait of James Rice in *My First Book*, ed. by Jerome K. Jerome	47
3	Portrait of Walter Besant in *My First Book*, ed. by Jerome K. Jerome	48
4	Portrait of Walter Besant in *My First Book*, ed. by Jerome K. Jerome	49
5	"The Oyster Shop" in *My First Book*, ed. by Jerome K. Jerome	49
6	Cover of *An Irish Cousin*, by Edith Somerville and Martin Ross	125
7	Monogram of Somerville and Ross, designed by Edith Somerville	153
8	*The World's Desire*, by Andrew Lang and Henry Rider Haggard	169
9	*The World's Desire*, by Andrew Lang and Henry Rider Haggard	170
10	Title page of *The Fate of Fenella*	187
11	Cover of *The Fate of Fenella*	190
12	Frontispiece of *The Fate of Fenella*	197
13	Prefatory Note to *The Green Bay-Tree*, by W. H. Wilkins and Herbert Vivian	227

Introduction

"Why shouldn't we collaborate?" said Henley in his most matter-of-fact way, as the Big Ben gave voice to the midnight hour. "Everybody does it nowadays. Two heads may be really better than one, although I seldom believe in the truth of accepted sayings. [...] I think you were born to collaborate, and to collaborate with me." (Hichens, 1896, 138)

These are the first words of a short story entitled "The Collaborators." Written by Robert Hichens and published in 1896, it portrays two long-time friends who dream of becoming novelists. The pragmatic Jack Henley believes that, by joining forces with his impulsive but imaginative colleague Andrew Trenchard, they will achieve "popular success" (139):

"We are both ambitious devils. We are both poor. We are both determined to try a book. Have we more chance of succeeding if we try one together? I believe so. You have the imagination, the grip, the stern power to evolve the story [...] I can lighten that way. I can plant a few flowers [...] on the roadside. And I can, what is more, check you when you wish to make the story impossibly horrible or fantastic to the verge of the insane. [...] Cheer up, old fellow, and be thankful that you possess a corrective in me." (140)

Recognizing the convenience of the proposal, Trenchard gives in: "'I believe you are right, and that I need a collaborator, an opposite, who is yet in sympathy with me. Yes. Either of us might fail alone; together we should succeed'" (140).

The arrangement may sound unlikely, even bizarre, to us, but it was not so when the story appeared in print. Actually, it must have sounded quite familiar to its contemporary readers. As a matter of fact, literary collaboration was a remarkably widespread practice in the last decades of the nineteenth century.[1] Several among the most celebrated writers of

---

[1] In collaboration studies, the terms 'collaboration' and 'co-authorship' are generally

the time tried their hands at it at least once: Rhoda Broughton, Wilkie Collins, Arthur Conan Doyle, Joseph Conrad, Charles Dickens, Henry Rider Haggard, Henry James, Rudyard Kipling, Margaret Oliphant, Robert Louis Stevenson, Bram Stoker, and Mark Twain – to mention just a few names – all took part in collaborative ventures. By the 1890s, collaboration was in its heyday. The hottest literary trend of the moment, it became the centre of a heated public debate raging in the pages of periodicals: how could the creation of a literary text – an act held almost sacred and so connected with the individual self – be shared among different people? How did collaboration work? What were its advantages, and what its limits? But also, why did it feel somewhat unnatural, if not utterly disturbing? Was it really something to be recommended? Whenever collaboration appeared, it always attracted people's attention and often aroused controversy. Novels co-written by two, three, four, and even more than twenty authors were serialized in popular weeklies and scored big sales. Collaboration was, truly, a money-making machine. Hichens's choice of topic and title for his story was part of a clever marketing strategy.

Collaboration and popular literature were strictly interwoven. Late Victorian co-authorship was by no means a phenomenon created by, or limited to, an intellectual elite. On the contrary, it sprang from, and was meant for, the popular market: first as a way to cope with it, later as a way to exploit it. By the 1870s the literary profession presented a crowded scene. The Education Acts, which were passed between 1870 and 1891, gradually led to a free, universal, and compulsory elementary education, creating the first true mass readership. All through the nineteenth century, the reading public had been expanding downwards through all levels of society. The population had been steadily growing, increasing from ten and a half million in 1801 to thirty-seven million in 1901 (Harrison, 2000, 2). The rise of the lower middle classes, the professional advancement of women, and the advent of New Journalism further contributed to widening the reading audience. Moreover, a cheaper kind of paper imported from North Africa and rapid technological progress in printing allowed for cheaper and faster methods of mass production. In the second half of the century, thanks to the gradual abolition of taxes on paper, advertising and the circulation of printed material, the number and accessibility of books and periodicals reached an unprecedented

> used interchangeably, with no fixed norm. Throughout this work, I will use 'collaboration' and 'co-authorship' as synonyms.

climax (Gabriele, 2009, 68; Patten, 2016, 482–88). The production and circulation of periodicals expanded to an unparalleled degree, along with the practice of publishing fiction in instalments. The Victorian age witnessed a shift from the predominance of the monthly serialization in a relatively expensive, low-circulation format for the bourgeois market to the weekly serialization in a cheaper, high-circulation format for the mass market (Gabriele, 2009, 43). By the mid-1860s, a wide variety of cheap weekly magazines combining instalment fiction with other instructive and entertaining features addressed a broad family audience ranging from the middle classes down to the servants (Law, 2000, 25). Popular weekly journals hosted the highest amount of fiction, and by the 1880s well-constructed syndicates for works by major writers could easily achieve well over a million sales in the UK alone (Law, 2000, 131).

The rise of the weekly miscellany, the emergence of the serialized novel as a major form of fiction publication, and the practice of syndication contributed significantly to the growth in both number and the economic security of novel writers. As the literary market expanded, new opportunities were created for authors (Patten, 2016, 496–97). Literature became a commodity, and for the first time in history the writing of fiction started to be not so drastically different from any other form of commercial or industrial production. The professionalization of authorship during this period remodelled and widened the ways in which writers practised and conceptualized their work. Such an atmosphere "enabled a proliferation of authors of all abilities and types" (Jamison, 2016, 5) and, within a few decades, the number of people "who could and did identify themselves as 'writers'" dramatically increased (Ashton, 2003, 2). The development of "the mass labour force of writers" (Ashton, 2003, 3) had two key consequences. The first was the creation of a professional group identity, which led to the establishment of leagues of writers, such as the Society of Authors, fighting for better pecuniary recognition; such associations marked late Victorian writers' sense of belonging to a professionalized class, increasingly concerned with the legitimization of the commercial position of the author. The second consequence was the intensification of the pressure to break from the pack.

A highly competitive literary market could be one of the reasons for the abundance of alliances of authors in this period – namely, for the phenomenon of literary collaboration. McDonald's (1997, 19) observation that "immediate commercial competitors are collaborators in the final analysis" proves true in this case: by competing for the same market and producing more or less similar products, authors of popular fiction were economic rivals who could also turn into allies following a two-heads-are-better-than-one strategy. Ashton (2003, 18) observes that "the frenetic literary marketplace of the late nineteenth [...] century was so complex that it is not at all remarkable that new ways to negotiate such terrain were explored." By forming alliances, authors managed to find their voice, to conquer the marketplace, or simply to profit from a public which increasingly hungered for novelties.

This book argues that it is not possible to fully understand the fascinatingly complex nature of nineteenth-century literary culture without acknowledging that, from the 1870s to the turn of the century, the practice of co-authorship constituted a significant feature of the marketplace. As the twentieth century advanced, however, the fashion for collaboration disappeared almost as quickly as it had arisen. What is more, it did not just vanish: collaborative authorship became looked down upon, held in contempt, its problems considered more relevant than its benefits. Late Victorian collaborators and their outputs were increasingly pushed to the margins and eventually forgotten.

An underestimated phenomenon

Late Victorian collaboration has received little attention so far, either from literary scholars and publishers or from the general public. Apart from some notable exceptions, Victorian collaborative novels are hard to find and mostly out of print. Major survey texts on nineteenth-century literature, such as *The Cambridge History of Victorian Literature* (Flint, 2012) or *The Oxford Handbook of Victorian Literary Culture* (John, 2016), do not take co-authorship practices into consideration. Scholars generally overlook collaborators and their texts, and studies that focus upon single writers tend to downplay their collaborative ventures or dismiss them altogether. The problem is not just with nineteenth-century collaboration: it goes far deeper, to literary collaboration itself. Therefore, before delving into a discussion of late Victorian collaboration, it is worth looking at the causes for such neglect.

Sustained scholarship on literary collaboration started in the 1990s and has generally ascribed the striking omission of collaborative texts from the canon to an overinvestment in the concept of "the solitary genius," to borrow Jack Stillinger's term (1991). Ever since the Romantic period, the concept of the artist as a solitary genius who creates original works of art in isolation in his garret (*his*, as the hero-artist is traditionally male) has imposed itself as a fundamental feature of the artistic process, excluding any other understanding of authorship. Jamison (2016, 15) argues that readerly and scholarly preference for the solitary genius stems from an oversimplification of the Romantic tenets of originality and authorship. The model of "the author as God the Father of the Text" (Moi, 1985, 2) ignores or displaces contribution from others as an important component of artistic creation. The result has been that "the traditional literary canon [...] rest[s] upon a belief in the individual author" (Karell, 2002, 20). Critical attitudes towards co-authorship, consequently, "derive from and arguably maintain the myth of the singular author-genius" (Jamison, 2016, 15).

Collaborative writing does not conform to the inherited Romantic model of authorship – even worse, it challenges it, as "[t]he sharing of textual spaces, and the dispersal of authorial ownership and control" (Jamison, 2016, 81) defy the notion of the "single, trustworthy authorial voice" (Bunting, 2019, 23). Ede and Lunsford (1990, 85) underline that collaboration breaks the "organic connection" between author and text, illustrating how the idea of the solitary author inherited from the study of literature has blinded us to the fact that writing is not generally a solitary practice; they also emphasize that the higher the literary value associated with a work, the less credit has been given to co-authorship. Boucharenc (2000, 100) comments on the subversive potential of the collaborative author, who "appears as a dissident in relation to the official figure of the Author." Indeed, argues Masten (1997, 16), traditional criticism has considered co-authorship as "a mere subset [...] kind of authorship, [...] the collusion of two unique authors whom subsequent readers could discern and separate out by examining the traces of individuality and personality [...] left in the collaborative text." Masten further suggests that many people experience the reading of a co-authored text as decentring: when we question long-standing definitions of authorship as an inspired, isolated, and isolating enterprise, we risk altering our understanding of the world and of our place at the centre of it.

Such a tradition of celebrating literature as the outpouring of an inspired genius has caused critical disregard for collaborative practices. However, the issues with literary collaboration do not end here: the term 'collaboration' is itself problematic. Koestenbaum (1989, 8), Laird (2000, 6), Karell (2002, 23), and Jamison (2016, 33) all point out that the OED defines collaboration as an act of working together, especially in intellectual work; however, it then gives "traitorous cooperation with the enemy" as a second meaning. Thus, a collaborator is "simultaneously friend and foe, partner and colluder, colleague and turncoat, teammate and mole" (Jamison, 2016, 33). In wartime, "collaborators are traitors who join the enemy" (Koestenbaum, 1989, 8). Collaboration somehow still suggests the meaning it acquired during the Nazi occupation of France, and the word has come to connote moral bankruptcy, treason, stratagems, and suspicious deals. Literary collaborators thus bear the stain of the term's political meaning: "the sense lingers that they, like collaborators in Vichy France, have compromised themselves, have formed new and unhealthy alliances, and have betrayed trusts" (Koestenbaum, 1989, 8). Therefore, collaboration is often viewed as "an inherently suspicious, even unethical process" (Karell, 2002, xxxiii). Ashton (2003, 15) highlights that in literature and the humanities collaboration is usually felt as "intrinsically subversive," whereas scientific co-authorship "has long been used to promote efficiency, production, and even authority. Many names on a scientific document can enhance its authority."

Dever (1995, 68) observes that collaboration has been relegated to the ranks of the creative freak show: the collaborator is "the two-headed author." Like anonymity, collaboration has been mostly understood as an enigma, as a riddle that engenders detective work, as Bunting (2019, 24) remarks. Indeed, the small amount of scholarship on collaboration traditionally focused on identifying and isolating individual contributions, viewed as the most intriguing and instinctive approach. "What is true for academic discourse," notes London (1999, 3), "appears even truer in the popular imagination, where the idea of the solitary author is so deeply entrenched as to leave no room for other possible configurations." The curiosity about sorting out individual responsibilities in a co-authored text seems to be just 'natural.' London (1999, 73) observes that readers inexorably "betray a fascination with the 'mechanics' of collaboration, with the nuts and bolts of 'how they did it.'" The question "who wrote what?" in front of a co-authored text "reflects both a fundamental disbelief in collaboration and a certain prurient interest – a desire to make collaboration rend up its bodily secrets" (26). Collaborative writing "has always invited the gaze even as it resists visualization" (26). All discourses surrounding literary collaboration indeed appear almost as discourses of voyeurism.

All these considerations apply to literary collaboration in the late Victorian era, which is the focus of this book. When looking at nineteenth-century articles on co-authored novels, it is notable that Victorians expressed a particularly intense curiosity – even anxiety – concerning the dynamics behind the collaborative process. Reactions from co-authors varied greatly: some indignantly refused to have their

INTRODUCTION

co-authorship dissected, claiming that it was impossible to separate their personal contributions, while others addressed (or, actually, further spurred) the public's curiosity by constructing deliberately opaque narratives in which they promised to reveal how collaboration worked, sometimes with surprising and contradictory results. Especially during the 1890s, many commentaries by popular authors on their experiences as collaborators appeared in print. Such accounts were often reflections of the writing process itself, almost an exposition of the physical act of writing. The insistence on questions about 'which hand held the pen' suggests that, as authorship became increasingly professionalized, writing itself – the act of putting pen and ink to paper – came to be seen as the last preserve of artistic integrity. Since co-authorship denies the 'author/ity' of a single holder of the pen – some co-authors even rejected the validity of the question – it was often perceived as denying the special claims of the literary. The difficulty or the sheer impossibility of authoring parts of a text triggered far-reaching questions about how and where authorship could be located: what constitutes an author? Who gets counted under the category? Does an author exist before the pen makes a mark on paper, or even without even the actual act of writing? What happens to the idea of textual property when even co-authors themselves cannot tell their hands apart? This book addresses such questions from two perspectives: the point(s) of view of collaborators (for they were many and diverse) and the perspective(s) of the Victorian reading public.

Drawing on articles in nineteenth-century periodicals and on the commentaries and metadiscourses by collaborators, this book also deals with the subsequent obscurity of Victorian collaborations due to late nineteenth-century aesthetic discourses on what constituted first- and second-rate literature and first- and second-rate authors. I argue that they have been forgotten because they were actually dismissed at the very moment they emerged, or shortly thereafter. In examining late Victorian co-authorship, I found that the idea of collaboration as an unhealthy alliance goes far back. After a first wave of enthusiasm, literary collaboration was seen as improper, even harmful, for the respectable man of letters. The Victorian imagination increasingly degraded it to an inferior and aberrant practice, collaborative works appearing as promiscuous and unnatural. As mentioned above, critical studies on collaboration mostly ascribe the absence of co-authors and co-authored works from the canon to the fact that co-authorship presents challenges to accepted notions of authorship. Although they provide insightful starting points, they do not examine what the practical consequences were of the Romantic conception of authorship for Victorian readers, editors, publishers, agents, and, most importantly, co-authors. Some prolific and successful collaborators astonishingly displayed a strong belief in the myth of the inspired solitary author, going so far as to deny collaborative texts – *their* texts – any artistic value. No wonder that Victorian co-authored novels quickly lost visibility. I argue that the exclusion of Victorian collaborators from contemporary critical attention is not simply ascribable to the unsettling implications of co-authorship itself; more concretely, such exclusion has its roots in their days, back in the nineteenth century, in the very context in which such collaborations developed, flourished, and perished.

Another possible cause for the obscurity into which late Victorian collaborative works have sunk might be related to genre issues. Writing for the popular market, co-authors adopted the trendiest genres of the time: mostly adventure, sensation, mystery, and sentimental novels. These genres have generally been marginalized and excluded from the body of literature worthy of critical attention. The absence of co-authored novels from the canon might thus be partly ascribed to the fact that they belonged to the genres liable to be read and put aside a week later. The fact that they were written in collaboration further demeaned them.

State of the art and aims of the book

This study explores how and why the phenomenon of late Victorian collaboration passed from obscurity to fame and vice versa. It argues that collaboration in novel writing – notwithstanding its popularity – has been marginalized by critics almost from the very beginning. It should not come as a surprise, then, that it plunged into oblivion as soon as the fashion wore out. Co-authorship's intrinsic destructive potential for established models of authorship, together with Victorian discourses meant to delegitimize it as both a professional and an aesthetic creative practice, have driven nineteenth-century collaboration to the margins. Indeed, looking at co-authored novels means looking at the margins. Marginality and invisibility are the ghosts that haunt co-authored novels: to study collaboration means studying not only the conditions of its existence but also those of its erasure.

As mentioned above, literary collaboration has recently started to receive critical attention. And yet the specific features of the phenomenon in the Victorian era still need to be explored: a study of late Victorian collaboration as a trend is lacking. So far, book-length studies on

INTRODUCTION

co-authorship have covered very wide temporal and spatial ranges and different genres. A quick overview will suffice.

Whitney Chadwick and Isabelle de Courtivron's 1993 *Significant Others: Creativity and Intimate Partnership* considers a range of twentieth-century British, American, and French artistic or literary unions, analysing the connection between creativity and intimate relationships. Wayne Koestenbaum's *Double Talk: The Erotics of Male Collaboration* (1989) takes into consideration writing relationships between men from 1885 to 1922, mainly Stevenson and Osbourne, Lang and Haggard, Conrad and Ford, Freud and Breuer, John Addington Symonds and Havelock Ellis, and Pound and Eliot. Like Koestenbaum, Jack Stillinger's *Multiple Authorship and the Myth of the Solitary Genius* (1991) focuses on prominent male authors and their personal and professional relationships with other male writers who, in various and often unacknowledged ways, had a share in the creation of their texts. Stillinger's attention centres mainly on Wordsworth, Coleridge, Keats, J. S. Mill, T. S. Eliot and Ezra Pound. Likewise, Jeffrey Masten's *Textual Intercourse: Collaboration, Authorship, and Sexualities in Renaissance Drama* (1997) deals only with male co-authors, though it focuses on sixteenth- and seventeenth-century theatre. Later on, feminist and queer critical works have boosted collaboration studies, and have finally called attention to women collaborators as well. Bette London's *Writing Double: Women's Literary Partnerships* (1999) and Holly Laird's *Women Coauthors* (2000) have inaugurated a restorative trend aimed at reinstating lesser-known female co-writers: London looks at British and Australian women's literary partnerships in the nineteenth and the first half of the twentieth centuries,[2] while Laird explores an incredibly wide array of British, American, and Canadian women who collaborated with other women or with men, from the mid-nineteenth to the late twentieth centuries.[3] Similarly, Lorraine York's *Rethinking Women's Collaborative Writing* (2002) analyses the power dynamics and ideological polyvalences of contemporary women's

---

2 The Brontë sisters, Michael Field, Somerville and Ross, E.D. Gerard, Mary and Jane Findlater, and M. Barnard Eldershaw.
3 The list includes John Stuart Mill and his wife Harriet Taylor, Michael Field, Somerville and Ross, Gertrude Stein and Alice B. Toklas, Louise Erdrich and Michael Dorris, Peter Redgrove and Penelope Shuttle, Daphne Marlatt and Betsy Warland, and Jael B. Juba (pseudonym for Lydia Fakundiny and Joyce Elbrecht). Laird devotes special attention to collaborations between Afro-American and white women, e.g., the Delany sisters with Amy Hill Hearth.

collaborations on drama, poetry, and novels in Britain, Italy, France, and the United States.

As can been seen from this brief survey, there has been a tendency to group several different instances of co-authorship from diverse genres, times, and geographical areas. This was something that had to be done in order to call attention to the significance of this neglected practice throughout history. However, the results have been somewhat confusing, albeit compelling. Only recently has research on collaboration focused on more specific genres and space- and time-ranges. In 2008, Jill Ehnenn published *Women's Literary Collaboration, Queerness, and Late Victorian Culture*, a study concerned with the construction of lesbian identity and the expansion of queer history, dealing with Michael Field, Somerville and Ross, Vernon Lee and Kit Anstruther-Thomson, and Elizabeth Robins and Florence Bell. Ehnenn maintains that the lives and works of these women collaborators "embody provocative strategies for resistance to, or at least negotiation of, social norms" (10). One of her points – which my discussion shares and hopes to expand – is that late nineteenth-century women, by entering into an exclusive creative relationship with another female partner, "not only invented texts, they invented themselves in ways that society otherwise did not permit" (12). In recent years, monographs on specific Victorian collaborators have started to appear. This is a sign that collaboration studies are an expanding field and that it is time for a re-evaluation. A fundamental starting point for my project has been the work of Anne Jamison, in particular *E. OE. Somerville & Martin Ross: Female Authorship and Literary Collaboration* (2016). Like Ehnenn, Jamison argues for women's literary collaborations as "a defiant cultural position within [...] Victorian literary society" (2). She provides a wide-ranging discussion of Somerville and Ross's partnership, taking into consideration most of their texts (the novels, the short stories, and the travel narratives). My book builds on Jamison's research but has a much more specific focus on how Somerville and Ross's literary partnership worked; in addition, I deal only with their co-authored novels. In 2019 a much-needed book-length study of Walter Besant was edited by Kevin A. Morrison (*Walter Besant: The Business of Literature and the Pleasures of Reform*). Morrison's collection devotes three essays out of twelve to Besant's literary partnerships, and although the rest of the book does not engage directly with him as a collaborator it is a first step toward a re-evaluation of this prominent

INTRODUCTION

Victorian novelist, activist, and philanthropist.[4] My book discusses Besant as a writer and co-author of popular novels, topics which have not received their due yet.

The present work follows in the footsteps of these recent studies and means to identify the patterns and features of collaboration within a specific historical moment (1870–1900), a precise geographical area (the UK), and a given literary genre (novels). By inserting itself into the expanding but still largely uncharted territory of collaboration studies, *Late Victorian Literary Collaboration* aims at filling a gap in nineteenth-century British literary history through a book-length study of literary collaboration on novel-writing in the late Victorian age. The book will guide the reader through late Victorian collaboration, trying not only to illustrate its trends but also to trace and explain the reasons for its success and subsequent decline. The goal of this volume is thus to unpack a significant practice of the Victorian literary scene, which, after its decay, has been unjustly neglected.

One of the main driving forces behind this work has been the desire to rediscover and integrate extinct lives and texts into literary history, and therefore to retrieve from obscurity long-forgotten authors and their writing practices. To reintegrate the presence of collaborators into memory means to gain a fuller understanding of the literary market and of the lively nature of Victorian culture. Sustained by a wide range of primary sources such as reviews, articles, essays, paratexts, private correspondence, and autobiographies, this book deals with popular authors widely acclaimed in their time but subsequently overlooked, unearthing forgotten and out-of-print collaborative novels.[5]

Another key goal of *Late Victorian Literary Collaboration* is to suggest a rethinking of the concepts of writing and authorship. Collaborators' untold stories can add something to the history of authorship: indeed, collaboration "provided a platform to return to certain fundamental questions" concerning authorship (London, 1999, 7). What can we learn about British culture of the fin de siècle by understanding how literary collaborations were imagined? Which forms of authorship were sanctioned and which forms marginalized? How can literary property be defined? Central issues examined here are the ways in which each

---

4 The three chapters are Bunting, 2019, 19–38; Storer, 2019, 39–54; and Bachman and Cox, 2019, 55–72.
5 The book does not examine unpublished private correspondence: all the letters by the collaborators employed here have been edited and published.

writer defined the (co-)authorial experience and how public discussion on co-authorship engendered vigorous legal and aesthetic debates over what it meant to be an author and about the act of authoring itself. Literary collaboration called into question the fundamental definition and purpose of authorship, even while the rigid notion of the singular author-genius was still privileged. Co-authorship had the merit of triggering discussion, of challenging what seemed natural ideas but were instead cultural constructions, thereby sparking reflection and even polemics: in brief, it took the Victorian imagination into the uncharted territories of authorship. It contributed to making it an era of discussion and broadened Victorian recognition of alternative literary practices, calling attention to the fact that authorship *could* be configured differently. The study of literary collaboration thus offers new perspectives on authorship, its meaning, and its configurations. The case studies discussed in this book are proof that authorship has followed multiple, if forgotten, paths.

The acknowledgement of the existence and significance of late Victorian collaborators has the potential of deepening, and perhaps challenging, our understanding of nineteenth-century literary culture in new, resonant ways. The late Victorian literary scene might actually look quite different from what we imagine it to be – in any case, much busier.

Criteria

Late Victorian Literary Collaboration has involved a series of key methodological choices. The first one concerned what counts as co-authorship, as there is as yet confusion on the proper parameters of the subject. Defining what co-authorship is remains a very pressing problem for every study on collaboration. "[C]ollaboration itself," noted London in 1999, is "still an unstable category" (18). In 2002, Karell reflected that "the meanings of the terms *collaboration* and *collaborative writing* are being debated, expanded, and refined; no final decision is in sight" (xix). These words might as well have been written today, as there is still no widely accepted definition for collaboration.

Stillinger (1991), Masten (1997), London (1999), and Witcher (2022), among others, intend collaboration in a broad sense: according to them, co-authorship can refer to a range of activities, such as acts of assistance and inspiration, mentoring, influence, revision, editorial input, posthumous completion of someone else's work, and transhistorical collaboration with figures of the past. Stillinger claims that "every work is necessarily the product of multiple authorship" (1991, 96). London

(1999) fully includes in her survey of women's literary partnerships the Brontë sisters' work, not just their juvenilia but also the novels they published separately but which were written in close contact with each other. Though undeniably fascinating, London's book considers automatic writing (such as that of Georgie Yeats) and mediumship as forms of collaboration: the final chapters are devoted to the activity of influential mediums such as Geraldine Cummins, Hester Dowden (who, in the 1920s, made a sensation by claiming to be in contact with Oscar Wilde), and Mrs Holland (Kipling's sister Alice). London aptly links mediumship to feminine empowerment, even though it can scarcely be considered a form of co-authorship. Karell's (2002) perspective is even more radical, as it includes not only acts of rewriting and of completing others' texts, but even "acts of writing in which one or even all of the writing subjects may not be aware of the other writers, being separated by distance, era, or even death" (xx). Karell goes as far as to claim that every act of writing is collaborative and that "absolute individual authority is ultimately impossible": (xxxiii) she argues that even a writer's reliance on a previous text or a passing conversation – typically described as influence or inspiration – should instead be included in the category of collaboration. In Karell's view, collaboration is "a multivoiced, multilayered process intrinsic to the writing virtually all writers do regardless of their conscious intentions or aspirations" (xxxiii). Karell has a point: if authorship is the product of social context, then all literary production is surely collaborative – but that would take us too far. Heather Bozant Witcher's *Collaborative Writing in the Long Nineteenth Century: Sympathetic Partnerships and Artistic Creation* (2022) adopts a wide approach to collaboration as well, as it takes into consideration the various connections and working relations of Mary and Percy Shelley, the Pre-Raphaelites, William Morris, Michael Field, and Vernon Lee.

This book, however, starts from a different premise, and focuses only on explicit acts of collaboration. A too-inclusive understanding of co-authorship, in fact, may end up depriving collaboration of any specific meaning. Following Koestenbaum (1989), Ede and Lunsford (1990), Laird (2000), and Ashton (2003), I define collaboration as acts of writing in which two or more individuals consciously work together, at every stage, to produce a common text which they (sooner or later) acknowledge. For a collaboration to be called so, mutual acknowledgment and intentionality are fundamental: the authors must sit down with the willingness to create a text together, with the deliberate intention of collaborating; at the end of the process, they must acknowledge each other's contribution. A double signature makes a co-authored text "most precisely and satisfyingly collaborative" (Koestenbaum, 1989, 2), but not all co-authors opt for this solution; many adopt singular, often composite pen names. This does not mean that they do not acknowledge the collaboration: the choice of a pseudonym can have marketing, personal, or many other reasons.

The reason for choosing to focus only on explicit acts of collaboration is twofold. First, explicit collaborations have received much less attention than unacknowledged ones: cases of plagiarism, ghost-writing, editorial alterations, unfinished novels completed by someone else, and other forms of hidden collaboration have been thoroughly examined; "unearthing unacknowledged collaborators," remarks Ashton (2003, 13), "is a tremendously popular activity for literary scholars." Second, hidden collaborations – however compelling and intriguing they might be – do not challenge traditional understandings of authorship as openly collaborative texts do, as this book will demonstrate.

A second methodological choice concerned the corpus of collaborative works to be discussed: this study looks only at collaboration in fiction writing, specifically the writing of novels. This is because collaboration in novel-writing reached an unprecedented peak at the end of the Victorian era and, although a relevant amount of other fiction and some poetry were written collaboratively, novels were the genre most exploited by co-authorship at that moment.[6] The time period this book considers, which roughly spans 1870–1900, is closely connected with the choice of genre.[7] My research is thus limited to a very specific time frame, when the practice of collaboration in novel-writing assumed the proportions of a literary fashion. As noted by Ashton (2003, 8) when discussing American co-authored novels, despite earlier and more recent occurrences of collaborative fiction, "the propensity for writers of the late nineteenth- and early twentieth-century America to write together was a distinct phenomenon." The same holds true for British writers.

Finally, this book does not focus on authors or texts of canonical stature. Although many writers now firmly established within the

---

6 If one excludes drama. However, collaboration had its own tradition in playwriting: early modern playwriting was collaborative in nature, a tradition which partially continued in the nineteenth century, and which, most importantly, was not considered a controversial practice.

7 I have occasionally included in my corpus novels published after 1900 since they were the later output of partnerships that had started in the Victorian age and simply continued, as in the case of Somerville and Ross.

INTRODUCTION

literary canon occasionally wrote collaborative fiction (Dickens, Collins, Stevenson, Kipling, Conrad, etc.), I do not directly engage with them.[8] It is true that the works they wrote collaboratively have generally been considered side production; still, they have already received at least some critical attention.[9] I look at more or less forgotten co-authors and out-of-print texts. And yet, although many names discussed here are rarely heard of, this study is not an egg hunt for the most obscure writers one may find buried in archives. Publication and success in the market of their day are criteria for entry here: the writers I consider were all acclaimed by readers and critics alike during their lifetime. In the introduction to her study, London states that her book "is not a bid for canonizing any of its writers" (1999, 29). The present work follows her premise. However, such writing partnerships are significant, and I believe in the need to give them due credit: first, because they existed, and their existence needs to be acknowledged; and, second, because in their time they made more than a respectable showing in the literary arena – publishing with the best publishers, hiring the top literary agents, receiving notice in the leading periodicals, and selling hundreds of thousand of copies.

As this research developed, it became clear that I was tracing more than the history of some authors and their texts: I was tracing the history of a peculiar practice at a moment of particular efflorescence; I was exploring an actual cultural phenomenon and the impact it had on late Victorian discourses of writing and authorship, on how people imagined the author and their activity. The cases discussed here have been selected because they offer new and challenging insights into the history of authorship, the nineteenth-century literary market, and late Victorian culture.

---

8 Dickens and Collins wrote together *No Thoroughfare* (1867); Stevenson collaborated with his stepson Lloyd Osbourne on *The Wrong Box* (1889), *The Wrecker* (1892), and *The Ebb-Tide* (1894); Kipling co-wrote *The Naulahka* (1892) with the American agent Wolcott Balestier; Conrad engaged in a literary partnership with Ford Madox Ford, which resulted in *The Inheritors* (1901), *Romance* (1903), and *The Nature of a Crime* (1909).
9 For example, see the recent *Robert Louis Stevenson and the Art of Collaboration* (2019) by Audrey Murfin.

Chapter outline

Late Victorian Literary Collaboration could be divided into two parts. The first three chapters examine different models of co-authorship in the late Victorian age – and consequently, different understandings of authorship – each represented by a partnership. Chapters 4 and 5 deal with questions of (co-)authorship and with the relationship between literary collaboration and the Victorian imagination, while discussing some crucial issues raised by the popularity of the practice: chapter 4 looks at the intense debate over literary collaboration in the periodical press of the time, while chapter 5 focuses on the point of view of the co-authors.

Chapters 1 and 2 respectively introduce two of the most popular literary partnerships of the last decades of the nineteenth century: the London-based friends and men of letters Walter Besant and James Rice and the Anglo-Irish cousins and feminists Edith Somerville and Martin Ross. Both partnerships epitomize what I have identified as the first stage of late Victorian collaboration: associations of friends or relatives who only (or mainly) wrote with each other, and whose partnerships lasted several years, often interrupted only by the death of one of the two. Such collaborations initially developed as experimental practices shared by amateurs who were not confident about how the public would react, and who therefore devised self-protective strategies such as the use of anonymity and pseudonymity. Chapter 1 tracks how, in the ten years of their partnership (1872–82), Besant and Rice played a prominent role in making collaboration one of the literary fashions of the time. Constantly compared to Dickens's works by contemporary reviewers, their novels were reprinted throughout the English-speaking world. Particular attention will be given to their first book, *Ready-Money Mortiboy* (1872), one of the best examples of Besant and Rice's joint fiction. After his partner's death, Besant went on successfully writing on his own, but he was still seen as the master of the art of collaboration. His ideas, expressed in a number of texts, had a great impact on public opinion. At first, Besant recalled his collaborative years in idyllic terms, but over time he grew colder on the subject, and right before his death he ended up advising against taking a collaborator, stating that "after all, an artist must necessarily stand alone" (Besant, 1902, 188). How could it be that a man who had spent a decade collaborating, whose reputation had been built largely on it, and who had repeatedly declared a perfect relationship with his former partner now came to express such

INTRODUCTION

destructive views? Chapter 1 argues that this is not a contradiction, because a detailed examination of Besant and Rice's partnership reveals that it was actually based on the principles Besant would outline later in his life. The chapter thus proceeds to analyse the model of collaboration proposed by Besant in his writings, most importantly in his 1892 essay "On Literary Collaboration," and the debate it sparked in the periodical press. Since Besant's essay was a direct reaction to "The Art and Mystery of Collaboration" (1890) by the Columbia professor and co-author himself, James Brander Matthews, the two works are discussed vis-à-vis one another. Crucially, both Matthews and Besant thought that a co-authored text had to appear as if it were the outcome of a single mind, but their opinions on how this unity was to be achieved differed substantially. Finally, chapter 1 unpacks Besant's opinions on fiction writing and the profession of letters by specifically looking at his lecture "The Art of Fiction" (1884), his practical guide *The Pen and the Book* (1899), and his posthumous *Autobiography* (1902).

Chapter 2 centres on the literary 'Firm' of Somerville and Ross, who, to this day, are arguably the best known of all late nineteenth-century collaborators. These women's partnership (1888–1915) has been read by criticism within two main discourses: the feminist one and the Anglo-Irish tradition of the Big House. The former has been predominant in recent decades, when Somerville and Ross have been recruited as a significant case study in the development of a wide and theoretically engaged approach to women's partnerships. Chapter 2 seeks to effectively move away from this approach: although it has been central in drawing a history of female collaboration, specialized studies of Somerville and Ross's partnership outside this perspective are still largely lacking. The goals of the chapter are, first, to reposition the collaboration within the specific historical and cultural context which constituted the fertile ground for it to flourish; and, second, to illuminate the features of their original literary alliance throughout its main phases over the decades. Since collaborative fiction is necessarily the product of relationships, to emphasize the connection between process and product is a major concern of this book. For this reason, special attention is paid to the relationship between the collaborators. In the case of Somerville and Ross, I suggest that their extremely close friendship constituted the bedrock and the secret of their co-authorship: without the emotional and intellectual bond, their writing method would not have worked, as chapter 2 carefully demonstrates, drawing mainly on their correspondence, on Somerville's autobiography *Irish Memories* (1917), and on her late-life essay "Two of a Trade" (1946). Somerville and Ross's co-authored novels are discussed, with a focus on their first one, *An Irish Cousin* (1889), and on the work they considered their masterpiece, *The Real Charlotte* (1894). After its mixed reception, Somerville and Ross struggled to write another "serious novel," as they used to call it. The chapter argues that their aspiration to become professional novelists somehow backfired: the turn in their careers from amateurs to professionals might be what, ironically, limited their subsequent literary production. Many of Somerville and Ross's contemporaries and subsequent critics denied them the status of authors worthy of study: such amazing disregard could be ascribed to a series of reasons, which chapter 2 identifies.

Chapter 3 looks at the later stage of Victorian collaboration: the occasional partnerships of the 1890s. Once it became a trend, co-authorship came to be regarded as something to experience out of curiosity or profit; the allure of the practice, the attention it attracted, and its publicity potential induced many authors to try collaboration out. The collaborations of the 1890s generally took place among popular writers who before and after the collaborative experience(s) pursued independent careers; normally, they did not work exclusively with one partner, but engaged in one-time collaborations with different people, sometimes at the same time, thus creating elaborate nets of collaborators. The chapter takes into consideration three case studies, representative of different kinds of 1890s occasional collaboration. First, it looks at the quirky alliance of the scholar and folklorist Andrew Lang with the king of fantasy fiction Henry Rider Haggard for *The World's Desire* (1890) as an example of a collaboration between two already prominent authors. The novel proved to be a commercial success, and the main business of the periodical press was to speculate on who had written what: as both Haggard and Lang already had established careers and were famous for specific areas of interest, the two hands were thought to be easily distinguishable. Second, chapter 3 deals with the intersection of Rhoda Broughton, then a well-known writer of slightly scandalous novels, and the young American journalist Elizabeth Bisland, who had just attracted worldwide attention for her sensational race around the world. Broughton and Bisland's literary partnership is an example of an alliance between an established novelist and an unexperienced one, and its result was *A Widower Indeed* (1891), a sentimental novel with a shocking ending. Despite its many flaws, the novel is remarkable for its criticism of English parochialism, voiced through the character of the young American co-protagonist. The last section of the chapter centres on the association of twenty-four celebrated writers (including Arthur Conan Doyle, Bram Stoker, and Florence Marryat) to produce a widely advertised sensational novel, *The Fate of Fenella* (1892), as an instance of the round robin craze of the fin de siècle. Even though the plot of *Fenella* was affected by the bizarre writing game, the transformation of the eponymous protagonist as the novel progresses is worth examining, as Fenella passes from being an emancipated woman to becoming the perfectly modest and passive Victorian wife, thus sending a clear message to the readers of the magazine where it was serialized.

Chapter 4 addresses the problematic relationship between literary collaboration and the reading public of the late Victorian era. The idea of a shared writing practice became very popular, but it remained tricky: collaboration seemed to elude definite understanding. How did the Victorian reader look at co-authorship? What were the most common questions people asked? Which aspects aroused more curiosity, and which more suspicion? To answer these and other crucial questions, the chapter delves into the discourse that developed around literary collaboration in the periodical press, exploring how it changed over time as the popularity of co-authorship grew, reached its climax, and eventually declined. It also demonstrates that co-authorship was a topic of interest not only for intellectuals: on the contrary, it took hold of the popular imagination, as testified by the many discussions in the regular, widely read newspapers of the time. The discourse in the press demonstrates that, from a certain point onwards, collaboration started to be linked with different, often contrasting, views. As the trend for co-authorship rapidly turned into an inclination for literary manufactures, thus sacrificing the artistic quality of the product, the response of the reading public grew more critical. The debate illustrated in chapter 4 seems to point to a problematic understanding of authorship: on the one hand, the idyllic representations of co-authors working together in blissful domesticity effectively challenged the paradigm of the solitary author; on the other hand, the tensions and the limits presented by collaboration seemed to confirm the urgency for solitude in order to create art. The coexistence for a certain period of these oxymoronic positions exposes an ambiguity in late Victorian conceptions of the author.

Chapter 5 further explores how the trend for collaboration affected concepts of authorship. This time, at the core of the analysis are the ways in which some collaborators conceived co-authorship and the author-figure, and how their ideas questioned hegemonic conceptions of author-ity. The first section briefly tracks how the author-figure changed over the centuries to identify the steps through which it acquired the traits late Victorians were so keen on. The second part investigates the unforeseen impact of the collaborative trend on the figure of the author at the end of the nineteenth century; to support and illustrate my argument, I rely on the experiences of some collaborators discussed in the previous chapters, in particular Somerville, Besant, and Matthews. Despite their substantial differences, these authors all talked about their collaborative practice in remarkably similar terms, emphasizing the final unity of the co-authored text and the shifted position of the author. One shared idea of authorship emerges when reading their commentaries: the authors of a collaborative work, being neither discernible nor perceptible, lose their primary importance; only the text in its unity and independence should be visible. In this perspective, the collaborative author fades away into an elusive presence that remains hidden behind the text. The chapter then points out that such dismantling of the myth of the author within the collaborative practice is not limited to the cases discussed here, but is in fact a much larger phenomenon. The final section calls attention to some points that the late Victorian collaborative trend shared with twentieth-century literary and critical movements that systematically dismissed the importance of the author, reaching the conclusion that Victorian collaboration might constitute an embryonic overcoming of the Romantic concept of authorship.

Overview of late Victorian collaboration

Late Victorian literary collaboration was not a homogeneous phenomenon. People who engaged in collaborative ventures did not think of themselves as belonging to a particular group or category. Although some of them occasionally commented on each other's public statements, they did not gather to discuss – let alone theorize – literary collaboration (at least, no such evidence emerged from my research). Each set of co-authors was motivated by different reasons; substantial differences in their sex, background, artistic aims, literary output, and professional status existed between people involved in collaborative relationships. And yet all the co-authors considered in this book share some common traits: they all wrote what can be labelled as popular fiction, were read by the mass reading public, and were extensively discussed in the leading periodicals.

Although in the 1890s collaborative ventures among several writers at a time were in vogue, late Victorian collaboration was mostly a dual practice. Significantly, it was quite common for pairs of friends

INTRODUCTION

or relatives to jointly assemble a novel. This is indicative of the need for intimacy and sympathy in order to write together. Large groups of co-writers were much less common than writing couples; moreover, group collaborations often resulted in serialistic turn-taking, which, while entertaining, was much less challenging to common notions of authorship: by providing clearly separated instalments, no merging of the authors' hands on the literary page took place.

Most pairs of collaborators were made up by men, significantly fewer by women; a few were mixed-sex couples, mainly husband-and-wife teams, such as Agnes and Egerton Castle, who started in 1898 and continued to sell well into the first decades of the twentieth century. The strong predominance of male co-authorship might come as a surprise in a period when publishers' catalogues presented almost as many women authors as men. The reason for this does not lie in the incompatibility of women with writing with someone else (as it was believed at the time), but rather in very practical details: men collaborated more than women because they had more occasions to meet. Confined to the domestic hearth and their usual coterie, Victorian women had far fewer opportunities to become acquainted with a variety of people, and therefore to find a suitable partner to write with. Indeed, it is not by chance that, when women collaborated, they often did so with a relative, generally a female one. In addition, even if they did find a partner with whom they decided to write, women had to face further practical difficulties: a woman was not supposed to stay away from home all day long and neglect her household duties in favour of remaining enclosed in a room scribbling a novel with somebody. Writing on one's own could be done safely and appropriately in the drawing room while keeping an eye on domestic affairs, but co-authorship required spending long hours away from home (at least for one of the partners), unless they lived under the same roof: here again the choice of collaborating with a sister or another female relative. Disruptions of all kinds, from housekeeping tasks to family matters and social commitments, always made it challenging for a woman to find the opportunity to sit down in 'a room of one's own'; when two women were involved, the practical problems doubled, as making schedules coincide was certainly not easy. This was something only well-off women, with housekeepers, servants and nannies available, could afford to do. It is no coincidence that many female collaborators were members of the upper-middle classes.

Among women partnerships made up of relatives, teams formed by sisters were quite common. Although this book will not engage directly with any of them, it is worth at least mentioning a few. Between 1880 and 1891, Emily and Dorothea Gerard published four sentimental novels under the signature 'E. D. Gerard.' Born into an upper-middle class Scottish family, the Gerard sisters travelled all their adult lives through Eastern Europe and introduced British readers to scenes and people from what was a still relatively unknown area, gaining a reputation as "purveyor of the exotic" (Laird, 2000, 5). From a very different social background there came another pair of sisters-collaborators: Mary and Jane Findlater were born in a poor and remote Scottish parsonage. Widely read and respectfully reviewed in their days, the Findlater sisters "wrote what was generally agreed to be accomplished fiction before, in the 1920s, retreating from the literary scene in the wake of modernism" (London, 1999, 5). At the turn of the century we find a partnership between two sisters of a much-celebrated family: Helen and Olivia Rossetti, nieces of Dante Gabriel, who, under the collective pseudonym 'Isabel Meredith,' experimented with collaboration.

Even if female partnerships were inferior in number to those made up by men, it must be noted that they were generally more enduring. The reason may lie in the fact that such relationships were grounded on a strong emotional bond, which in all cases preceded and informed the collaboration. When women collaborated, they tended to do so for a long time, with one single partner, in an exclusive relationship.

Relatives were very few instead among men collaborators. We have the case of Stevenson and his stepson, or Walter H. Pollock and his son. But most male collaborators were friends or simply colleagues who, out of fun or profit, undertook joint authorial projects. The majority were one- or two-time collaborations, spread over the years while the writers were engaged in individual work or in temporary intersections with other people (only Besant and Rice sustained a continuing writing relationship for a decade). A great part of these occasional collaborations took place between 1889 and 1899, the decade when co-authorship was most in vogue. They were made up of authors who were already popular and prolific, sometimes coupled by publishers or magazine editors. Many male collaborators of the 1890s were the representatives of the new professionalized authorship, like H. Rider Haggard, Francis Charles Philips, Walter H. Pollock, and Arnold Bennett.

Among late Victorian collaborators, we find both famous and wealthy writers by profession living in fashionable London and obscure women from the margins of the country. Some co-authors achieved a professional status thanks to their collaboration, as in the cases of Besant and Rice or Somerville and Ross; others had already obtained a stable position within the literary market. In the main, established authors collaborated with other established authors. However, there were cases when a popular writer engaged in a collaboration with an unknown and unexperienced partner, as in the case of Broughton with Bisland.

Writing together strengthened the authors' sense of themselves as professionals: as Ashton suggests (2003, 171), co-authorship "gave them community and it gave them clout." The first case discussed in this book is precisely an example of two struggling writers who, thanks to their association, succeeded in becoming authors by profession. Like Henley and Trenchard, the collaborators in Hichens's story mentioned at the beginning of this introduction, Besant and Rice started out as two ambitious but unsuccessful men of letters who decided to try a new way of writing: they decided to become literary collaborators. In the fiction, Henley and Trenchard's partnership, however promising, proves disastrous: the book proceeds "by slow degrees and with a great deal of discussion" (Hichens, 1896, 143). What is more, Trenchard keeps writing on his own during the night, ignoring his friend's ideas. Exasperated with his companion's stubbornness, and feeling that the book is not his at all, Henley quits. But a final surprise awaits him and the reader. Trenchard has been writing night after night what was actually happening to him: the story of his drug addiction and his love/hate for the woman who introduced him to it. At the end, he leaves the unfinished manuscript for Henley to complete, as he proceeds to murder his evil lover and drown himself into the Thames: it will be his collaborator's task to write the last chapter.

Unlike Henley and Trenchard's, Besant and Rice's collaboration worked quite well – more than that, it proved tremendously successful. Besant in particular ended up being the popular novelist everyone knew, and the very embodiment of collaborative and professional authorship, as chapter 1 will illustrate.

CHAPTER ONE

Walter Besant and James Rice

Two long-standing mysteries surround the figure of the collaborator, novelist, philanthropist, and authors' rights campaigner Walter Besant (1836–1901). The first one concerns his highly contradictory position about literary collaboration; the second one is the striking contrast between the fame he enjoyed in his lifetime and the oblivion he slipped into after his death.

Besant was probably "the most collaborative literary figure of the nineteenth century": he "thrived in spaces of literary discussion, community, and collaboration," which were probably "the very reason for his success" (Bunting, 2019, 37–38). His literary partnerships were many and various.[1] But he also greatly contributed to the Victorian era's increasing fascination with the author as a personality to be interviewed, portrayed, and photographed. Even though a prolific co-author, Besant saw himself as eminently a single professional man of letters: all his commentaries testify to that. Curiously enough, at times he questioned the tenet of the solitary genius; at other times, he just seemed eager to embody it.

The first, the most lasting, and the most prolific of Besant's collaborations was with James Rice (1844–82). He and Rice "are unique in the level of success they achieved as partners" (Storer, 2019, 43): for ten years, the two of them collaborated "seriously and systematically" ("Lit.

---

1 In his life, Besant collaborated with at least eleven co-authors in both works of fiction and history books. Besides the decade spent collaborating with James Rice, he was involved in several occasional collaborative ventures. Among others, he worked with Walter Herries Pollock on a novel (*Sir Jocelyn's Cap*, 1885) and a collection of dramas (*The Charm and Other Drawing-Room Plays*, 1896). In 1871 he and Edward Palmer, professor of Arabic at Cambridge, co-wrote *Jerusalem: The City of Herod and Saladin*, and ten years later they published *The Survey of Western Palestine*, together with C. R. Conder. In 1879, Besant collaboratively wrote *Constantinople: A Sketch of Its History* with W. J. Brodribb.

Coll.," 200) and made literary collaboration fashionable. When their partnership began in 1871, co-authorship in novel writing was only an eccentric writing practice rarely heard of; when Rice died in 1882, it had become the literary fashion of the time, and hundreds of aspiring authors were begging Besant to take them on as his new co-authors, as he remembered in his *Autobiography*.[2]

Years after his collaborative phase had ended, Besant, by then a prominent literary figure, was still seen as the master of the art of collaboration; his opinions on the subject were continuously looked for. His 1892 essay "On Literary Collaboration" sparked a vigorous debate in the press of the time, probably the largest wave of articles on the topic ever.[3] In the prefaces to the many re-editions of his co-authored works and in various commentaries and interviews, he remembered Rice with sentimental nostalgia and recalled their collaborative years in idyllic terms. Strangely enough, though, with the passing of time Besant became increasingly cold on taking a long-term collaborator. He repeatedly came to affirm that collaboration was good for humour and storytelling, but "to touch the deeper things one must be alone" ("Lit. Coll.," 203). In his public treatment of collaboration, he often derided collaborative acts, particularly when the partners aimed at an equal share of work. Just before his death he ended up strongly advising against it. In his 285-page-long *Autobiography* only seven pages are dedicated to his decade with Rice, and Besant concluded that "after all, an artist must necessarily stand alone" (188). Though this may seem a contradiction, this chapter demonstrates that in fact it is not: once examined in detail, Besant's model of collaboration was based on the principles he would theorize later in his life.

The second mystery involving Besant concerns the erasure of his name after his death, notwithstanding the fame he had enjoyed in his lifetime. That Besant "was probably the most popular author of his day in England" (Spilka, 1973, 103) has by now been acknowledged by a

---

2 Besant died before finishing the manuscript; he left a hand-written draft, which was completed and typed by his friends and appeared in print the year after his death.

3 Over the following months, Besant's essay was reprinted in several periodicals. The British Newspaper Archive is very helpful in identifying reprints. See, for example: *St. James's Gazette*, 1 February 1892, p. 5; *Yorkshire Evening Post*, 2 February 1892, p. 1; *Birmingham Daily Post*, 2 February 1892, p. 7; *Glasgow Evening Post*, 2 February 1892, p. 8; *Morning Post*, 3 February 1892, p. 2; *Inverness Courier*, 5 February 1892, p. 3; *Grantham Journal*, 13 February 1892, p. 2.

growing corpus of scholarship. Boege (1956a, 249) remarks that, when Besant declared that his name was "known all over the English-speaking world" (*Autobiography*, 215), "he was stating an obvious truth that any of his readers would have assented to." Morrison (2019) underlines that in the last quarter of the nineteenth century Besant was "one of Britain's most lionized living novelists" (1) and a central figure in British society and culture (3). The list of Besant's achievements is a long one. His novels – more than forty, both those written in collaboration and those written alone – were bestsellers. He made substantial profits exclusively from his literary work.[4] He founded and directed the Society of Authors, the first successful association of writers, which greatly changed the status of the profession of letters in the United Kingdom; he went to great lengths to "undo the stigma of market relations" (Çelikkol, 2019, 142) when talking about literature, and tirelessly advocated the author's right to possess their own work and profit from it. He was the key figure in the building of the first institution aimed at offering education and recreation to the inhabitants of the London East End, now a part of Queen's University. His activities brought him in close connection, both personal and professional, with the principal men of letters of the period, and they all – Tennyson, Collins,[5] Kipling, Stevenson, Hardy, James – talked of him with respect. In 1895, Queen Victoria knighted him. Doubtlessly Besant had an impact on his age: he was probably more in the public eye than any other author of his time.

And yet, after his death he was forgotten. Besant finds no place in reference works; at best, he is mentioned and dismissed in a few lines or in

---

4 For a discussion of Besant's income as a full-time novelist in the 1890s, see Eliot, 2019. Eliot estimates Besant's income from each of his major 1890s novels to have been almost always between £1,700 and £1,800.

5 In 1889 Besant was asked by Wilkie Collins, then in his last illness, to complete his novel *Blind Love*. The story was already planned, and Besant had to finish the writing "without any obvious break in the style" ("Lit. Coll.," 202) by following the extensive set of notes left by Collins. Collins's choice probably fell on Besant not only because of mutual esteem but also because Besant was used to dealing with someone else's work: it was common knowledge that the first chapters of Besant and Rice's first novel had been written by the latter, with Besant stepping in to develop and write the rest of the book. Thanks to his vast experience as a collaborator, Besant would not be daunted by the challenging task of completing Collins's novel. For a discussion of Besant's completion of *Blind Love*, see Bachman and Cox, 2019, 55–72. Bachman and Cox compare the notes provided by Collins with the final manuscript completed by Besant, and unpack the major differences between the two.

a footnote.⁶ "Even popular novelists," notes Boege, "are seldom so utterly neglected; yet Besant was so much more than a popular novelist" (1956a, 249). Boege ascribes such a spectacular fall to Besant's overwork in his last twenty years, leading him to do too many things at the same time. From the end of his partnership with Rice, Besant kept writing an average of one novel per year; he was daily engaged with the Society of Authors and its journal, which he edited; his commitment to a series of philanthropic causes was impressive; he carried on researches for a colossal project called *A Survey of London*, which ambitiously aimed at reconstructing the history and topography of the capital from prehistoric times to the end of the nineteenth century. An exhausted imagination and having probably too many things at hand affected the quality of his literary work. In the 1880s he had been in high repute as a novelist: then, an unceasing flow of inferior books characterized by machine-like dreariness caused his fame to wane.

Morrison (2019) adds two very plausible reasons for twentieth-century neglect of Besant, suggesting that he had been too outspoken about two issues then at the centre of public discussion: fiction writing and gender. He remarks that Besant's "The Art of Fiction" provocatively argued that literature was an art form governed by rules, which could be taught in specific schools. To claim that "the creative process was reducible to a quantifiable number of laws and techniques" (Morrison, 2019, 4) was something quite disconcerting. In addition, Besant has come down in history for his vociferous polemic on the New Woman question: his novella *The Revolt of Men* (1882) and his short story "The Doll's House – and After" (1890), a sequel to Ibsen's *A Doll's House*, are overtly anti-feminist works and express deep concern about what Besant pre-figured as sexual anarchy in the future. The positions adopted by Besant on such hot topics may have contributed to make him unpopular in the twentieth century.

Boege's and Morrison's insights are undoubtedly intriguing, and deserve to be more accurately developed. Building on their studies, I expand on these intuitions and advance some more reasons for Besant's fall into oblivion. In the last eighteen years of his life, he published several commentaries on co-authorship and the craft of fiction writing,

---

6 Even the recent *Oxford Handbook of Victorian Literary Culture* (John, 2016) mentions Besant only twice, and quickly dismisses him: the first time as ranking among his age's "anti-feminists" in launching "a defence of traditional patriarchal values" (171); the second time for his role in the Society of Authors (499). In *The Cambridge History of Victorian Literature* (Flint, 2012) Besant makes only a fleeting appearance in connection with slum life fiction for his reformist novel *All Sorts and Conditions of Men* (524).

and they all plainly exposed his practical and commercial views. But it was his *Autobiography* that did utterly harm his reputation. There, as in the previous commentaries, Besant stated that fiction could be practised as a job like any other. He gave details of his daily working routine; he set down extremely precise, almost pedantic guidelines, which according to him would enable aspiring authors to write saleable novels. Although clinging to the concept of the literary genius, Besant frankly admitted that his novels were wares of commerce. His engagement with the Society of Authors, whose main aim was the recognition and the protection of literary property, was not perceived positively by many of his contemporaries, as the association of literature and money was widely disliked. His attitude lowered him in the eyes of the public, who liked to think of their favourite writers as geniuses who worked following sudden inspiration. This chapter argues that Besant's too straightforward commentaries on novel writing and money and his direct engagement with the Society of Authors contributed to lower his reputation as much as, or perhaps even more than, his later novels.

The second reason I suggest is that Besant's association with literary partnership further contributed to his debasement. In the Victorian imagination, collaboration in novel writing did not enjoy a high reputation: as we will see, it was perceived as a funny or stimulating experimental writing method or as a useful stepping stone to gain the confidence necessary to write alone; in any case, it was not deemed good for producing valuable literary work. Besant himself contributed to feed such views, and his opinions had a great impact on his contemporaries. Ironically, then, Besant had a hand in his own ruin; collaboration was the final nail in the coffin of his posthumous reputation.

In his introduction to the first collection of essays about Besant, Morrison (2019, 13) suggests that "the time is ripe for a re-evaluation." This is indeed true, as critical interest in Besant has substantially grown in the last years.[7] However, it must be noted that the expanding corpus of studies on Besant has focused mainly, if not exclusively, on his role as a social reformer and/or as a campaigner for authors' rights.[8]

---

7 Morrison (2019) observes that the number of critical studies on Besant published in the last ten years equals the number of studies published in the preceding fifty years. See Bivona and Henkle, 2006; Swafford, 2007; Banerjee, 2014; Gannon, 2014; McCann, 2014; Ghosh, 2017; and Ginn, 2017.
8 On Besant as a social reformist see Neetens, 1990; Weiner, 1994; Joyce, 1996; Bivona and Henkle, 2006; Swafford, 2007; Gannon, 2014; Ghosh, 2017; and

Among Besant's fictional works, the ones to attract the most scholarly attention have been his social novels (only *All Sorts and Conditions of Men* and *Children of Gibeon* are available in critical editions).[9] Morrison's collection itself aims at discussing the mutually constitutive interplay between Besant's social activism and his efforts to professionalize authorship. Yet much more needs to be said about Besant: his prominence as a novelist and most of all as a co-author has not received its due yet. This chapter makes it its focus, specifically for what regards Besant's partnership with Rice. Their relationship, their working method, and the different role each partner played in the collaboration will be examined in detail.[10] The aim of the chapter is ultimately to shed light on the issues with which I opened this discussion, and hopefully to suggest new directions of study on Walter Besant as an author and collaborator.

The goblins, or, before the collaboration

When Walter Besant and James Rice started to collaborate in 1871, the former was thirty-five and the latter twenty-eight. Both had already tried their hands at novel writing. Both had been unsuccessful: Rice had dashed off a novel in the magazine he edited, but it was never printed in book form; Besant had worked for years on a novel which "was read and refused" by publishers and consequently "consigned, while still in manuscript, to the flames" by its author (*MFB*, 3–4). The two evidently had literary ambitions but seemed unable to realize them.

In Besant's *Autobiography*, which begins in Robinson Crusoe style enumerating the benefits of being born into the middle class, he extensively accounts for his childhood in Portsmouth, the town where Dickens was also born, twenty-four years before him. About seventy pages of the *Autobiography* are devoted to his childhood, narrating in

---

Ginn, 2017. On Besant as a campaigner for authors' rights see Colby, 1990, and Eliot, 1999.

9 Two critical editions of *All Sorts and Conditions of Men* have appeared so far: one edited by Helen Small (1997), which is no longer in print, and one edited by Kevin A. Morrison (2012). As for *Children of Gibeon*, there is currently only one critical edition, edited by Kevin A. Morrison (2015).

10 No comment on their collaboration and how it worked was made by either Besant or Rice while it was still ongoing. After his partner's death, Besant waited five years before revealing some details and expressing his opinions. I have not found any written comment on the collaboration left by Rice.

exasperating detail anecdotes of his youth, his family, his neighbourhood, and his teachers. In 1855 he entered Christ's College, Cambridge, with a view of becoming a clergyman, despite being never really convinced about taking holy orders: since his childhood, he had dreamt of being a writer.[11] During his years at Cambridge, however, Besant became absorbed in mathematics, and "for three years almost ceased to think of writing at all" (*Autobiography*, 78). After a university career "not greatly distinguished" (*Autobiography*, 88) he was just about to enter the clergy when a chance to escape came his way: the opportunity to work as a professor of mathematics at the Royal College in Mauritius. Besant applied and got the job, and in 1861 he left England to spend the next six years in Port Louis. Since his job left him with a lot of free time, he devoted himself to a series of "voracious and indiscriminate" readings (*Autobiography*, 150) and went back to his first passion:

> I was writing all the time. I wrote essays for the most part, which have long since been torn up. In truth I was not in the least precocious, and I spent these years in getting control over my pen, which at first ran along of its own accord, discursive, rambling, and losing its original purpose. No one would believe the trouble I had in making the pen a servant instead of a master; in other words, in forcing the brain to concentration. (*Autobiography*, 141)

The fact that he showed no natural talent for writing did not hinder him. In his late-life commentaries he would insist on the importance of practice, as he distinguished between what he called "facility of the pen" and "writing well":

> [a]s a first rule, I advise the student to write something every day. This rule does not mean that he should write in order to acquire facility of writing. Mere facility is nothing [...]. Indeed, it is a dangerous and suspicious gift. The writer who has facility of the pen finds that his pen is his master: it runs away with him: it will not stick to the subject; in other words, the writer's brain is not under his control. (*PB*, 49)

The section "Preparation for the Literary Life" of *The Pen and the Book* explains that daily exercise is not aimed at writing fast, but rather at writing about "one thing, and one thing only," without digressions

---

11 In his solo novel *All In a Garden Fair* (1883), Besant portrayed himself in one of the protagonists, a boy with literary aspirations. This novel would later inspire Kipling to leave India and follow his dream to make a career as a writer, as he remembers in *Something of Myself* (see Kipling, 1987, 71). For a discussion of *All in A Garden Fair*, see Ue, 2019.

(*PB*, 49). The greater the gift of imagination, the harder it is to acquire mastery over one's pen: "[t]he brain must be trained to obey, and the will must be taught to command" (*PB*, 50). Besant repeatedly said that he acquired his capacity for writing well through "painstaking practice" (*Autobiography*, xvii). He also reported in many of his life-writings that his first novel, written in two years during his time in Mauritius, had been a failure. The returned manuscript, and the disappointment it represented, became a source of anxiety:

> [t]he papers lay in my chambers for a long time afterwards in a corner covered with dust. They got upon my nerves. I used to see a goblin sitting on the pile; an amorphous goblin, with tearful eyes, big head, shapeless body, long arms and short legs. He would wag his head mournfully. "Don't make another like me," he said. "Not like me. I couldn't bear to meet another like me." At last I plucked up courage and burned the whole pile. Then my goblin vanished and I saw him no more. (*Autobiography*, 141–42)[12]

After the destruction of the work of two years, Besant began to feel burdened by "an increased tendency to a form of melancholia" (*Autobiography*, 142). He therefore took a vacation and went to visit the island of Réunion in 1864. The written account of his sojourn on the island was what would put Besant in contact with his future collaborator: once back in England, he sent the manuscript to a London paper, the 2d. illustrated weekly *Once a Week*. He heard nothing in reply, nor did he receive the manuscript back. In the autumn of 1869, while browsing *Once a Week* at a railway bookstall, he found that it had been published without him being informed.[13] Moreover, the article was full of misspelt names and other mistakes. Indignant at the treatment of his work, Besant wrote to demand an explanation. He "received a note in reply, signed James Rice, begging that [he] would call upon him" (*RMM*, vi). The explanation was simple: Rice had just taken over the magazine, and, on finding Besant's paper with no indication as to the name of the author or anything to show that it had not been corrected, had published it:

> I found my Editor a pleasant and friendly creature, anxious to set himself right with me, and desirous of hearing again from me. I departed with a

---

12 Almost identical accounts of this episode are present in Besant, 1884, 91–93; Besant, 1887, vii; *MFB*, 2–3. This is not infrequent: since Besant's ideas on topics connected with writing were often requested, he made economies by reusing the same bits.

13 [Unsigned], "The Island of Réunion: In Two Parts," *Once a Week*, 16 October 1869, pp. 224–28; 23 October 1869, pp. 250–54.

promise on my part to send him sketches, notes of travel, notes on literature, essays – anything that I chose; and on his, to receive and consider everything that I should send.

Very soon I got into the habit of dropping into the little back office in Tavistock street, generally with some small contributions, and of staying for a talk. (*RMM*, vi)

For the next two years, Besant worked as a regular contributor to the paper and formed a friendship with its editor.

Samuel James Rice is "a surprisingly elusive figure" (Storer, 2019, 46). Not much about him has come down to us; even the details of the date and place of his birth are full of discrepancies.[14] We do know that he too was a Cambridge man (he entered Queens' College in 1865), that he studied law, and that for a short time he practised at the Temple. Soon enough, however, his literary ambitions led him to seize the opportunity to become the editor (and possibly the owner) of *Once a Week*.[15] At first, Rice contented himself with editing, but he wanted more: he wrote a serial called *The Mortimers* that he published in the magazine from February to October 1870. The novel had a promising plot, but was crude and mechanically written. "The result was not satisfactory," commented Besant, "and he wisely resolved not to republish it until he could find time to rewrite it. That time never came" (*RMM*, vii).[16]

14 Besant wrote that Rice was born in 1843, but the entry in the Register of Births in Northampton gives Samuel James Rice's year of birth as 1844. *The Oxford Dictionary of National Biography* states that Rice was born in Bridge Street, All Saints, Northampton, on 26 September 1844. See Storer, 2019, 47.

15 As with Rice's date of birth, Storer (2019, 40–41, note 5) warns that Besant's carelessness in dating the early events of the collaboration in his various accounts has led to confusion in more than one aspect. Through a careful investigation, Storer proves that Besant and Rice's first meeting could not have occurred earlier than July 1869: in the 1887 preface to *Ready-Money Mortiboy* and in his *Autobiography*, Besant stated that he first met his future collaborator as owner and editor of *Once a Week* in 1868; but this statement is problematic, as the publishers Bradbury and Agnew (the former Bradbury and Evans, who had founded *Once a Week* in 1859) owned it until mid-1869. In addition, Besant claims that Rice bought the magazine, maintaining the ownership as well as the editorship until 1873. However, once again there is no independent evidence of this. The *ODNB* simply repeats the details from Besant's statement (even repeating his inaccurate date). It is therefore important to note that there may be a problem with the accuracy of Besant's accounts.

16 Besant, 1887 is written in a sentimental tone, and Besant tries to save Rice from a bad reputation by adding that "it was not a work of which he had any reason to be ashamed" (vii). The only other work by Rice alone is a two-volume *History of the*

On his return to England, Besant had resolved to become a writer: "I would not go back to the Royal College of Mauritius, nor would I take a mastership in any English school. I was never a teacher to the manner born [...]. I understood that my opening was to be made – somehow or other, as yet I knew not how – by literature" (*Autobiography*, 150). Disliking the prospect of living in privation, he got a job as a secretary of the Society for the Systematic and Scientific Exploration of Palestine, a place he kept for the following eighteen years.[17] Only in 1885, at the peak of his fame as a novelist, did he resign from the job: "my office was continually crowded with editors and publishers and visitors, who came to me not on account of their interest in Palestine. I therefore left off drawing the salary" (*Autobiography*, 179). So, Besant turned to literature as his sole profession only at fifty, when his fame was more than solid, and his novels "gave [him] an income which would be called handsome even at the bar" (*Autobiography*, 180).

The job at the Society allowed Besant to live comfortably (the annual salary was £300),[18] and left him with enough spare time to pursue his literary ambitions:

> although my office hours were supposed to be from ten to four, [...] there was not enough work to occupy a quarter of the time. [...] After the letters had been answered I could carry on my work in a perfectly quiet office, I could give the afternoons to visitors, and from four till seven I was again free to carry on my work without interruption in my chambers. (*Autobiography*, 168)

A point much insisted upon in all Besant's commentaries was to avoid relying exclusively on literature to earn a living, as that would lead to hack writing. Besant always showed contempt for the figure of the hack, as, being obliged to live on their writing, they would care more for the quantity than for the quality of their work: "I was resolved that I would not become a publisher's hack; that I would not hang about publishers' offices and beg for work; nor write introductions and edit new editions at five guineas the job with a preface, an introductory life,

---

Turf. It was referred to in *The Times* (21 November 1879) as a very unmethodical work.

17 On the Palestine Association, see Kark and Goren, 2011.

18 Besant's *Autobiography*, like all his writings, displays an extremely practical and precise attitude towards every subject, including money matters. It reports minutely the cost of everything at the time, thus becoming an interesting source of information about the cost of life in London in the late 1860s and the early 1870s.

notes, and an index thrown in. I meant to [...] live an independent life" (*Autobiography*, 151–52). Besant advised "everybody who proposes to make a bid for literary success to do so with some backing," like "a mastership in a school, a Civil service clerkship, a post as a secretary to some institution or society; anything, anything, rather than dependence on the pen, and the pen alone" (*Autobiography*, 168). Such insistence on this issue reveals Besant's preoccupation with the financial position of writers. He also lamented the solitude of his beginnings: he started to notice that writers usually stood alone, and that they lacked the possibilities to make connections with one another.

With time on his hands and no pressing need for money, Besant pondered what to do. Not feeling confident enough to try another novel, the first big work he completed and managed to have published was a book on French literature, the result of his readings in Mauritius. *Studies in Early French Poetry* (1868) gained him a reputation as a scholar and opened the doors of magazines (*Autobiography*, 169).[19] He wrote reviews, articles and essays on motley subjects for various periodicals, but he deeply disliked the idea of being a critic – a figure repeatedly and bitterly attacked in his *Autobiography*:

> there is no branch of the literary life more barren and dreary than that of writing notes upon poets and other writers dead and gone. I have seen the effect of this left upon so many. First, everybody can do it, well or ill; therefore there is a striving for something distinctive, resulting in extravagance, exaggerations, studied obscurity, the pretence of seeing more than other people can see in an author, the parade of an inferior writer as a great genius; so we have the revival of a poet deservedly forgotten – all *pour l'effet*, and all leading directly to habitual dishonesty, sham, and the estimation of form above matter. [...] I am continually grateful for the accident which took me out of the ranks of reviewers and criticasters and placed me in the company of the story-tellers. (*Autobiography*, 182–84)

The "accident" was a short story Besant wrote, entitled "Titania's Farewell," which struck Rice and made him think of a collaboration: "[t]o me this flimsy trifle became of the utmost importance, because it changed the whole current of my life. In place of a writer of 'studies,' 'appreciations,' and the lighter kind of criticism, I became a novelist" (*Autobiography*, 182). However, like other parts of the *Autobiography*, the information provided by Besant is inaccurate: he states that "Titania's

---

19 Besant published a sequel in 1873, *The French Humorists*. On Besant's life-long love for French literature, and Rabelais in particular, see Ginn, 2019, 163–70.

Farewell" was published in the 1869 Christmas number of *Once a Week*, but the story is nowhere to be found in any issue of the magazine around that time (nor in any other magazine; or, at least, I could not find it).[20] Whether or not it was a story called "Titania's Farewell" that attracted Rice's attention, we do know that, at some point in 1871, Rice made a curious proposition to his paper's contributor.

The authors of *Ready-Money Mortiboy*

> After the appearance of "Titania's Farewell," Rice came to me with a proposal. It was that I would collaborate with him in writing a novel. (*Autobiography*, 186)

> It was not until the autumn of 1871 that Rice first made a serious proposition to me which changed the whole of my work for life. He proposed that I should join him in writing a novel. (*RMM*, vii)

> One day [...] [Rice] told me that he had an idea [...] which seemed to him not only possible, but hopeful. He proposed that we should take up this idea together, work it out, if it approved itself to me as it did to him, and write a novel upon it together. (*MFB*, 10)

All Besant's accounts of the beginning of his literary partnership with Rice are more or less the same. After the serialization of *The Mortimers*, Rice had thought of another story. He had planned the plot, drawn the main characters, and written the first chapters: however, he must have realized that the work would not come out well this time either. He needed an ally. So, he thought of joining forces with someone who could write with facility and with whom he was becoming increasingly familiar. Besant agreed to the proposal, but put as a condition that "the thing, whether good or bad, was to be anonymous" (*RMM*, viii). As a matter of fact, Besant and Rice's first five novels were published anonymously, both in instalments and in book form.

The first result of the writing partnership was *Ready-Money Mortiboy*: originally serialized in *Once a Week* from January to June 1872, it was then published in three volumes by Tinsley.[21] The edition had no authorial

---

20 We know with certainty that it was included in a collection of short stories entitled *The Case of Mr. Lucraft, and Other Tales* (1876), which came out under Besant's and Rice's joint names some years later. *The Graphic* described the story as the weakest of the collection (27 May 1876, p. 527).
21 Besant's novels (whether with Rice or alone) were all produced for periodical

identification at all, but the authors played with a visual element to subtly provide hints about their identities: the frontispiece presents an emblem consisting of a circle, within which the initials of the authors' names were drawn; the letters 'SJR' on the left, and 'WB' on the right, though separate, are intertwined.[22] When the novel came out, however, reviews talked about 'the author' of *Ready-Money Mortiboy*. The use of the singular reveals that the public was not aware of the double authorship – in fact, people did not even think of that option. Apart from the emblem, no other hint was given as to the collaborative nature of the work, and the public's assumption of single authorship was proof of the textual unity Besant would talk about in "On Literary Collaboration."

The double authorship was revealed by the end of the year, with the first instalment of *My Little Girl* in *Once a Week* (then published in volume by Tinsley in 1873), which presented the formula "by the authors of *Ready-Money Mortiboy*." This shows that the partners had no intention of concealing the collaborative nature of their novels, but rather to double the mystery by doubling anonymity. By looking at a few reviews of *My Little Girl*, it emerges that the double authorship struck the critics, and many reflected on the originality of this practice.[23] The *Standard* remarked that

> [a]n English novel by two authors, working conjointly, is a phenomenon of rare occurrence, and deserves notice, if only on that account. But the

---

publication, except for *The Revolt of Men*. He and Rice wrote for a variety of periodicals, but the most typical venue was the London weeklies. Besant seems to have been particularly suited to the rhythm and constraints of serial publication. In addition, he was not inclined to major revisions of his stories before publication in volume. Perhaps due to the influence of Rice and then Watt, his agent (both well acquainted with the London periodical market), Besant seems to have often shaped his stories specifically according to the nature of the journal in which they were to appear. For more details, see Law, 2000, 207–08. For the complete table of the periodicals in which Besant's co-authored and solo novels were originally serialized see Law, 2000, 241–44.

22 This visual element appeared for the first time on the title page of the book edition of *Ready-Money Mortiboy* and was reprinted on the title pages of their second and third novels, both published by Tinsley. Then, starting from the fourth novel, *The Golden Butterfly*, by the same publisher, it disappeared. This emblem is not present in any instalment of their works. The artist was F. Waddy, illustrator for *Once a Week*.

23 Reviews printed at the end of vol. III of the first edition of *By Celia's Arbour* (London: Sampson Low & Co., 1878). From now on I will refer to this source as *CA*.

READY-MONEY MORTIBOY.

A Matter-of-Fact Story.

(REPRINTED FROM "ONCE A WEEK.")

IN THREE VOLUMES.
VOL. II.

WITH INITIAL DESIGNS BY F. W. WADDY.

LONDON:
TINSLEY, BROTHERS, 18 CATHERINE ST., STRAND.
1872.

(All rights reserved.)

249. c. 1!.

Figure 1. Title page of *Ready-Money Mortiboy*, by Walter Besant and James Rice (London: Tinsley Brothers, 1872, II). Source: Archive.org

book before us needs no such recommendation; as, for vigour, conception, brightness, freshness of style, and general originality, it altogether stands apart from and above the ordinary run of recent fiction. (*CA*)

The novelty of double authorship alone sufficed to make the novel stand out, a fact that, within less than two decades, would no longer be enough. The review in the *Athenaeum* praised the partnership highly and reasoned on its benefits:

> [t]he principle of co-operation seems to be extending itself to every branch of life. Scientific research has long been indebted to it, and now our novelists are

making the experiment of its use. The authors of *Ready-Money Mortiboy* have, we think, reason to be satisfied with the result. A joint capital of experience of life, the friction of separate modes of thinking, with the advantage of mutual criticism, and something of conversational emulation, should have much influence in maintaining the authors' energy, and eliminating those lapses into weakness, from which the single muse is seldom absolutely exempt. (*CA*)

In particular, the arguments that collaboration implies are seen in a positive light: according to the critic, they purify the novel from the taints a solitary work is inevitably subject to.

Besant and Rice's next three novels (*With Harp and Crown*, *The Golden Butterfly*, and *This Son of Vulcan*), though still anonymous, all present the formula "by the authors of" on their title page. In a review of *With Harp and Crown* (first serialized in *Tinsley's Magazine* and then printed in volume by the same publisher in 1875),[24] *The Hour* commented that "[i]t is a phenomenon really worth notice that we should have in England two authors who work so wonderfully well together as the 'eminent hands' which have given us *Ready-Money Mortiboy*" (*CA*). Building on their realism and ironic treatment of humanity's common faults, the *Examiner* compared Besant and Rice to Dickens and Thackeray, advocating for the novel's place among the classics:

> our authors supply with dignity the gap in current literature hitherto left by the loss of Thackeray and Dickens. *With Harp and Crown* merits more than the most brilliant ephemeral success – namely, a permanent and honourable place in the classical literature of the country. We find therein liveliness of manner united with seriousness of purpose, keen discernment of the rottenness of society evinced without either coarseness or cynicism. (*CA*)

When Besant and Rice started to collaborate Thackeray had been dead eight years and Dickens had died the year before. Besant and Rice's fame was growing, and the comparison with Dickens and Thackeray became a common one.[25]

---

24 For a discussion of *With Harp and Crown*, see Storer, 2019, 51–53.
25 An analysis of the parallels between Dickens and Besant has been made by Diniejko, 2019. Similarities between the two authors are indeed many, partly accidental, partly due to a precise intent of Besant's, who loved and assimilated Dickens's works. In his second year at Cambridge he won a contest based on a set of absurdly precise questions on *The Pickwick Papers* (the whole text of the exam is reported in the *Autobiography*, 99–102). They both wrote extensively about the London poor and contemporary social problems, embracing an idea of the novel as a combination of entertainment and moral purpose (Diniejko, 2019, 230–39); they were famous for being able to deeply move their readers, indirectly contributing

By the publication of *The Golden Butterfly* (serialized in *The World* and then published by Tinsley in 1876), the "eminent hands" had become a guarantee of success, with eccentric and endearing characters as their trademark: "[a]s long as they can draw Phillises and Gilead P. Becks, they will not want readers, or an adequate popularity at the circulating library, with the pecuniary reward thereto appertaining" (*The Spectator, CA*). Not only: by then, people's curiosity over the workings of their partnership must have been intense, and the two collaborators could not resist satirizing such interest. Interestingly, literary collaboration features in the novel: two main characters of *The Golden Butterfly*, Captain Ladds and Jack Dunquerque, write a novel together about their adventures in America under the pen names 'the Dragoon and the Younger Son.' The book is a success, they get invited to dinners in the best London houses, and people invariably inquire who wrote which parts. The answers given by the fictional co-authors are too amusing not to be reported here:

> "It is fair to ask," the lady went on, "how you wrote the book?"
> She was one of those who, could she get the chance, would ask Messieurs Erckmann and Chatrian themselves to furnish her with a list of the paragraphs and the ideas due to each in their last novel.[26]
> Ladds looked as if the question was beyond his comprehension.
> At last he answered slowly –
> "Steel pen. The other man had a gold pen."
> "No – no; I mean did you write one chapter and your collaborateur the next, or how?"

to legal reforms. Both Dickens's and Besant's fiction had a philanthropic aim, and they were reformers but not radicals (Diniejko, 2019, 236). Both promoted a code of values based on duty, hard work, respectability, and charity. They were men of phenomenal energy and dedication: despite their extremely busy lives, both Dickens and Besant were engaged in philanthropic work and various public commitments. Both were clubbable men and dedicated Londoners (Diniejko, 2019, 229, 233). Finally, Besant's Society of Authors recalls the abortive efforts of Dickens in the same direction as a campaigner for authors' rights, as both believed that the novel was an aesthetic object but also a mass-market commodity to profit from.

26 Emile Erckmann (1822–1899) and Alexandre Chatrian (1826–1890) were a very popular pair of French co-authors who, in the course of a forty-year-long partnership, wrote an impressive amount of fiction and drama, a great part of which was translated into English. Besant and Rice were repeatedly called the Erckmann and Chatrian of English literature by the periodical press, and here they refer to the French collaborators as a model for successful co-authorship. The partnership of Erckmann and Chatrian and its impact on Victorian culture will be discussed in Chapter 4.

"Let me think it over," replied Ladds, as if it were a conundrum.
(Besant and Rice, 1877, 93)

Ladd's replies also give voice to Besant and Rice's impatience with questions about 'who did what.' Jack Dunquerque and Captain Ladds further enjoy confusing nosy readers by attributing to each other the "wicked parts" (93) of the novel:

> "O Captain Ladds!" this was one of two ladies, she who had read up the book before coming to the dinner, and had so far an advantage over the other – "that is just like one of the wicked things, the delightfully wicked things, in the *Little Sphere*. Now we know which of the two did the wicked things."
> "It was the other man," said Ladds. [...]
> "Of course, if you write wickedness you are sure of an audience. I don't think, Mr. Dunquerque," [Mrs. Cassils] added, with a smile, "that it is the business of gentlemen to attack existing institutions."
> Jack shook his head.
> "It was not my writing. It was the other man. I did what I could to tone him down." (Besant and Rice, 1877, 93, 94)

Besant and Rice's novels were not only praised: they bore pecuniary fruits. Evidence can be found in the preface to the first book edition (Besant and Rice, 1876a) of their fifth and last anonymous novel, *This Son of Vulcan* (originally serialized in *London Society*). This is the only preface written when both authors were alive. Though it makes no explicit comment on co-authorship, it is worth looking at for another telling visual element and for the information it provides about the reception of the novels. The preface is signed 'W.B.' and 'J.R.' with a curly bracket that embraces both initials. The bracket unites the two names, so that a connection is established between them even if they are separate.[27] As for the content of the preface, it mainly consists of a strong attack on pirate editions in America, Canada, India, and Australia. From it we learn that, by the mid 1870s, Besant and Rice's works circulated widely outside Europe. They ironically thanked their "friends the pirates" for the notoriety they contributed to give them by paying them "the honour of unlicensed reproduction." The duo reminded publishers that "the

---

27 Bracketed names of co-authors were not an invention of Besant and Rice's publishers: the tradition goes back at least to the 1647 Beaumont and Fletcher folio, which in its title-page reads *Comedies and Tragedies Written by Francis Beaumont and John Fletcher, Gentlemen*, with Beaumont's and Fletcher's names bracketed together.

eight commandment is still supposed to be binding," thus indirectly calling them thieves (Besant and Rice, 1876a, iv). They also warned readers that *The Toronto Globe* was the only non-British paper with which they had made arrangements: such insistence on copyright issues was an early sign of Besant's interest in the cause he would advocate in the later part of his career.

The first novel to be published under Besant and Rice's names was *By Celia's Arbour*, first serialized in *The Graphic* and then printed in volume by Sampson Low & Co. in 1878, the same year as their seventh novel, *The Monks of Thelema*.[28] Nevertheless, their names would not appear as often as the formula 'by the authors of *Ready-Money Mortiboy*.' Exhibiting the title of their first and very successful novel was thought a more effective strategy than displaying their names. In reviews and blurbs, the duo's *oeuvre* was referred to as 'The *Ready-Money Mortiboy* Novels.' The fact that their first novel came to indicate a whole category, including non-novels such as collections of short stories, is evidence that Besant and Rice remained, first and foremost, 'the authors of *Ready-Money Mortiboy*.'

The praise was not unjustified: *Ready-Money Mortiboy* must indeed be counted among Besant and Rice's best works The title introduces the main theme of the book, money, and the influence it has on people – how it deeply affects social relationships, how it can corrupt some (as in the case of the eponymous, elderly protagonist) or improve others (as in the case of his son): "wealth that works in many ways, turning the unselfish man into the voluptuary; or the selfish man into one who lives and cares wholly for others. Wealth brings with it its curse or its blessing, just as its recipient is disposed" (Besant and Rice, 1872, III, 233). The basic idea stemmed from the parable of the Prodigal Son, who comes home apparently repentant, but actually "ten times worse than when he went away" (*RMM*, viii); yet Besant and Rice managed to make the story evolve in unexpected ways. *Ready-Money Mortiboy* is the story of an extremely rich, hardened banker called Richard Mortiboy – nicknamed

---

28 For a discussion of *The Monks of Thelema* with a focus on social reform see Storer, 2019 (50–51) and Ginn, 2019. Ginn especially offers an accurate analysis of Besant and Rice's only social novel, which foreshadows Besant's later interest in philanthropy and reform. *The Monks of Thelema* was subtitled "An Invention," just as *All Sorts and Conditions of Men* (Besant's first solo book and his most famous social novel) was subtitled "An Impossible Story." Such telling subtitles, according to Ginn, were intended to "romanticize the possibilities of a positive human vision" (2019, 169).

by his fellow citizens Old Ready-Money Mortiboy – and of his only son, Dick. The narration begins when the latter, after an absence of twelve years (his father had thrown him out at nineteen for forging a cheque) unexpectedly comes home. He professes to have reformed, to have become respectable, and – most importantly in the eyes of his materialist father – to have made a fortune in America. Actually, in those twelve years Dick has been living by various expedients, including the slave trade, and is a gambler who intends to rob his father. Little by little, he gains back the old man's trust, who decides to retire and leave him the bank and all his estates, only to find out, the very moment after the passing of property, that Dick has been lying all the time. Shocked, Old Ready-Money Mortiboy is struck with paralysis. Ironically enough, the stroke gives him the benevolent expression he has never had before: "[h]is face is drawn curiously out of shape, and it gives him a happy and pleasant look he never used to have. He actually looks as if he was smiling all the while – a thing, as you know, he did not often do" (Besant and Rice, 1872, II, 100–01). Dick has finally had his revenge: his father brought him up without love, teaching him to value only money, and received what he gave. From this moment on, Dick undergoes a gradual, profound change, so that he does not act as the villain any more: now the richest man in town and free from worries, he behaves generously and is beloved by the people. Unlike his father, he uses his wealth for good causes. He immediately raises the salaries of the bank's employees and devotes himself to individual but effective charitable actions, being deeply critical of institutions. Dick's reformation is effected by his love for his cousin Grace, who does not love him back but who teaches him the joys of an honest and simple life (the influence of a good woman is one of Besant and Rice's most recurrent motifs). When Dick meets Bill, a poor child whom at first he believed to be his son from a hasty marriage he contracted as a teenager, he is deeply moved and decides to adopt him even if he has proof that the child is not his. The scene of the baby farm (Besant and Rice, 1872, III, ch. 4) offers a vivid picture of the life of the London poor, especially destitute children: this would become a characteristic trait of Besant's solo fiction. Dick resolves to raise the child as his own, teaching him different values from the ones his own father brought him up with. Through Grace and little Bill, the former scoundrel starts to know what love is:

> [a]s he looked down at the child's thin face and deep blue eyes, his heart grew soft. It seemed as if he had missed something all his life, which he

was finding now. What he had missed were the influences of love: now they were upon him. He loved a woman. True, she did not love him; but she cared in a way for him. It was something to know that Grace loved him "as a brother" [...] – all this touched Dick, and moved him: it was the first step upwards – to something like repentance. (Besant and Rice, 1872, III, 169–70)

Dick even repents of what he did to his father and starts to behave more gently towards the invalid old man. He decides to go back to America, taking little Bill with him and leaving the bank and all his property to Grace's family. At this point, however, his former partner in gambling, an evil Frenchman named Lafleur, reappears, claiming a part of Dick's money. Dick offers him a generous sum, on condition that he would leave immediately and never come back; Lafleur accepts but also proposes to play a card game for the last time. When Dick finds out that his former partner is cheating, a fight ensues; Dick manages to floor him, but Lafleur unexpectedly takes a gun out his pocket and shoots him: "Dick was dead. Dick the generous: Dick the noble: Dick the true and brave. Dick was dead" (Besant and Rice, 1872, III, 247). The protagonist's reformation process and his plans for a bright future are thus put an end to by the return of his past. Dick's sudden, violent death leaves the reader with a sense of deep injustice, repeatedly emphasized by the narrating voice. In the same exact moment of Dick's death, his old father has another stroke, this time fatal, and dies too.

The novel presents a secondary (though much less interesting) subplot, the story of Frank Melliship, Dick's cousin and his opposite. Frank has been raised by a loving but weak father – the very opposite of old Ready-Money – who, at the beginning of the narration, commits suicide because of the debts he has accumulated, leaving his family in a state of destitution. Frank is left to survive by his own means, but he has been brought up as a gentleman and lacks the means to enter a profession. Too proud to ask for help, he unsuccessfully tries to make a living first by painting, then by singing. He and Grace are in love, but they cannot get married until his financial situation is more stable and his father's debts are paid off. Frank's situation seems without solution; his story is dragged on chapter after chapter, and is finally solved by Dick, who, with an act of generosity just before his death, makes him a partner of the Mortiboy bank, so that Grace can be happy with the man she loves. The story closes with the inauguration of a statue in memory of Dick Mortiboy in the centre of his native town.

Despite the many digressions and a very intrusive narrator's voice, *Ready-Money Mortiboy* is remarkable for the realistic handling of the characters, the acute observations on middle-class life, and the slyly satiric humour. It celebrates most Victorian values; and yet, through Dick's character, it also presents a sharp critique of some pillars of Victorian morality. In particular, Dick is harshly critical of his countrymen's attitude towards the lower layers of society; his analysis of the hypocrisy of teaching children to be content with the position they are born into, but at the same time putting so much importance on money and social status, is an interesting aspect of the novel. At a feast he organizes for the poor country children of the area, Dick delivers an inspiring speech which alienates "the affections of all the spiritual leaders of the town" (Besant and Rice, 1872, II, 113): "'[a]nd now, my boys and girls, remember this. Don't you believe people who tell you to be contented with what you've got. That's all nonsense. You've got to be discontented. The world is full of good things for those who have the courage to get up and seize them'" (Besant and Rice, 1872, II, 128). Dick attacks charity institutions and the Church throughout the narration, for instance during a confrontation with Grace:

> "[y]ou subscribe a million a-year to convert the niggers. You send out people you call missionaries, who live in comfortable houses, and bully and bribe the natives. I've seen them. [...] All the time, you've got all your paupers at home starving [...]. Your charities make the people paupers: your Church helps to make them hypocrites; your poor laws make them slaves: your trading interest grind them to the dust." (Besant and Rice, 1872, III, 11–12)

In addition, the comments on the dullness of middle-class women's lives are noteworthy. Referring to Grace and the women of her family, chapter eighteen reads:

> [i]t is the way of things. A man works and hopes, and is sure to be disappointed. A woman waits and hopes, generally getting disappointed too. [...] [T]hey talked, and made each other unhappy. This, I believe, is not uncommon in English households – the sweet domesticity on which we pride ourselves covering an infinite amount of petty miseries, tiny bullyings, nagging, and prickings with tongues as sharp as needles. Sister against sister – mother against daughter. They love each other fondly, of course, because they are always supposed to love each other: domestic affection being as necessary in modern life as a shirt to one's back. [...] The lower classes of England [...] are much superior to the middle classes in this respect. I have found out the reason why. They don't sit at home so much. (Besant and Rice, 1872, II, 303–04)

By 1880, Besant and Rice's fame was well established and they were considered among the best novelists of the moment: the *London Evening*

Standard (28 October 1878, no. 16931, p. 2) referred to them as "the prolific joint authors of some of the shrewdest and cleverest novels of the day," and stated that there were "only a very few living authors" producing novels with such "fun and the satire [...] infinitely better than the fun and satire of most other living novelists." They were called "writers [...] of contents of unrivalled reputation, so far as interest and entertainment [...] are concerned" (*Belfast News-Letter*, 5 April 1879, no. 18838, p. 5), and "our brightest and most piquant novelists" (*Northern Whig*, 22 December 1878, no. 22, 275, p. 5). Besant and Rice's penultimate work, *The Chaplain of the Fleet* (1879), ran simultaneously in England (*The Graphic*), the United States (*American Queen*), Canada (*Toronto Globe*), and Australia (*Melbourne Argus*); it was immediately translated into different languages and serialized on the continent as well (*London Daily News*, 12 November 1880, no. 10787, p. 2).

Re-editions were also continuously issued. In the Chatto & Windus 1887 edition of *Ready-Money Mortiboy* a portrait of Rice appeared with the words "yours faithfully, James Rice" inscribed below in an etched facsimile of the writer's handwriting (Besant and Rice, 1887, ii). This frontispiece fulfilled a commemorative intent, as Rice had been dead five years. Such intent was reinforced by the content of the preface, in which Besant went through the various steps of their collaboration. The frontispiece explicitly follows the model established by Charles Dickens in 1839 for the final double number of *Nicholas Nickleby*, painted by Daniel Maclise and engraved by William Finden. Dickens's frontispiece presented a picture with a text: below the portrait the phrase "faithfully yours" is added with the well-flourished signature "Charles Dickens." The "faithful" that used to be meant as a comment to the content of the novel ('a faithful account') had now come to describe the relationship between the author and his readers, establishing a connection of trust between them. The author's face and signature, rather than their prose, became the guarantors of identity, "a seal of authenticity" (Curtis, 1995, 241), as if visuality had replaced the uncertainty of a mere name, of mere words, with a recognizable and authentic image. Dickens thus complicated the concept of authorial identity: to know the writer we must *see* their face – that is, formally portrayed by a major contemporary painter. The iconography of Dickens's portrait became the canonical way of representing the bourgeois writer (Patten, 2001, 31). By association, Chatto & Windus was placing Rice, and consequently his former partner Besant, in that realm of the middle-class, respectable household authors that Dickens had inaugurated.

Figure 2. Portrait of James Rice in *My First Book*, ed. by Jerome K. Jerome (London: Chatto & Windus, 1897), p. 5. Source: Archive.org

The same portrait appeared seven years later in *My First Book*, a collection of essays by twenty-two popular novelists recounting their beginnings, edited by Jerome K. Jerome and published by Chatto & Windus in 1894, re-issued in 1897. Significantly, Besant was given the opening chapter. Apart from Jerome's, his portrait is the first to appear in the book, on the very second page (*MFB*, 2). The style is the same as Rice's portrait, which appears only on page five, but some crucial differences characterize Besant's picture: Rice is represented looking away, staring into the distance (maybe a reference to him no longer being alive?), and only his face and shoulders are visible; Besant instead looks directly at the reader, and in the foreground a pen is present in his hand. Another sketch of Besant appears some pages later: this time a full-length image, representing the author in his study, with a meditative expression, seated by his writing table, a pen in his hand, and surrounded by a setting showing comfortable middle-class status, evoking once again the portrait of Dickens by Maclise (*MFB*, 9). Although the main topic of the chapter is Besant and Rice's partnership, there is only one illustration representing them together, which, however, depicts them in a very different context: they are having dinner in a restaurant, in a relaxed and non-professional setting; their eyes are focused on the waiter in the foreground: they are neither looking at, nor speaking with, each other, and there is no sign of any interaction between them (*MFB*, 12). This detail is interesting, as the literary partners are not pictured at any stage of collaboration (talking, arguing, or writing) or in the office of *Once A Week* where they used to sit and work. Besant was the only one represented holding a pen (not once but twice), and at a desk. All the images bespeak a conception of the author as a solitary genius, embodied by Besant: even if the chapter in *My First Book* centres on the beginning

Figure 3. Portrait of Walter Besant in *My First Book*, ed. by Jerome K. Jerome (London: Chatto & Windus, 1897), p. 2. Source: Archive.org

Figure 4. Portrait of Walter Besant in *My First Book*, ed. by Jerome K. Jerome (London: Chatto & Windus, 1897), p. 9. Source: Archive.org

Figure 5. "The Oyster Shop" in *My First Book*, ed. by Jerome K. Jerome (London: Chatto & Windus, 1897), p. 12. Source: Archive.org

of his collaboration with Rice – narrated in a very positive light, too – the illustrations suggest an individualized understanding of authorship.

The fact that Besant was the only one depicted with a pen in his hand may also be ascribed to the fact that, by the publication of *My First Book*, it was common knowledge that he had played a certain role in the collaboration. Indeed, from Besant's accounts and from a number of other sources it appears that the duo had followed a precise division of tasks, as the next section will show.

Collaboration and professionalism

A week after Besant's death, an article appeared in *The Times* by a Percy Fitzgerald, who claimed that Rice had described to him how the team carried on its work:

> Besant was the skilled writing partner – he did the description, dialogues, characters; but Rice thought out the plot and construction. They met at each other's rooms, over a pipe and glass of grog, and debated the story chapter by chapter. Rice, having read his friend's daily portion of the work, would arrive furnished with many ingenious expedients for unravelling or complicating the situation [...]. Most of these were put aside, and the most striking and eligible were chosen. Besant had a gift for seizing on and developing what was thus put before him. Rice, too, often told some of his commercial efforts to exploit the stories – what elaborate treaties he entered into with the colonial booksellers, etc. In all these things Rice was the business manager and worked the "show" thoroughly well [...]. (17 June 1901, p. 16)

There is no reason to doubt Fitzgerald's account: all evidence supports it. James Brander Matthews, a personal friend of Besant's and a co-author himself, had commented on a previous occasion:

> of the long series of stories bearing the names of Besant and Rice, all that the late James Rice actually wrote with his own pen was the first chapter or two of their first book [...]. This assertion, whether well founded or not, gains color of truth from the striking similarity of style, not to call it identity, of the Besant and Rice novels with the novels of the surviving member of the partnership. (Matthews, 1891, 8–9)

Besant's own remarks on the collaboration seem to confirm this hypothesis. He dropped hints by making short, general comments, although he never plainly declared that he took care of the writing and his *collaborateur* worked as a sort of assistant. If Besant's narratives of how the partnership had begun are long and detailed, his accounts of how it had worked are brief and deliberately opaque.

When Besant died, expectations of a revelation in his posthumous *Autobiography* were high. "The remarkable and almost unique feature of his literary career is the fact that for the first ten years of it [...] he did his work in collaboration. When his autobiography is published we shall probably know the exact truth as to what Besant did and what Rice did in the series of novels which bear both their names," wrote *The Bookman* in July 1901 (vol. 20, no. 118, pp. 111–12). However, when the *Autobiography* finally appeared in print, it disappointed readers by (once again) dismissing the subject in a few sentences. Besant asserted that it was "impossible" for him to "offer any explanation or give any account" of "the method of collaboration adopted by Rice and [himself]" (187). He only wrote that

> [i]t is enough to state that we worked without disagreement; that there was never any partnership between us in the ordinary sense of the word; but that the collaboration went on from one story to another always without any binding conditions, always liable to be discontinued; while each man carried on his own independent literary work, and was free to write fiction, if he pleased, by himself. (*Autobiography*, 187–88)

The casual, non-binding nature of collaboration seems to be a relevant point for Besant, who was anxious to let readers know that he was never bound by any contract to Rice, but that the arrangement had gone on spontaneously from novel to novel. He despised the idea of a settled partnership – a point he had already stressed in "On Literary Collaboration," where he affirmed that a partnership, "though it may result in many volumes when the partners are happily able to work together evenly and harmoniously, without jealousy, without measuring each other's share, can only [...] be one from book to book" ("Lit. Coll.," 209). Indeed, there had been a gap year in the collaboration after their second novel. By 1873 *Once a Week* was no longer profitable for Rice, who had to give it up (*RMM*, viii). Since the earnings from their fiction were not yet enough, Rice went back to the Temple, working as an attorney for some time: "[t]he question then arose whether he should not seriously address himself to the Bar. For a while he did this, conducted several cases [...] and talked of giving up all attempts at literature" (*RMM*, ix). However, Rice soon accepted a post as a London correspondent for the *Toronto Globe*, "and the Bar knew him no more" (*RMM*, ix). Meanwhile, Besant was busy with journalistic work, and for a year they did nothing together. "Then Rice came to me again. He had found an opening – two openings – and was ready, if I would join him, to try again" (*RMM*, ix).

He had secured the sale of the serial rights for a new novel with *Tinsely's Magazine*, where *With Harp and Crown* appeared in instalments.

In this case, Rice acted as a manager: "[t]he collaboration had its advantages; among others, that of freeing me, for my part, from the worry of business arrangements. I am, and always have been, extremely averse from making terms and arrangements for myself" (*Autobiography*, 188). Eliot (1989, 73–76) explains that Chatto and Windus dealt exclusively with Rice as long as he was alive. Ashton (2003, 108–09) maintains that Besant totally depended upon Rice to handle business transactions, as he "spent much of his life avoiding what he considered a vital, but annoying, part of authoring." The literary marketplace, indeed, had become so complex that Besant felt that "outside help was needed in order to retain the artistic integrity necessary to write" (Ashton, 2003, 108). Crucially, according to Besant, "[a]n author is as a rule endowed with an artistic temperament; he knows little of farming an estate and is wholly unbusinesslike in making commercial bargains" (*PB*, 298). Thanks to his partnership with Rice, he was free from the worries of practical issues and could focus solely on writing; when Rice died, Besant's plunge into professional dealings must have been traumatic. He lost no time in availing himself of the services of one of the first and most prominent literary agents in London, Alexander Pollock Watt, who, later helped by his son, would handle Besant's affairs for the rest of his career.[29] Besant always talked enthusiastically of his agents, saying that thanks to them he had "always been engaged for three years in advance" and "relieved from any kind of pecuniary anxiety," and that his income had been "multiplied by three at least" (*Autobiography*, 204). *The Pen and the Book* offers a detailed picture of the British literary market around the turn of the century and underlines that "[t]he Literary Agent has now become almost indispensable for the author of every kind, but especially for the novelist" (*PB*, 215). Besant strongly advised novelists to put themselves in

---

29 The literary agent as a professional figure arrived on the scene between the late 1870s and the early 1880s and was a key factor in the transformation of literary culture. Three men are generally recognized to have played a central role in the agent's rise to prominence: A. P. Watt, J. B. Pinker, and Curtis Brown. Watt (1834–1914) is usually regarded as the first true agent: though he did not invent the job, he played the leading role in defining the functions of agents. Besides Besant, he acted for Collins, Hardy, Yeats, Conan Doyle, Kipling, Mrs Oliphant, H. G. Wells, and Rider Haggard, among others. For an account of Watt's handling of Besant's affairs and their dealings with Chatto & Windus see Eliot, 2019.

the hands of an agent for three main reasons: to begin with, the agent was a businessman, and was therefore "able to meet the publisher [...] on an equal footing. It is now one business man with another: *and one knows as much as the other*" (*PB*, 220). The second reason was that the market was too thriving to be dealt with on one's own, especially with regard to securing copyright in all the different forms of publication (the English serial rights; the American serial rights; the English volume rights; the American volume rights; the Colonial rights; the Continental rights; the translation rights; and the dramatic rights, if the novel was turned into a play). Third, an agent was in touch with the periodical press and publishing houses, and knew all about their requirements and openings: those who wanted articles or serials, those who had no empty room in their agenda, those that would be open at certain dates. For all these reasons, Besant maintained that an agent's usual commission of 10 per cent was "dirt cheap" (*PB*, 215).

Besant devoted a great deal of effort to uprooting the widespread idea that literature ought not to be connected with money. This is one of the points where his position has been mostly misunderstood, first of all by his contemporaries. He fought the "false and foolish" prejudice that it was "unworthy the dignity of letters to take any account at all of the commercial or pecuniary side" (*Autobiography*, 226–27). He remarked that the same prejudice was not so pervasive with regard to any other form of artistic and intellectual effort: the painter, the sculptor, the inventor, the musician, the singer "might blamelessly acquire by his work as much money as was attainable. Every kind of worker – except the author" (*PB*, 133). He noted that, the moment any writer begins to make some money out of his work, "a hundred voices arise," especially from "those of his own craft," voices that "cry out upon the sordidness, the meanness, the degradation of turning literature into a trade" (*Autobiography*, 227). Besant reflected that the only rational objection that could be made to writers making money by their books was that they may be tempted to work too fast and too much (*PB*, 134); this objection, he added, could nevertheless be applied to all who work with their brain.

He theorized a distinction between two kinds of value of a text: literary and commercial. The former was connected with a text's "artistic, poetic, dramatic value," and "[o]n that value is based the real position of every writer in his own generation, and the estimate of him [...] for generations to follow" (*Autobiography*, 228). The commercial value, instead, "is just measured by the public demand for it – that and nothing more" (*PB*, 5). Besant pleaded for these two values to be kept distinct: "[a] failure to hit the popular taste does not always imply failure in Art" (Besant, 1884, 77); "[i]f a good book is not in demand, that fact does not make it a bad book. If a bad book is in demand, that fact does not make it a good book" (*PB*, 4). According to him, authors need not think of the commercial value of their text while they are writing it. That is the key to keep Art untainted: "an author of any kind cannot write at all – cannot at least write anything worth having, if he is not entirely absorbed in his work, and careless while he is engaged upon it, as to any other consideration at all" (*PB*, 16). Once the book is finished, "then comes in the other value – the commercial value," and at this point "the artist ceases and the man of business begins" (*Autobiography*, 228). Once the writing part is completed, the artist has created a property of a certain value, and "[h]e is free to deal with it then as he thinks best. Why should he not?" (*PB*, 16). Çelikkol (2019, 133) emphasizes Besant's innovative point of view in suggesting that "price tags did not demean literature," but, on the contrary, "exchange value made the production of art possible" (133).[30] Authoring, claimed Besant, was a profession, and hence it should be both lucrative and respectable: it should not be "beggarly" with "no money" and "no dignity" in it (*PB*, 16–17). He particularly insisted that to raise the status of authorship to a respectable profession would mean not only to improve the material conditions of authors, but also their social standing, as society generally measured the value of a professional according to the income earned. Three requisites are identified as necessary for a profession to be held in public esteem: first, "it must be independent" – that is, "the members must not be servants of anyone"; next, "it must be entitled to share in the national distinctions as much as a soldier, a sailor, or a statesman"; last, it must have "great prizes, whether of distinction, or of money, or both" (*PB*, 20). The focus of Besant's first condition was the economic situation of writers, who had

---

30 Çelikkol (2019) points out that Besant "implicitly acknowledge[d] that literary and commercial value overlap" when "he writes of the process of composition as 'production.'" The literary and the commercial value are indeed "inseparable components of a unified process" (131–32). Çelikkol convincingly illustrates that the dominant ideal of pure aesthetics untainted by economic considerations was not shared by Besant, who claimed that "the commodification of the work of art in the marketplace is not unfortunate, but a welcome element of interpersonal exchange that ensures its social status" (134). Besant also included his view that art should not be isolated from trade relations within his works of fiction. For a discussion of the co-existence but mutual independence of the aesthetic value and the exchange value in Besant's *All Sorts and Conditions of Men* see Çelikkol, 2019, 132–41.

to be educated about publishing practices or have an agent who would manage their business. The second condition was explained in this way: "the people [...] of every country are accustomed to consider those men and women worthy of honour whom the State honours, and those men and women unworthy of honour whom the State refuses to honour. [...] [O]ur men of letters are not honoured by the State. The conclusion seems to me obvious" (Besant, 1893, 35). This second condition was the most criticized by Besant's contemporaries, who sometimes claimed that "literary men, of all men, ought to feel that authorship of good literature is its own reward" (*The Spectator*, 24 May 1884, p. 675, quoted in Gillies, 2019, 87). Exactly as with the economic aspect, popular opinion put national distinctions out of authors' reach, as they should simply be above such things. The "dream of pure aesthetic" (Çelikkol, 2019, 132) once again condemned authors to exclusion from material enjoyments. Yet Besant acknowledged that symbols such as titles mattered, and that they had an influence on people's perceptions, perhaps more than they were willing to recognize. Moreover, the accusation that a writer should not care about material validation missed Besant's key argument: as Gillies (2019, 88) highlights, Besant's interest in titular rewards was not for the sake of the individual author, but rather for authorship collectively. As to the third condition – the "great prizes" – here Besant meant the possibility for "a good steady man of letter" to "live in comfort and to educate his children properly" (*PB*, 24–25). Obviously, substantial economic profits would go to those authors whose work had great commercial value, not necessarily an artistic one; but, if one's work was in demand, there was nothing wrong in being compensated appropriately.

Besant further noticed that, unlike the other professions, novelists were not associated: "they hold no annual exhibitions, dinners, or conversazioni; [...] they have no President or Academy; and they do not themselves seem desirous of being treated as followers of a special Art" (Besant, 1884, 11). Worse than that, little or no solidarity was expressed among writers:[31]

> [e]very other profession holds itself in honour. You never find a lawyer ridiculing other lawyers because they are unsuccessful. You never find an artist ridiculing another because nobody will buy his pictures. Yet the literary

---

[31] Besant also dealt with the lack of social bonds among authors in his fiction, specifically in two of his solo novels, *Herr Paulus* (1888) and *Armorel of Lyonesse* (1890). Both works explore the issue of intellectual property and the absence of proper profits for fiction writers. See Gabriele, 2019, 106–12.

man has been constantly engaged in writing enviously and savagely against his brethren. This, I think, is the very worst feature of all: [...] envy and jealousy consumed him [the literary man] [...] The mere fact that another man was simply an author, was sufficient to fill his soul with hatred against that man. (*PB*, 12–13)

Noticing such "lonely displacement" and feeling "the need to elevate authorship and connect disparate networks of authors" (Bunting, 2019, 38), Besant set out to find a remedy. In September 1883, he and twelve members of the Savile Club set up a working party "to form an association or society of men and women engaged in letters" (*Autobiography*, 216). It would become the Society of Authors:[32]

> Some Literary Gents the other day did meet
> All in a private chamber, which looks on Garrick Street;
> There did they meet together, and solemnly they swore
> That as they had been done enough they would be done no more … .
> (*The World*, 12 March 1884)

> It was only vaguely felt, as it had been felt for fifty years, that the position of literary men was most unsatisfactory. The air was full of discontent and murmurs; yet, when any broke out into open accusation, the grievance, in some mysterious way, became insubstantial, and the charge, whatever it was, fell to the ground. It was impossible to find a remedy, because the disease itself could not be diagnosed. (*Autobiography*, 216–17)

In the first year of its creation the Society of Authors counted sixty-eight paying members; a decade later, in 1892, the number had reached 870. Besant's "first and greatest success" (*Autobiography*, 218) was Tennyson's acceptance of the Society's presidency, an accomplishment that gained it respectful consideration. The Society quickly came to include many great names. Its council counted J. M. Barrie, A. Conan Doyle, H. Rider

---

[32] Besant's Society of Authors was preceded by a series of similar projects, all unsuccessful, the most famous being Dickens's short-lived Society of British Authors, established with Thackeray and Carlyle in 1843. Besant also became a member of, or established, several clubs: in 1873 he joined the prestigious Savile Club; in 1879 he founded the Rabelais Club (to whose journal, *Recreations*, he was a major contributor); in 1891 he established the Authors' Club, which counted among its members George Meredith, Thomas Hardy, Oscar Wilde, Arthur Conan Doyle, J. M. Barrie, Jerome K. Jerome, Ford Madox Ford, and H. G. Wells; he was a member of the United Universities Club and honorary vice-president of the Royal St George's Society, which promoted English culture; in 1900 he established the Atlantic Union, aimed at the improvement of the relations between English-speaking countries.

Haggard, Thomas Hardy, Rudyard Kipling, and Charlotte Yonge; Wilkie Collins, Charles Reade, and Matthew Arnold acted as members of the representative body. Under Besant's supervision, the Society started its work by offering assistance to writers in their dealings with publishers; as a rule, it preferred private action to litigation in court, and in the cases of publishers who refused to mend their ways it simply tried to keep business out of their hands.[33] The Society never supported its allegations against publishers by naming names: it published facts but no names, and that saved it from legal suits.

Beside day-to-day tasks, the Society focused on the definition and defence of literary property, the consolidation and amendment of the laws of domestic copyright, and the promotion of international copyright. Colby (1994, 147) underlines that Besant's most important result was indeed that of institutionalizing, once and for all, the principle that the author can and must exercise control over his text. Since literary property was, more than any other, "the actual production of the individual," it had to be "in his eternal possession" (*PB*, 270). In the first issue of *The Author*, the Society's monthly journal, literary property was defined "as real a thing as property in every other kind of business" (15 May 1890). "In lucidly identifying literary creation as property," notes Gabriele (2019, 105), *The Author* "dispelled the Romantic mystifications that would make writing a disinterested act of a divinely inspired author."

Copyright law was "a means of defining this valuable property" (Gillies, 2019, 81). When the Society of Authors was established, only minor revisions had been made to the Revised Copyright Act of 1842, whose promotion had engaged Dickens, Carlyle, Wordsworth, Southey, and Browning. The Copyright Act of 1842 had been a crucial step, but by the last decades of the century it was already outdated as a result of technological and cultural changes in the publishing industry. Besant lucidly understood that literary property was becoming increasingly profitable because of the many ways in which it could be commercialized, and produced clear and detailed accounts of the problems concerning the copyright situation.[34] His advocacy for copyright revision certainly had

---

33 Two books published by the Society, entitled *Methods of Publication* and *Costs of Production*, shed light on every form of publishing, with relative costs and possibilities of profit, complete with real accounts and cases.

34 See, for instance, Besant's article "Literary Conferences," published in *Contemporary Review* 65, 1894. See Gillies, 2019, 79–80.

a key role in the Copyright Act of 1911.[35] As to international copyright, the Society denounced the lucrative trade in pirated editions. Although sometimes publishers made informal arrangements with authors as part of "the courtesy of the trade," no international copyright law protected writers, leaving them at the mercy of publishers' generosity. Revision of the American copyright law was a particularly pressing issue, as American publishers could legally reprint British books without any payment.[36] Gabriele (2019, 100) foregrounds the Society of Authors' innovative position in dismissing "the simplistic, nationalist terms of the debate on the question of copyright." In fact, it also worked to stop the circulation of pirated editions within the UK, recognizing that "it was absurd to keep calling the Americans thieves and pirates while our people did exactly the same thing on a smaller scale" (*Autobiography*, 224).

It might not be too daring to establish a connection between Besant's collaborative experience with Rice and his founding of the Society of Authors. Ashton (2003, 109) intriguingly suggests that "[t]he trauma of losing his personal cushion against the marketplace forces" was what might have given Besant the necessary impetus to start the first professional association for writers. Ashton wonders whether there is any direct connection between collaboration and advocating literary professionalism: Besant's experience with co-authorship must have taught him that association leads to success. This hypothesis sounds more than plausible. Neither he nor Rice had succeeded on their own; by working together, they had created far better works they could possibly have done alone – Besant's solo later novels are strong evidence of this. Furthermore, Rice had taught him what a good agent could do, and the difference it could make to rely on someone who knew how to move in the field. Thanks to his partner, Besant had learned that literature could be turned into a profession, and a profitable one too. Coming from a

---

35 For a detailed discussion of Besant's major role in British copyright reform, see Gillies, 2019, 75–98. For a history of copyright law in Britain see Saunders, 1992; Rose, 1993; Feather, 1994; Woodmansee and Jaszi, 1994; Seville, 1999; Saint-Amour, 2003; Deazley, 2006; Alexander, 2010; and Spoo, 2013.

36 In 1886 Great Britain, France, Germany, Belgium, Spain, Italy, Switzerland, Haiti, and Tunisia, reunited in the Berne Convention, signed the International Copyright Act. The USA was not a signatory to the treaty and continued to pirate British authors until 1891, when copyright was granted under certain conditions. For a discussion of the circulation of works of fiction in continental Europe and international copyright law see Gabriele, 2019.

collaborative background, he noticed how, in contrast, the majority of authors stood alone and how this could only be a disadvantage. Hence, it may be argued that the collaborative experience with Rice lay the foundations for Besant's remarkable efforts for the community of authors for which he is mostly remembered today.

Defining collaboration and redefining authorship

If Besant did the writing and Rice acted as the assistant and the manager, how can their partnership be considered a proper literary collaboration? The answer lies, once again, in Besant's own words, as he repeatedly and vigorously defended Rice's status as a full co-author. He claimed that Rice contributed significantly to the composition of the novels published under their double signature, even if he did not write: he had a hand in the development of the stories, extensively discussing the characters and the plot with Besant, and providing inputs and corrections. Such a method, presented in "On Literary Collaboration" and partly in the *Autobiography*, was described by Besant as the most efficient way to collaborate. Since "On Literary Collaboration" was a direct reply to another essay on the topic of co-authorship, "The Art and Mystery of Collaboration" by James Brander Matthews (1852–1929), the two works will be now discussed in conversation.

A few words on Matthews first. Brought up in New York's high society, he was the only son of a millionaire; his father lost his fortune when Matthews was twenty, but enough money remained so that he never had to earn his living. He counted among his friends writers, critics, and politicians, including Theodore Roosevelt. A professor of Dramatic Literature at Columbia University from 1892 to 1924 (a professorship created especially for him), he was generally acknowledged to be the foremost expert on dramatic theory and criticism in the United States. Like Besant, Matthews was indefatigable: beside his academic career, he wrote sixty-five books, which included three novels, many collections of short stories and a number of plays, some in collaboration with different partners (all men). Ashton (2003) reads Matthews's collaborations as the spontaneous outcome of his fondness for clubs and social activities: he strongly believed that "friendly association has power for mutual inspiration" (Ashton, 2003, 107). According to Matthews, the identity of a professional man of letters could not be separated from his ability to socialize. Significantly, his life and work "epitomized the last stand of writers who sought the cultural status of 'the artist' even as they participated in the marketplace" (Ashton, 2003, 92).[37] For the young moderns of the 1920s, Matthews embodied all that was conservative: mocked as "an outdated Victorian" (Ashton, 2003, 124), he has since then fallen into oblivion. Yet, as I shall discuss later, Matthews promoted an innovative and in many respects subversive understanding of authorship. Although he never explicitly theorized it, the importance he placed on conversation, dialogue, sociability, and friendship seems to suggest an idea of authorship at its best as a collaborative effort.

"The Art and Mystery of Collaboration" was originally published in *Longman's Magazine* in 1890 and was reprinted the following year as a preface to Matthews's collection of short stories, *With My Friends: Tales Told in Partnership*, co-written with (one partner at a time) H. C. Bunner, W. H. Pollock, G. Jessop, and F. Anstey. Besant read the essay "with a sense of relief" that a discussion on collaboration had finally been written by someone who had experienced it: co-authorship was a subject "on which a good deal has been written of late years, hitherto by those who know nothing about [it] and have never attempted it" ("Lit. Coll.," 200). Since he too had "seriously and systematically" worked in partnership ("Lit. Coll.," 200), Besant set out to clarify his own point of view. Besides, Matthews repeatedly mentioned Besant in his essay, calling him "that past master of the art" (1891, 24).

In their essays, both Besant and Matthews placed great emphasis on the importance of collaborative talk for the creation of a work of fiction. Besant stated that "the novelist can find nothing more helpful to his work than to talk it over" ("Lit. Coll.," 208) and that "the main advantage of partnership lies in the discussion of the plot and its situations, and the hammering out of all the effects of which they are capable" ("Lit. Coll.," 207). As a matter of fact, "two minds working upon the same idea, having the same object in view, and agreed upon the group of characters to carry out the plan of the piece, ought to arrive, more certainly and more clearly than one mind alone, not only at the possibilities but also at the certainties of the subject" ("Lit. Coll.," 207). He explained that when a plot, an incident, a situation, or a character are discussed, a thousand combinations occur and rise up in the mind; those which are useless or unnecessary are more easily picked out and thrown away in discussion

---

[37] Ashton refers to the 1890s in the USA as years of "a sociability of authorship [...] promoted to reap the advantages of a collective identity without sacrificing the patrician identity of the nineteenth-century writer" (2003, 92). For a discussion of Matthews's life and work, see Ashton, 2003, 91–126.

than on one's own, while the most promising are developed to their full potential. Similarly, Matthews wrote that

> the main advantage of a literary partnership is in the thorough discussion of the central idea and of its presentation in every possible aspect. Art and genius, so Voltaire asserted, consist in finding all that is in one's subject, and in not seeking outside of it. When a situation has been talked over thoroughly and traced out to its logical conclusion, and when a character has been considered from every angle and developed to its inevitable end, nine-tenths of the task is accomplished. (Matthews, 1891, 7)

Besant nostalgically recalled the infinite conversations and the almost symbiotic lives he and Rice had led when writing their first novel:

> I wish I was five and twenty-years younger, sitting once more in that dingy little office where we wrangled over this headstrong hero of ours [...]. The office was handy for Rule's and oysters. We would adjourn for the "delicious mollusc," and then go back again to the editor's room to resume the wrangle. [...] In the evening we would dine together, or go to a theatre, or sit in my chambers and play cards before resuming the wrangle. [...][38] And always during that period, whatever we did, wherever we went, Dick Mortiboy sat between us. (*MFB*, 11–14)

Thus, the phase of oral collaboration that preceded and surrounded the writing was declared fundamental by both Matthews and Besant. Both writers also believed in the importance of a "unity of impression" (Matthews, 1891, 7): "the very essence of literary partnership is that the result must appear just as spontaneous, just as entirely individual, as if it had been the creation of a single mind and the work of a single pen" ("Lit. Coll.," 202); "[t]he *presentement* of the story must seem to be by one man. No one would listen to two men telling it together. We must hear – or think we hear – one voice" ("Lit. Coll.," 205). However, they differed in their opinions as to how this unity was to be achieved. According to Matthews, it had to be the result of harmonious equality: through discussion, the minds of the partners became one. For him, discussion was *the* most important part of the creation, the "nine-tenths of the task." He explained that "the subject was always thoroughly

---

[38] It is worth noting that within two pages the word "wrangle" is used multiple times. By repeatedly employing this term Besant conveys the feeling that co-authoring a novel involves prolonged, exhausting discussions, an association that emerges from many accounts by other co-authors.

discussed between us; it was turned over and over and upside down and inside out; it was considered from all possible points of view and in every stage of development. When a final choice was made [...] the mere putting on paper was wholly secondary" (Matthews, 1891, 27). After the discussion, then, the material was ready, and the writing was "but the clothing of a babe already alive and kicking" (Matthews, 1891, 7). He therefore affirmed that "in a genuine collaboration, when the joint work is a true chemical union and not a mere mechanical mixture, it matters little who holds the pen" (Matthews, 1891, 7).

This assertion must have annoyed Besant, who devoted a great portion of his article to contradicting it. According to him, the unity of impression had to be attained through the domination of one partner. Drawing on his personal experience, he argued that the writing had to be carried out by one of the co-authors only: discussion was fundamental, "[b]ut literary style is another thing. It is individual. One of the two must impress his own individuality upon the work" ("Lit. Coll.," 205). He reiterated this point in the *Autobiography*: "[i]f two men work together, the result must inevitably bear the appearance of one man's work; the style must be the same throughout; the two men must be rolled into one" (188). After discussing with one's partner, then, the one in charge of writing had to take a final decision on the points on which an agreement could not be found, and had to mould the text on their own literary taste and style, otherwise the work would result in an uneven mixture: "in literary partnership, one of the two must be in authority: one of the two must have the final word: one of the two must be permitted to put the final touches" ("Lit. Coll.," 204). To this end, "one man must finally revise, or even write, the whole work" (205).

Besant remarked that this point was "the rock on which many literary partnerships get wrecked" ("Lit. Coll.," 205), as many co-authors thought that each had to write as much as the other. On the contrary, "the general notion of collaboration, that it must be carried on by each man contributing every other word, every other page, or every other chapter, is absolutely erroneous" (200). Besant reported the example of a manuscript sent to him by two co-authors who had made "the great mistake of writing it in alternate chapters":

> [n]ow, the style of one was not in the least like the style of the other; the effect was that of two men taking turns to tell the same story, each in his own way and from his own point of view. Nothing could have been more grotesque; nothing more ineffective. Every one of the characters talked

with two voices and two brains, and had two faces. The thing was a horrid nightmare. ("Lit. Coll.," 205)

The clearly split division of tasks between Besant and Rice projects the former as the artist who writes and the latter as the helpmate who offers suggestions and acts as a mediator between the creative artist and the surrounding world. Hence, in Besant's conception of co-authorship, the idea of the solitary author still remains to some degree.[39] Yet, as mentioned above, Besant insisted on calling Rice a co-author: "[c]an, then, the other man who has contributed only rough drafts here and there, or even perhaps nothing at all in writing, be called a collaborator? Most certainly he can" ("Lit. Coll.," 205). He provocatively asked: "if he throws into the work all the harvest of his life shall he not be called a partner?" ("Lit. Coll.," 206). Since Rice took part in the development of their books in every way except the writing, Besant affirmed that neither of them could "be held responsible for plot, incident, character, or dialogue" and that it was "impossible for [him] to lay hands upon any passage or page and to say 'this belongs to Rice – this is mine'" (*Autobiography*, 188, 189). Matthews's position was similar to Besant's in the fact that "in a genuine collaboration each of the parties [...] ought to have so far contributed to the story that he can consider every incident

---

[39] Archibald John Stuart-Wortley's 1882 portrait of Besant and Rice, intriguingly analysed in detail by Storer (2019, 47–48), seems to allude to the different roles played by each partner in the collaboration. The picture was donated to the National Portrait Gallery by the Chatto family in 1929, but it is dated 1882, the year of Rice's death; according to Storer, it was probably commissioned by the publisher with a commemorative intent. The two literary partners are depicted behind a table, apparently after sharing a meal. The table is laid with several objects: bowls of fruit may hint at their enjoyment of the fruits of their work; Besant's glass is full, while Rice's is empty – a possible reference to his premature death; the difference in the content of the two glasses might also suggest their different contribution to their stories. Storer remarks on the strong contrast in the appearance of the two men: Besant stands in a formal pose, towering over Rice, who is seated; he holds a bundle of papers in one hand (a hint at him being in charge of the writing and thus the partner in authority?) and stares away in the distance, absorbed in his thoughts or looking for inspiration. Rice is enjoying a cigarette, his posture is more relaxed, and he looks directly at the viewer – a detail which, according to Storer, makes sense as Rice was the one to handle the business part and was the most approachable partner. Note how the gazes of the two partners are reversed in this painting compared to their portraits in *MFB* analysed above, where Rice stares away and Besant looks at the viewer.

to be his, and his the whole work when it is completed" (Matthews, 1891, 15). Besant went on:

> [t]he first idea suggests leading situations, these suggest characters; these again other characters; in the discussions concerning these it is obvious that there must be many divergencies into paths perilous, many turnings back, many experiments, many failures, many happy discoveries, many checks, before the whole is concluded. Surely, when two minds are engaged in producing this result, both may be called partners in the work. ("Lit. Coll.," 205–06)

Even if Besant wrote, Rice made vital contributions to the planning of the plot, revised everything his partner wrote, and provided new solutions for the development of the stories. Besant advocated for the recognition of these kinds of collaborator as authors, crucially detaching the noun 'author' from the act of writing. He was aware of the subversive power of his position: "[i]n the recognition – for the first time – of this fact lies, I think, the chief value of the essay before us" ("Lit. Coll.," 205). Besant further supported his argument by explaining that "[i]t is not possible for a child to have two mothers, but a child may be watched, trained, educated, and moulded by two women" ("Lit. Coll.," 205). The image of the text as child had already been employed by Matthews: "any endeavor to sift out the contribution of one collaborator from that of his fellow is futile – if the union has been a true marriage. […] Who shall declare whether the father or the mother is the real parent of a child?" (Matthews, 1891, 9).

Predictably, the point Besant was advocating presented some risks: "the allowing of any claim to partnership of one who has written none of the book is a thing which might lead to great abuses and preposterous pretensions" ("Lit. Coll.," 206). He therefore took care to make some specifications and put forward three cases that should not be considered fit for collaboration. To start with, a man who only suggested a few situations afterwards adopted by the novelist could not claim partnership; mere suggestion of ideas was not enough:

> I have […] received dozens of proposals from persons wishing to enter into partnership with me. One man offers a magnificent plot on the trifling condition that his name shall appear on the title page as collaborator. It is difficult to make this person understand that much more than a plot must be expected of a partner. ("Lit. Coll.," 206)

Then, he specified that manuscript revision was not collaboration at all: "another [man] sends a bulky manuscript. If I will only revise it and put his name with mine in the title page, it is at my service. That man cannot understand that the work of an editor is not the work of collaboration" ("Lit. Coll.," 206). These first two cases underline that one had to be a part of the literary creation from the beginning to the end, even if not contributing to the writing moment itself. Besant specified that collaboration was a "work which may bring mind closer to mind than in any other task" ("Lit. Coll.," 204), precisely like Matthews, who had written that "in literature collaboration is more complete, more intimate than it is in the other arts" (Matthews, 1891, 2). Like marriage, collaboration was perceived by these authors as the union of two minds: "[i]n marriage husband and wife are one, and that is not a happy union when either inquires as to which one it is: the unity should be so complete that the will of each is merged in that of the other. So it should be in a literary partnership" (Matthews, 1891, 23–24). The third case put forward by Besant introduced a crucial point in his discussion:

> [a] third simply puts himself, his genius, his experience, his reputation – all – at my service in return for literary partnership. That man cannot understand that one would as soon offer to marry a girl met once at an evening party – or perhaps never met at all – as to take into partnership a complete stranger. ("Lit. Coll.," 206)

The metaphor of collaboration as marriage had been, as several other points in Besant's argument, already employed by Matthews. Both set down more or less the same rules for a successful collaboration, strikingly similar to the ingredients for a happy marriage: "[p]erhaps the first requisite is a sympathy between the two partners not sufficient to make them survey life from the same point of view, but yet enough to make them respect each other's suggestions and be prepared to accept them," wrote Matthews (1891, 23). Similarly, Besant suggested that:

> [a]s in the partnership of marriage, so in that of literature, these unions are happiest and best where the two partners have many points of unlikeness as well as some of likeness. There should of course […] be equal invention, equal dramatic power, equal perception of proportion, equal artistic sense. With these there may be – and, perhaps, should be – unlikeness in pursuit, learning, experience, private life, birth, social connections, tastes, training, and temperament. ("Lit. Coll.," 207)

The co-authors thus should not be too much alike in temperament in order to have a stimulating relationship. Here Matthews brought up the De Goncourt brothers, a pair of French novelists and playwrights who were inseparable in life as well as in their writing, as an example of "morbid" (23) collaboration: "although not twins, [they] thought alike in most subjects; and so close was their identity of cerebration that, when they were sitting at the same table at work on the same book, they sometimes wrote almost the same sentence at the same moment" (23). Matthew was referring to the brothers' incredibly laborious method of collaboration: apparently, when working on a novel, each chapter was written separately by each, and "then the two products were fused together by a process that must have cost inconceivable labour" (*The Sketch*, 22 July 1896, p. 2). This kind of interdependent personal and professional relationship was, Matthews warned, "collaboration carried to its abnormal and unwholesome extreme" (23).[40]

Openness of mind and willingness to put oneself in another's shoes were deemed vital for the good functioning of a collaboration. The partners should be able "to take as well as to give" and "be tolerant of the other's opinions" (Matthews, 1891, 23, 5). However, at this point Besant's and Matthews's positions parted again: while for Matthews each partner "must be ready to yield a point when need be" and "there must be concessions from one to the other" (5), Besant limited his advice to general remarks such as having a "spirit of compromise and the readiness to sacrifice personal vanity" ("Lit. Coll.," 204). Indeed, as seen above, in Besant's opinion one partner had to have the final word. According to him, it was inevitable that in every partnership "one will be stronger than the other" ("Lit. Coll.," 204). On the contrary, Matthews professed a strong belief in the equality of the partners: carrying on the marriage metaphor, he wrote that "[i]n collaboration as in matrimony, again, it is well when the influence of the masculine element does not wholly overpower the feminine" (Matthews, 1891, 25). In this light, Besant and Rice's partnership could be seen as a traditional Victorian marriage in which the former acted as the husband, generally benevolent but domineering, and the latter embodied the ideal wife,

---

40 Edmond (1822–1896) and Jules (1830–1870) de Goncourt were French naturalism writers. Their 1865 play *Henriette Maréchal* caused a sensation in Paris, but they received a mixed reception in England: the *Morning Advertiser* described them as "the tawdriest scribblers of the realist school" (11 December 1865, p. 6), while the *National Observer* commented that "the brothers are rather honoured than read," and remarked that "their literary partnership is probably the most curious example of the kind on record," being "a most puzzling mystery" and inspiring all sorts of "investigations" (25 July 1896, p. 6) – comments probably triggered by their almost symbiotic relationship.

ready to yield to the authority of the man. Matthews also advanced a distinction between literary monogamists and polygamists: "we may consider MM. Erckmann-Chatrian and Messers. Besant and Rice as monogamists," while those who are "ready to collaborate at large" are literary polygamists (Matthews, 1891, 23).

A careful choice of one's collaborator was deemed fundamental by both Matthews and Besant. The latter indeed remarked that "[t]he great – the very great – objection to literary partnerships is the difficulty of finding your partner" ("Lit. Coll.," 208). Once again linking collaboration to marriage, Matthews commented: "[a]s there are households where husband and wife fight like cat and dog, and where marriage ends in divorce, so there are literary partnerships which are dissolved in acrimony and anger" (Matthews, 1891, 25). He thus introduced another crucial point in his argument and consequently in Besant's, the fights involved in collaboration:

> [t]o take a man into partnership even for a short story [...] is a step attended with great risks: it may lead to certain failure, with certain quarrels, recriminations, and pretensions. Why did the novel fail? Because of the other man. Or, if it was not a failure, why did the thing succeed? In spite of the other man. ("Lit. Coll.," 208)

Matthews noticed that "in general it is when the work fails that the collaborators fall out" (25), and added that "[t]he quarrels of collaborators [...] are the height of folly. The world looks on at the fight, and listens while the two former friends call each other hard names; and more often than not it believes what each says of the other, and not what he says of himself" (Matthews, 1891, 26). Fights were generally so connected with co-authorship that collaborating would immediately be equated with quarrelling, as Matthews ironically reported: "M. Dumas is said to have answered a request to collaborate with the query, 'Why should I wish to quarrel with you?'" (25).

Strangely enough, though, Matthews and Besant distanced their personal experiences from this apparently pervasive aspect of collaboration. Both talked of their partnerships in utterly idyllic terms:

> I can declare unhesitatingly that I have never had a hard word with a collaborator while our work was in hand and never a bitter word with him afterwards. My collaborators have always been my friends before, and they have always remained my friends after. [...] There was never a dispute as to our respective shares in the result of our joint labors [...]. Sometimes I may have thought that I did more than my share, sometimes I knew that I did

less than I should, but always there was harmony, and never did either of us seek to assert a mastery. (Matthews, 1891, 26–27)

Since Matthews's collaborations were mostly occasional, and restricted to one or few works, one could believe him. But that Besant and Rice never had a squabble in ten years of joint work seems unlikely. And yet Besant began his very first commentary on his and Rice's partnership, the 1887 preface to *Ready-Money Mortiboy*, in the following terms:

[t]en years of continuous work, cheered by such a measure of success as we had not ventured to hope for, and undisturbed by the least jar of disagreement, cannot be looked back upon without mingled feelings of sorrow that the end came in so unexpected a manner, and of gratitude that the work was so successful. (*RMM*, v)

However, Besant's position towards his literary partnership underwent a radical change in his *Autobiography*. The novelist moved from a romanticized commemoration of his literary partnership to its brusque dismissal – almost a repudiation. In unexpectedly blunt terms, he unceremoniously dismissed his long collaborative experience in a total of seven pages; moreover, he kept mixing the discussion of the collaboration with various digressions totally unconnected with the topic, as if he were unwilling to talk about it;[41] his tone was cold and reluctant, totally different from that of 1887. At one point, he abruptly declared:

[i]f I were asked for my opinion as to collaboration in fiction, it would be decidedly against it. I say this without the least desire to depreciate the literary ability of my friend and *collaborateur*. The arrangement lasted for ten years and resulted in as many successful novels. I only mean that, after all, an artist must necessarily stand alone. (*Autobiography*, 188)

So, even if in "On Literary Collaboration" Besant had foregrounded the importance of a partner, he now declared that, in the long run, a writer has to be alone. A few lines later, he commented that, after some time, every collaboration is doomed to end:

---

41 Besant first introduced his collaboration with Rice on p. 169, only to break off on the following page to talk about his journalistic work; then he picked up the topic again on p. 181, interrupting himself again on p. 182 to launch a long attack on critics and reviewers; on p. 186 he resumed the subject, finally giving some concrete information, until p. 190, when he made a digression on the practice of serializing novels until p. 193; after that, we find another attack on reviewers which lasts until p. 197; pp. 197–98 are dedicated to general information and to the account of Rice's death.

[t]here will come a time when both men fret under the condition; when each desires, but is not able, to enjoy the reputation of his own good work; and feels, with the jealousy natural to an artist, irritated by the loss of half of himself and ready to accept the responsibility of failure in order to make sure of the meed of success. (*Autobiography*, 188)

A writer needs to keep himself intact, he stated, as collaboration leads only to a sort of dismemberment. Even if he never plainly wrote that he himself had "fretted" about his collaboration, it seems quite obvious that Besant was talking about his own experience. Indeed, in the following page he started referring again to his own partnership, and reflected that, had not Rice died, "the collaboration would have broken down" anyway, although "amicably" (*Autobiography*, 189). Furthermore, he regretted that the collaboration had not "broken down five years before the death of Rice" (*Autobiography*, 189). He justified such a strong statement by saying that in that way Rice "might have achieved what has been granted to myself – an independent literary position" (*Autobiography*, 189). Although this explanation is not illogical, one has the impression that Besant himself had been increasingly impatient with the collaboration, which he had probably come to feel more and more as a cage. Some lines later, he returned to the point: "I repeat that I desire to suggest nothing that might seem to lessen the work of Rice in the collaboration, while, for both his sake and my own, I regret that it ever went beyond *The Golden Butterfly*, which was quite the most successful of the joint novels" (*Autobiography*, 190). After the success of *The Golden Butterfly*, Besant must have felt confident enough to start working on his own.[42] Why, then, did he allow the collaboration to go on, if he was sick and tired of it? In the first place, as illustrated above, he was deeply averse to handling the business part of authoring himself; in addition, he probably thought that Rice was not able to achieve "an independent literary position." For Rice, the end of the partnership would probably have meant the end of his career as an author,[43] and it is likely that Besant felt restrained by this awareness.

There was only one type of literary partnership that Walter Besant

---

42 Storer (2019, 42) suggests that Besant's wish for the collaboration to have ended after *The Golden Butterfly* may also have been motivated by the fact that after its publication the name of 'Besant and Rice' became public, thus connecting him with Rice in the public's mind.

43 Rice tried to get some of his own fictional work published but was always unsuccessful. For instance, Eliot (1989, 93) shows that in 1879 Rice offered a collection of short stories to Chatto & Windus, which was rejected.

felt sure to recommend "to every young literary workman": "I would advise him to find among his friends – cousins – sisters' friends – a girl, intelligent, sympathetic, and quick; a girl who will lend him her ear, listen to his plot, and discuss his characters" ("Lit. Coll.," 209). He then proceeded to illustrate the qualities such a girl should possess: "[s]he should be a girl of quick imagination, who does not, or cannot, write – there are still, happily, many such girls" (209). The young author would simply have to discuss his ideas with the girl, and

> [w]hen he has confided to her his characters all in the rough, with the part they have to play all in the rough, he may reckon on presently getting them back again, but advanced – much less in the rough. Woman does not create, but she receives, moulds, and develops. The figures will go back to their creator, distinct and clear, no longer shivering unclothed, but made up and dressed for the stage. Merely by talking with this girl everything that was chaotic falls into order; the characters, which were dim and shapeless, become alive, full grown, articulate. (209)

This kind of collaboration was to be preferred to all others, since "[a]s in everyday life, so in imaginative work, woman should be man's best partner – the most generous – the least exacting – the most certain never to quarrel over her share of the work, […] her share of the pay" (209). A girl, he believed, would never claim any right to the text, but would selflessly step back: in this way "the resultant text would remain singly authored" and "the agency of the female partner" would be "erased" (Bunting, 2019, 25).[44] Besant's unequal model of collaboration as a male genius assisted by a female helper is most explicit in this case.

Besant carried his point even further, taking collaboration from a metaphorical marriage to an actual one: "[p]erhaps he would like to get engaged to her – that is a detail: if he does it might not injure the

---

44 Bunting (2019, 25–26) quotes an essay by journalist Elizabeth Banks called "New Paid Occupations for Women" (*Cassell's Family Magazine*, 1894, pp. 585–88), which echoed Besant's collaborative model: among other small moneymaking schemes for women, such as dog-walking, table-decorating, and the breaking in of clients' new boots, Banks suggested a kind of ghost-writing for male authors, providing them with new ideas for their stories. She told her female readers that "their thoughts have commercial value" and could be sold to male writers who could "take the children of their brain" and "dress them up and give them to the world" (588). Bunting argues that this model was "rooted in a domestic, familial economy of female procreativity and patriarchal ownership of children" (26).

collaboration" ("Lit. Coll.," 209).[45] The bizarre suggestion triggered a series of reactions from the periodical press. The number of papers from February 1892 that reported and commented on Besant's article is impressive, and most of them replied to his final advice. Although many articles found Besant's idea stimulating and pasted the passage in their first page under titles such as "the most agreeable collaborator" (*Yorkshire Evening Post*, 2 February 1892, no. 445, p. 1), sarcastic comments were not spared. One newspaper remarked that "it would be interesting to hear what a lady novelist would think of the converse of this suggestion" (*Greenock Telegraph and Clyde Shipping Gazette*, 5 March 1892, no. 9467, p. 2). Another one imagined the possible practical obstacles to Besant's idyll:

> Mr. Besant [...] gives us a capital account of the system of literary collaboration. There is one point of it quite idyllic. He recommends the novelist to discover some young girl. [...] I can fancy the tender passages especially improving wonderfully under the arrangement. [...] In the case of a young and rising storyteller, it may be easy to find a collaborator of this engaging kind; but when a novelist is getting on in years there may be a difficulty in getting her to "lend him her ear": it is probable that somebody else may have been promised the loan of it. If he is married, it is also just possible [...] that his wife may object to such an arrangement. One can imagine a dramatic situation arising from it not included in the author's plot. A feeble voice pleading that "we were only collaborating," and a more resolute one replying that that system of composition must be put a stop to. (*Illustrated London News*, 13 February 1892, no. 2756, p. 2)

The *London Daily News* observed: "Mr. Besant suggests that a nice girl is the best kind of partner, but that would lead to indolence, flirtation, or even to the altar. After marriage, the nice girl who 'collaborated' so pleasantly will no longer do so, nor, to be sure, will she let the novelist work with other nice girls" (13 February 1892). *Hearth and Home* sharply criticized Besant's recommendation with a long, hilarious article entitled "Walter Besant's Guide to Matrimony," which begins in the following way:

45 The question arises whether Besant was talking from experience, but we know very little of his private life. We only know that in 1874 he married a woman named Mary Garat Foster Barham, and that they had four children. In his *Autobiography* Besant dismissed his marriage in a few lines, in connection with a crisis in the Palestine Exploration Fund that made him shorten his honeymoon (167). From his statements one might think that, after Rice's death, Besant's wife took the place of his last partner in discussing his novels with him. However, we have no evidence and this remains pure speculation.

> Mr. Besant – who likes to have a saying in all things literary – has pointed out a new method of collaboration which is likely to find great favour with match-making mammas. He advises the young writer male who can write to collaborate with the young thinker female who cannot write, and declares that by talking things over with a charming girl of quick imagination and ready sympathy everything that was chaotic will fall into order, and the dim, shadowy characters "become alive, full grown, articulate." In fact, to put it bluntly, Mr. Besant says to the youthful and aspiring author: "Flirt, and you will be able to write; but flirt with someone who has got an intellect." A literary flirtation! (11 February 1892, vol. 2, no. 39, p. 383)

Hearth and Home went on to foreshadow the possible catastrophic consequences for the literary market if Besant's "delicious recipe" was to be taken seriously:

> [i]s Mr. Besant, however, wise in setting such a very sparkling torch to the smouldering ambition which lurks in so many – fools? For, alas! The foolish ones of literature are a large and growing class. People who have nothing to say and say it at great length, bound in green cloth, this style two-and-six, abound, and literary tares are day by day springing up in such quantities as to choke much literary wheat.
>
> The sowers of tares will certainly increase and multiply if men in authority like Mr. Besant give such delicious recipes for the making of books. You are a young, and probably a foolish, man. Floating through what you are pleased to call your brain are certain nebulous phantoms named by you thoughts or ideas. They float shadowly and refuse to take real shape, eluding you like the Fata Morgana. You are puzzled until Mr. Besant comes to your aid, crying on the housetops, "Collaborate!" Forthwith you look about you for a young maiden of quick imagination, and to her you convey your nebulous phantoms. She thinks you handsome and therefore declares your phantoms beautiful. Cause and effect. You beg her to make them take shape, to clothe them in flesh and blood. She is eager to do so. You talk the matter over – you are always talking it over – while probably the censorious world, which understands not collaboration, begins to talk you over. The phantoms take shape. They are shadows no longer. The magic touch of this girl of quick imagination has waked your brain Galatea from a marble sleep. She opens her eyes, and you are entranced. So you send her forth to the long-suffering world bound in boards. What matter if the critics – vultures you term them – say your Galatea is a Frankenstein's monster? You have collaborated, and the chances are you are looking out for a nice little house, and are dreaming domestically of a sweet dual life crowned with orange blossoms throned by a glowing hearth in a snug home. (p. 383)

Sarcasm reached its highest inflection at the end of the article:

[i]n point of fact, Mr. Besant is coming forward as the apostle of matrimony. He says "collaborate heads," but he means "collaborate hearts." He is a new St. Valentine bidding, in rounded, literary phrases, the birds to pair. He should have called his article "Walter Besant's Guide to Matrimony," and he might even set up a bureau, which would completely cut out his Society of Authors. If his advice be followed, we shall have more books, more weddings, fewer bachelor's clubs, and more publishing houses. Literature and love will join hands and trot merrily along together to the chime of wedding bells, and the author of *All Sorts and Conditions of Men* will find his name changed upon the lips of the world. It will no longer call him Besant; it will smile upon him and murmur the word "Hymen." (p. 383)

Besant's linking of literary collaboration with romance ended up permeating the late Victorian imagination to the degree that in the columns of newspapers it is possible to find advertisements by people looking for a romantic collaboration. In the section "Situations Vacant and Wanted" of *The Standard* advertisements such as the following appeared:

Widower, without encumbrance, 40, with moderate private means, of quiet and studious habits, engaged in literary work, is desirous of meeting with a cultured lady of literary taste [...] possessed of independent means, with a view of sharing expenses of a refined home and collaboration. – Full particulars, in strict confidence, write Litterateur, 54, New Oxford-street. (22 June 1894, no. 21831, p. 9)

One last key topic of Besant's and Matthews's essays remains to be explored: both set out to assess the benefits and the limits of collaboration. Interestingly, they reached the same conclusions. Matthews remarked that "two heads are indubitably better than one" in the attaining of "ingenuity, construction, compression" (Matthews, 1891, 11). "Collaboration succeeds most abundantly," he went on, "where clearness is needed, where precision, skill, and logic are looked for, where we expect simplicity of motive, sharpness of outline, ingenuity of construction, and cleverness of effect" (12). Besant confirmed that "two heads will prove better than one" where there is need for "construction, compressions, selection, and grouping" ("Lit. Coll.," 201). On the other hand, Matthews reflected, "with its talking over, its searching discussion, its untiring pursuit of the idea into the most remote fastness," co-authorship could lead to "an over-sharpness of outline, a deprivation of that vagueness of contour not seldom strangely fascinating" (Matthews, 1891, 14). Besant agreed that "[t]here is the danger that there may be too much distinctness – a loss of atmosphere – not enough left to the imagination" ("Lit. Coll.," 208). The American co-author explained that the presence of a partner and the necessity of talking things over and over restrained the flow of imagination:

> [w]here there may be a joy in the power of unexpected expansion, and where there may be a charm of veiled beauty, vague and fleeting, visible at a glimpse only and intangible always, two men would be in each other's way. In the effort to fix these fugitive graces they would but trip over each other's heels. A task of this delicacy belongs of right to the lonely student in the silent watches of the night, or in solitary walks under the greenwood tree and far from the madding crowd. […]
>
> No doubt in the work of two men there is a loss of the unexpected, and the story must of necessity move straight forward by the shortest road, not lingering by the wayside in hope of wind-falls. There is less chance of unforeseen developments suggesting themselves as the pen speeds in its way across the paper – and every writer knows how the pen often runs away with him "across country" and over many a five-barred gate which he had never intended to take. (Matthews, 1891, 11–12, 14)

Owing to mutual criticism, "an intuitive attaining of the ideal, the instinctive artistic creation of poetic wholes, is not to be expected from a partnership – indeed, it is hardly possible to it" (Matthews, 1891, 13). Consequently, "[c]ollaboration fails to satisfy where there is need of profound meditation, of solemn self-interrogation, or of lofty imagination lifting itself freely towards the twin-peaks of Parnassus" (11). Besant remained on the same wavelength when he affirmed that "[s]atire, fun, humour, and pathos all may be exhibited at their best in partnership" ("Lit. Coll.," 203), but "[t]o touch the deeper things one must be alone. Two men talking together, using the same words, on solemn subjects, like a church congregation, might look ridiculous. One must, alone, speak to the alone. To treat of the graver things one must, alone, construct the machinery" (203). Besant's conclusion was that "[n]either in the study of the wanderings and development of the individual soul, nor in the development of character, nor in the work of pure and lofty imagination, is collaboration possible" (204).

In storytelling, conversely, collaboration "may be not only possible but useful" ("Lit. Coll.," 204). According to Besant, authors like Charles Dickens, Wilkie Collins, and Charles Reade were able to collaborate because they were, "first and foremost, storytellers" (204). He included himself in their ranks, and in the *Autobiography* he voiced his pride in being part of "the company of the story-tellers" (184). In drama, too, collaboration may be precious: "[p]erhaps the drama is the only form of literature in which so painstaking a process would be advantageous, or in which it would be advisable even" (Matthews, 1891, 28). Since a play must follow rigid limitations of time and space, "the structure can hardly be too careful or too precise, nor can the dialogue be too compact or too polished" (Matthews, 1891, 28–29). Matthews observed that France was the country "with the most vigorous dramatic literature" (18) and that it was also the country where collaboration had been and still was most frequent; he linked the two facts, proposing that one was the consequence of the other: "in any country where there is a revival of the drama, collaboration is likely to become common at once. [...] I venture to suggest that one of the causes of immediate hopefulness for the drama in our language is the prevalence of collaboration in England and in America" (18).[46] Besant's and Matthews's ideas about the pros and cons of literary collaboration had a massive impact on late Victorian conceptions of co-authorship and on the ways in which it came to be represented, which will be explored in chapter 4.

The art and craft of fiction

In 1882 Besant and Rice's partnership was put to an end by the latter's death. Rice's fatal illness – probably a cancer in the throat – lasted from January 1881 to his death in the April of the following year, and was narrated by Besant in both *RMM* (xi, xiii) and in his *Autobiography* (198). However, as can be expected, the two accounts are very different. *RMM* deals with the topic in great detail, following the ups and downs of Rice's disease in a sentimental and participatory tone, until the final, unexpected decline:

> [h]e maintained his cheerfulness of tone until the very end. I received, in fact, so many letters from him, and all so hopeful, that I never had any serious fears about his recovery.
>
> The last letter I had from him was written only three or four days before he died. He told me [...] that the doctor held out hopes of his being able to travel as far as Brighton in a few weeks, and made me promise to go

---

46 It is worth noticing that Besant and Rice attempted to write drama as well as fiction: they dramatized *Ready-Money Mortiboy*, but the play was "received with indifference" (*RMM*, x–xi) and withdrawn within a few weeks; then they tried again with a text written specifically for the stage, *Such a Good Man* (later converted into a story), which was performed, again unsuccessfully, in 1879.

there with him. The sea air, he said, would complete his cure, which was at length assured. Nothing could have been more hopeful. Yet on the following morning he collapsed altogether, and died two days after. (*RMM*, xii)

From the account in *RMM*, one can feel the close bond between the two: the frequent letters, the promise to go to Brighton together to complete Rice's recovery, Besant's cheerful hope for his friend. Rice is presented in a heroic light, facing his illness with optimism and carrying on his work as the manager of the duo until a few months before his death, when he went to London to arrange a serial publication in the *Illustrated London News* for the following summer, "the very subject of which he did not live to discuss," though it appeared, as it had been advertised, under their joint names (*RMM*, xi). The *Autobiography*, instead, presents a shorter and much more pragmatic description, all the more astonishing if we consider that it was the last comment Besant ever passed on his friend and collaborator: "[a]fter lingering for six months in great suffering, he died in April 1882 at the age of thirty-nine; the cause was a cancer in the throat" (*Autobiography*, 195). Such a dry account may be a reaction to the insistent curiosity the press had showed about their partnership over the past twenty years; for once, maybe, Besant wanted to be the only hero of his own story. It was as if he took the occasion to reclaim his status as an individual novelist.

When the collaboration with Rice ended Besant was forty-six; he had become a writer loved by the public and respected by the critics. In the years that followed he not only talked about collaboration but also devoted a great deal of time and energy to theorize what he considered the laws of fiction writing. Questions of authorship were the focus of Besant's famous commentary *The Art of Fiction*, originally a lecture delivered at the Royal Institution in London on 25 April 1884. On 30 April, a long response appeared in the *Pall Mall Gazette* – also called "The Art of Fiction" – written by Andrew Lang. In May, Chatto and Windus published Besant's lecture in volume form with notes and additions. In the autumn of the same year, Henry James joined the debate in *Longman's Magazine* with his own version of "The Art of Fiction," to which R. L. Stevenson rejoined in the winter with "A Humble Remonstrance."[47]

---

[47] Besant's *Art of Fiction* was preceded in 1882 by two articles: "Henry James, Jr." by William Dean Howells in the *Century Magazine*, and "A Gossip on Romance" by R. L. Stevenson in *Longman's Magazine*. Some reactions had followed, but it was only two years later that the debate really started through Besant's contribution.

Henry James's "Art of Fiction" is now a celebrated piece of criticism; on the contrary, Besant's has been virtually ignored by twentieth-century scholars. Doubtlessly, when the two essays are placed side by side, Besant appears at his worst. He approaches the topic in a rather simplistic way, using a tone "more suitable for telling his listeners how to finish a piece of furniture than how to write good fiction" (Boege, 1956b, 38). Nevertheless, I believe it is worth looking at, as Besant's ideas were extremely popular and, after all, it was his contribution that fuelled the subsequent debate: before Besant, wrote James, "there was a comfortable, good-humored feeling [...] that a novel is a novel, as a pudding is a pudding, and that this was the end of it" (1885, 52). The success of Besant's talk aroused public interest and prepared the field for James, as he admitted to being "anxious not to lose the benefit of this favorable association, and to edge in a few words under cover of the attention which Mr. Besant is sure to have excited" (51). The choice of the same title as Besant's was clearly aimed at exploiting the interest generated by it. James stressed the lack of intellectual fellowship between writers, a problem identified by Besant, thanks to whom "the era of discussion," as James named it, was opened (52).

The main tenets of Besant's lecture constituted the starting points of James's manifesto. The former's *Art of Fiction* was essentially a discussion of three propositions: that fiction must be recognized as the equal of the other fine arts; that it is governed by some general laws, which may be laid down and taught; and that, fiction being no mechanical art, no laws can be taught to those who do not already possess "the natural and necessary gifts" (Besant, 1884, 6). Most controversially, Besant pleaded for the establishing of schools of fiction, and pointed out that fiction was the only fine art that had "no lectures and teachers, no school or college or Academy, no recognized rules, no text-books" (14). He made the question of the teachability of fiction a public issue and a matter for debate: by the late nineteenth century, the novel had a history, a distinct variety of subgenres, and a rather large body of important works behind it; it was time, Besant argued, to take it seriously as an academic subject. His plea was the first systematic and influential appeal for creative writing courses. He criticized the idea that novelists should

Discussion was revived in 1891, when the *New Review* published two symposia: "The Science of Fiction," by Besant, Hardy and Paul Bourget, and "The Science of Criticism," featuring James, Lang, and Edmund Gosse. In 1895 Vernon Lee added her contribution "On Literary Construction," in the *Contemporary Review*.

not speak about their art, and observed that not one single writer had ever tried "to teach his mystery, or spoken of it as a thing which may be taught" (15). The only way open to those who wanted to try their hand at fiction was to acquire the art "unconsciously, or by imitation" (15). The widespread belief that one did not need instruction to write fiction had led to the idea that anyone who had "talent" could write a novel: "why not sit down and write one?" (15). The result was the flood of "bad, inartistic" novels that was "every week laid before the public" (34). Conversely, Besant believed that people should approach fiction with the same seriousness with which they would undertake the study of music or painting. Following rules "will not make a man a novelist, any more than the knowledge of grammar makes a man know a language, or a knowledge of musical science makes a man able to play an instrument. Yet the Rules must be learned" (33).[48]

Since, according to Besant, the aim of fiction was to portray humanity ("the human interest must absolutely absorb everything else," 21–22), the first rule to learn was that everything "which is invented, and is not the result of personal experience and observation, is worthless; [...] never go beyond your own experience" (34, 36). For instance, he claimed, a young lady brought up in a country village should avoid dealing with garrison life; or a writer belonging to the lower middle class should not introduce his characters into Society. But this first rule was already highly problematic: "[w]hat kind of experience is intended, and where does it begin and end?" wondered James, to which he answered: "[e]xperience is [...] an immense sensibility, a kind of huge spider-web, of the finest silken threads, suspended in the chamber of consciousness and catching every air-borne particle in its tissue" (James, 1885, 64). The American author complicated the concept of experience and claimed that an imaginative mind had "the power to guess the seen from the unseen" (65), and thus needed only a glimpse in order to be able to give a true impression of something.

According to Besant, in order to be able to write from experience the novelist had to acquire the ability of description, which consisted in the combination of observation and selection. Observation could be trained by keeping a notebook, while selection required "that kind of special fitness for the Art which is included in the much-abused word Genius"

---

[48] Besant's plea for schools of fiction was reiterated in the 1891 symposium "The Science of Fiction" in the *New Review* (IV, 304–19) occasioned by the announcement that one was to be established in the United States.

(47), but whose general principle was that everything "which does not either advance the story or illustrate the characters, ought to be rigidly suppressed" (48).

Besant's next point became a debated one as well. He claimed that the modern English novel should have a moral purpose, but that "fortunately" it was "not possible in this country for any man to defile and defame humanity and still be called an artist": (57) the development of modern sympathy, the appreciation of a life of devotion and self-denial, the deep-seated religion, together with "the sense of responsibility among the English-speaking races" act strongly upon the artist and lend to their work, almost unconsciously, "a moral purpose so clearly marked that it has become practically a law of English Fiction" (58). This point was overtly condemned by James, who argued that most people would find "moral timidity" (1885, 82) rather than moral purpose, in the English novel. The "usual English novelist," according to James, was "apt to be extremely shy" and the sign of his work was "a cautious silence on certain subjects" (82). James believed that the moral and the artistic sense "lie very near together," as "[n]o good novel will ever proceed from a superficial mind; that seems to me an axiom which, for the artist in fiction, will cover all needful moral ground" (83). What James was calling for was a change in sensibility; his coupling of the moral and the artistic senses introduced modern moral consciousness into the Victorian arena.

Next, Besant's *Art of Fiction* claimed that style was to be cared for – but not as much as most critics thought; the story, instead, was everything: "[t]here is a school that pretends that there is no need for a story: all the stories, they say, have been told already; [...] One hears this kind of talk with the same wonder which one feels when a new monstrous fashion changes the beautiful figure of woman into something grotesque and unnatural" (65–66). The material for fiction, according to Besant, is infinite, because it concerns humanity, which is like a kaleidoscope: one can turn it about and look into it again and again, but they will never find the same picture twice – "it cannot be exhausted" (43). Besant's distinction between style and story puzzled James, who declared that he could "not see what is meant by talking as if there were a part of a novel which is the story and a part of it which for mystical reasons is not" (76). Since the novel is "a living thing, all one and continuous, like every other organism" (68), the story and the style, the idea and the form are like the needle and thread: "I never heard of a guild of tailors who recommended the use of the thread without the needle or the needle without the thread" (77).

Overall, Besant appears to have too definite ideas of what a good novel should be. He seems too confident, too didactic, too fond of rules. For his part, James distrusted precise prescriptions; although he was very careful to shape his criticism as mildly as possible, he ended up debunking most of Besant's positions. For all his insistence that Besant's lecture was "suggestive" (84) and "excellent," and that it was "difficult to dissent" and "surely impossible not to sympathize" with his recommendations (63), in fact James threw them out of the window. His "single criticism" (60) was actually the most significant part of the essay, when he affirmed that Besant was mistaken "in attempting to say so definitely beforehand what sort of an affair the good novel will be. [...] The good health of an art which undertakes so immediately to reproduce life must demand that it be perfectly free" (60). The "only obligation to which in advance we may hold a novel," he concluded, "is that it must be interesting" (60). There should be no limit to what the novelist may attempt: such freedom, he observed, was "the advantage, the luxury, as well as the torment and responsibility" of the novelist (61).

R. L. Stevenson's contribution to the debate, "A Humble Remonstrance," opened by briefly describing James and Besant: the former "the very type of the deliberate artist" and the latter "so genial, so friendly, [...] the impersonation of good nature" (Stevenson, 2009, 309). Stevenson's praise of Besant immediately sounds somewhat demeaning: it looks as if he was highlighting Besant's human qualities in order not to pass too harsh a judgement on his literary skills. As a matter of fact, he quickly dismissed Besant: it was James that Stevenson addressed throughout his reply, "with the emphasis and technicalities of the obtrusive student" (315). "A Humble Remonstrance" dissented on some key points from James's "Art of Fiction," most importantly on the American author's conviction that art could compete with life, which, according to Stevenson, was impossible, since "[l]ife is monstrous, infinite, illogical, abrupt, and poignant; a work of art, in comparison, is neat, finite, self-contained, rational, flowing and emasculate" (312). Crucially, Stevenson recommended to "the young writer" to "bear in mind that his novel is not a transcript of life, to be judged by its exactitude": on the contrary, a novel is "a simplification of some side or point of life, to stand or fall by its significant simplicity" (316). He suggested that authors "choose a motive" and "carefully construct his plot so that every incident is an illustration of the motive" (315). In this respect, Stevenson's position is actually closer to Besant's: his tone was more practical than James's, his suggestions more precise and down-to-earth, as "the young writer will not so much be helped by genial pictures of what an art may aspire to at its highest, as by a true idea of what it must be on the lowest terms" (315). Stevenson recommended avoiding a sub-plot, "unless, as sometimes in Shakespeare, the sub-plot be a reversion or a complement of the main intrigue" (315–16). The novelist should in no case "utter one sentence that is no part and parcel of the business of the story or the discussion of the problem involved" (316). So, even if Stevenson did not mention him when offering his advice, his ideas sound more similar to Besant's that to those expressed by James.

In the following years Besant went on with his mission of theorizing on the art of fiction in *The Pen and the Book* and the *Autobiography*. The tone is still that of a pedantic instructor, and prolixity and repetition are constant features.[49] But, unlike the serene preaching of *The Art of Fiction* and *The Pen and the Book*, the *Autobiography* was written in a defensive and rather polemic tone, as can be glimpsed from an extract from the chapter dedicated to the years between 1882 and 1900:

> [e]ighteen novels in eighteen years! It seems a long list; how can one write so much and yet survive? My friends, may I ask why a painter is allowed to produce a couple of pictures and more every year and no one cries out upon him for his haste in production; yet if a story-teller gives to the world a novel every year, the criticaster yaps at his heels and asks all the world to observe the haste which the novelist makes to get rich. (*Autobiography*, 200)

As usual, in defending his point Besant made a comparison with other professions. He then revealed how he managed to write so much while keeping up with his many activities. He presented a sort of scientific method of writing, giving very precise information: he explained that he worked at his novels every morning from nine to half-past twelve; that a novel generally took him from eight to ten months of work; consequently, "if you turn this statement into a little sum in arithmetic, you will find that it means about a thousand words a day" (*Autobiography*, 200). It little helped that, in the next line, he hastened to specify that he did not exactly write a thousand words every day, and that it was only a general line of conduct. What people perceived was that he was talking about the profession of letters as if it were an accountant's job. In his explanation

---

49 Mark Twain, invited by an editor to review *The Pen and the Book*, refused the assignment because it would have compelled him to disparage Besant: "Besant is a friend of mine, and there was no way of doing a review that wouldn't cut into his feelings and wound his enthusiastic pride in his insane performance […]. The book is not reviewable by any but a sworn enemy of his; for so far as I can see, there isn't a rational page in it" (quoted in Boege, 1956b, 36).

there was no mystery, no idealistic view of literature, no exalted tone, no desire for a higher aim. It is the account of a man who loved to write, and who practised literature as a profession. That was not what people wanted to read; that was not how many of his fellow writers wanted to think of themselves. George Gissing – who in *New Grub Street* (1891) set the "profiteers" against the "purists" of literature[50] – met Besant at a dinner at the Authors' Club in 1894 and described the experience as a "mere gathering of tradesmen, and very commonplace tradesmen to boot"; to him, Besant was "[c]ommonplace to the last degree; a respectable draper [...] his face that of an owl – a resemblance strengthened by his gold-rimmed *pince-nez*" (Coustillas, 1978, 354, quoted in Ue, 2019, 220). In his view Besant epitomized "the degradation that our time has brought upon literature" (Mattheisen et al., 1990–97, vol. 5, 251, quoted in Ue, 2019, 220).[51]

In the subsequent pages of the *Autobiography*, Besant described with precision the steps he religiously followed when writing a novel: first, one has to decide upon one "plain, clear, and intelligible *motif* – one which all the world can understand" (201); around this theme, a collection of well-drawn characters must be grouped, whose actions, conversations, and motives form a clear and consistent story; the third step is what Besant called the presentation of the story, the phase that "involves practice and study in the art of construction" (201). Besant's recipe was to keep the different parts of the story in proportion to each other and avoid long descriptions of characters, as "it is best for the ordinary novelist to make his characters describe themselves in dialogue" (202). He compared his writing method with the digging of a tunnel: at first he wrote at headlong speed the first two or three chapters; then he laid them aside for a few days, and, when the heat of composition was over, took them up again, so that he could estimate in cold blood the things

---

50 In *New Grub Street* Edwin Reardon represents the purist, for whom literature exists in and for itself; his opposite is embodied by Jasper Milvain, the profiteer, for whom writing is an instrument to achieve financial security and social status. Milvain knows that he will never do anything of solid literary value: his aim is to write a certain number of pages a day to earn as much as possible. Reardon's failure and Milvain's success convey Gissing's bitter view of the literary market of his time.

51 Despite such harsh comments, Gissing was ambivalent towards Besant and his novels. On his part, Besant wrote with enthusiasm about *New Grub Street* and its honest depiction of literary life. On the relationship between Gissing and Besant, see Ue, 2019.

that held promise and those that did not; he then rewrote everything, correcting, cutting, or expanding; meanwhile, he went on to another rough draft of a future chapter: "[s]o the novel is constructed much on the principle of a tunnel, in which the rough boring and blasting goes on ahead, while the completion of the work slowly follows" (202–03). He added that, at the outset, "when the work was difficult and the way thorny" (204), it was necessary to exercise upon oneself a certain amount of pressure; but, after a little while, the characters would become alive and start to work out the story in their own way, and their talk would become "incessant" (203).

Besant's case is far too similar to that of Anthony Trollope not to draw a quick comparison between the two. Trollope had been one of the most prolific and widely read novelists from the 1850s to his death in 1882. Then, just after his death, the demand for his books suffered a precipitous drop, and his name was nearly forgotten. This abrupt decline has often been attributed to the damaging effect of his autobiography upon his reputation (Smalley, 1969, 6). Like Besant's, Trollope's autobiography appeared posthumously the year after his death, and it made its author unpopular for the following decades. Like Besant's, it charted the methodical ways in which the novelist worked and articulated Trollope's belief that the writing of fiction was a profession no more sacred than that of a shoemaker or a grocer. Trollope candidly admitted that he wrote for money and that he thought of himself as just another tradesman providing a product at a price for public consumption. The (in)famous passage in which he described his way of writing is strikingly similar to Besant's:

> [i]t was my practice to be at my table every morning at 5.30 a.m.; and it was also my practice to allow myself no mercy. [...] By beginning at that hour I could complete my literary work before I dressed for breakfast.
>
> All those I think who have lived as literary men – working daily as literary labourers – will agree with me that three hours a day will produce as much as a man ought to write. But then he should so have trained himself that he shall be able to work continuously during those three hours – so have tutored his mind that it shall not be necessary for him to sit nibbling his pen, and gazing at the wall before him, till he shall have found the words with which he wants to express his ideas. It had at this time [from 1859 to 1871] become my custom [...] to write with my watch before me, and to require from myself 250 words every quarter of an hour. I have found that the 250 words have been forthcoming as regularly as my watch went. (Trollope, 1883, 250–51)

With his three hours every morning, wherever he was, whether on ship or on shore, on trains or in hotels, totting up to his 250 words every quarter-hour, his watch before him, Trollope managed to produce his prodigious output:

> [t]his division of time allowed me to produce over ten pages of an ordinary novel volume a day, and if kept up through ten months, would have given as its results three novels of three volumes each in the year – the precise amount which so greatly acerbated the publisher in Paternoster Row, and which must at any rate be felt to be quite as much as the novel-readers of the world can want from the hands of one man. (Trollope, 1883, 250–51)

He followed a method similar to Besant's principle of the tunnel: each morning, before going on writing, he read and corrected what he had written the day before, "an operation which would take me half an hour, and which consisted chiefly in weighing with my ear the sound of the words and phrases. I would strongly recommend this practice to all tyros in writing" (251). Like Besant, Trollope was very open about the amount of money he made from his pen: he declared that from 1862 to 1874 his income averaged the impressive sum of £4500 a year. Thanks to his industry and self-discipline, Trollope was able to carry on simultaneously many different activities and to write a huge quantity of fiction. Trollope and Besant were the embodiment of hard work, precision and perseverance, some of the virtues most celebrated by Victorian society. And yet, such qualities were not supposed to be possessed by artists, who were held as a self-standing category. People did not like to read what Trollope first, and later Besant, wrote; their fellow-writers felt a kind of disloyalty to the conventions of their craft: it was as if they "went out to deny [their] literary caste" (Sadleir, 1961, 364). Strangely enough, Besant did not mention Trollope when he illustrated his working method. Still, their paths are remarkably similar, even if Trollope has been re-evaluated and Besant's name is still covered with thick dust.

More than a novelist, less than a novelist

An obituary notice in *The Bookman* may be the best appraisal of Besant's fictional work:

> the main characteristic of his novels, one which may have helped them at the time [of their publication], but may be fatal to their chances of life, is that they are all "impossible" stories. Wherever the scene is laid,

whoever the personages may be, a kind of prosaic phantasy is almost always introduced. [...] His prosaic phantasy was at once his making and his undoing. (July 1901, vol. 20, no. 118, pp. 111–12)

"As a novelist he is a child," *The Outlook* had commented a few years before (8 October 1898, vol. 2, no. 36, pp. 306–07). In his bitter assessment of Besant, Spilka (1973, 103) states that he "was anything but a serious thinker and could not even follow his own good advice." If perhaps too aggressive, Spilka has a point: although Besant preached extensively in favour of learning to master one's pen, and warned young writers not to lose themselves in episodes and digressions that do not advance the story, his writing – both in the joint novels but much more so in the solo ones – has a distressing tendency towards prolixity. Besant and Rice's production abounds with irrelevant material and miscellaneous comments by the narrating voice; such garrulity became more and more pronounced in Besant's solo works. "Mr. Besant is going down among the babblers," the *Nation* observed in 1892 (vol. 55, p. 436). Boege defines Besant "an irresponsible novelist" (1956b, 51), especially in his later years: according to him, the author's irresponsibility consisted in the fact that, in order to turn out novels at a steady pace, he resorted to verbosity, flights from reality, and a general carelessness. In my opinion, rather than "resorting to," Besant let himself indulge in a tendency that had been his problem since the beginning of his literary activity, and had only temporarily been kept under control by the partnership with Rice. Besant did not *need* to turn out a novel a year: it was not hack writing, it was not necessity, it was the self-indulgence of an established name of literature. Most of his later work lacks serious intention, or rather, the declared serious purpose is not fulfilled. Much like Wilkie Collins's novels 'with a purpose,'[52] part of Besant's later fiction professed to be studies of specific problems: for instance, spiritualism (*Herr Paulus*),[53] alcoholism ("The Demoniac"), heredity (*The Fourth Generation*), and ill-gotten wealth and its corrupting influence (*Beyond the Dreams of Avarice*). However, he increasingly ended up dallying with the supernatural to reveal information or to motivate characters. Besides,

---

52 Although Besant never declared an explicit intention to follow Collins's example in this field, in reading his later work one is reminded of Collins's 'novels with a purpose' such as *No Name* (dealing with the position of illegitimate children), *Man and Wife* (marriage laws and the mania for muscular sports), and *Heart and Science* (vivisection).

53 For a discussion of *Herr Paulus*, see Gabriele, 2019, 106–12.

the level of sentimentality and improbable events – scattered here and there in the co-authored fiction, and not necessarily to a bad effect – soared. Besant and Rice's novels present some romanticized characters, idealized situations, and an occasional dose of saccharine. Some of their plots contain strange acts whose motivations are inadequate. But the improbable events blend with the dominantly realistic material in an enjoyable way that was recognized by reviewers as a distinctive quality of Besant and Rice. But in Besant's solo novels the improbabilities multiply in an alarming way and cease to blend with realism. Furthermore, the eccentric characters with whom he had achieved success become mechanical, unbelievable, and all more or less derivative from the same types: they were no more the endearingly quirky figures of the co-authored novels. Even if he did not seem to acknowledge it, the partnership with Rice represented Besant's best and most creative phase: Rice's contribution, whatever form it took, made the collaborative novels more lively and unpredictable; it also kept Besant grounded, keeping his tendency towards verbosity and exaggerated idealism under control. It is a pity that he never realized what he had lost in Rice as a co-author.

In the *Autobiography* (205–15) Besant said little of his solo novels: they are listed one after the other with superficial and irrelevant remarks. He affirmed that *The Fourth Generation* was "the most serious of all my novels" (210), but did not give a reason for this choice. Although he professed the pleasure of living with the characters of his novels while writing them, in reading such works one does not feel that they were real to him. The feeling is that he produced more and more fiction without the full engagement of his imagination.

Even the comparison with Dickens, so common in the 1870s and 1880s, started to become unfavourable in the following decade. An article in *The Outlook* (7 October 1899, p. 312) pondered that both Dickens and Besant were to be classified as popular authors, but in very different ways: the former is said to please the crowds "by throwing into its life new conceptions of its own life," while Besant pleases them by "reflecting back its ideas, its tastes, its prejudices," as he "embodies in himself those characteristic limitations, outlook, and mental horizons of the special crowd he pleases." The article asserted that authors like Besant "are popular because they introduce nothing new to the crowd which loves to have its own conclusions popularly set forth in a series of pretty pictures and bound up in gilt-edged volumes to be laid in the sitting-room table." *The Orange Girl*, Besant's latest novel when the article appeared, was described as "a pier glass, reflecting nothing but the average mind of the average middle-class man now around us." The formerly celebrated novelist was now classified as a "third-class popular author":

> [i]t is because we cannot find anything original in Sir Walter Besant's mind (save his excessive optimism) that we must class him strictly with those third-class popular authors who work hard at amusing, instructing, and teaching their age, and then fall straightway into the dust, it is because they themselves are altogether the work of their age, and have struck nothing *out* of it, and have added nothing *to* it. (312)

The verdict is then announced: "in the case of ninety-nine out of a hundred novelists the term popular means that the works are destined to a speedy death" (312).

The Outlook was right. When Besant died, his fame as a novelist had already declined dramatically.[54] His reputation was based more upon philanthropic and social activities than creative writing: he had come to be seen more as a public figure than as a novelist. A wave of obituary notices appeared, which may help us understand how he was perceived at the time of his death. The general feeling may be summed up by another extract from the article in *The Bookman* mentioned above:

> it has been said that his books are already forgotten, but he will be held in memory for what he did as the founder of the Authors' Society, as the originator of the People's Palace, and as a most earnest student of the history of London. Without disparaging any of these achievements, we venture to think Sir Walter Besant's name will live just as long as his books live. (July 1901, vol. 20, no. 118, pp. 111–12)

Even though Besant never expressed any anxiety concerning the fate of his books, it seems that he used to sell most of his copyrights outright (Eliot, 2019, 129). Maybe he sensed that his luck would not last. *The Academy* (15 June 1901, no. 1519, pp. 515–16) wrote Besant's obituary

---

54 Notwithstanding his declining popularity, Besant was still earning conspicuously from his novels when he died. Eliot (2019, 128) ascribes this apparent contradiction to the mechanisms of the 'New Journalism': in the new miscellany magazines of the 1890s – a blend of stories, pictures, factual pieces, letter pages, and gossip – serialized novels were present but played no crucial role (not as central, at least, as they had played in the literary magazines of the previous decades, such as Dickens's *Household Words* or *All the Year Round*). Thus, if the story was particularly weak (or strong), it made no huge difference. A writer with a good name and solid reputation such as Besant, argues Eliot (2019, 128), "could go on asking, and probably go on getting, a standard fee, whatever happened to his novels once they had appeared in book form."

together with that of Robert Buchanan, who had died on the same day. The article drew a comparison between the two authors, observing that Buchanan "studied life in the nude, while Sir Walter Besant arranged its draperies"; Besant "offered kindly, masterful guidance to rather ordinary minds. His own mind was somewhat ordinary, though very strong and well-furnished. His genius was social, and a little coarse of grain." *The Academy* also criticized Besant's attitude towards writing as a profitable profession:

> [w]hile recognising the rightness of Sir Walter Besant's efforts to improve the author's relations to publishers, and accepting the value-for-money principle which he held so dear, we think that his view of literature was too professional; and that in his very eagerness to secure the dignity of letters he was, to some extent, defeating his own aims. Neither by his writings nor in his practical literary life did Sir Walter Besant add to the romance of letters; but he was in harmony with his age in bringing commercial common sense to bear on the literary life, [...]. All his own work was sound, and nearly all of it had a high market value [...]. His death leaves a gap in the organised literary life of London which will not soon be filled, or filled so worthily. No such gap is created by the death of Robert Buchanan; but in the world of ideas, and in the literature of sincere but vexed spirits, his vacant place is very noticeable. (pp. 515–16)

Nevertheless, not all judgements were negative: "[e]ven a good writer may write too much, may exact from himself too abundant an output, suffer from the disease of superactivity" (*Athenaeum*, 19 April 1902, no. 3886, pp. 492–93). W. H. Pollock wrote a letter to the *Saturday Review of Politics, Literature, Science and Art* (21 June 1902, vol. 93, no. 2434, pp. 805–06) arguing that it was not true that Besant "never reached first rank as a novelist"; the problem, according to Pollock, was that "after he had attained great success the very multiplicity of his interests may [...] have interfered with the concentration that he was wont to apply to his novels." *The Athenaeum* did not try to evaluate Besant's literary work, stating that "[t]he great critic Time will pronounce judgement soon enough, and with regard to literature the ultimate question, With what share of creative power was Walter Besant endowed? will be finally answered" (19 April 1902, no. 3886, pp. 492–93).

From this brief survey of obituary notices, it is clear that when Besant died doubts were already being cast about his literary legacy. His identity had not coincided with being a novelist, as Dickens's, Thackeray's or Trollope's had been. He had been somewhat more and somewhat less than that.

After all, the Prefatory Note to Besant's *Autobiography* first presented him as a campaigner for authors' rights; second, he was described as a scholar, who popularized early French literature (xii); only in the third place was Besant identified as a novelist ('novelist' first appears at p. xv). The space in the *Autobiography* that Besant himself devoted to his novels was considerably less than the space in which he discussed the Society of Authors or his philanthropic work. The fourth field which the Prefatory Note identified as a very important one to Besant was his activity as historian and antiquarian: his engagement with his massive project *A Survey of London* almost entirely came to occupy his last six years; when he died, he had completed the work down to the end of the eighteenth century. Lastly, Besant was characterized as one of the century's most active philanthropists. Though largely paternalistic and melodramatic, his slum fiction touched his contemporaries. In *All Sorts and Conditions of Men* (1882), *Children of Gibeon* (1886) and "One of Two Million in East London" (1899),[55] the East End became almost a living character, as it had never been represented in fiction before. The Victorian age was famously a time of causes, but among the socially conscious novelists Besant stands out for achieving the most spectacular result of all: the People's Palace was the direct outcome of *All Sorts and Conditions of Men*, where Besant had envisioned such a place; the

---

[55] *All Sorts and Conditions of Men* has been thoroughly discussed in Morrison's edited collection (2019), especially by Swafford and by Cheng and Kim. Swafford explores how and why Besant's most famous social novel is neither a sensational slum narrative nor a condition-of-England novel, but rather a hybrid text combining realism with romance, comedy, and mystery; he also illustrates how Besant groundbreakingly portrays the infamous inhabitants of the East End in terms of a shared humanity, seeking to normalize their perception by the middle class. Finally, Swafford discusses the concept of class consciousness in the novel and Besant's 'ethical' solution to class differences: to improve the lives of the East Enders, they must be given access to culture. The chapter suggests that Besant drew on and expanded the line of thought developed by Matthew Arnold's *Culture and Anarchy* (1869) (Swafford, 2019, 185). Cheng and Kim discuss *All Sorts and Conditions of Men* in conversation with *Children of Gibeon*, and explore Besant's shifting ideas regarding social reform. The fictional premise of both novels rests on a social experiment undertaken by a well-meaning upper-class character who aims at a connection with the alienated working class. *Children of Gibeon*, unlike Besant's first social novel, emphasizes the importance of 'universal community,' to be reached through sympathetic mutual understanding. On how *Children of Gibeon* effectively prompted a public critique of factory working conditions and safety regulations, and on how it contributed to the development of working women's trade organizations, see Diniejko, 2019, 238.

combination of his influence with a pre-existing project (which had not succeeded in attracting public attention) made the building of the Palace possible: his role was to fire public imagination in unprecedented ways.[56] In *Children of Gibeon* he dealt with women's work in the East End, especially with those who worked as sewers in their lodgings. The book led Besant to be introduced to clubs for working women; he championed their cause, went to their meetings, and raised funds.[57] He managed to create the Women's Bureau of Work, which facilitated and made safer women's search for work. However, he was not a subversive reformer, let alone a socialist: Besant was convinced that hope lay in gradual improvement. He did not support the feminist cause and shared his age's conception of women as primarily wives

---

56 In 1841 John Beaumont left a fund of £12,000 to provide intellectual improvement and amusement for the inhabitants of the East End; however, the sum was not enough to accomplish anything significant, and the project lagged until Besant became involved. Besant's vision was taken as inspiration, and a campaign was started to raise more funds: a huge portion of English society, from royalty to aristocracy, businessmen, workers and their unions (the Drapers' Company was the largest contributor), emptied their pockets to make Besant's vision come true. In 1886 the sum of £75,000 was raised and works began. The first section of the People's Palace was opened on 14 May 1887 by Queen Victoria as the first major event of the jubilee celebration (Waller, 2008, 888). The place included a concert hall, a swimming pool, a gym, a library, a winter garden, billiard-rooms, art schools, and lecture rooms (*Autobiography*, 245–46). Besant edited a weekly magazine, the *Palace Journal*, and was mainly concerned with the library and the recreational features of the Palace. But his hopes were disappointed: from 1889, the Palace came increasingly under the influence of the Drapers' Society, which aimed at strengthening the educational rather than the recreational side: "[t]hey have turned the place into a polytechnic and nothing else," he lamented in his *Autobiography* (247). As a consequence, he lost interest in the Palace and dropped out of its committee (*Autobiography*, 251).

57 Not everyone appreciated Besant's approach to the working women's cause, though. On 12 December 1893 an article entitled "A Note on Walter Besant" appeared in *Fun* (vol. 58, no. 1492, p. 257), written from the point of view of an East End working-class girl, mimicking the style of an uneducated person and reacting against Besant's patronizing attitude: "I should jest like to 'ave a talk with this 'ere Mr. Besant, who sets 'isself up to paternise people as don't want it." To the speaker, Besant is a man "who kids every body as he knows all abaht the East End." The fictional girl finally addresses Besant directly: "Mr. Besant, [...] [y]our note on the Young Gel is unctuous, snobbish, unmanly libel on a girl whose lot is a hard and a lonely one, but whose character, notwithstandin' her poverty and her temptations, is, taken all round, as good as those of her more happily-situated sisters."

and mothers. He exposed his ideas in a moralistic sequel to Ibsen's *A Doll's House*, entitled "The Doll's House – and After," which first appeared in the *English Illustrated Magazine* (1890, vol. 7, pp. 315–25) and was later included in *Verbena Camellia Stephanotis Etc.* (1892). The story, set twenty years after Nora slammed the door, begins with her return in town. She has become a wealthy novelist, acclaimed as the representative of the independence of women, supporting the theory that selfishness is the secret of happiness. Nora's violation of the sacred family ties has resulted in the ruin of her husband and children: Torvald has become an idle drunkard; one of their sons is his companion in drink; the other son is an employee at the bank his father used to work at and has just embezzled some money; only Emmy, the daughter, has remained virtuous, but she is condemned to a life as a social outcast due to the stain on her mother's reputation. She and Krogstad's son are in love, but Krogstad (who meanwhile has gained control of the bank) manages to prevent the wedding by blackmailing Emmy: he promises not to prosecute her brother if she gives up his son. The girl agrees for the sake of her family, and drowns herself. At the end, we see Nora learning of her daughter's death with indifference and, after a moment's emotion, she reflects that she cannot be saddened by the death of a stranger. She then leaves again, this time never to come back. When writing the story, Besant was obviously worried by the possible effects of feminism on society: as Boege puts it, he was "too deeply shocked to see the difference between a symbolic drama and a manual of conduct for unhappy wives. If it was good for Nora to leave her husband, why not for Mrs. Doe, Mrs. Smith, or Mrs. Besant?" (Boege, 1956b, 44).[58] Yet Besant's ideas can sometimes be surprising. In 1894, the *New Review* conducted a symposium on how to educate girls in preparation for marriage. Fourteen authors were called to contribute: some claimed that parents and the Bible were the only proper sources of education; on this occasion, Besant advocated instruction in physiology and sex (though carefully supervised) as part of the school curriculum for both boys and girls (vol. 10, pp. 675–90).

Besant also became the object of satire by his contemporaries. The character of Verena Tarrant in James's *The Bostonians* (1886) clearly shares some features with him: beside the rhyming surnames (Besant–Tarrant), Verena is exuberant and brilliant in society, and her extraordinary

---

[58] Besant's piece provoked two more sequels, one by Eleanor Marx, daughter of Karl Marx, and one by Shaw.

oratorical gifts bring her to become the embodiment of a cause – in her case, women's emancipation – but she is too naïve, and not too sharp either. In *The Green Carnation* by Robert Hichens (1894), Esmé Araminth, looking for something to slow him down, turns to Besant's novels as he hopes their dullness will help him: "intelligence is the demon of our age. Mine bores me horribly. I am always trying to find a remedy for it. I have experimented with absinthe, but gained no result. I have read the collected works of Walter Besant. They are said to sap the mental powers" (Hichens, 1992, 91). *Punch* parodied Besant in *The Curse of Cognac* by "Walter Decant," recommended by its author "as calculated to lower the exaggerated cheerfulness which is apt to prevail at Christmas time [...] Married men who owe their wives' mothers a grudge should lock them into a bare room, with a guttering candle and this story. Death will be certain, and not painless" (*Punch*, 13 Dec 1890, p. 277, quoted in Waller, 2008, 889). In the 1890s, 'Besantine' became a familiar label to the public. It was variously used to refer to a number of aspects connected to Besant, from the campaign for authors' rights to a certain type of character (especially female ones) or a sentimental or zealous attitude. An article entitled "The Besantine Craze" in *The Glasgow Evening Post* called the suspicious attitude of writers against publishers a "Besantine fad" (30 Nov. 1893, no. 8016, p. 4). 'Besantine' was used in a pejorative sense to indicate a new class of authors too concerned with their economic status and eager to steer clear of the alleged tyranny of publishers. "Besantine chivalry" (*Sunderland Daily Echo*, 14 April 1891, no. 5440, p. 2) was connected with Besant's efforts in favour of aspiring young novelists. A certain category of literary figure, usually unrealistically good and idealistic, was indicated as "Besantine characters," as opposed to "more human characters" (*The National Observer*, 20 June 1891, vol. 6, no. 135, p. 124). In particular, a "Besantine young woman" (*The National Observer*, 6 Jan. 1894, vol. 11, no. 268, p. 197) or a "young lady of Besantine architecture" (*The Scots Observer*, 15 Nov. 1890, vol. 4, no. 104, p. 667) was an innocent, unfailingly well-meaning girl. More generally, 'Besantine' came to indicate sentimental idealism and dream-like optimism. It could also refer to a kind of enthusiastic but unnecessarily eager altruism:

> hard-working, cheery, God-fearing yearners who will yearn to improve their fellow creatures, and, having done so by founding, with the aid of an opportunely bequeathed fortune, an institution for the benefit of a section of the people, will be left yearning to improve their fellow-creatures some

more and found another institution for the benefit of another section of the people. (*The Scots Observer*, 13 Sept. 1890, vol. 4, no. 95, pp. 431–32)

Puns with 'Besantine' and 'Byzantine' flourished in the periodical press, as 'Byzantine' "would be a not inapt description for Mr Besant's style" (*Glasgow Evening News*, 7 March 1892, no. 7473, p. 2).

In conclusion, there is no denying that Besant was a wide-ranging and influential figure of his age. He triggered debates on authorship, fiction writing, and on the role of literary collaboration in it. He sparked and played a key role in the "era of discussion," through which "the novel in England and in America acquired its first modern credo" (Spilka, 1973, 101). He had the gift to inspire people, a power that made him a leader of public opinion. It seems that whatever Besant touched became gold; he was the King Midas of his age. In *The Longman Companion to Victorian Fiction*, Sutherland (2009, 58) describes Besant as "a perfect Victorian." When studying nineteenth-century culture and society, indeed, Besant's role and achievements cannot be overlooked. His impact on his time deserves to be recognized, because Besant was, first of all, a man of his time: in a strange coincidence, his lifespan almost exactly corresponds to the Victorian age, which he marked in so many ways. Queen Victoria died on 22 January 1901; Besant followed her less than six months later, on 9 June: with them, an epoch had come to a close.

CHAPTER TWO

E. Œ. Somerville and Martin Ross

To this day, E. Œ. Somerville and Martin Ross – respectively Edith Œnone Somerville (1858–1949) and Violet Florence Martin (1862–1915) – remain the best known of all late nineteenth-century co-authors. Between 1888 and 1915, they jointly published five novels, various collections of short stories, four travel accounts, and a variety of periodical literature. Defined as "the most brilliant, successful literary collaboration in our times" (Graves, 1913, 436), this duo's popularity in the first decades of the twentieth century was considerable, and their partnership widely celebrated. Although in subsequent years their fame decreased significantly, they have never completely dropped out of the canon of Irish literature and have recently been acknowledged as key figures in the study of women's literary partnerships (London, 1999; Laird, 2000; York, 2002; and Ehnenn, 2008).

However, as Jamison (2016, 9) points out, the main problem with studies of female literary collaboration is that they have "variously recruited" Somerville and Ross as a significant case study to develop a theoretically engaged approach to women's collaborative practices, thus ending up disembodying the cousins' outstanding partnership "from both its historical roots and the cultural politics of the texts that it engendered." Most critical investigation have indeed discussed Somerville and Ross within a motley, ahistorical grouping of other female collaborators. Although these approaches are meaningful and have been fundamental in (re)discovering the significance of their collaboration and in tracing a history of women's co-authorship, more specialized studies of Somerville and Ross's partnership outside these perspectives are still largely lacking. Apart from Jamison's contribution, monographs on their collaboration have so far been mainly biographical studies (among others, see Collis, 1968; Cronin, 1972; and Lewis, 2005). As for critical discussions of Somerville and Ross's novels, they are scattered among histories of the Ascendancy and the Big House, including McCormack, 1985; Genet, 1991; Rauchbauer, 1992; Frehner, 1999; and seminal works by Vera Kreilkamp (1998; 2006; 2010; 2020). Kreilkamp's studies are largely parts of companions to Irish literature or histories of the Irish novel. Among this last category, Kiberd (1996; 2001) has included a couple of chapters on two of Somerville and Ross's novels.

For authors whose major work has been compared in import to those of George Eliot or James Joyce, the record of critical interest remains meager.[1] The aims of this chapter are thus to identify and discuss the most significant features of Somerville and Ross's partnership throughout its main steps over time, while, crucially, relocating it within the historical, social, and cultural context in which it developed and prospered. Somerville and Ross, their collaborative relationship, and their novels were deeply of their time; indeed, their collaboration could not have flourished in any other time or place: late nineteenth-century Ascendancy Ireland presented a unique atmosphere, which was about to fade forever at the time of the collaboration of the two cousins, who managed to capture it in their works in a masterly fashion.

Literary foremothers

Somerville and Ross came from ancient families.[2] Their mothers were first cousins, granddaughters of the judge and statesman Charles Kendal Bushe (1767–1843), Chief Justice of Ireland, known as Silver-tongued Bushe after his vehement speeches against the Act of Union of 1800. Yet perhaps more pervasive for his great-granddaughters' imagination was the figure of Bushe's wife, Anne (Nancy) Crampton, whom he married in 1793.

Mrs Bushe was a woman of culture, an artist, and a well-known friend of Maria Edgeworth's. Somerville and Ross were proud of their ancestor's famous friendship with one of the women writers they looked up to, and

---

1 Cahalan (1988, 94) identifies *The Real Charlotte* as "the greatest Irish novel of the nineteenth century"; Moynahan (1995, 183) defines it "a serious contender for title of the best Irish novel before Joyce," while Eagleton (1995, 215) champions it as "one of the few truly totalizing works of Irish fiction […] with all the synoptic assurance of a *Middlemarch*."

2 From now on, I will follow the common practice among readers of Somerville and Ross by referring to the latter as Martin, as did Edith Somerville. When I refer to both authors, I will call them by their pen names 'Somerville and Ross,' but when I refer to Violet Martin alone, I will use 'Martin.'

talked gladly of the mutual admiration between them. In Somerville's autobiography *Irish Memories*, one long chapter (III) is dedicated to the bond between Crampton and Edgeworth; some of their correspondence is also reported in order to highlight how the latter "lost no time in falling in love with her 'very dear Mrs Bushe'" from their first meeting in 1810, and how the attachment "remained unbroken to the last," until the novelist's death in 1849 (*IM*, 53). Indeed, the letters tell us of a sincere affection and of a communion of minds.

Although the friendship between Mrs Bushe and Edgeworth did not lead to a writing partnership, Somerville and Ross were fascinated by it and portrayed it in a romanticized light, using the same sentimental vocabulary they employed to describe their own friendship. If Edgeworth and Mrs Bushe's first meeting was like falling in love, Somerville described her first meeting with Martin in a similar way: "[f]or most boys and girls the varying, yet invariable, flirtations, and emotional episodes of youth, are resolved and composed by marriage. To Martin and to me was opened another way, and the flowering of both our lives was when we met each other" (*IM*, 125). Edgeworth's description of Mrs Bushe as her "delight and admiration, from her wit, humour, and variety of conversation" (*IM*, 53) could have easily been written by Somerville or Martin about each other. The correspondence between Edgeworth and Mrs Bushe reported in *Irish Memories* is often concerned with contriving ways to meet; likewise, Somerville and Ross's letters are full of planning, timetables, and ticket prices, with mutual offers to pay for them.

These might seem inconsequential biographical details, but they offer in fact an enlightening starting point to better understand Somerville and Ross's literary partnership. The fact that their great-grandmother had developed an intimate, lifelong friendship with a woman they considered a literary foremother was inspiring. Somerville and Ross have often been compared by critics to Maria Edgeworth because of the many similarities between their works, such as the use of Hiberno English or the interest in representing with irony the decline of the Ascendancy to whom they belonged. Mrs Bushe died in 1857, only one year before Somerville's birth and five before Martin's, so she was not a faded ancestor but a very vivid presence in their families' memories. Her relationship with Edgeworth provided Somerville and Ross with an early model of female friendship based on affection, esteem, and shared literary interests. Both relationships lasted more or less thirty years and were interrupted only by the death of one of the two.

The figure of their great-grandmother, however, affected Somerville and Ross in other ways: they admired Mrs Bushe not only for her friendship with Edgeworth but also for her own talents as an intellectual and an artist. Somerville seems to have regretted that she had not had the chance to fully express her potential, as "marriage had subdued the artist in her" (*IM*, 52). To Somerville's distress, Mrs Bushe had devoted herself to her large family, thus neglecting her many other talents: "[in] her time there were few women who gave even a moment's thought to the possibilities of individual life as an artist, however aware they might be – must have been – of the gifts they possessed" (*IM*, 52). Even if she proceeded immediately to reassure the reader that her great-grandmother had been "well satisfied enough with what life had brought her – honour, love, obedience, troops of friends" (*IM*, 52), her frustration with her ancestor's wasted talents surfaces clearly enough. That a young Somerville vowed to be self-supporting and remained unmarried could be a reaction to Nancy Crampton's fate as a married woman and mother of six – a woman she felt so akin to herself, but to whom circumstances had not given the chance to realize her potential. It is likely that Martin shared her cousin's opinion, but we have no explicit written evidence of her thoughts about it.[3]

Many others among Somerville and Ross's relatives were amateur painters and writers. "[T]here was scarcely one of them without some touch of that spark which is lit by a coal taken from the altar, and is [...] called originality" even if "the reputations of neither Shakespeare nor Michael Angelo were threatened" (*IM*, 61–62). The Martin family in particular counted many respected names in the literary scene of the time: Martin's father had written for leading London magazines to earn extra money at the time of the Great Famine; her mother was an amateur poet; her elder brother Robert became a renowned journalist and a playwright, and would promote Somerville and Ross's first works; her mother's cousin William G. Wills was a famous playwright, poet,

---

3 We have many metadiscourses by Somerville, the most significant ones being *Irish Memories* and the 1946 article "Two of a Trade," while we have very few written accounts by Martin, apart from the letters she used to write to family and friends. Thus, I will necessarily base many of my reflections on statements made by Somerville, though keeping in mind that they are the point of view of only one of the partners: even if Somerville declared on many occasions the perfect correspondence of her and her cousin's thoughts – and by reading their letters to each other it is easy to trust her – it is important to remember that we often have only one perspective.

and painter; and Lady Augusta Gregory was a cousin of Martin's. The web of the Martins' connections also laid a strand on Oscar Wilde via the Wills family (his middle names were Fingall O'Flaherie Wills).[4] The list could be longer, but this will suffice to give an idea of the background Somerville and Ross came from.

An almost lost world

It has often been remarked that Somerville and Ross's *oeuvre* is tinged with nostalgic tones for the waning world of the Big House.[5] Some of their novels can indeed be included in the Big House novel genre, most overtly *An Irish Cousin* (1889), *The Real Charlotte* (1894), *Mount Music* (1919), *An Enthusiast* (1921), and *The Big House of Inver* (1925), and all their texts present the same partly elegiac, partly ironic longing for the old rural system. Like Edgeworth, Somerville and Ross not only wrote about Big Houses but were born within their walls and spent their lives managing them, perpetually engaged in a painful struggle to save them from ruin.

The Somervilles and the Martins were long-established Ascendancy families, the former based in County Cork, the latter in County Galway. They belonged to the Anglo-Irish class of landowners, that oligarchy who occupied the Big Houses first satirized by Edgeworth.[6] *Castle Rackrent*

---

4 Unfortunately, there was little love left between Somerville and Ross and Oscar Wilde. In 1887 Wilde was the editor of the *Lady's Pictorial* and refused to publish Somerville's French sketches. In an indignant letter to Martin she gave an account of her meeting with him: "[h]e talked great rot that 'French subjects should be drawn by French artists' – I was near telling him, as Dr. Johnson said – 'who drives fat oxen must himself be fat.' He assumed deep interest in the 'Miss Martins,' asked if they were all married: I said, 'mostly all.' He was kind enough to say that Somerville [one of Martin's sisters] was so pretty and nice – and bulged his long fat red cheeks into an affectionate grin at the thought of her. He then showed me a book of very indifferent French sketches – was foully civil, and goodbye" (*Letters*, 68). Somerville's general opinion of Wilde was that he was "a great fat oily beast" (*Letters*, 68).
5 As is well known, the collocation 'Big House' refers to a country mansion owned by an Anglo-Irish family presiding over a substantial agricultural acreage leased out to Catholic tenants who worked the land. The Protestant oligarchy was eager "to display its wealth and power – and indeed its permanence – through a classically inflected building programme," in a sort of fantasy to visually transform Ireland into a replica "of an England that was increasingly imagining itself as the modern version of the imperial Roman estate" (Kreilkamp, 2006, 60).
6 See Welch, 1996; Kreilkamp, 2006; and Cotta Ramusino, 2019.

(1800) inaugurated the Big House novel and established its conventions: a crumbling mansion as symbol of family and class degeneration, the irresponsible landlord alienated from his duties, and the native Irish middle-class usurper. Unsurprisingly, the peak of the Big House novel can be found in the late nineteenth and the early twentieth century, when, under assault from new land laws and emerging nationalism, the Ascendancy was struggling to keep up with modern times; in Edgeworth's time the Anglo-Irish gentry was already in crisis, but by the end of the century it was evident that its ruling role had ended. Somerville and Ross experienced the crisis first-hand: despite their social status and the stately houses, their families were moneyless because of non-payment of rents. The heirs of the Big Houses were left to their own means to earn a living: the sons were generally placed in the army, navy, or Church; to Somerville and Ross, "the ability to earn their own money was a matter of life or death, or at least life or marriage" (*Letters*, viii). Lack of money, and how to raise it, were two of the most recurrent topics in their letters. As Lewis points out (*Letters*, viii), at the end of the nineteenth century the Ascendancy was "an enormous confidence trick, shored up by faithful servants and good horsemanship." The fact that they still owned the Big Houses was what saved appearances. Yet the running of these ancient, large estates cost money, so much so that a good part of their income was swallowed by their upkeep. Ross House, the Martins' family home, was built in 1777 in the peculiar style of the Big House, "a tall, unlovely block, of great solidity" (*IM*, 7). Somerville described the apparently unromantic Ross House with sentimental melancholy:

> there is a special magic in Galway, in its people and its scenery, and for me, Ross, and its lake and its woods, is Galway. The beauty of Ross is past praising. I think of it as I saw it first, on a pensive evening of early spring, still and grey, with a yellow spear-head of light low in the west. [...] On higher ground above the lake stands the old house, tall and severe, a sentinel that keeps several eyes, all of them intimidating, on all around it. (*IM*, 98–99)

After the death of Martin's father in 1872 Ross House was leased, and the family returned to live there only in 1888, after sixteen years of absence, during which time the tenant had stripped the estate bare and the house had fallen into utter neglect. This was a common occurrence in those days, when gentry families were moving to England or Dublin after getting the best bargain they could. The tenant of Ross House, whose aim was just getting the most out of the land, left it in an appalling state, as Martin told Somerville:

[i]t takes a long time to patch the present Ross and the one I remember on to each other. [...] I do not know anything gives such desolation as the loss of trees and shrubs and that *devil* who was our last tenant has laid about him for pure spite. [...] In the garden the old apple trees were cut down by this brute that he might have more room for planting his potatoes [...]. (27 June 1888, *Letters*, 77)

Somerville felt the decline of her class somehow less, at least in her youth, as Drishane House, in Castletownshend, was still the place of a comfortable life. The situation got worse over the years, and in later times they had to let the house for the summer. In her letters to Somerville Martin expressed her heartbreak at the condition of Ross, now fallen from the almost royal status it had held; she dedicated her adult life to try and bring Ross House back to its past glories, clinging to its preservation with all her strength, not out of vanity or snobbery, but out of affection for the estate and the quasi-feudal bonds with the local families that had been in the service of the Martins for generations: "[t]he tenants have been very good about coming and working here for nothing – except their dinners – and a great deal has been done by them. It is of course gratifying, but in a way very painful, and makes one want money more than anything" (Martin to Somerville, 27 June 1888, *Letters*, 80). In Somerville and Ross's biased perception, Big Houses were traditionally not only the seat of the landlord, but "places that were once disseminators of light, of the humanities; centres of civilisation; places where the poor people rushed, in any trouble, as to the Cities of Refuge" (*IM*, 154–55). By the 1880s, however, those mansions had become "desolate, derelict" (*IM*, 154–55). In her autobiography, Somerville romanticized Martin's struggle to keep the house going: when the Martins returned to Ross, "there was everything to be done, inside and outside that old house, and no one to do it but one fragile, indomitable girl" (*IM*, 154).

Despite belonging to the Ascendancy, Somerville and Ross's loyalties tended to lie more with Ireland than England, and they saw their class as an intermediary group who simultaneously tried to improve the condition of Ireland and its relationship with the United Kingdom. Chief Justice Charles Kendal Bushe had been the very embodiment of that attitude. Hence, if the Big House was a presence in the Irish landscape that embodied political, economic, and cultural control of the remote English colonial power structure – and thus a symbol of division (Kreilkamp, 2006, 60) – it was also the site of an in-between class, a "race of hybrids," to use Elizabeth Bowen's term (1950, 4), neither alien nor native, who sympathized with the local lower classes and were suspicious of English visitors in the land they were born in and loved. "In our parts of Ireland we do not for a moment pretend to be too civilised for superstition," declared Somerville (*IM*, 181). "Nonsense about being 'English'!" she wrote passionately to one of her brothers, "my family has eaten Irish food and shared Irish life for 300 years, and if that doesn't make me Irish I might as well say I was Scotch, or Norman, or pre-Diluvian!" (quoted in Lewis, 1985, 165).

In a study aimed at introducing Oscar Wilde, George Bernard Shaw, and Somerville and Ross within the late nineteenth century Irish Literary Revival, Clare (2014) argues that, despite being Anglo-Irish and writing mainly for English audiences, Somerville and Ross deserve a place among the Revivalists. Like Wilde and Shaw, Somerville and Ross are usually "disqualified" from the movement because of a "perceived Britishness" in their work (91). Clare claims that the entire Irish Revival "was underwritten by [...] the cultural Britishness of most of its key participants" (93), as they all had had upbringings heavily influenced by Britishness. The article calls attention to the difference between "English" and "British," and underlines that "Britishness" and "Irishness" are not necessarily mutually exclusive terms (92). Many Irish Protestants traditionally felt a more or less active antipathy towards the English. A kind of anti-Englishness surfaces in Somerville and Ross's novels, from the base opportunist soldier Hawkins or the pretentious Miss Hope-Drummond in *The Real Charlotte* through the invading pack of English idiots in *The Silver Fox* to the fastidious, class-conscious Jean Masterman in *Dan Russel the Fox*.[7] In their novels, English people are always the Other, mainly visitors in a country whose ways and customs they ignore and cannot understand. One of the main characters in *The Silver Fox* falls out with her English suitor because of their radically different views on the superstitions of the local peasants. Somerville and Ross's last joint novel in particular, *Dan Russel the Fox*, revolves around a visit by a group of English friends to Ireland; they are introduced to Irish

---

7 Clare (2014, 98) also considers Somerville and Ross's travel book *In the Vine Country* (1893), in which the two cousins repeatedly expressed their "defiant Irish pride and an anti-Englishness as strong as that of any Revival writer." During a stay in France, Somerville and Ross were irritated to be called *les Anglaises* by the French, and so they got used to immediately declaring their true nationality, with positive consequences: "we found ourselves at once on a different and more friendly footing, and talk had a pleasant tendency to drift into confidential calumny of our mutual neighbour, perfidious Albion, and all things ran smoother and more gaily" (Somerville and Ross, 2001, 117).

ways and pastimes by their host, the witty Irish widow Lily Delanty. The young English protagonist, Katharine Rowan, is captivated by what she perceives as the bewitching Irish country life and falls in love with the Irish huntsman John Michael. Her fellow-travellers, on the contrary, do not share Katharine's fascination, and, after a brief sojourn, would like to go back to their usual life. Ireland appears to the eyes of the English as a weird country, quite apart from England. Such a view of Ireland as a foreign land that enthrals the English or American visitor was already present in Somerville and Ross's first novel, *An Irish Cousin*, in which Theo, a young American girl, comes to Ireland to visit her Irish relatives; like Katharine Rowan, she becomes acquainted with Irish country life and people, and feels all their strange charm.

Despite a tendency to idealize the world of the Big House, in their novels Somerville and Ross portrayed the decline of their own class without embellishments, mercilessly showing its faults and inadequacy. Dominick Sarsfield in *An Irish Cousin*, Christopher Dysart in *The Real Charlotte*, Major Talbot-Lowry in *Mount Music*, and Captain Jas Prendeville in *The Big House of Inver* are incapable of effectively managing their responsibility, and therefore guilty of the downfall of the Ascendancy. Still, the waning of the Ascendancy is depicted with a tinge of melancholy, and this has usually contributed to Somerville and Ross's exclusion from studies of the Revival. In addition, their contempt for the rising Irish middle classes, who were taking the place of the Anglo-Irish, is evident: the most patent case is that of the social climber Charlotte Mullen, the anti-heroine at the centre of *The Real Charlotte*. Charlotte's greediness and ruthlessness damage both the Irish peasants – who have to pay unreasonably high rents for squalid lodgings – and the Anglo-Irish Julia Duffy, whose farm ends up in Charlotte's hands. I agree at least partially with Clare's argument that Somerville and Ross's Anglo-Irishness, and their sentimental nostalgia for the golden days of the Big House, do not make them more English than their contemporary Irish Revivalist.[8] However, it must be pointed out that, in his plea to include Somerville and Ross in the Revival, Clare does not take into account the aims of these writers' work: one of the main goals of

---

8 Clare adds to his argument that Somerville and Ross's rendering of West Cork speech in texts such as the *Irish R.M.* stories is more precise and authentic than the peasant speech in works by many playwrights writing for the Abbey Theatre (Clare, 2014, 97). Lewis (1989, 25) also maintains that "the exactitude and build of their record of Irish speech is unique."

Revivalist authors was decleredly to rediscover ancient Irish texts and traditions, an ambition that Somerville and Ross did not share, so that they were not keen at all on the Irish Revival. When Lady Gregory invited them to write for the Abbey Theatre, they refused the offer as they "did not really approve of something that had been brought back to life with so much artificial respiration" (*Letters*, 238). Somerville and Ross also did not appreciate the plays staged at the Abbey Theatre because they felt that the French influences overwhelmed the Irishness of the plays (Lewis, 2005, 209–10; see also Clare, 2014, 97). In this light, proposing to include Somerville and Ross in a movement they disliked and whose purposes they did not share seems an unnecessary forcing.

Women who live by their brains

"It was, as it happens, in church that I saw her first; in our own church, in Castle Townshend. That was on Sunday, January 17, 1886" (*IM*, 120). After growing up apart, Somerville and Ross met on an occasional visit of Martin and her mother to Drishane. Somerville was twenty-eight, Martin was twenty-four. Each had already had some experience of life: "[w]hen we first met each other we were, as we then thought, well stricken in years. [...] Not absolutely the earliest morning of life; say, about half-past ten o'clock, with breakfast (and all traces of bread and butter) cleared away" (*IM*, 1). Somerville described their first encounter as "the hinge of my life, the place where my fate, and hers, turned over, and new and unforeseen things began to happen to us" (*IM*, 122). She probably exaggerated its importance, as apparently the new acquaintance became significant only some time later: it seems that Martin was fascinated with Somerville's brilliant personality, but that Somerville, for her part, was not immediately struck by this shy, younger cousin. Somerville was the eldest of eight children, and throngs of cousins came and went through Drishane (just in her own family, Martin was the youngest of twelve); besides, she had already a favourite cousin, her childhood companion Ethel Coghill.[9] One more cousin made no difference to her. Somerville was what Martin defined as "a popular girl" (19 May 1886, *Letters*, 6) and far too busy with her social life and her artistic aspirations to notice

---

9 Somerville's friendship with her first cousin and 'twin' Ethel Coghill lasted until the end of their lives, despite the fact that in 1880 Ethel married out of the family circle (leaving Somerville "bereft") and preferred – like many Anglo-Irish – to live in England, where she died (Lewis, 2005, 35, 40, 42).

Martin. In March 1886 she left her hometown to spend a few months studying in a Paris studio, and did not trouble to answer Martin's first letters. Lewis (*Letters*, 5) supposes that it would have been unlikely that a relationship would have developed had Martin not been so persistent in trying to get her attention.

Moreover, Somerville had to earn the money to pay for her studies in Paris (she made illustrations for *The Graphic* and other magazines) and did not want to lose time writing unnecessary letters. At that time she had published a sensationalist short story and some humorous pieces, but did not worry too much about a career as a writer: she considered herself a painter and all her energies were directed towards becoming a professional illustrator. She had briefly studied art in London at seventeen, but her serious artistic education started later, thanks to the help of her older cousin Egerton Coghill, who was also studying painting and invited Somerville to join him in Düsseldorf. When Coghill moved to Paris Somerville followed suit, notwithstanding her mother's objections to a young woman living on her own in a city she termed "the Scarlet Woman" (*IM*, 110). In the French capital she lived a bohemian and relatively free existence for an upper-class girl of the 1880s, in a cosmopolitan environment of artists from all over Europe and America:

> [w]e had rooms in a tall and filthy old house in the Rue Madame, one of those sinister and dark and narrow streets that one finds in the Rive Gauche, that seem as if they must harbour all variety of horrors, known and unknown, and are composed of houses whose incredible discomforts would break the spirit of any creature less inveterate in optimism than an Art student. [...]
> I find myself thinking how good it would be to be five and twenty, and storming up that rickety staircase again, with a paint-box in one hand, and a *Carton* as big as the Gates of Gaza in the other. (*IM*, 113, 118)

Somerville would spend many periods of her life in Paris, sharing house and expenses with other women artists. During her Paris stays, no chaperone was around to supervise her, and she could come and go as she pleased, at least as long as she had money:

> we knew that when [money] ended there would be no husks to fall back upon; nothing but one long note on the horn, "Home!," and home we should have to go (I once ran it to so fine a point that I could buy no food between Paris and London, and when I arrived at my uncle's house in London, it was my long-suffering uncle who paid the cabman). (*IM*, 114)

Art was already the main object of Somerville's life, and she was determined to be an independent professional woman. The friendship with her apparently negligible cousin changed the way in which she would pursue her goals.

On her part, at the time of their first meeting Violet Martin was just beginning to turn into Martin Ross. Since her father's death when she was ten she had lived a rather secluded life with her mother in a north Dublin house; she had had little experience of life and had not travelled much, "growing quite a solitary little prodigy" (Lewis, 2005, 27). Yet she had already, like the men in her family, published a few serious articles. She did not think of herself as a novelist, even less as a humorous entertainer, but rather as a politically engaged essayist, who wrote "in the grave columns of the *Irish Times*" (*IM*, 124).

Why, and how, did a struggling painter and a shy aspiring journalist ended up co-authoring fiction? Actually, the idea of the literary partnership did not come out of the blue; both were familiar with the idea of collaboration. Somerville, as an illustrator, knew well the close collaborative relationship between painter and writer; Martin had been exchanging ideas for stage plots with her cousin William Wills, with whom she was considering a more formal collaboration (Jamison, 2016, 90–91).[10] Moreover, they already had an example of collaboration in their family, as Wills and another cousin of the clan, Mrs Greene, had collaborated on a shilling shocker around 1885–86. In addition, the Somerville siblings and their cousins, like many other children, used to set up plays and co-write stories.[11] Collaboration was in the air that

---

10 Jamison (2016, 90) points out that the kind of collaboration with Wills placed Martin in a subordinate position, as he claimed authority and regarded her not as a partner, but rather as an assistant and amanuensis. Yet, despite Wills's downplaying of Ross's contribution, Stevens (2001, 67) argues that he paid her and attempted to get her more work with other playwrights and directors. When *An Irish Cousin* appeared, Wills claimed his share of merit: "I am sincerely delighted and proud of you, because it was I who reared you. Loftus has been here talking of your novel [...] I spoke and claimed the praise for myself – I formed her, I said, I developed her nascent qualities, in fact *I* am the author of that book" (William G. Wills, letter to Martin, quoted in Jamison, 2016, 91).

11 For example, before publishing her first work of fiction, Louisa May Alcott collaborated on plays with her sisters; the Rossetti children produced a collection of tales and two family journals, completed with poems and stories; Rudyard Kipling and his sister Alice 'Trixie' published a co-authored collection of tales and a collection of verse parodies; most famously, the Brontë sisters, together with their brother Branwell, collaborated on a voluminous series of works varying from

Somerville and Martin breathed. It does not sound so strange, then, that by their third meeting Somerville had already suggested to Martin that they should write a book together, which she should also illustrate (*IM*, 124).

In June 1886 Somerville returned home from Paris and her friendship with Martin bloomed. Their first collaborative project was an article for *The Graphic* (11 October 1886) entitled "Palmistry," written by Martin and illustrated by Somerville. The step towards a full literary collaboration was not far, and the key to it was the friendship that developed between the cousins. The summer of 1886, spent "in sheer idling" (*IM*, 126) in Castletownshend, proved vital for the development of their personal and literary partnership. The two young women got to know each other, took long walks, played lawn tennis, chatted for hours, "lying in the warm, short grass of the sheep fields," and it was "the beginning [...] of a new era" (*IM*, 125). Somerville and Ross built the foundation of their partnership on their intimate, exclusive, and, in many respects, romantic friendship. Their habit of taking time only for themselves, spending mornings outdoors walking and talking (the afternoons were dedicated to their respective social schedules) became a basic element of their collaborative model. The fact that they talked their stories into existence is well known and has been emphasized by many critical works, but few have taken the pains to point out the importance of their first summers together when they, by becoming friends, were actually preparing the ground for their careers as professional writers.

In a celebrated passage of *Irish Memories* Somerville reflected that "[t]he outstanding fact, as it seems to me, among women who live by their brains, is friendship. A profound friendship that extends through every phase and aspects of life, intellectual, social, pecuniary. Anyone who has experience of the life of independent and artistic women knows this" (*IM*, 326). Surely, Victorian society recognized female friendship as a much more significant bond than we normally do, comparable to kinship and conjugal love. For a number of reasons, including the gender theory of the separate spheres, female friendship was a vital component of nineteenth-century conceptions of proper femininity, as increasingly acknowledged by women's and queer studies, such as Marcus (2007). Before "psychiatrists popularized the concept of the deviant lesbian" (Marcus, 2007, 30), female emotional intimacy and passionate friendship

> tales, plays, poems, little magazines, and multi-volume novels that they shared only with each other.

were integral elements of domestic life, as they were seen as important in cultivating the 'feminine' virtues of sympathy, altruism, and selflessness. Physical contact and effusive displays of affection were encouraged: women "were expected to touch, caress, and fondle each other" (Flint, 2016, 205). Looking at Victorian women's letters or reading their autobiographies can be a puzzling experience, as they used a startling romantic language to describe how they felt about female friends. Female homoeroticism "did not subvert dominant codes of femininity, because female homoeroticism was one of those codes" (Marcus, 2007, 113).[12] In the latter half of the nineteenth century, when more and more women started to assert their right to independence and work, their ties to each other became even more important. Higher education and employment opportunities for women, though still limited, increased, and a woman with ability and motivation could make her way as she could have seldom done in earlier times.[13] If a woman chose not to marry and pursue a career that would enable her to earn a living, then friendship with other women in her same position was what provided the support she would need. Somerville had already experienced something similar in her early Paris days, when she had lived with other "independent and artistic" women.[14] With Martin, she took this idea to a further level, making their friendship the most significant relationship of her life and the underlying rock of her career.

Feminist studies in North America and Britain generally identify

---

[12] On female friendship and its various forms in the Victorian age see Faderman, 1981; Vicinus, 2004; Marcus, 2007; and Flint, 2016. See also Chapman, 2015: within her wider analysis of the community of expatriate women poets living in Florence in the 1840s and the 1850s, Chapman explores the intellectual, social and sometimes homoerotic bonds that these women shared; she also considers some cases of female cohabitation – described as female marriages – that provided mid-Victorian women writers living in Italy with opportunities to reimagine their identity in creative, fertile, and liberating ways.

[13] On Victorian women and employment, see Young, 2019. Young focuses on the typist and the nurse as pioneering figures in women's professional advancement.

[14] Lewis (*Letters*, 36) underlines that Somerville did not work with "feeble amateurs." On the contrary, to most of her Paris friends it was a matter of great consequence that they should train to a professional level. Their goal was to be self-supporting and many went on to become teachers or illustrators. In 1887 Martin visited Somerville in Paris to see what studio life was like, and thought it awful: Somerville's friends in the French capital were a motley collection of women from Scandinavia, central Europe, and America who lived bohemian lives, a kind of company Martin was not used to.

a first generation of New Women, born in the 1850s and 1860s, educated, autonomous and single, who were active in the feminist movement from the 1890s to World War I and who pursued personal and economic independence by rejecting their mothers' domestic roles. These women would turn to romantic friendships as the alternative to the male-dominated, heterosexual family structure (Newton, 1989, 238; see also Smith-Rosenberg, 1985, 245–96). The fact was that many of them believed marriage to be incompatible with their life ambitions. A husband would demand what nineteenth-century men were taught to reasonably expect from a wife; housekeeping and child care would have absorbed most of the time and energies necessary for a woman's personal and professional pursuits. But even if practical reasons were strong enough, their emotional reasons were even stronger. In Victorian society, men and women inhabited different spheres; their worlds were separated, not only in their daily occupations but in their leisure interests as well. Women were taught to see other women as kindred spirits and men as the Other. In addition, a proper Victorian marriage would imply that the wife be inferior to the husband and selflessly sacrifice her ambitions to his. Even if the husband did not claim superiority over her, "society would nevertheless attribute that superiority to him, and she would have to live with the injustice" (Faderman, 1981, 205) or at least play a role in which she did not fit. These New Women, instead, sought equals, partners who were striving for their same goals and who could sympathize with them. Many found in female friendship what they needed in an otherwise quite isolated condition. A "profound friendship" was so vital because the lives of these women who "lived by their brains" could be extremely lonely: an unmarried woman who did not seek support from a male relative and lived by her own means was normally ostracized. In a society that idealized marriage and reduced the role of women to wife and mother, New Women represented a threat, something to be made fun of or scorned. They needed companions who understood and were there for them, for whom they would do the same.

As seen above, Somerville and Ross talked of their friendship in gushing, overtly romantic terms, and compared it to a marriage. This has led twentieth-century critics to infer that a sexual relationship existed between them, and many biographies and studies of Somerville and Ross have focused on either proving or negating their lesbianism.[15] In

---

15 Collis (1968) states categorically that "Somerville could only fall in love with a woman" (37). Lewis (1985; 2005) negates the sexual nature of their relationship,

Somerville and Ross's time there were some famous couples of women writers for whom love – or, at least, romantic, monogamous friendship – and literary work were interrelated: Katherine Bradley (1846–1914) and Edith Cooper (1862–1913), who published poetry, plays, and various fiction under the pseudonym 'Michael Field,' are the most prominent instance of lesbian lovers/writers, but Marie Corelli and Bertha Vyver, Alice French (who wrote under the name of Octave Thanet) and Jane Crawford, and Rosa Bonheur and Nathalie Micas, to name a few, were also independent women who formed long-lasting Boston marriages. These women lived together for a significant part of their adult life, did not include a man in what they felt to be their household paradises, and were perfectly integrated into respectable society. Nevertheless, it must be remembered that Victorian women were assumed to be asexual, acquiescing to sexual activity only for the sake of their husbands and for the supposedly higher, more fulfilling purpose of procreation. Since there was no possibility that women, at least respectable ones, might have sexual urges, they were permitted a level of intimacy and public display of affection that in the twentieth century would become suspect. Since "Victorians saw lesbian sex almost nowhere" (Marcus, 2007, 113), a woman in bed with another woman would have raised nobody's eyebrows. Precisely because women were believed to be "unsullied by the evils of carnality," "a sex-hating society" (Faderman, 1981, 203) could view their relationships as ideal and even admire the purity and the devotion of such relations. In addition, a modest woman would always have to restrain herself with a man, even within marriage: a wife with too strong a sexual appetite transgressed against codes of domestic sexuality and could even be seen as deranged – active and 'uncontrolled' female sexual longing being conceived as one of the defining symptoms of insanity in women (Heilmann and Llewellyn, 2016, 163). With another woman, in contrast, the shield of restraint could be put aside: women could express all the intensity of their feelings for a female friend without fear of being improperly labelled. Since "the language of sexual desire falls so very close to that of passionate female attachment" (Flint, 2016, 207) it is misleading to try to distinguish – should one wish to do so – erotic desire from emotional attachment in

---

asserting that it was merely platonic, and so do a number of other studies: Cahalan, 1999; Cowman, 1997; Kiberd, 1996; Kreilkamp, 2010; London, 1999; O'Connor, 2010; and Weekes, 1990. Others characterize their relationship as lesbian: Stone and Thompson, 2006; Wood, 1994; and York, 2006.

nineteenth-century women's declarations of 'love.'¹⁶ Ultimately, I agree with Mooney (1992, 173) that using "unhelpful heterosexist bias" in order to prove or disprove lesbianism in the case of Somerville and Ross "obscure[s] and distort[s] the creative, emotional and probably sensual centrality of the[ir] relationship." Whatever the sexual nature of their relationship, what is relevant for this study is what they thought essential for their literary careers. Emotional commitment, intellectual affinity, and constant support made Somerville and Ross's daring life choices possible and their collaboration successful. They strongly believed that, without their passionate friendship, their professional achievements as "women who live by their brains" would have been impossible.

Two Irish cousins

Somerville emphasized how her and Martin's special empathy had developed not only from personal affinity but also from shared family heritage: "[b]eing Irish, I have to acknowledge its spell, and I think it is indisputable that a thread, however slender, of kinship adds a force to friendship" (*IM*, 42). And it was precisely from that shared background that their first joint literary effort sprang: in 1887 the cousins engaged in the compilation of the "Buddh Dictionary," a collection of words and phrases used by the network of families that descended from Charles Kendal Bushe and who called themselves 'Buddhs.' Somerville referred to Buddh terms as

> the froth on the surface of some hundreds of years of the conversation of a clan of violent, inventive, Anglo-Irish people, who generation after generation, found themselves faced with situations in which the English language failed to provide sufficient intensity, and they either snatched at alternatives from other tongues or invented them. (*Letters*, 297)

The dictionary of family slang points to the already underlined problematic position Somerville and Ross occupied within nineteenth-century Ireland: the terminology examined in it is a prominent element capable of setting them apart from both the world of the proper English and the world of the native Irish. London (1999) sees in the "Buddh Dictionary" the first seeds of Somerville and Ross's later production:

---

16 Indeed, critical work over the last decades has tried to unpick the complexities of applying contemporary theoretical and conceptual frameworks onto the Victorian age. See Heilmann and Llewellyn, 2016.

like the dictionary, their works of fiction document and preserve the morals and manners of the Irish and Anglo-Irish people in a precise moment in history, and "perform a service for the 'language' – a way of life – passing out of existence, and hence in need of translation and transcription" (123). Somerville and Ross's works have been often praised for their accurate reproduction of the living language of the Irish people, and their early interest in language is certainly proven by the Buddh project.[17]

Noticing how easily they could work together, Somerville proposed that they might try with a novel. The literary atmosphere of the late 1880s was full of what were then known as shilling shockers, and Somerville and Ross thought it would be funny to try their hands at something of that kind. Thus, just after completing the dictionary, in October 1887, they began writing a sensationalist story, affectionately called between the two of them 'The Shocker.' The joint literary venture began in a light-hearted spirit, as something they did for the fun of it. They did not have the support of their families, who dismissed their efforts at times with sarcasm, at other times with open hostility:

> we began what was to be known to us as "The Shocker," and "The Shaughraun," to our family generally, as "that nonsense of the girls," and subsequently, to the general public, as "An Irish Cousin." Seldom have the young and ardent "commenced author" under less conductive circumstances. We were resented on so many grounds. Waste of time; the arrogance of having conceived such a project; and, chiefly, the abstention of two playmates. They called us "The Shockers," "The Geniuses" (this in bitter irony), "The Hugger-Muggerers" (this flight of fancy was my mother's); when not actually reviled, we were treated with much the same disapproving sufferance that is shown to an outside dog who sneaks into the house on a wet day. (*IM*, 128–29)

The difficulties of those early times are almost identically repeated in Somerville's late-life essay "Two of a Trade":[18]

---

17 Somerville and Ross "foraged among the country people in search of phrases and habits of speech" (Cronin, 1968, 10), and recorded what they heard "with all the tender precision of a folk-lorist" (Lyons, 1970, 120). They kept notebooks in which they annotated words and sentences heard in the streets; once they had used the phrase in one of their works, they scratched it out.

18 This essay was commissioned to Somerville in 1946 for the opening number of *Irish Writing: The Magazine of Contemporary Irish Literature*, edited by David Marcus and Terence Smith.

[the books] were resented on so many grounds. Waste of time. Unjustified Conceit, and chiefly the *Mutiny* of two playmates. They were called "the Shockers," the "Geniuses (this in savage irony) and they found themselves the victims of a kind of *inverted Boycott*, a determination to *pursue* them to any *retreat* in order to *compel* participation in the sport of the moment. This on one typical occasion, being only *evaded*, and the *escape* of the *fugitive* Shockers being only secured by their overhearing sounds of a *search party* on their track, and by their *fleeing* instantly to the kitchen garden where they laid themselves at full length between rows of umbrageous Cabbage, remaining motionless while the *pursuit* swept by. ("Two," 184; my emphases)

Humour, excess and the grotesque combine in this passage. The use of so many words from the field of warfare (mutiny, boycott, evaded, escape, fugitive, fleeing, pursuit), even if half-playfully, evokes the opposition that the two aspiring authors suffered at the hands of their families. Ehnenn (2008, 53) notes that, notwithstanding the humorous tone, the passage employs violent images to delineate the consequences "of stepping outside of the accepted realm of female behaviour." As women, whose function was chiefly social, not taking part in the social occasion of the moment for the sake of writing a book was seen as failing a duty, a mutiny, a rebellion against what the authority expected from them. As appointed companions for the members of their family circle, taking time for themselves was not seen as a right, let alone taking time to write. Since Somerville and Ross put writing with each other over other, more feminine occupations, they became "fugitives," outlaws who had to "flee" and "escape" from their relatives. The pursuit ended up resembling a fox hunt (an activity they were, as members of the gentry, well familiar with): Somerville and Ross, accomplished hunters and horsewomen, became sport themselves. Ehnenn (2008, 53–54) underlines that, like a fox, there was nothing they could do but hide motionless among the leafy shadows of the cabbages, waiting for the hunt party to go away.

And yet a sort of pleasure emerges from the account: the scheme and its repetition – the two friends' resistance to patriarchal forces, their families' resentment, and the following chase – are presented as a kind of adventure. Being together against "every man's hand" (*IM*, 129) turns into a game, and one to play in team. Also, "persecution had its usual effect" on rebellious spirits, and "deepened somewhat tepid effort into enthusiasm" (*IM*, 129): standing alone against everyone else around them made the two cousins closer and their purpose stronger. What began "in idleness and without conviction" (*IM*, 129) turned into a goal. The support provided by friendship thus proved vital from the very beginning of Somerville and Ross's literary career: without it, the determination to keep writing might have wavered; being in disgrace, but being in each other's company, not only made the burden lighter but even made it a game that could be funny to play. Like the impertinent magic fox that keeps tricking the hunters in *The Silver Fox*, Somerville and Ross turned the persecution into a source of amusement.

Another event concurred to give the partners the inspiration they needed. In *Irish Memories*, Somerville related how inspiration came to them after a visit to a neighbouring Big House. However, from their letters we know that it was only Somerville who went.[19] This, together with the exaggerated importance of their first meeting, was part of Somerville's romantic attempt at making Martin a central presence in her life from the early moments of their acquaintance. In the autumn of 1887 she paid a visit to a family friend, an elderly lady who lived alone in an old manor some twenty kilometres from Drishane. The place, in the best Big House tradition, was in a state of semi-abandonment: "it was the old house, dying even then, that touched our imaginations" (*IM*, 129). By the end of the visit the sun had set and

> it was at that precise moment that into the *Irish Cousin* some thrill of genuineness was breathed. In the darkened façade of the long grey house, a window, just over the hall-door, caught our attention. In it, for an instant, was a white face. Trials of ivy hung over the panes, but we saw the face glimmer there for a minute and vanish. [...] As we rode home along the side of the hills, and watched the fires of the sunset sink into the sea, and met the crescent moon coming with faint light to lead us home, we could talk and think only of that presence at the window. (*IM*, 130)

In a suggestive description, Somerville places the origin of their inspiration:

> [t]he shock of it was what we had needed, and with it "the Shocker" started into life, or, if that is too much to say for it, its authors, at least, felt

---

19 In a letter of 21 August 1898 Martin remembers when Somerville told her of her visit: "I seem to remember very much the first beginnings of the Shocker just now – when I was humping over the Dumpy [the studio stove] and you were mucking with paints at the window you told me of the old maniac's face at the window over the White Hall door – and remember you were the person who suggested that we should try together to write a shocker or story of sorts on that foundation – and you were also the person who lifted us through the first chapters" (*Letters*, 142–43).

that conviction had come to them; the insincere ambition of the "Penny Dreadful" faded, realities asserted themselves, and the faked "thrills" that were to make our fortunes were repudiated for ever. [...] [A]n ideal of Art rose then for us, far and faint as the half-moon, and often, like her, hidden in clouds, yet never quite lost or forgotten. (*IM*, 130–31)

In reality, she must have reflected on the apparition by herself on her way home and told Martin only later. The shared ecstasy is fictional, but the whole episode, however romanticized, gives us a first instance of the inspiration from real life that was to be so fundamental to Somerville and Ross's subsequent production. Somerville's vision and her account of it resembles Martin's much later visit to Tyrone House (reported in a letter dated 18 March 1912), which provided Somerville with the material for *The Big House of Inver*, written on her own after her partner's death. The fact that Somerville never went to Tyrone House, and could nevertheless write about it and its history, was thanks to Martin's enthusiastic description and her exhortation "if we dare to write upon that subject!" (*Letters*, 294).

With their wills set and inspiration on fire, Somerville and Ross plunged into the composition of their first novel. Famously, their writing was far from being a smooth process: they would discuss every single matter, argue over it, then write and rewrite. Much of the process was carried out by letter, because each of them was expected to live with her family and not stay away too long. Although they frequently travelled or spent periods of time together, Somerville and Ross did not live under the same roof until the death of Martin's mother in 1909. From that date to her death in 1915 Martin resided at Somerville's family house in Castletownshend. Their union was different from many Boston marriages as neither of them ever set up house independently: they were family women, rooted in their family homes. Notwithstanding their apparent disregard for their relatives' opinion, Somerville and Ross cared greatly about what they thought of their books. They regularly read the new parts aloud to their families, who "offered criticisms, incessant, and mutually destructive" (*IM*, 135). Their letters are full of reported comments and suggestions by their mothers and siblings.

A particularly indulgent attachment was shown for their mothers: they laughed at their mothers' absurdities but kept close to them, and stoically accepted their criticisms. Even after the success of their first novels, and the enthusiastic reactions from the most respected literary figures of the day, their mother's opinions were still the topic of many letters. Martin's mother was generally affectionate and supportive, while Adelaide Somerville made no mystery of disapproving of her daughter's ambitions. She had very reluctantly tolerated Somerville's stays in Paris, believing that, sooner or later, she would settle down; when she did not, and her time was devoted more and more to writing, her mother did not conceal her dissatisfaction. But her disapproval did not prevent her from being intrusive: the "tall, and fervent and flaming" (*IM*, 87) Mrs Somerville would always expect to be consulted for her opinion, which she never failed to provide. In January 1888 Somerville noted in her diary: "[g]ave [the Shocker] to mother to read. She loathes it" (*Letters*, 134). In particular, she complained of the lack of love affairs – a remark she would make for the subsequent books too – which she, as "frankly mid-Victorian" (*IM*, 82), thought necessary in a good novel. It seems that it was Martin who insisted on keeping the writing detached: "[m]other has complained bitterly of the want of love interest. […] I said that I had urged you in vain to insert many such – and she declared that you were quite wrong" (Somerville to Martin, 21 January 1888, *Letters*, 63). Adelaide Somerville died a few years later, in 1895:

> [s]he did not live to see many of our books, but I fear that such as she did see, with their culpable economy of either love-makings or happy endings, were a disappointment to her. In her opinion the characters should leave a story, as the occupants left Noah's Ark, in couples. (*IM*, 90)

Mrs Somerville provided the model for the aristocratic, opinionated, stiff-upper-lipped Lady Dysart in *The Real Charlotte*, while the "ideal daughter" she never had, with "hair of dazzling gold, blue eyes as big as mill-wheels, and […] incessantly enmeshed in the most lurid flirtation" (*IM*, 92), came alive through *The Real Charlotte*'s co-protagonist Francie Fitzgerald; the unhappy fate Francie faces at the end of the story may suggest what Somerville thought of her mother's feminine ideals.

An Irish Cousin was completed in May 1888. The continuous revisions and rewritings had cost a great deal of time and energy, and the end of the novel had seemed "further off than the end of the world" (*IM*, 136). As also reported by Walter Besant and James Brander Matthews in their essays on collaboration, co-authoring a novel did not make the process faster. The clean copy – made by Somerville, as she had what she disparagingly referred to as a clear commercial hand – was sent to a London publisher, Sampson Low, who after a month returned the manuscript without comment. Somerville tells us that they accepted the refusal with tranquillity, decided to place it "in the hands of a friend to do with it as he saw fit, and proceeded to forget all about it" (*IM*, 136). Actually, they did not. Lewis (*Letters*, 141) remarks on the key role Martin played in the promotion of *An Irish Cousin*. She used the connections of her brother Robert in the London literary world and pulled strings shamelessly. In December 1888 the situation took a favourable turn: Bentley & Son offered £25 on publication, plus £25 on sale of 500 copies of the book. The reality of their shocker being published struck the cousins: "[a]ll comment is inadequate. [...] Wrote a dizzy letter of acceptance to Bentley, and went to church, twice, in a glorified trance" (*IM*, 136).

The novel was published in two volumes in the autumn of 1889. As a perfectionist, Martin was not fully satisfied with the work, but vividly recognized its significance in their lives:

> [a]ny period of good work has a nice honest romance about it. I do not think much of the Shocker all around I am bound to say. It has its points but it is indifferently written – with awkwardness and effort. However the tone is very sound and the sentiment is genuine and it is sincere and unusual. That is my opinion.
>
> You once said a little thing about it and what the writing of it did for us – if you don't remember it I do – that is good enough. Anyhow it was a nice little thing. Goodnight now. (Martin to Somerville, 3 December 1887, *Letters*, 62)

Martin pondered on the personal gains of the joint writing activity, the "nice little thing" that it did for them. The outcome of the partnership, the novel, did not seem to her as important as the experience of the collaboration itself. On the eve of publication, a thrilled but nervous Martin went back to the beginning of the enterprise:

> [w]e little thought then that I, at Ross, should take the *World* with a view to seeing my own writing in it, and should see the Shocker in large type heading Bentley's list therein. [...]
>
> Here's good luck to the Shocker and even if it doesn't do much to making our fortunes I do not think it was time wasted. It taught us a lot – in a literary way – and I don't think we shall ever forget it. And the long time that we fought over it, it was my fault – isn't that true? [...] Goodnight again – you were a nice woman to write with. (Martin to Somerville, 21 August 1889, *Letters*, 143)

Again, it is the act of writing together and the pleasure deriving from it that count the most for Martin. Somerville was, above all, "a nice woman to write with."

After the publication, the literary partners went to great lengths to bring the novel to the attention of reviewers and circulating libraries. Martin dealt more with the practical aspects of authoring, showing greater facility for publicity and distribution. Her connections with Edmund Yates, then the editor of the sixpenny weekly *The World*, proved important. She had written some articles for the magazine under her name only; the first one, "A Delegate of the National League," had appeared in July 1889, and was welcomed with mingled emotions by Martin's family: "[t]hat 'a Shocker' should preach, that 'one of the girls' should discourse on what was respectfully summarised [....] as 'Deep subjects of Life and Death,' was not quite what anyone enjoyed" (*IM*, 198). Yates's role as propagandist for Somerville and Ross would always be remembered with gratitude by the two cousins – the naming of the Irish R.M. as Major Sinclair Yeates was actually a tribute to him, and not to the poet W. B. Yeats, whom Somerville and Ross did not particularly admire.

A letter from Martin to Somerville of August 1889 attests to the cousins' persistence in promoting the book, showing ambition, a good commercial eye, and an early determination to profit from their work – a very different attitude from an amateur's contentment with publication as a goal in itself:

> [m]ama did not come home today, but she shall at once be set to work tomorrow. I into Oughterard to fetch Rose out in the afternoon and shall set Molly and Edmond on the trail. In fact anyone I meet or can think of shall not be ignorant of the Shocker. [...] You will have to take to getting up early & religiously writing a certain number of letters before breakfast. I am afraid this is a baddish time for books to come out, but we must make up for that by energy. What about Egerton's man on the *Saturday*? I have incensed Edith about Willie Wilde and Desart, and must concoct a discreet line or two to Edmund Yates – Edith is going up to the horse show, and accordingly will see everyone she knowns in Ireland, and can go round the book shops – and the Grays are trusty people of large acquaintance. (Martin to Somerville, 21 August 1889, *Letters*, 142)

A few days after writing the letter, Martin communicated good news to her partner: Carnegie Libraries agreed to subscribe to and circulate *An Irish Cousin*, as well as recommend the book to the booksellers Eason and Son. The family collaboration in sponsoring the novel went on:

> Molly Helps has been very kind about it – and said at once that she would write to Charlie Graves, who reviews the light literature for the *Spectator*, to give us a good word. [...] I wrote the best letter I could to Edmund Yates

today. Indeed I write letters all the time and Rose is very good about it too – Mama of course ploughs away, but her eyes come against her. I should make Aylmer ask for it at every station on the Underground if I were you. I am sure that your mother is magnificent in the matter of letters, and if the family really put their shoulders to a wheel they could do a great deal. (Martin to Somerville, 24 August 1889, *Letters*, 144)

Lady Gregory was asked to advertise the book among her social and literary circles. She encouraged Martin's artistic endeavours with Somerville, and, after reading the novel, predicted "great fame and popularity" for them (Jamison, 2016, 88).

The publication of *An Irish Cousin* presented the two co-authors with a new problem: under which names was the book going to appear? Martin's pseudonym was ready at hand, her precedent articles in *The World* having been signed 'Martin Ross,' coupling her surname with the family estate. Now it was Somerville's turn to make up a pen name. That they would not use their birth names was taken for granted, as an early letter by Martin to Somerville – dated December 1887 – tells us: "[y]ou must think of a name for yourself. Two New Writers is every day more odious to me – Gallantly invent something like Currer Bell, George Eliot, or any of them [...] but anyhow do try for a name" (*Letters*, 61). In *Irish Memories*, Somerville reveals that her mother opposed her using the family name "for some reasons that I have now forgotten" (*IM*, 137). As hinted above, Mrs Somerville did not like the idea of the prestigious family name being associated with fiction writing. After "much debate and searching of pedigrees," the name of a Somerville ancestress, Geilles Herring, "was selected to face the music" in her place (*IM*, 137). However, the career of 'Geilles Herring' was brief. The name sounded kind of comic, and provoked hilarious reactions, even from themselves: "[y]esterday in telling Rose the title of the book to put in one of her letters, I called it 'An Irish Herring' and then laughed so interminably that Rose nearly wept from boredom and fury," wrote Martin (*Letters*, 143–44). Yates seems to have asked Martin "the reason of her collaboration with a grilled herring" (*IM*, 137). Another name was needed, and the occasion came very soon: the first edition of the book sold well, and a second edition was printed by the end of the same year; this time Somerville tried with 'Viva Graham.' However, 'E. Œ. Somerville' was about to make its appearance on the cover of their next books. Stories report that Adelaide Somerville gave up her doubts when her daughter's literary work proved successful: now that there were not only excellent reviews but also cheques to be put in the bank, the atmosphere changed in Drishane.

Begun in imitation of the fashionable shilling shockers, *An Irish Cousin* turned out to be much more. Towards the end of the nineteenth century, in Ireland the Gothic was becoming increasingly intertwined with the Big House novel. The political situation of the time certainly played a crucial role in this association; proprietors of Big Houses were surrounded by the material and psychic conditions encouraging a turn to the Gothic: stuck in their decaying mansions, isolated from the native Irish Catholic community, threatened by acts of local violence, and burdened by financial crisis and utter instability over their political role, they practically lived in a Gothic scenario. Ascendancy anxieties found their expression in allegorical Gothic motifs that intruded upon and interacted with the conventions of the realistic Big House fiction. Kreilkamp (2006, 67) illustrates how Charles Maturin, Sheridan Le Fanu, Bram Stoker, and Somerville and Ross developed full-blown Gothic Big House novels, and identifies some characteristic motifs: decaying houses, deranged and demonized landlords, class obsession with racial pollution and cultural decline, and sadistic threats against helpless young women.[20] *An Irish Cousin* includes each of these tropes. Theo, an orphaned American girl, goes to Ireland to visit a brooding uncle, Dominick Sarsfield, who belongs to the landed gentry and lives in an estate near Cork, Durrus, "a long, low house, looking wan and ghostly in the moonlight" (Somerville and Ross, 1889, I, 43). In the best Big House tradition, Durrus is a mixture of past greatness and present decay: imposing, gloomy, and neglected, it provokes in Theo "an unexplainable shudder" (Somerville and Ross, 1889, I, 50–51). Uncle Dominick is, as mentioned above, the master of a Big House who lacks the energy and the business acumen to run it:

> "This place is shockingly neglected," my uncle said, [...] "in old days it was a whole different affair. [...]" We had by this time come to the dilapidated old hothouse, and we both stood and looked at it for a few seconds. [...] "I wish I had the energy and the money to get this whole place put to right [...] but I have neither the one nor the other. [...]" (Somerville and Ross, 1889, I, 87–88)

When the wind blows, the portraits of the Sarsfield ancestors shake in their frames in the draughty corridors (I, 68). The room assigned to

---

20 For a discussion of Protestant Gothic see also McCormack, 1991; Foster, 1993; and Eagleton, 1995.

Theo, her father's room, is menacingly out of proportion and seems to hold promises of violence:

> [t]he room was large and bare. The paper and the curtains of the two windows were alike detestable in colour and pattern. The enormous bed had once been a four-poster, but the posts had been cut down, and four meaningless stumps bore witness to the mutilation it had undergone. A colossal wardrobe loomed in a far-off corner; a round table of preposterous size occupied the centre of the room. Six people could comfortably have dined at the dressing-table. In fact, the whole room appeared to have been fitted up for the reception of a giantess [...]. (Somerville and Ross, 1889, I, 49)

Theo spots a secret door in her bedroom, which leads to another, smaller room and a passage. The Gothic setting is thus ready. The villain, Uncle Dominick, impeccably embodies the doomed satanic landlord. His past is full of dark secrets, including the death of his elder brother Owen, Theo's father, under mysterious circumstances. A vague, instinctive dread seizes Theo each time she is in her uncle's presence. Detached, intellectual, and ceremonious, he behaves with "strained and glacial geniality" (Somerville and Ross, 1889, I, 47) towards Theo when they meet at meals; he usually spends the rest of the day alone, leading a solitary life walking restlessly about the house or absorbed in meditation in his studio. In his ways and appearance, Dominick resembles the charming but treacherous vampire after the model created by Polidori: although "decidedly a handsome man" (I, 56) there is "something repelling in his manner" (I, 67); his dark hair and eyes contrast with an "unwholesomely pallid skin" (I, 56); an iron-grey moustache conceals yellow teeth, "long and slightly prominent" (I, 56).

Fortunately for Theo, Dominick's son, Willy, seems good-natured and friendly.[21] He and Theo become friends and spend many pleasant weeks hunting or simply riding in the beautiful Irish countryside. However, soon enough Willy too starts to behave in an increasingly disquieting way: he gets more and more possessive, and when Theo rejects him he is subject to violent bouts of anger. Estranged from her cousin and afraid of her uncle, Theo spends her days alone in Durrus's solitary rooms, almost as a prisoner – following the Gothic trope of the heroine incarcerated in

---

21 The figure of Willy seems to be a fictional version of Hewitt Poole, a cousin of Somerville's with whom she had a flirtation in 1878. They exchanged poems and drawings; after staying at Drishane in the autumn of that year, when he probably asked for Somerville's hand, he departed and was never seen in Drishane again. In 1880 he married another woman (*Letters*, 109; Lewis, 2005, 47–48).

isolated estates, with a male relative, representing patriarchy, to act as her oppressor. To make things worse, a madwoman called Moll Hourihane keeps wandering about Durrus, especially at the full moon, when she alternates ghostly dances to moments of utter desperation:

> raising her arms above her head with a wild gesture, she began to step to and fro with jaunty liftings and bendings of her body, as though she was taking part in a dance. [...] [p]lacing her hands on her hips, she danced with fantastic lightness and vigour some steps of an Irish jig. Suddenly, however, she checked herself; she knelt down, and, turning a pale face to the sky, she crossed her hands on her breast and remained motionless. Her absolute stillness had in it an intensity almost more dreadful than the strange movements she had previously gone through, and I [Theo] stood staring in inert terror at the grey kneeling figure, with a face as white as that which was still turned rigidly skywards in what appeared to be the extremity of supplication. (Somerville and Ross, 1889, I, 93–94)

A tall and vigorous woman, Moll never speaks, but she occasionally howls.[22] When Moll appears for the first time, Theo thinks she is seeing a ghost, and "the frightened glare of Moll Hourihane's eyes" haunts her (Somerville and Ross, 1889, I, 112). One night the woman steals into Theo's room through the secret passage and tries to suffocate her with a pillow. The figure of Moll Hourihane inevitably calls to mind *Jane Eyre*'s madwoman: although in Somerville and Ross's correspondence there is no mention of Bertha Mason, the similarities between the two characters are patent. They do not speak, but at best emit guttural beastly sounds; they are presented as more similar to animals than human beings: Moll haunts the Sarsfield family graveyard, where she claps her hands and beats her breast in her keening (Somerville and Ross, 1889, II, 46); when Jane finally sees Bertha in the attic, she depicts her as a "wild animal" that "grovelled, seemingly, on all fours," running backwards and forwards (Brontë, 2006, 338). Both can count on robust, strong bodies, and in their youth were extremely attractive women; the events of their tragic lives made them lose their beauty and their minds. Both Bertha and Moll have been wronged by the man they loved, whether husband or lover, who considered himself their superior: both Edward Rochester and Dominick Sarsfield belong to the Protestant landed gentry (both second-born sons), while Bertha is 'only' a creole heiress in Jamaica, and Moll an Irish servant; both men have been attracted to their wild, fierce

---

22 The howl is a trope in Irish Gothic, possibly representing the demonization or repression of Gaelic culture. See Kilfeather, 2006, 88.

beauty, only to reject them when they realize they cannot be controlled. Finally, both Bertha and Moll creep into the heroine's bedroom with murderous intentions at some point (Somerville and Ross, 1889, II, 173–77; Brontë, 2006, 326–27).

At the end of the novel the truth concerning Moll and Dominick's past is revealed: in her youth, Moll was a maid in the Big House; after the premature death of Dominck's wife she acted as nurse for little Willy and started an affair with Dominick; when his elder brother Owen, the heir to the estate, came home from America seriously ill, Moll killed him in his sleep with a pillow, believing this act would please her lover and hoping that he would marry her. Dominick was appalled by Moll's actions, but nevertheless helped her to secretly remove the body from the house and bury it in a bog nearby. Those were the years of the Famine, and few people were around to notice that something was wrong: in this way, Dominick became the master of Durrus and their secret was safe. However, Moll's hopes were disappointed: Dominick, obsessed with class pride and blood purity, had never intended to marry her. On being rejected and turned out of the house, Moll went mad. She married the lodgekeeper, a good man who did his best to take care of her, and they had a daughter as beautiful as her mother. Her mental illness, though, increasingly worsened. The horrific consequences of stepping out of one's social class and racial miscegenation between Protestant landlords and their Catholic underlings reminds one of Le Fanu's *Uncle Silas* (1864), where the degeneracy of the eponymous protagonist is completed through his marriage to an Irish barmaid and his fathering of a debased son. Even if in *An Irish Cousin* the master doesn't marry the Catholic servant, and their relationship does not produce a child, their affair nevertheless engenders criminality and madness.[23]

Twenty years later, Dominick's son Willy starts an affair with Moll's daughter, Anstey, thus repeating the previous generation's pattern. Dominick condemns their union as unnatural; during a discussion at a dinner party, the violence of his argument strikes all the guests:

> I cannot believe that any sane person can honestly hold such absurd theories. What! Do you mean to tell me that one of my tenants, a creature whose forefathers have lived for centuries in ignorance and degradation, is my equal? [...] What I maintain is that any fusion of classes [...] would have

---

23 Transgressive sexual relations between the Protestant landlord and a Catholic servant, engendering an illegitimate child, are also present in *The Big House of Inver*.

the effect of debarring the upper while it entirely failed to raise the lower orders. [...] It is absurd to suppose that the natural arrangement of things can be tampered with. This is a subject I feel very strongly [...]. (Somerville and Ross, 1889, I, 186–87)

Dominick hopes that the arrival of Theo will distract Willy from what he perceives as a degrading relationship. His desires are satisfied, as Willy falls in love with his cousin and abandons Anstey – now a ruined girl. However, in the final chapters Willy finds out his father's crime and, when Moll's husband threatens to reveal everything, thus bringing public disgrace to the whole Sarsfield family, he agrees to marry Anstey and move to Australia. The day after Willy's elopement Dominick falls mentally ill and Theo finds him dead in the bog where he and Moll had buried his brother. Unlike Bertha, Moll does not die in the end: here, it is the man who wronged the madwoman who dies. Though shocked by the events, Theo can finally have her happy ending with the man she loves, a neighbour of the Sarsfields', who plays a very small part in the narration.

Gothic conventions were immediately suggested by the cover of the first edition of *An Irish Cousin*, which is worth looking at: medieval-style green letters stand out against a black background, a twig with drops (of blood?) falling from it, the 'I' of 'Irish' resembling a dagger, and the 'C' of 'Cousin' reminiscent of a horn. The font evokes Celtic folklore, underlining the 'Irish' quality of the novel. Martin recognized the commercial strength of the choice of font and colours, even if she did not completely agree: "[t]he books have come – I was a little disappointed with the first sight of them [...]. Black and green are of course fashionable, but at the same time it is a trifle funereal and gloomy" (*Letters*, 144).

Notwithstanding the many conventional Gothic tropes, the insightful portrayal of Anglo-Irish society and the local peasants and the vivid drawing of the characters placed the novel above the deluge of sensationalist stories that were being published at the time. The book met with popular and critical acclaim. *The Standard* wrote: "[t]he interior of a modern Irish squire's house has seldom been drawn with such skill, and never since Miss Edgeworth's time with such absolute faithfulness and want of exaggeration, as Durrus, the home of the Sarsfields" (Somerville and Ross, 1903, 307). Somerville herself ascribed the success of the book to the fact that Edgeworth "had been the last to write of Irish country life with sincerity and originality, dealing with both the upper and the

Figure 6. Cover of *An Irish Cousin*, by Edith Somerville and Martin Ross (London: Bentley, 1889). Source: Archive.org

lower classes, and dealing with both unconventionally" (*IM*, 138). Indeed, Edgeworth's successors as realistic chroniclers of the Big House, William Carleton, Charles Lever, and George Moore, did not convey the same ironic poignancy. In particular, Somerville lamented that Lever's stories "merely created and throned the stage Irishman" (*IM*, 138), thus corroborating English stereotypes about Ireland. The favourable reviews by the main London magazines struck the incredulous Somerville and Ross and strengthened their purpose to become (co-)authors: "we were justified of our year of despised effort; the hunted Shockers emerged from their caves to take a place in the sun" (*IM*, 139). They had struggled to bring their novel to the attention of the press, had mobilized their families and friends, but had somewhat prepared themselves to be ignored, or, worse, attacked – an understandable attitude from young women used to receiving little consideration for 'their nonsense.' Success and validation was what they had hoped for but had not dared to expect: "[i]t is very much like a dream – that I should sit down and write about a flourishing critique of the Shocker [...] but there it is, in black and white," wrote Martin (4 September 1889, *Letters*, 147).

An Irish Cousin, like all Somerville and Ross's subsequent works, was "an undoubtedly lifelike Irish story" (*Athenaeum*, 31 August 1889, no. 3227). At the end of the nineteenth century Ireland, especially provincial Ireland, was still perceived by the English audience as a rather distant part of the empire, its ways and traditions seen as exotic. Somerville and Ross presented themselves as purveyors of this strange land, a reputation they maintained throughout their career. They depicted "the gloom of the Celtic character and the tragic possibilities that underlie it," but managed to balance and lighten it with humorous passages and "cheerful views of the oddities of rustic society in a distant district" (*Athenaeum*, 31 August 1889, no. 3227). The *Morning Post* caught what was to become the core of Somerville and Ross's production when it remarked that "the authors understand the management of light and shade, so that tragical as are the main incidents of the book, it is frequently relieved by pages that would not be out of place in a purely humorous novel" (reported in *Letters*, 149).

From amateurs to professionals: the struggle for the 'serious novel'

After the success of *An Irish Cousin*, Bentley offered Somerville and Ross £100 for a three-volume novel. At that time the two cousins were already engaged in turning a short story they had published in the *Lady's Pictorial* into a novel, which was to become *Naboth's Vineyard* (1891), their second novel. A simple, linear story in one volume dealing only with lower- and middle-class characters, the book was another triumph with both the public and the critics, who reviewed it "with a respect and seriousness that almost alarmed" Somerville and Ross (*IM*, 211). Having achieved another unexpected success, the two cousins now felt confident enough to devote themselves exclusively to writing: "we decided forthwith to abandon all distractions and plunge solemnly, and with single-hearted industry, into the construction of the three-volume novel desired by Messrs. Bentley" (*IM*, 211). Unfortunately, they never managed to do that. This is one of the main issues with Somerville and Ross's partnership: they had huge potential, and they saw it; and yet, for a series of reasons we shall presently explore, they did not give it full expression. The fact that they wrote only five novels in almost thirty years of collaboration, but plenty of short stories and various periodical literature, is telling. They struggled to write what they called "serious literature" (*IM*, 211), but pressing family obligations, endless social functions, the managing of their families' Big Houses, the constant need for ready money, and Martin's increasingly poor health would more and more distract them from their purpose. Short stories and articles were quicker to write and required less constant application. Their letters are full of exasperated complaints about lack of time to work. A couple of extracts will suffice to give an idea:

> [t]his is a torn and broken day and the week does not promise to be much better. [...] Tomorrow a hideous tennis function at the Broughams – Wednesday Herbert goes – some of us will probably be dragged to the Powells. Thursday, we have a tennis party to which *every* bounder in the whole country is coming and on Friday we have a dinner. My whole being heaves and curdles alternatively at the prospect. To attempt anything serious or demanding steady work is just simply impossible here – and I feel sickened of even trying. We are all so tied together – what ever is done must be done by everyone in the whole place and as the majority prefer wasting their time, that is the prevalent amusement. (Somerville to Martin, 10 September 1888, *Letters*, 118)
>
> I never had a more frenzied morning than this; the drawings to fix, gum on, write letters about, and then the drawing room to arrange for a crowd of female tea drinkers [...] I am finishing in bed at 11.30 p.m., after a fiery argument. [...] The entertainment was not amusing. (Somerville to Martin, 15 January 1891, *Letters*, 169)

Although they tried to make time for their work, Somerville and Ross could not, nor did they want to, exclude themselves from their large, sociable, and intruding families. Most of the time, they liked the convivial life of the Big House. In order to find time to work, they travelled as often as they could afford to. Not only busy social schedules but also the running of their estates took up much of their time. Martin in particular was the first to be encumbered by the task when she and her mother went back to Ross in 1888. By 1890 she had succeeded in making it comfortable again, and, with visitors coming and going continuously, as was common for great residences, it was difficult for her "to devote herself to literature, especially serious literature" (*IM*, 211). During the summer and autumn relatives came for long stays at the house. Her brother Robert often came to reside at Ross with his wife Connie, an uncultivated woman with drinking problems. Martin's mother did not get along with her daughter-in-law and much of Martin's time was given to smoothing things over in the household. Somerville enjoyed more freedom in her youth, but her mother's sudden death in 1895 left her mistress of Drishane, as her brother Cameron, the heir, never married; although she felt satisfaction at running the household and holding the family together, this left her with less time to write. Due to shortage of money, Martin used to do manual labour about the residence herself. This affected her health, which had never been particularly sound: she was painfully short-sighted, suffered from neuralgia, and sometimes had to spend whole days in bed; the "vague lassitudes and neuralgia bouts" were called by Martin her "mysterious sickness" (4 August 1888, *Letters*, 91). She went to see various specialists in Dublin, settling in the end with Dr Stoker (Bram's brother), but no real remedy could be found. In 1898 her health deteriorated after she was badly hurt in a riding accident, after which she had to spend several months in bed as an invalid and never fully recovered.

Notwithstanding the difficulties, at the close of 1889 Somerville and Ross set out to write what they referred to as their serious novel, *The Real Charlotte*. Its writing was completed in erratic, intermittent spells over three years: "*The Real Charlotte* can claim resemblance with Homer in one peculiarity at least, that of a plurality of birthplaces" (*IM*, 22). Its planning began in November 1889, but then, provoked by an "intolerably vulgar" (*IM*, 214) guide-book of Connemara sent to Martin by an English friend, the two cousins decided to undertake a tour of the district and themselves write a travel book on the subject.[24] The commercial industri-

---

24 This resulted in the publication of *Through Connemara in a Governess Cart* (1893). For a detailed analysis, see Jamison, 2016, 105–30. Jamison observes how travelling in Connemara as both tourists and natives mirrors in many ways Somerville and Ross's own ambiguous position as both Irish and English. Beside Connemara, in the next few years the cousins made other tours aimed at the publication of travel books: Bordeaux in 1891, Wales and then Denmark in 1893, and the Aaran Islands in 1895. Somerville made three more significant tours after Ross's death: in 1920 she went to Sicily (a description of which was included in *Happy Days! Essays of*

alization of travel in the second half of the nineteenth century had spurred the market for tourist literature, and Ireland was at the centre of many inexact and stereotypical accounts. Somerville and Ross felt the urge to correct them. In addition, though reluctant to interrupt their fictional work, the many practical and intellectual attractions of travel writing appealed to them: as with humorous short stories, travel pieces provided them with a steady income and were more easily managed than novels. So, in spite of their "excellent resolutions, the serious novel was again put on the shelf" (*IM*, 214).

They took the project again in their hands in November 1890. From this time on, despite the continuous interruptions,

> those unattractive beings, Charlotte Mullen, Roddy Lambert, the Turkey-Hen, entered like the plague of frogs into our kneading-troughs, our wash-tubs, our bedchambers. With them came Hawkins, Christopher, and others, but with less persistence. But of them all, and, I think, of all the company of more or less tangible shadows who have been fated to declare themselves by our pens, it was Francie Fitzpatrick who was our most constant companion [...] We knew her best; we were fondest of her. Martin began by knowing her better than I did, but, even during the period when she sat on the shelf with her fellows, while Martin and I boiled the pot with short stories and the like [...], or wrote up tours, or frankly idled, Francie was taking a hand in what we did, and her point of view was in our minds. (*IM*, 229–30)

The Real Charlotte revolves around two women, the Machiavellian Charlotte Mullen and her naïve cousin, Francie Fitzpatrick. Charlotte and Francie are each other's opposites and embody two different models of femininity: Francie is nineteen, conventionally beautiful, playful, spontaneous, and irresponsible; on the contrary, Charlotte is middle-aged, unmarried, painfully ugly, scheming, and cynical. No love is lost between them. At the death of a common aunt, Charlotte cheats Francie out of her inheritance and starts climbing the social ladder.[25]

Sorts, 1946), in 1926 she visited Spain ("Some Spanish Impressions," *Blackwood's Magazine*), and in 1928 she toured the United States (*The States Through Irish Eyes*, 1930). All travel accounts included illustrations by herself.

25 Notoriously, the character of Charlotte Mullen was based on a cousin of Somerville's called Emily Herbert, who had cheated Somerville out of an inheritance. A common aunt had left all her money to Somerville and her brother Jack (about £4000), but the will was destroyed (supposedly) by Emily Herbert. Somerville and Martin gaily admitted to whoever asked that Charlotte's original was Herbert, as if finding pleasure in their ironic revenge. In different points in Somerville

But after some time, Francie, who is orphaned and has always lived with some poor relatives in Dublin,[26] is forced by their disastrous economic situation to go to live with Charlotte in her small town, Lysmoyle, where she attracts the attention of the local community. The novel follows Francie's love relationships with three suitors: Roddy Lambert, Christopher Dysart, and Gerald Hawkins. Lambert is a charming land agent who likes to live beyond his means and always finds himself in need of cash. Charlotte has been in love with him since her youth, and it is hinted that something had passed between them in the past. After a marriage of convenience with an easily manipulated widow, nicknamed 'the turkey hen,' Lambert exploits Charlotte's faithful attachment to borrow money from her, conveniently misleading her about his true feelings. He also indirectly makes her believe that, should his wife pass away, he would marry her. However, when Francie arrives, Lambert falls in love with the girl who, for her part, just likes attention. Christopher Dysart is the heir of the local Big House and the representative artist figure in Lismoyle: sensitive but inept, he does not succeed in anything in particular – neither his diplomatic career nor his attempts at poetry and painting. He settles for the new art form of photography: as Hand (2011, 111) remarks, Christopher's interest in photography displays "the stunted nature of his character; he is drawn to it [...] because it is much easier than the hard work associated with either painting or writing poetry. Its accessibility and easiness reinforces his claim to a certain aristocratic languidness." Christopher falls in love, in spite of his snobbish taste, with Francie's genuine and straightforward ways. The third suitor, Gerald Hawkins, is a vain English soldier; thanks to his good looks and gallant manners, he is the only one who succeeds in winning Francie's affection – deliberately omitting to tell her that he is already engaged. Once his secret is found out, Hawkins promises to break his previous engagement, without any intention of doing so. Blinded by her passion for Hawkins, Francie rejects Christopher Dysart's proposal. Her refusal destroys Charlotte's grand plan of a marriage between her cousin and a

and Ross's correspondence we find mention of Emily Herbert, and their tone is unforgiving, as in the account of her death: "Emily was an awful drunkard, & when she finally drank and cat-poisoned herself to death, they found her dead body in the bed with fourteen cats sitting round it!" (Somerville to Martin, 27 July 1908, *Letters*, 284).

26 Descriptions of Dublin were mostly supplied by Martin, as she had spent her schooldays in a North Dublin neighbourhood. The description of a Dublin Sunday School in the first chapter is derived from Martin's memories (*IM*, 102).

member of the gentry, thus putting an end to her ambition to count an aristocrat among her relatives. Infuriated at her cousin's disobedience, Charlotte kicks Francie out of the house.

Meanwhile, Lambert's wife dies, leaving him a free man. The death scene is deeply disquieting, as it is implied that Charlotte has a hand in it: she first makes the weak-hearted woman read Lambert and Francie's flirtatious correspondence, thus shocking her; then, when she has a heart attack, Charlotte intentionally fails to give her the pills that could save her. At this point, Charlotte has managed to acquire the farm she had always wanted, and her financial success is complete; she has also succeeded in convincing Lambert to set up a business with her to keep him close. Now that he is widowed, her hopes of a union are higher than ever. Yet her plans are involuntarily destroyed, once again, by Francie. Back in Dublin, abandoned by Hawkins, with no prospects and helpless, Francie ends up marrying Lambert. Her marriage is an act of desperation and feels like a surrender of her free and cheerful nature; even if Lambert proves a loyal husband, from this moment Francie loses the *joie de vivre* that characterized her.

When the news of Lambert's unexpected marriage with Francie reaches Charlotte, all her pursuits suddenly appear empty to her. The 'real' Charlotte, who has stood lurking from the beginning, uncovering herself only occasionally, now takes over:

> [a] human soul, when it has broken away from its diviner part and is left to the anarchy of lower passions, is a poor and humiliating spectacle [...]. [...] now that she had been dealt the hardest blow that life could give her, there were a few minutes in which rage, hatred, and thwarted passion, took her in her fierce hands, and made her for the time a wild beast. When she came to herself she was standing by the chimney-piece, panting and trembling; the letter [written by Lambert to inform her of his marriage with Francie] lay in pieces on the rug, torn by her teeth, and stamped here and there with the semicircle of her heel; a chair was lying on its side on the floor [...].
> (Somerville and Ross, 2011, 291–92)

Then, Charlotte spots the photograph of Lambert that she keeps in her drawing room, and

> the biting thought of how she had been hoodwinked and fooled, by a man to whom she had all her life laid down the law, drove her half mad [...]. She plucked it out of its frame with her strong fingers, and thrust it hard down into the smouldering fire. [...] "The cur, the double-dyed cur! Lying and cringing to me, and borrowing my money, and – and – " Even to herself

she could not admit that he had gulled her into believing that he would eventually marry her – "and sneaking after her behind my back all the time! [...]" she tried to laugh, but instead of laughter came tears as she saw herself helpless, and broken, and aimless for the rest of her life – "I won't break down – I won't break down – " she said, grinding her teeth together with the effort to repress her sobs. She staggered blindly to the sideboard, and, unlocking it, took out a bottle of brandy. She put the bottle to her mouth and took a long gulp from it, while the tears ran down her face. (Somerville and Ross, 2011, 292)

Charlotte's only aim, from now on, will be revenge. She starts by insistently asking Lambert for her money back, thus pushing him to steal from the Dysart estate, which he manages. Then, she denounces his theft to his employer, Christopher, who feels compelled to fire him, leading him to financial and social ruin. In the meantime, she sabotages Lambert's marriage by arranging apparently accidental meetings between Francie and her old suitor Hawkins, thus rekindling the passion between them. Now that she is the property of another man, Hawkins finds Francie irresistible; she, bored with her life as a married woman, finds new vitality in the renewed romantic attachment. Blinded by empty passion, Hawkins wants Francie to elope with him to Australia. She agrees, but after learning of Lambert's imminent ruin feels pity for him and reconsiders her decision. When Christopher changes his mind and agrees to give Lambert another chance at the job, she falls into utter indecisiveness. Her torment is put to an end by a riding accident in which she dies. Moments before Francie's sudden death, Charlotte reveals to Lambert that she is the cause of his ruin, thus cutting off all possibilities of attracting him in the future. The ending is full of bitter irony, as Charlotte is defeated a few minutes after defeating Lambert and Francie. Her revenge backfired, and nobody wins.

In *Irish Memories* Somerville revealed that it was Martin who first developed the character of Francie, but then, as with everything they wrote together, it became a familiar presence for her as well. Francie became such a constant company for the two cousins that, when they wrote the scene of Francie's death in the summer of 1892, "it felt like killing a bird that had trusted itself to you" (*IM*, 231). Somerville recorded the writing of the final chapters:

[w]e had sat in the cliffs, in heavenly May weather, with Poul Ghurrum, the Blue Hole, at our feet, and the great wall of Drishane Side rising sheer behind us, blazing with yellow furze blossom, just flecked here and there with the reticent silver of blackthorn. [...] We and the dogs had achieved as

much freedom from social and household offices as gave us the mornings, pure and wide, and unmolested. There is a place in the orchard at Drishane that is bound up with those final chapters, when we began to know that there could be but one fate for Francie. (*IM*, 231)

These lines give us a sense, again, of Somerville and Ross's writing as something illicit, clandestine, furtive. In addition, they tell us of a habit of theirs: they wrote a lot outdoors. This speaks volumes about their lives: within the house, whether Drishane or Ross, they would always be interrupted, their attention would always be requested for something else; within the house, time was not theirs. Only by 'fleeing' outside they could find a space for themselves. Unlike the stereotypical image of the male author who locks himself up in a study and writes, Somerville and Ross produced a great deal of their work in the open air. If a man was in his rooms, nobody would disturb him; if a woman did the same, her privacy would seldom be respected. Once again, the image of the two women hiding themselves somewhere outside the house, in full contact with nature, resurfaces: to avoid pursuit during the writing of *An Irish Cousin* they had found a safe hiding place in the kitchen garden; *The Real Charlotte* was completed in the orchard. However external, these were still domestic spaces, belonging to the realm of the house, and yet outside it so that the two women could taste some freedom. Working outdoors was a habit Somerville and Ross maintained for the rest of their partnership. The origins of the *Irish R.M.* stories and of *Dan Russel the Fox* are recalled in a similar way:

> [i]t was among Cazin's sand-dunes, [...] that the "Irish R.M." came into existence. [...] [w]e sat out on the sandy hills, roasting in the great sunshine of Northern France, and talked until we had talked Major Sinclair Yeates, R.M. and Flurry Knox into existence. (*IM*, 258)
>
> While we were at Amélie, we wrote the beginning of "Dan Russel the Fox," sitting out of the mountain side, amidst the marvellous heaths, and spurges, and flowers unknown to us, while the river [...] stormed "in confluence" in the valley below us, and the pink mist almond blossom was everywhere. Dan Russel progressed no further than a couple of chapters and then retired to the shelf, where he remained until the spring of 1909 found us at Portofino [...]. We worked there in the olive woods, in the delicious spring of North Italy [...]. (*IM*, 305)

Somerville and Ross's partnership debunks in many ways the conventional image of the solitary author. One may try to imagine and contrast the scenarios described by Somerville with the iconic painting of Dickens by Maclise: here the author is sitting alone by his desk with a meditative expression, in the undisturbed silence of what is perhaps his study, thinking (or listening to the Muses?), his hand touching a manuscript, pen on the desk, ready to write when inspiration comes. In Somerville and Ross's case, instead of a single male author, we find two women; instead of writing under inspiration, in silence, they talk and discuss before and after the proper writing; instead of sitting at a desk, they often create their stories in unconventional, casual outdoor settings, rambling outside the garret of the Romantic mythology. The creative moments could not be more different.

As was the norm with Somerville and Ross, after the writing of *The Real Charlotte* was concluded a process of intense revision started. It was only in February 1893 that the manuscript was sent off to Bentley. However, the offer of £100 no longer seemed adequate to the cousins, who "wrote breathing forth fire and fury, and refused" (*IM*, 232). Only five years before they had accepted in dizzy incredulity £25 for their debut novel; now their confidence had grown, and the awareness of the value of their work made them reject four times that sum. They believed that *Charlotte* was their best work, a conviction that would remain steady for the rest of their lives (*IM*, 238). This marked the beginning of Somerville and Ross's self-perception as professional writers, capable of producing goods of a certain value and determined to be paid accordingly. They went to London and began a long process of negotiations with different publishing houses, during which they "saw and heard many cheerful things" (*IM*, 232). *The Real Charlotte* was finally sold to Ward and Downey for £250, and was published in three volumes in May 1894. The publisher promised them half of the American rights as well, which, however, never materialized.

When the novel came out Somerville and Ross were in Paris, the former working in a studio, the latter writing some articles on France. But reviews reached them quickly – and they were bad. Although the book was universally declared clever and original, and the humorous passages of the first volume were appreciated, its increasing grimness annoyed critics. It was proclaimed to be "unsympathetic, hard and harsh" (*Weekly Sun*, reported in *IM*, 236) and the characters vulgar and nasty. A reviewer advised Somerville and Ross to "call a third coadjutor, in the shape of a judicious but determined expurgator of rubbish" (*IM*, 236). The point most insisted upon was the general unpleasantness of the characters and the fact that they did not call for sympathy from the reader. The *Lady's Pictorial* lamented that

[t]he picture it gives of lower middle class life in Ireland is not altogether agreeable.[...] The happy go-lucky mode of life, the curious mingling of shrewdness and childishness, [...] the irrepressible love for fun and frolic, are so admirably hit off by the observant and clever collaborateurs, that we feel instantly that they are drawing, for the most part, from life [...].

But [...], as the story and the characters develop, and the seamy side of Charlotte Mullen, Mr. Roddy Lambert, and others, is brought prominently into view, [...] my pleasure [...] in reading the book, gradually declined; and not even the undoubted cleverness of the writers could reconcile me to the way to which the tale is worked out. The worst side of human nature has just now a strange fascination for novelists [...]. English people who read this novel will be confirmed in their mistaken idea that Ireland is a nation of barbarians, for the authors have forgotten unfortunately, that without light and shade there is no real art, and as their story grew under their hands the light that glimmered in vol. I went out completely, and the book winds up in unrelieved gloom.

I am sorry that it is so, for the authors have the gift of delineating character very strongly developed [...]. But what is worth while to expend such an amount of cleverness upon such a sorry crew? The next time that E. Œ. Somerville and Martin Ross combine to write a novel of Irish life I hope they will [...] devote their clever and graphic pens to the task of delineating men and women who are brave, generous, and noble, instead of wasting their powers upon elaborately finished pictures of the sordid-minded Charlotte Mullens and Roddy Lamberts, whose ill-spent lives need no historian. (19 May 1894)

What had been so admired in their previous work, the balance of light and shade, of humour and tragedy, was felt to be lacking in *The Real Charlotte*, which proceeded in "unrelieved gloom." Another review declared it one of the most disagreeable novels ever written, and stated that "we can hardly imagine a book more calculated to depress and disgust [...]. The amours are mean, the people most repulsive, and the surrounding depressing" (source unknown, reported in *IM*, 236).

Charlotte was, predictably, the most heavily criticized figure of the book. Her different versions of herself – she even has different voices and uses different registers according to the mask she is wearing – and her machinations disgusted the press. Crucially, her plots and her greediness were not compensated by youth and beauty: the ambitions of a plain, middle-aged spinster had rarely, if ever, been the central focus of a novel. Thackeray's equally wicked Becky Sharp, or Collins's forger Lydia Gwilt, for instance, had outraged the press, but at least they remained within the role traditionally expected from evil women:

the charming seductress, the ambitious temptress, the man-eater. Their climbing of the social ladder was facilitated by beauty, marriage, and flirtation. Charlotte's rise, instead, is carried out exclusively through her efforts: no man helps her. That an unattractive spinster could have so great an authority (she practically runs the community of Lysmoyle) was unheard of; her desperate independence was destabilizing. Charlotte has failed to become a wife and a mother, and, instead of selflessly accepting her destiny and settling into a quiet, uneventful life, she carefully devises and carries out an ambitious plan for her personal realisation through financial and social achievements – however mean they might be. She rejects the passive, religious life that Victorian unmarried women were supposed to be contented with. On the contrary, she is active, demoniacally active, "an agent of upward mobility for herself and downward mobility for her enemies" (Laird, 2000, 114). In her relationship with Lambert, she turns from his victim into his executioner: he has conveniently given her the illusion that sooner or later he will propose, thinking she will always be compliant; but Charlotte reverses the situation.

Though her bad actions are set down plainly, Charlotte is not presented entirely unsympathetically, and cannot be reduced to the role of the villain. The reader is disgusted by her actions but feels intensely her pain behind them. Indeed, the narrator makes sure that the reader gets acquainted with her deep suffering: her ugliness is continuously, almost obsessively remarked, and she is perfectly aware of her lack of attractiveness. Her outlets for her repressed sentimental life are the French novels she devours and the exaggerated affection for her cats. In a society that places such high value on women's looks, the devaluation of her appearance is internalized by Charlotte as a failure, and triggers an urge for revenge:

> [i]t is hard to ask pity for Charlotte, whose many evil qualities have without pity been set down, but the seal of ignoble tragedy had been set on her life; she had not asked for love, but it had come to her, twisted to burlesque by the malign hand of fate. There is pathos as well as humiliation in the thought that such a thing as a soul can be stunted by the trivialities of personal appearance, and it is a fact not beyond the reach of sympathy that each time Charlotte stood before her glass her ugliness spoke to her of failure, and goaded her to revenge. (Somerville and Ross, 2011, 300)

Somerville and Ross do not explicitly condemn Charlotte, but simply lay her actions and her reasons in front of the reader. The title proves of crucial importance in the reading of the novel, as it immediately invites us to expect a drama of appearances and reality, truth and falsehood, mask and self – and, above all, a drama of layers. On a superficial level, Charlotte seems quirky and honest to the people around her, but her real self is aggressive, domineering, and egocentric. On a deeper level, the title might refer to Charlotte's motives behind her actions, to a real suffering Charlotte against the evil one. Three layers of Charlotte's personality thus emerge: the external respectable and amiable one; the in-between evil, greedy, and beastly Charlotte; and, lastly, the suffering soul underneath. Therefore, although Laird (2000, 119) and others claim that the real Charlotte is as ugly as she physically appears, or ever uglier, I agree with Ehnenn (2008, 157–59) in arguing that it is not so easy to categorize Charlotte and judge her. Charlotte is simultaneously demonic, sympathetic, and tragic. The novel asks what is real morality and who possesses it, but, in the light of everyone's reasons, moral evaluations become blurred.[27]

Written with sceptical realism, *The Real Charlotte* nevertheless presents Gothic elements, like the many strange coincidences that punctuate the narration. Francie's fatal fall from her horse is foreshadowed by other, increasingly serious falls. Her carelessness when riding is remarked at different points, for example in the seventh chapter, when she lets

---

27 Ehnenn (2008, 159) also notes the similarities between Charlotte and Somerville and Ross: they are unmarried, independent women, excellent in their managerial skills, and struggling to assert themselves "in a world of male privilege." Drawing on Reynolds' study of women in Irish literature and legend (1983), Ehnenn intriguingly connects Charlotte with the mythological figure of the Mórrígan, thus highlighting the impossibility of reading Charlotte's character through normative identity, social constructions of femininity or morality (157–60). The Mórrígan is the primordial war goddess of Irish mythology and is characterized by continuous shapeshifting – which reminds us of Charlotte's constant change of mask. Masterful, wrathful, power-loving, and uninhibited, she can be a powerful ally to those she loves, but when scorned she turns into a ruthless enemy. The Mórrígan's fraught relationship with CúChulainn (like Charlotte's relationship with Lambert) is characterized by his refusal to treat her with the reverence she desires; she attacks him three times, in the shape of a wolf, an eel and a heifer; when in the guise of a crow she perches on his shoulder at his funeral, it is not clear whether she does so in mourning or in triumph. Irish Revival versions of the Mórrígan were greatly softened to maintain Victorian decorum; they generally focused on her appearances in the shape of a pretty girl, depicting her transformations so that she could be perceived as being really a beautiful young woman. Somerville and Ross's Charlotte can be seen as a more faithful modern version of the Mórrígan, as she never becomes beautiful and is never toned down.

fall both reins to settle her hat (Somerville and Ross, 2011, 57). On that occasion, Lambert predicts her final fall: "'[s]ome day you'll be breaking your neck, and then *you'll* be sorry.'" (57). During a boat trip in chapter fourteen a sudden gust of wind throws Francie off the boat into the lake; she is saved by Christopher, who has a horrific vision of her death: "[s]he lay horribly still, with the water washing over her face; and as Christopher caught her dress, and turned, breathless, to try to fight his way back with her to the wrecked yacht, he seemed to hear a hundred voices ringing in his ears and telling him that she was dead" (108). When she is rescued and taken back onto the boat, Charlotte flings herself on her knees beside her cousin and utters "yell after yell of hysterical lamentation" (108). Towards the end of the narration, in chapter forty-four, Francie is almost run over by a herd of galloping horses, somewhat anticipating her forthcoming death (321). The funeral of Julia Duffy, who has spent her last days in a workhouse as a consequence of Charlotte's acquisition of her farm, is highly reminiscent of the funeral in *An Irish Cousin* which horrifies Theo. Both are Irish country funerals characterized by keening and violent demonstrations of grief. Lastly, Charlotte herself contributes to make *The Real Charlotte* a Gothic novel in many aspects: despite the force of her reasons, sometimes she is depicted as simply succumbing to another self, a demonic part which does not know empathy or humanity – as when she fails to give Lambert's first wife her medicine or when she is tempted, even if just for a few moments, not to close the gate so the running horses would kill Francie. In these moments, Charlotte becomes worse than wild, worse than a beast: she becomes satanic.

The lack of a happy ending for any of the characters and the absence of lofty feelings, brave actions, and at least one pure love affair particularly displeased the press. Francie, though basically well-meaning, was declared vulgar and insolent for her unladylike love of flirtation. The novel does not allow love to find its ideal realization: nobody's affection is requited, as each of the characters loves someone who does not reciprocate. Moreover, they are all distorted kinds of love: what Charlotte feels for Lambert is a possessive and controlling passion; Lambert's feelings for Francie are blinded by physical attraction, so that he does not see that they are not a good match; Hawkins's passion for Francie is a product of his vanity; and, finally, Francie's attraction to Hawkins is a childish romantic attachment. Only the figure of Christopher Dysart found some supporters among the critics, who saw in him the only gentleman in the story. However, Christopher's infatuation for Francie is an idealized love that does not allow its object to be herself: he sees the girl as a soul to be saved and instructed, and likes to spend afternoons reading poetry to her, which she does not understand but is too polite to interrupt. Christopher is also the only character who sees the real Charlotte behind the façade, as he feels an instinctive distrust towards her. When Charlotte denounces Lambert's theft to him, he is not grateful but only feels repugnance for her meanness. Yet he does nothing; he does not even try to alert the others of Charlotte's manipulative schemes; he is passive, just like all Charlotte's other victims. Christopher simply lacks backbone, and this prevents him from being the hero of the story.

Reactions from Somerville's and Ross's families and friends were not much better. Somerville reports that a friend objected that the novel "would give English people the idea that in all ranks of Irish life the people were vulgar, rowdy, and gave horrible parties" (*IM*, 237). One of Somerville's brothers wrote to her "in high reprobation," saying that "such a combination of bodily and mental hideosity as Charlotte could never have existed outside of [her] and Martin's diseased imaginations" (*IM*, 238). That two women could have conceived such a grim prospect was even worse. Adelaide Somerville "summarised the general opinion," when she affirmed that "[a]ll here loathe Charlotte" and that "Francie deserved to break her neck for her vulgarity" (*IM*, 236–37).

On receiving such heavy criticism, Somerville declared that they "laughed rather wanly" (*IM*, 237). Yet a certain depression was inescapable, as she added in the next line. Even the few positive reviews seemed to have misunderstood them. Their initial gratification at what seemed to them "the best & best-written" (*Letters*, 216) review they got, penned by T. P. O'Connor for *The Weekly Sun*, turned into indignation when they realized that O'Connor had taken them for *shoneens* – an Anglo-Irish term of abuse for those who aped English behaviours and attitudes.

Notwithstanding scathing reviews, the novel scored "steadily improving sales" (*IM*, 241). In January 1895 Martin went to visit some friends in Scotland, and understood for the first time that Somerville and she had made "a mark that was far deeper and more impressive than had been hitherto suspected by either of [them]" (*IM*, 241). Finding herself a celebrity almost overnight had its effects on the shy Martin:

> [s]ince I last wrote various have been the dissipations. Afternoon teas, two dinners, an organ recital, a concert. It is very amusing. They are all, as people, more interesting than the average, being Scotch. And they have a high opinion of *Charlotte*. I am beginning to be accustomed to having people

introduced to me, and feeling that they expect me to say something clever. I never do – I am merely conversational, and feel in the highest spirits, which is the effect of the air. It is pleasant to hear Mrs. Jackson [her host] tell how she went into an assembly of women […] and heard them raving of *Charlotte*. (Martin to Somerville, 23 January 1895, *Letters*, 213)

> I shall not come back here again – having created an impression I shall retire on it before they begin to find me out. (Martin to Somerville, 29 January 1895, *Letters*, 217)

She also affectionately reproached Somerville for not coming with her to Scotland (she was once again away at her art studies): "[w]hy aren't you here to take your share?" (23 January 1895, *Letters*, 215). "It will be your turn next. Though Mrs Jackson says she will not rest till she has had us here together" (29 January 1895, *Letters*, 217). Martin was all the more amazed when Andrew Lang expressed his admiration for the novel, especially for its eponymous protagonist, and told her "that *Charlotte* treated of quite a new phase – and seemed to think that that was its chiefest merit" (*Letters*, 215). Lang had put a notice of the novel into an American magazine for which he wrote, and was eager to discuss it with Martin when they were introduced at a dinner. However, in front of a scholar such as Lang, Martin found herself at a loss, and half-jokingly wrote to Somerville:

> I haven't the face to discuss *Charlotte*. […] Talking to Andrew Lang has made me feel that nothing I could write could be any good – He seems to have seen the end of perfection – I will take my stand on *Charlotte* I think and learn to make my own clothes – and so subside noiselessly into middle age. (*Letters*, 209, 210)

During her stay in Scotland, Martin and Lang developed a friendly relationship. She soon regained her confidence, and they went sightseeing and visited the offices of *Blackwood's Magazine*, from which Martin was trying to get a review (even during a leisure stay, she could not forget her role as promoter of the duo).

After their respective breaks in Scotland and Paris, Martin and Somerville reunited in London in February 1895. They decided to write another novel, a second "ferocious narrative" (*IM*, 252), this time focused on the contrast between the Anglo-Irish and the English. It was settled that the new novel should appear in weekly instalments in the *Badminton Magazine*. However, the arrangement soon turned out to be a problem, as serial publication involved a steady rate of production which did not fit in with Somerville and Ross's schedules: "[the publisher] said that as we purpose to run the story serially we ought to arrange it to be no more than between 70 & 72.000 words, to be equally divided into 12 parts, not necessarily chapters, & to arrange a curtain for each part" (Somerville to Martin, 25 April 1897, *Letters*, 243). *The Silver Fox* was written in a hurry, among the usual interruptions, and was finished in 1896. As soon as the serial publication was over, it was sold to Lawrence and Bullen, and appeared in book form in 1898.

By the time they started to write *The Silver Fox*, Somerville and Ross were set at making a living out of their pens. To this purpose, they decided to avail themselves of all the newest means of the literary profession. They were among the first women to join Besant's Society of Authors. Lang advised Martin to hire an agent, suggesting A. P. Watt; after some consideration, in 1897 they chose instead James B. Pinker, who, along with Watt, was one of the most prominent names in the London scene. The decision of hiring a literary agent points to a shift in Somerville and Ross's self-perception: the two girls writing a shilling shocker in the kitchen garden had turned into professional women writers.[28] Now, they "had a taskmaster, a little man of iron determination, a Literary Agent (which is the modern equivalent for an Egyptian taskmaster)" (Somerville and Ross, 1946, 9). That the choice fell on Pinker and not on another agent is significant as well: if Watt was the man "for people whose position was assured" (Martin to Somerville, 29 January 1895, *Letters*, 220), Pinker had made a name for himself championing new names and female authors. His attitude towards women's suffrage was something that Somerville and Ross appreciated and used to discuss with him. Moreover, unlike Watt, who acted as an agent for both authors and publishers, Pinker worked only for authors. In this way, he became well-known for defending authors' rights against the snares of the publishing trade.[29]

Pinker managed to secure some of Somerville and Ross's most lucrative deals. Before him, they had largely relied on their own circle

---

28 When her brother Robert died in 1905 Martin was asked to write an account of him for a memoir a group of his friends was preparing. The meeting with one of them was a disaster: "[h]e said 'about twelve columns of The Times – but you write all you like, and we can select what is wanted –' I at once said that I was too busy to write stuff that might not be wanted, and he seemed quite surprised – I don't think he at all realises the position, or that I am a professional writer. I shall not put you in a passion by telling more of his recommendations and advice" (Martin to Somerville, 10 July 1906, *Letters*, 278).

29 Gillies (2007) takes Somerville and Ross as a case study to investigate Pinker's professional relationship with his clients.

of acquaintances to promote their work, often pushing male members of their families to intervene on their behalf with publishing issues. This took up a lot of their time. Although they had often met with success, they also fell foul of rogue middlemen, as well as editors and publishers who were tardy with their payments.[30] It is not surprising that, when they hired Pinker, one of the first tasks they assigned him was to recover a debt owed by a magazine. As a matter of fact, money was an increasingly pressing issue. Need of cash had always been a major preoccupation in the women's lives, as their letters at the time of the writing of *The Real Charlotte* attest:

> the sooner you can come, without seeming unkind to your family, the better. I must make money – so must you – . (Martin to Somerville, 18 September 1890, *Letters*, 164)

> I am also very poor, only for the Art Journal – as yet unpaid – I should be bankrupt. [...] [*The Real Charlotte*] is our best chance and you will honestly tell me if you are able to work as we ought to work. Not if you are willing, I know you are that, but genuinely *able*? [...] I would rather die in the workhouse than kill you by making you work when you are not fit for it. The only thing that occurs to me is that if you don't work with me you will be toiling about the vile house and I don't know which is worse for you. (Somerville to Martin, 29 September 1890, *Letters*, 165)

By the second half of the 1890s Somerville and Ross were in their mid-thirties, unmarried, and determined to keep up their costly family homes, as their siblings were more and more indifferent to the fate of their Big Houses in the increasingly explosive Irish social and political situation. Their desire for financial independence was stronger than ever. Glimpsing at the possibility of achieving it, they did not want to lose any opportunity:

> you must come back to Drishane or else meet me in a desert place as soon as possible [...]. Some other Irish Devil who can hunt and write will rise up & knock the wind out of our sails, & we can't afford to be jockeyed like that – *The Silver Fox* money will make us fairly independent. (Somerville to Martin, 25 April 1897, *Letters*, 244)

One can feel the urgency in this passage. Somerville exhorted her partner to set to work (the desire for "a desert place" expresses, once again, the

---

30 Jamison (2016, 83) discusses some examples of the snares into which Somerville and Ross fell, as well as their problems connected with underpayments and delayed payments.

cry for a 'room of their own'), before someone "stole" their signature style.

Money, thus, became a necessary priority. At around this time the duo's literary output took a very precise turn: despite their wish to keep writing what they called 'serious' literature, their agent, their publishers, and their families encouraged them to write humorous hunting stories set in the Irish countryside:

> [t]hey then all – including the little Pinker – swore we had got hold of a very good thing in this serio-comic hunting business – "To use literary slang," said Pinker, "this is *your own stuff* & no one else does anything like it –" [...] "No one on earth could write incessantly about hunting & keep it amusing & interesting [...]." (Somerville to Martin, 25 April 1897, *Letters*, 243)

As seen above, Somerville and Ross believed that *The Real Charlotte* was their best work. Yet its writing had been a struggle and a source of anxiety for years. They had also been puzzled by its mixed reception and hurt by the harsh criticism. Lewis (*Letters*, 264) suggests that "it is almost as if they shrugged their shoulders and moved away into the safer territory of funny short stories." Such conclusion seems a little hasty: Somerville and Ross did not simply "shrug their shoulders"; reading their correspondence and Somerville's autobiography, their frustrated aspiration to write 'serious' literature repeatedly comes to the surface; circumstances led them to temporize, to do what was more practical, what produced more immediate income, and they ended up writing what was expected of them and neglecting what they really wished to do.

This affected their production. *The Silver Fox* started on a good basis, but was not developed to its full potential. After it, they did not embark upon the writing of any other novel for more than a decade. Their next and last joint novel, *Dan Russel the Fox,* appeared in 1911, and in reading it one has the feeling that something is missing: the novel betrays lack of concentration and results in little more than an episode, as the subtitle, *An Episode in the Life of Miss Rowan*, specifies. The reason for the long silence between *The Silver Fox* and *Dan Russel the Fox*[31] is that, just after the publication of the former, Somerville and Ross had devoted themselves to the work that was to give them money

---

31 The presence of 'fox' in both titles is not a coincidence. Like the comic stories, they present several scenes of fox-hunting and horse-riding, two features appreciated by their audience. To put 'fox' in the titles was probably a marketing strategy to reassure readers that the novels had the same qualities as the short stories. *An Irish Cousin* has some long fox-hunting scenes as well, but they did not need to advertise

and long-lasting fame: the twelve stories about the adventures of the Irish Resident Magistrate, Major Sinclair Yeates, were published monthly in the *Badminton Magazine* and collected in book form in 1899 under the title *Some Experiences of an Irish R.M.*[32]

The writing of the R.M. stories coincided with Martin's hunting accident in the autumn of 1898, resulting in "a nightmare effort" (*IM*, 262). Once more, respecting the strict publication times of serialization cost much energy: "[l]ooking back at the writing of them, each one, as we finished it, seemed to be the last possible effort of exhausted nature. [...] By the time the last bundle had been dispatched Martin and I had arrived at a stage when we regarded an ink-bottle as a mad dog does a bucket of water" (*IM*, 262). Despite some unfavourable reviews claiming that the stories gave a "depressingly squalid and hopeless" picture of Irish life, describing them as "unfeminine" and "devoid of any sentiment or refinement," and lamenting the lack of "romance, seriousness, or tenderness" (*IM*, 291), the invention of the R.M. rescued Somerville and Ross's finances. It gave them a steady stream of income, also thanks to continuous re-editions and the sequels that followed, collected in *Some Further Experiences of the Irish R.M.* in 1908 and *In Mr. Knox's Country* in 1915. Somerville confessed to her brother Cameron that the stories were "such good business" that they could not "afford to fall out with them [...] only that we both want money so badly we would chuck them for the present" (quoted in Jamison, 2016, 102). Pinker encouraged Somerville and Ross to make such stories their hallmark: "I asked his advice about the next book. He still says that a short story volume would do just as well as anything else. [...] We could take characters out of *Dan Russel* or anything else" (Martin to Somerville, 25 October 1911, *Letters*, 292). In reply to Somerville and Ross's request to look for publishers for a more serious line of work – potentially a new novel – Pinker wrote: "I think your happiest work is in this semi-sporting vein, and, moreover, there is, so far as I know, no one who can touch

---

them at the time. When fox-hunting became their hallmark, Somerville and Ross remained somewhat bound to this particular aspect and were told to emphasize it.

32 The stories start when Major Yeates decides to resign from the British Army and accepts an appointment as a magistrate in a small town in the west of Ireland. Other central characters are Yeates's wife Philippa, Flurry Knox, a local squire whose main aims in life are horse-dealing and fox-hunting, and Mrs Cadogan, the ever-dramatic cook. The adventures of the Irish Resident Magistrate became so famous that copies of the books were distributed to soldiers during World War I to cheer them up. A television series based on the books was made in the 1980s.

you [...] I should say from all points of view, that is the work to do" (quoted in Jamison, 2016, 102). The appetite of the English public for the stories of Irish life and fox-hunting was great, and continued well into the twentieth century. The "dirty Irish realism" (*Letters*, 25) of the novels simply did not sell as much.

This new direction in their production gave Somerville and Ross all sorts of benefits, yet it was also a hindrance to their literary ambitions. The turn in Somerville and Ross's career from amateurs to professionals might be what, ironically, limited their subsequent output. *Experiences of an Irish R.M.* and its sequels are a brilliant example of comic short fiction, and nothing to be ashamed of – quite the contrary. However, they were not the kind of literature the two co-authors had wanted to build their whole reputation upon; they felt they had somewhat remained stuck with it. Moreover, when it came to an overall evaluation of their professionalism, their reputation as humorous writers hindered and demeaned them. The debasing of Somerville and Ross's artistic status is well exemplified by Jamison (2016, 92–104) in her account of the cousins' legal allegations of plagiarism against the authors of *By the Brown Bog* (1913), a collection of stories clearly written after the model of the *Irish R.M.* tales. Jamison shows how Somerville and Ross found little support in the matter, either from their agent or from Longmans, who, despite being the publisher of all the *Irish R.M.* collections, did not hesitate to issue the *Brown Bog*.

Interestingly, the language used by Pinker and by those around them suggests that Owen Roe and Honor Urse, the authors of *By the Brown Bog*, had simply written within the same 'class' of writing, thus denying Somerville and Ross's work any original or artistic quality.

After her accident of 1898, Martin's health never fully recovered:

> [o]ne of the pummels of the saddle had bruised her spine, and the shock to a system so highly-strung as hers was what might be expected. [...] The effects of the hunting accident, and the strain of writing, too soon undertaken, were [...] beginning to come to their own. Neuralgia, exhaustion, backaches, and all the indescribable miseries of neurasthenia held her in thrall. [...] We wrote, desultory, when she felt equal to it, and I worked. (*IM*, 260–63)

For the following years, it was impossible for Martin "to undertake any work that would demand steady application" (*IM*, 294). The two women started to spend long periods of time in health spas, often in France, also because Somerville was beginning to suffer from the rheumatism that eventually crippled her. As a result of the injury caused by her horse rolling over her (or so her doctor thought), a tumour had formed at the back of Martin's brain. When she died on 21 December 1915 they had not written any other 'serious' novel. In the last chapter of *Irish Memories*, Somerville went back once again to that frustrated desire:

> [t]o return to our work, which for us, at all events, if for no one else, was serious. [...] I suppose it was the result of old habit, and of the return of the hounds,[33] but, for whatever reason, during the years that followed the appearance of "Dan Russel the Fox," Martin and I put aside the notions we had been dwelling upon in connection with "a serious novel," and took to writing "R.M." stories again. (*IM*, 325, 327)

A sentence like "our work, which for us, at all events, if for no one else, was serious" in an autobiography written in a light tone is remarkable: it betrays a not-even-veiled indignation on Somerville's part towards the treatment their literary work had received. Many of Somerville and Ross's contemporaries (and many subsequent critics as well) denied them the status of authors worthy of study. Such disregard may be ascribed to two main factors: in the first place, to the comic short fiction for which they became largely popular; second, to the fact that they wrote in collaboration. Significantly, Somerville and Ross's "own stuff," as Pinker shaped it, was the type of stuff – satire, fun, humour – which collaboration had been deemed fit for by Besant and Matthews in their influential 1890s essays on co-authorship. This fed back into the discourses that delegitimized co-authorship as both a professional and an artistic practice: within the aesthetic hierarchy, collaborative works were removed from the realm of great art. A third factor may be added. Not only were Somerville and Ross collaborators: they were women collaborators, and so doubly devalued by virtue of their gender. Female collaboration with a relative, whether sister or cousin, was generally perceived as little more than a pastime between amateurs. Somerville and Ross had at first reinforced this narrative: as seen above, they declared to have started their shared literary activity half-jokingly. Such claims are common to several female co-writers when recounting their beginnings. For instance, the Gerard sisters claimed to have begun their first novel out of boredom of Hungarian country life. In 1877, the twenty-two-year-old Dorothea was living with her elder sister Emily and her husband:

---

33 In 1903 Somerville had followed her brother Aylmer in the mastership of the West Carbery Hunt. She was the first Irish woman to be master of foxhounds. This role took up much of Somerville's time and added to her already numerous daily occupations.

being consigned to the deadly monotony of a little Hungarian country town, where the landscape was a desert and the society *nil*, the idea of writing a novel as "something to do" was suddenly and almost without premeditation born in upon them. [...] Up to that time there certainly was in neither sister "a deep poetic voice," anxious to utter anything in particular. They simply wanted an occupation. (Black, 1896, 155)

From this account, the practice of collaboration emerges as a form of private entertainment, without any serious literary intent, let alone that of becoming professionals. Their declarations are strikingly similar to those by Somerville and Ross; altogether, their attitude is totally different from the one with which Besant and Rice set out on their collaboration. This may be ascribed to notions of Victorian femininity: since codes of respectability required women to be modest, it would have been too bold to declare ambitions of any sort. It was safer to say that their literary beginnings had been an unpretentious pastime.[34]

In the course of their career, Somerville and Ross repeatedly described their literary partnership as both work and play: "writing together is [...] one of the greatest pleasures I have. To write with you doubles the triumph and the enjoyment, having first halved the trouble and anxiety," confided Martin to Somerville on the eve of *An Irish Cousin*'s publication (*IM*, 134). Very soon they dreamt of counting themselves among professional authors. Unlike the Gerard sisters' partnership, the collaboration of the two Irish cousins survived the transition from amateur to professional. Neither Somerville nor Ross, even after they had acquired a large readership, ever expressed the wish to enjoy fame on her own. Just after the publication of *An Irish Cousin* Martin exhorted Somerville to write with her again for both professional and personal reasons: "you shall write another story with me or without me. It would be too bad to let go such an opening as we now have [Bentley's offer], and I am not man enough for a story by myself" (Martin to Somerville, 6 September 1889, *Letters*, 153). She playfully voiced the need for her female partner to be "man enough" to compete in the literary marketplace. From the moment they started to collaborate, the two cousins produced only co-authored fiction: their popularity came entirely from being part of the duo. After

---

34 On the complicated relationship between gender, creativity, and professionalism during the long nineteenth century see Hadjiafxendi and Zakreski (2013). They call attention to the fact that there were continued backlashes against female professional activities and dismiss the naïve idea that there was continuous progress for women from amateurs to professionals.

the *Irish R.M.* stories their joint names became a trademark, and they accomplished what in business is the ultimate professional achievement – brand-name recognition – so much so that after Martin's death Somerville went on for another thirty-four years to publish fiction under their double signature. The name of Martin is still present in virtually every single piece written after 1915. Significantly, *Irish Memories* not only presents the double signature but even begins by talking about Martin and deals extensively with her, so that it results more in a joint biography than Somerville's own life-writing. Somerville's treatment of her former writing partner is very different from Besant's treatment of Rice in his autobiography, and this mirrors their different attitudes towards collaboration.

Sixteen books appeared with their trademark signature before 1915, and another fourteen came out after this date. In "Two," Somerville gave voice to her unwillingness to give up the cherished double signature: "our signature is dual, as it has ever been, and I recognize no reason why I should change it" (185). In an Author's Note at the beginning of the first edition of *The Big House of Inver* (1925), Somerville justified her choice:

> [a]n established firm does not change its style and title when, for any reason, one of its partners may be compelled to leave it.
> The partner who shared all things with me has left me, but the Firm has not yet put up the shutters, and I feel I am justified in permitting myself the pleasure of still linking the name of Martin Ross with that of
> E. Œ. SOMERVILLE
>
> (Somerville and Ross, 1925)

She referred to her and Martin's literary partnership as "the Firm," as Besant had done before her: they both used the vocabulary of the commercial field, which well conveys the professional and financial aim of their partnerships, beside the artistic one. Besant too, on one occasion, had deployed the dual signature after Rice's death: when he published his first solo novel, his publishers advertised it as a Besant & Rice work. Only after being reassured that his books would be successful anyway did they drop Rice's name (Eliot, 1987, 27–30).

In contrast, Somerville and her publishers were convinced that the trademark signature was an essential factor for the success of the books she continued to write, as their partnership had become a source of endless fascination. But Somerville did not limit herself to the use of her dead cousin's name: she became convinced that Martin's death did not necessarily mean the end of their relationship. She declared that they continued to communicate and argued that their writing method had only had to be modified ("Two," 185). She started automatic writing practices, referring to them as "writing with Martin." Somerville had always had an interest in spiritualism, and members of her family had been early supporters of the Society for Psychical Research. With the occasional help of mediums, she would report messages from Martin from the afterlife, and put it as a condition that the honorary degree from Trinity College Dublin in 1932 should be awarded to her deceased partner as well.[35]

Such extravagances surely did not help their already underrated partnership, which came to be seen as even less worthy of serious study. Somerville's insistence on her spiritualist relationship with her former collaborator cast doubts on the partnership's earlier professionalism; her theatrical gestures opened the collaboration to ridicule and contributed even more to make it a curiosity. So much was collaboration a defining characteristic of her public and private image that Somerville ultimately risked her professional reputation over it.

Unbroken conversation

> To me then Andrew Lang with a sort of offhand fling – "I suppose you're the one who did the writing –" I explained with some care that it was not so – He said he didn't know how any two people could equally evolve characters etc. – that he had tried, and it was always he or the other that did it all – I said I didn't know how we managed, but anyhow that I knew little of bookmaking as a science. He said I must know a good deal – On which I had nothing to say – and talked of other things. (Martin to Somerville, 16 January 1895, *Letters*, 209)

On their first meeting during Martin's stay in Scotland Andrew Lang tried to make her admit that she was "the one who did the writing." Lang had assumed that there was one main author in Somerville and Ross's collaboration, or at least that the tasks of authorship were split between them. He was speaking from his own experience. He had also supposedly declared that "in most collaborations one man did all the work while the other man looked on" (Matthews, 1891, 5). He expected Somerville and Ross's partnership to be no different. Taking for granted that their collaboration was a façade, he tried to make Martin privately confess the

---

35 On Somerville's automatic writing see Collis, 1968, 177; London, 1999, 5, 116–17; and Jamison, 2016, 131–65.

secret. When she answered that they actually did everything together, Lang, still half in disbelief, asked for an explanation, a revelation of the mysterious system. To Martin's reply that there was no system ("I said I didn't know how we managed"), he provocatively remarked that she "must know a good deal." Lang admired Somerville and Ross's work, but he simply could not understand their collaboration; he saw the intertwining of two different hands in one single text as a mystery to be solved.

He was not the only one. Somerville and Ross's writing partnership, during and after their lifetime, has led to incessant interrogations. Their collaboration has remained cloaked in mystery up to our day; it has been referred to in most critical studies as something mysterious, hard to explain, and confusing. At the end of her study of the uncanny in Somerville and Ross's novels, Laird (2000, 125) concludes that "their collaboration itself counted among the more uncanny of their stories." She remarks that the various "mysteries" regarding Somerville and Ross – their writing process, their sexuality, their spiritualist intercourse – have become oddly intertwined in biographers' and critics' accounts, and remain "ghoulish 'shockers'" (Laird, 2000, 126). Greene (2016, 198) laments that the "mystery" of the writing process has been fused with commentators' inability to understand the exact nature of the women's relationship, also characterized as mysterious and scandalous; she attempts to "demystify the writing collaboration, not by examining the personal relationship between the two women, but by grounding [her] argument on collaborative writing theory," referring to the composition studies by Ede and Lunsford (1990) (Greene, 2016, 199). She declares that her focus is solely Somerville and Ross's "writing process or method" (200). However interesting Pepinster Greene's approach, from my perspective it is impossible to understand Somerville and Ross's collaborative writing method without taking into consideration their personal relationship. Their extremely close friendship formed the bedrock of their co-authorship: the latter sprang from the former. Without their private, emotional bond, Somerville and Ross's writing method would not have worked. In this light, their writing process does not appear (so) mysterious any more, as the next paragraphs will demonstrate.

The problem with the study of Somerville and Ross's collaboration is that Andrew Lang and his many successors insisted on seeing their co-authored texts from the same perspective that one would adopt when looking at a single-authored work. York (2006, 299–300) aptly notes that commentators usually set out to "decollaborate" co-authors – that is, to identify who wrote what and who was the better writer of the two. After the success of *An Irish Cousin*, a relative of Somerville and Ross's declared that she "found it impossible to believe in the jointness of the authorship, though she admitted her inability to discern the joints in the writing" (*IM*, 133–34). The lady further commented:

> [b]ut though I think the book a success, and cannot pick out the fastenings of the two hands, I yet think the next novel ought to be by *one* of them. I wonder by which! I say this because I thought the conception and carrying out of "Willy" much the best part of the character drawing of the whole book. It had the real thing in it. If Willy, and the poor people's talk, were by one hand, that hand is the better of the two, say I! (*IM*, 134)

The speaker here considered collaboration, successful as it might be, as a stepping stone: now that the authors had gained confidence, they could – should – go on independently. Of course, since the lady thought of co-authorship as a division of tasks, the most probable to succeed would be the one who managed certain parts of the novel. It seemed pointless – nay, wrong – that the authors should continue writing together, if they could do it alone. A few years later, Somerville reported another telling conversation with a woman she met at a tea party:

> [l]ater on in the conversation, which lasted, most enjoyably, for half an hour, "Are you the Miss Somerville who writes books with Miss Martin? Now! To think I should have been talking to you all this time! And is it you that do the story and Miss Martin the words?" (etc. etc., for some time). "And which of you holds the pen?" (To this branch of the examination much weight was attached, and it continued for some time.) (Somerville to Martin, winter 1894, reported in *IM*, 132–33)

Not only the reading public but also people in the publishing trade were curious to find out 'who did what.' In 1897 Mr Bullen (of Lawrence and Bullen) and Hedley Peek, art editor and sub-editor of the *Badminton Magazine*

> both attacked me [Somerville] to know which of us wrote which parts – by chapters or how – the usual old thing. – I assured them that we did it all together – "Well" says H.P. "I have formed a theory, comparing these stories, & I think the person of these sentences" here he whirled to the G.F.,[36] "wrote these" and here to the 19th Cent. Mag. I was very arch and told him

---

36 "A Grand Filly" (1896), a short comic hunting story Somerville and Ross had published in the *Badminton Magazine*.

he was quite wrong, as they also were joint stock [...]. (Somerville to Martin, 25 April 1897, *Letters*, 243)

Not to mention that Somerville's and Ross's mothers were each "comfortably aware that her own daughter had done all the work" (*IM*, 208).

Such approaches to collaboration – the mechanical division of labour or the predominance of one partner over the other – were fiercely rejected by Somerville and Ross. However, as with Lang's provocative assertions, they offered no explanation in reply. As long as Martin was alive they limited their answers to a few remarks. Somerville drew on her background in art and made some meaningful visual representations: a non-verbal comment was devised in the shape of a monogram, inspired by their Irish heritage, which combined Somerville's and Ross's initials (E. Œ. S. on the left, M. R. on the right) so that they remained apart and distinct on the page, but connected by the interlacing motif of two serpents (or dragons?) looking at each other. The bodies of the serpents are intertwined so fluently that it is hard to see where one ends and the other begins. The monogram reflects the intermingling of two distinctive elements into a larger, united whole, and wonderfully conveys the character of Somerville and Ross's collaboration.[37] Curiously, in the chancel of Castletownshend church, where Somerville used to play the organ on Sundays, there is a floor mosaic designed by her featuring two serpents with intertwined tongues, adapted from a motif in the Book of Kells. Lewis (2004) suggests that the mosaic is a representation of their partnership, which – also given its similarity to the monogram – sounds more than likely.[38]

It was only two years after her partner's death that Somerville ventured to spend some words on the dynamics of their collaboration. She did that in *Irish Memories*, and the following extract is the clearest description of their writing process Somerville ever gave. She explained that it was wholly based on what she called a conversational method:

> [t]he question [...] as to which of us held the pen, has ever been considered of the greatest moment, and, as a matter of fact, during our many years of collaboration, it was a point that never entered our minds to consider. To those who may be interested in an unimportant detail, I may say that our

---

37 The monogram is present in some editions of Somerville and Ross's novels, but not in first editions published before 1900, so we may suppose that Somerville devised it after the turn of the century.

38 On how Somerville's expertise in visual art was central to the fiction she co-authored with Martin see Stevens, 2017.

Figure 7. Monogram of Somerville and Ross, designed by Edith Somerville (*An Irish Cousin*, London: Longmans, 1910). Source: Archive.org

> work was done conversationally. One or the other – not infrequently both, simultaneously – would state a proposition. This would be argued, combated perhaps, approved, or modified; it would then be written down by the (wholly fortuitous) holder of the pen, would be scratched out, scribbled in again; before it found itself finally transferred into decorous MS. It would probably have suffered many things, but it would, at all events, have had the advantage of being well aired. (*IM*, 133)

Somerville revealed that their collaboration drew heavily on conversation, and accorded special significance to the act of talking. The writing came secondarily, since it was not as important as the discussion that preceded and followed it. In this way, like Besant and Matthews before her, she subverted the common assumption that associated authorship with writing: the putting of pen to paper, she affirmed, was not the defining act of authorship. Moreover, the role of the "holder of the pen" was neither hers nor Martin's: it was "wholly fortuitous." Once they had made up their minds upon the course of a chapter, or any other issue, it was chance that dictated who wrote it down. Somerville's statements echo Matthews's words: "when a final choice was made of what seemed to us best, the mere putting on paper was wholly secondary" (Matthews, 1891, 27). Against the significance the Victorian imagination accorded to the writer with their pen in hand – "that autocratic, commanding pen, which has – as is so generally known and believed – so much in its power!" ("Two," 186) – Somerville bluntly downplayed the act of writing as a matter of chance. Most importantly, it simply did not matter who had written what, because she and Martin would plan and revise everything together: after one had written a part, the other would always revise it, and suggest corrections and alterations; then they would write it all down once again, and so on, until they both agreed on everything. As a result, the identification of who first wrote something lost its meaning in the process of mutual revision.

Since Somerville and Ross did not live continuously together until late in their partnership, a large amount of this process was carried out via letters, by sending drafts back and forth between Drishane and Ross House. Reading Somerville and Ross's correspondence is illuminating, as it provides evidence of the lengthy and taxing procedure of mutual revision.[39] The letters started as the space to get to know each other, as recorded at the beginning of this chapter; later on, they cemented their mutual affection in the long periods they spent apart and were used as the space for the plotting of their works, the sharing and the debating of ideas, and as a source of raw-life material for their fiction. The exhortation by Martin "[l]et us take Carbery and grind its bones to make our bread!" (*Letters*, 135) well expresses their purpose. For instance, the account of the suicide of a local boy in the bogs near Ross House in December 1893 was dramatized into the tragic life and drowning of Tom Quin in *The Silver Fox*. Martin's letter containing the report of the tragedy reads: "[i]t is the making of a story almost," and "[i]t fills my mind in its dramatic aspects mostly and perhaps after a talk with you it might take shape" (3 January 1894, *Letters*, 198). Perhaps the most famous example is one of the last surviving letters from Martin to Somerville, which contains an account of her visit to Tyrone House and the illicit relations of its inhabitants. The letter ends with the exhortation "if we dare to write upon that subject!" (18 March 1912, *Letters*, 293–94). Somerville eventually drew on the letter to compose *The Big House of Inver*.

The letters were also the site for revision of the manuscripts and for mutual criticism. Criticism and debate were indeed crucial ingredients of the collaboration: they were unrelenting, and ranged from minutely detailed suggestions of alterations to phrasing and ideas to plot changes and practical comments on publishing. Drafts were usually accompanied by a letter that explained what changes had been made and praised or rejected the adjustments that had been received. An example from the composition of *An Irish Cousin* will give an idea:

> for pity's sake try and write by return of post to say if you like pages 71 and 72. I have always felt something like that there – don't say it is premature

---

39 Jamison (2016, 68–79) argues that letter-writing acted as a site for rebellion and exhaustively explores Somerville and Ross's correspondence with each other.

– it isn't – and I do think that that is the kind of thing that seems to me probable. Of course add, if you like, but I would not sweep or modify – don't anyhow till you have given it good consideration. [...] I know you must loathe my sticking in these putrid things and then fighting for them. [...] Please goodness we will have many a tooth and naily fight next month – but don't let us combat by post; it is too wearing. (Somerville to Martin, 21 January 1888, *Letters*, 63)

Drafts manuscripts, for their part, reveal the extent of the authors' revisions, but we can learn little from them about the creative process. Somerville and Ross used to write on the right-hand page, with the left-page left blank for annotations (Greene, 2016, 203). The drafts do not help 'decollaborate' Somerville and Ross, also because their hands are virtually indistinguishable. London (1999, 73) notes that collaborators come to write like each other, often displaying handwritings that are strikingly similar. As one would expect, the manuscripts are chaotic, but, significantly, "the fluency with which they are written indicates [...] that most of the early invention and composition stages were done conversationally and not written down" (Greene, 2016, 203). So, apart from some passages in the surviving letters, we can have no written testimony of their conversational method. By virtue of its nature, the conversational method of Somerville and Ross is lost with them.

From the description of their working process in *Irish Memories* as well as from their letters, an image of co-authorship as a site of conflict emerges. Somerville and Ross never tried to conceal the practical difficulties of collaboration, and the language of collision repeatedly characterizes their comments. Somerville went as far as using a war metaphor, "combated" (*IM*, 133) – a much more intense term than that employed by Besant, "wrangle" (*MFB*, 11–14). The passage in the letter "[p]lease goodness we will have many a tooth and naily fight next month" (*Letters*, 63) attests to the complex process of two minds trying to work as one. In "Two" Somerville ironically treated "the question as how two people can write together, without battle, murder, and sudden death ensuing immediately" (180), and reported Martin's comment in response to the woman who refused to believe in the jointness of their writing:

> [n]ever mind what she says about people writing together. We have proved that we can do it, and we shall go on. The reason few people can, is because they have separate minds upon most subjects, and fight their hands all the time. I think the two Shockers have a very strange belief in each other, joined to a critical faculty. (Martin to Somerville, September 1889, *IM*, 134)

To this, Martin added that the collaboration with Somerville was, as already underlined, "one of the greatest pleasures" she had (*IM*, 134). In addition, Somerville's expectation to "have many a tooth and naily fight" anticipates with a sort of excitement their moments of debate. Somerville and Ross's partnership thus confirms York's theory (2002, 5) that all successful collaborations are, of necessity, relationships enhanced by discordance: "difference and disagreement strengthen rather than disable collaboration." For the two cousins, co-authorship implied fighting, and certainly did not shorten composition times, but it was also about having fun together, and finding intellectual stimulation. The fact was that, as combative and critical as they could be, Somerville and Ross had faith in, and respect for, each other as women, friends, and authors. Thanks to their profound personal bond, they allowed mutual criticism to flow freely but to remain constructive and never be followed by rupture. This "very strange belief in each other" was what kept the collaboration going for almost thirty years.

The acknowledgement of these dynamics deflates the assumption, made by many, that Somerville and Ross's partnership was at all times harmonious, and that their imaginations magically became one when they wrote. A few years after Somerville's death, her nephew Nevill Coghill fostered the view of Somerville and Ross's partnership as something involving a miracle:

> [t]he nature of their collaboration is as simple as any other miracle. Anybody can understand it at once and nobody can explain it. [...] I once asked Dr. Edith which of them held the pen. She replied: "I'm sick to death of that question!" [...] As a matter of fact they *talked* their stories and their characters and their every sentence into being. As soon as anything was agreed it was written down and not a word was written down without agreement. So they would sit in the studio, or in a Railway carriage or wherever it might be; the two imaginations became one, working with the equal harmony of a pair of hands knitting a scarf. (reported in *Letters*, 145)

The collaborative writing is compared here to the domestic image of knitting. This simile goes back to a series of metaphors employed by reviewers in Somerville and Ross's lifetime. For instance, a suggestive metaphor for their co-authorship was proposed by *The Graphic* in a review of *The Real Charlotte*: "the authors have united their work without leaving a single visible seam" (reported in Somerville and Ross, 1903, 310). This is a very material, practical image, evoking the two women working together on a novel with the same perfect harmony as if it were a piece of knitwear; it also conveys the strength of Somerville and Ross's collaboration: although the product of two people, the completed work is perfectly joint and defies any untangling of the two hands involved, with no "visible seam" left. Yet the choice of the traditionally female activity of sewing seems to relegate the two authors once again into the box of amateurism and domesticity, thus depriving them of the professionalism they were trying so hard to build for themselves.

In Coghill's account, Somerville's and Ross's imaginations miraculously become one and, like two hands belonging to the same person engaged in knitting, they proceed simultaneously and without any friction. As we have seen, their reality was very different, not because there was no harmony, but because harmony persisted notwithstanding disagreements and criticism. Once this notion of the miraculous unity of thought has been proved wrong, the mystery of Somerville and Ross's collaboration becomes less cloudy: we can picture two women, totally open with each other, engaged in constant, sometimes highly combative but always rewarding conversation. Lewis (*Letters*) points out that Somerville and Ross often referred to their letters as 'talking,' and Jamison (2016, 78) remarks that letter-writing "actively manifests itself as an imagined conversation." When her mother died, Somerville sought consolation in writing a letter to Martin: "I can't go to sleep, I have tried but it is no use, so I have lighted my candle and will try to think that I am talking to you" (December 1895, *Letters*, 227).

The critical debate characterizing Somerville and Ross's collaborative process affected their individual creative efforts as well. While writing an essay on education, Martin automatically pictured her partner at her side, and an imaginary discussion started in her head: "I got a sort of grip of the 'Education' thing today [...] I feel you saying 'Well, but I don't see' – and then I don't see either. But it is good for me" (18 May 1889, *Letters*, 135). Even when writing on one's own, then, the collaboration would remain a constant presence, the dialogue would never end. Such real or imagined ongoing conversation not only shaped Somerville and Ross's literary collaboration but also impacted on their individual identities. The collaboration arose from their friendship, but, at the same time, it ended up affecting each individual's sense of self.

Somerville's claim that she was 'writing with Martin' after 1915 is ascribable to this perpetual inner dialogue, beautifully portrayed by Martina Devlin in her novel *Edith* (2022). When the narration begins, Martin has been dead for six years, and a sixty-three-year-old Somerville has come to a standstill in her writing career; she also has to face the increasingly difficult management of her family estate, her brother

Cameron's squandering habits, and the turmoil of the Irish political situation during the War of Independence. A dialogue with Martin automatically starts in Somerville's mind when dealing with problems of any sort, helping her see things more clearly. Martin is a very real presence throughout the narration, at times comforting her former partner, at other times – as happened when she was alive – confronting Somerville with the harsh reality and providing her with practical advice: she is not spared from Martin's criticism even in the inner dialogue. The novel does not present Somerville as on the verge of losing her lucidity: in fact, she perfectly "knows the voice is inside her head" (Devlin, 2022, 9). She never sees Martin, but only hears her voice within her consciousness. When, early on in the narration, Somerville finds out how irresponsibly Cameron has been managing Drishane, Martin steps in:

> "You know what you have to do, Edith."
> "He can't be left in charge. I thought he could. But I was wrong."
> Edith waits for a denial, a defence of Cameron.
> A sigh, whisper faint. It's corroboration.
> When Martin doesn't speak, Edith does. "I'm going to have to do something about him." (Devlin, 2022, 9–10)

The close-knit relationship is still working, with the flowing exchange that characterized it: "[w]hen Martin doesn't speak, Edith does." Somerville is still in perfect harmony with her partner, they still get each other – and that is the fascinating aspect which Devlin masterfully emphasizes. The novel presents some seance scenes as well, with Somerville entranced to lend her hand to Martin's spirit in her automatic writing sessions. However, the trance scenes are not, in my opinion, the real strength of the book, which lies instead in how convincingly and naturally Devlin renders Somerville's subjectivity as a collaborator, even now that her partner is gone. Somerville's bond with Martin continues to characterize her, but that does not prevent her from looking at the future with energy, initiative, and optimism. She stays loyal to her former friend – repeatedly claiming that "Martin is as real to [her] as she ever was" (Devlin, 2022, 242) – but she is projected into the future.

After the description of their writing process in *Irish Memories*, and as the years went by, Somerville increasingly recoiled from further comments on how the collaboration (had) worked. She declared how "abhorrent" it was to her "all the senseless curiosity as to which hand holds the pen" (quoted in Robinson, 1980, 47). Towards the end of her life she dismissed once and for all questions by stating that their collaboration was "what can never be explained" ("Two," 186). She offered only two last evocative descriptions. The first one was related to dancing:

> [s]ometimes the compelling creative urge will come on both, and we would try to reconcile the two impulses, searching for a form into which best to cast them – one releasing it, perhaps as a cloudy suggestion, to be caught up by the other, and given form and colour, then to float away in a flash of certainty, a completed sentence – as two dancers will yield to the same impulse, given by the same strain of music, and know the joy of shared success. ("Two," 186)

Then she talked about her and Ross's joint style by drawing on her painting background: she argued that their styles were as different as blue and yellow on the mixing palette, but that the final product was neither blue nor yellow, but green, which constitutes a proper style on its own. Exactly as green is a secondary colour resulting from the merging of two primary colours, so was Somerville and Ross's joint style: the "resultant green" obscured the individual colours that went into its composition and stood on its own, defying any untangling of the two hands involved ("Two," 186).

In this way, at the end of her life Somerville herself contributed to feeding the aura of mystery that veiled the collaboration with her few suggestive and elusive comments. Her attitude was ambiguous: at the beginning of "Two" she cut short with "[u]nfortunately, much as I should enjoy giving away a secret, there is none to tell" (180). She probably meant that there was no trick, that they simply "did it." However, her reticence to talk about their writing method, together with the declaration that the partnership was "what can never be explained" and the vague metaphors she presented seemed to contradict what she had said before. Moreover, Somerville and Ross wrote of themselves as having an almost religious faith in each other, and the exact nature of their relationship is difficult to define. The fact that all the post-Martin texts continued to be co-signed ("Two" is no exception) adds to all this. At the end of the essay Somerville reproached herself for having "done little or nothing in elucidating this difficulty of two minds and two hands, and only one pen" (186). Yet this might be precisely what she had wanted to do, and Somerville and Ross's collaboration has since then remained a source of fascination.

CHAPTER THREE

Fashionable Collaborations

This chapter moves away from long-term collaborative relationships and turns instead to occasional partnerships. This kind of collaboration was extremely fashionable in the last decade of the nineteenth century: by the 1890s, literary collaboration had become a widespread practice and many popular writers experimented with it. Occasional collaborations were generally the product of already established authors who before and after the collaborative experience(s) pursued independent literary careers. They did not usually work exclusively with one partner, but in the course of their life took part in different collaborations with different people, sometimes even simultaneously, giving origin to a series of intricate nets of collaborators.[1] In this period, co-authorship was confidently asserted and deployed as a marketing strategy: it was no longer a means to face and conquer the literary market, a tool to gain the confidence needed to pursue, eventually, an independent career; on the contrary, it came to be regarded as something experienced out of curiosity and for economic gain. Collaborative novels scored big sales: indeed, the possible economic benefits of a collaboration between best-selling authors were a strong motivation. By the time we are considering, authors' names had become crucial selling factors, and collaborating with a popular colleague could make the difference. Editors and publishers would couple blockbuster authors in order to produce easy-to-sell popular fiction.

1 Just to give some examples, in 1877 Alexander J. Duffield co-authored a novel with Walter H. Pollock (editor of the *Saturday Review*), who in the late 1880s wrote four novels with Andrew Lang, who was himself a co-author with H. Rider Haggard in 1890 and with A. E. W. Mason in 1899. The novels Lang co-authored with Pollock were parodies of Haggard's solo works. Pollock was involved in collaborations with other writers beside Lang and Duffield, including his son Guy Cameron Pollock and Walter Besant (with whom in 1885 he co-authored a collection of short stories, *Uncle Jack*).

Going through every occasional collaboration of the 1890s would be time consuming, and scarcely worth the effort, since the products of most of these partnerships were ephemera, meant to entertain the public and then be put aside to make space for the next ones. They did not aspire to literary greatness: they were made for the public to consume. What matters most is how these books bear witness to the playfulness and liveliness of the literary market of the fin de siècle, and how they illuminate significant aspects of late Victorian culture. This chapter considers three case studies, each representing a kind of occasional collaboration, all published more or less in the same years: to start with, the fantasy novel *The World's Desire* (1890), as an example of a collaboration between two established authors; second, the sentimental novel *A Widower Indeed* (1891), as a case of an alliance between an elder, well-known novelist and an unexperienced young writer; and, last, the sensational *The Fate of Fenella* (1892), co-written by twenty-four celebrated authors, as an example of the gimmicky round robin novels that enjoyed great popularity around the end of the century.

"Two sworn friends" having fun: Henry Rider Haggard and Andrew Lang[2]

In 1890, a strange novel set in ancient times and far away spaces made its appearance on the marketplace. Its production had involved two well-established names of the literary scene, although in very different areas: H. Rider Haggard and Andrew Lang. The association could not have been odder.

Henry Rider Haggard (1856–1925) was a prolific writer of popular adventure novels. He had spent his early twenties in Africa, serving as a secretary to the governor of Natal. His African stay provided him with the material for most of his future fiction, swashbuckling novels like *King Solomon's Mines* (1886) and *She* (1887). Besant, whom he used to meet at the Savile Club, did not hide his pleasure at reading Haggard's stories and, on the publication of *She*, wrote to him assuring him that the novel put him "at the head – a long way ahead – of all contemporary imaginative writers. If fiction is best cultivated in the field of pure invention then you are certainly the most modern of novelists"

---

[2] "Those two sworn friends Mr. Rider Haggard and Mr. Andrew Lang have conspired together to produce a book" (*Dundee Advertiser*, 4 December 1890, no. 9266, p. 2).

(Besant to Haggard, 2 January 1887, reported in Haggard, 1926, I, 249). Among his literary friends Haggard counted the Scottish writer, folklorist, anthropologist, and critic Andrew Lang (1844–1912), who, after becoming a fellow of Merton College, left the position in 1875 to become a writer. Lang was a Greek scholar who devoted himself to Homer, publishing prose versions of the *Odyssey* (1879) and the *Iliad* (1883), and whose *Tales of Troy and Greece* (1907) were long regarded as a children's classic. To the general public he became known as a collector of folk and fairy tales (helped by his wife Leonora), although he also wrote poems and melodramatic novels. Before collaborating with Haggard, Lang had written, in partnership with Walter H. Pollock, parodies of *King Solomon's Mines* and *She*, respectively *King Solomon's Wives* (1887) and *He* (1887).[3]

Unfortunately, not much has arrived to us concerning the relationship between Haggard and Lang; in this respect, Haggard's autobiography, *The Days of My Life* (1926), proves valuable. He wrote it between 1910 and 1912, but left instructions to publish it after his death. Here, the bond between the two emerges clearly. Before their collaboration, Haggard and Lang were already in the habit of corresponding, meticulously commenting on each other's work; Lang helped Haggard plan and revise *She*, *Allain's Wife*, *Beatrice*, *Eric Brighteyes*, and *Nada the Lily*, and added poems to *Cleopatra*, about which Haggard wrote "[p]erhaps Lang and I shall collaborate in the final copy" (Higgins, 1981, 118). When, in a moment of crisis during the late 1880s, Haggard had become "sickened of the novel-writing trade" (Haggard, 1926, I, 273) and was considering giving up literature, Lang pushed him: "[i]f you jack up Literature, I shall jack up reading. […] I was infinitely more anxious for your success than for my own, which is not an excitement to me" (Lang to Haggard, reported in Haggard, 1926, I, 273–74). They also dedicated to each other some of their works: Haggard included Lang in his dedications of *King Solomon's Mines* and *Allan Quatermain*, and dedicated *She* to him alone; in 1887, the Scottish writer composed a warm dedication to Haggard at the beginning of a collection of essays, *In the Wrong Paradise*.

3 In *He*, Lang and Pollock reversed the sexes of all the characters in *She*, turning She into He, Holly into Polly, and Leo into Leonora; they also turned Queen Victoria into a man. They replaced She's matriarchal kingdom of Kôr with the world of men's literary clubs: *He* is set in Grub Street, London, instead of Africa. Another parody of *She*, also entitled *He*, appeared in the same year by John De Morgan. De Morgan also wrote another parody of *King Solomon's Mines* (also called *King Solomon's Wives*) and of *Jess* (which he entitled *Bess*).

Surely, the connection between the two was strong. Lang once wrote to Haggard: "[y]ou have been more to me of what the dead friends of my youth were, than any other man, and I take the chance to say it, though not given to speaking of such matters" (20 February 1896, reported in Haggard, 1926, II, 78). Haggard answered that the "friendship to which you make such touching allusion always has been, is and will be returned by myself. I will say no more" (Haggard to Lang, reported in Haggard, 1926, II, 78). Before he died, Lang asked his wife to give Haggard a ring once belonging to the Egyptian Queen Taia, and Haggard always wore it (Haggard, 1926, II, 82). Koestenbaum (1989, 153) suggests some homoerotic tension between them, and, drawing on the account of Lang's early biographer (Green, 1946, ix), he underlines how Lang's widow systematically destroyed her late husband's correspondence, sparing just the letters where statements of mutual affection were restrained.

The two friends started to think about *The World's Desire* (whose title initially should have been *The Song of the Bow*) in early 1888. Haggard gave only a brief account of how the collaboration had begun: "[r]oughly the history of this tale, which I like as well as any with which I have had to do, is that Lang and I discussed it. Then I wrote a part of it, which part he altered or rewrote. Next in his casual manner he lost the whole MS. for a year or so" (Haggard, 1926, I, 280). Therefore, after the first few pages, "not having the heart to recommence the book, the idea of writing it was abandoned" (281). However, the lost manuscript "was unexpectedly found, and encouraged thereby, I went on and wrote the rest" (280). Apparently, Lang had "thrust the MS. into a folio volume, which was replaced among his numerous books, where it might have remained for generations had he not chanced to need to consult that particular work again" (281). So the writing was resumed, mainly done by Haggard (at least according to his autobiography), with Lang providing material, revising, and writing some parts: "the MS. contains fifty-three sheets [...] written or re-written by Lang, and about 130 in my writing" (280). A good amount of the collaboration was carried out by letter, with the two co-authors sending the manuscript back and forth, along with letters commenting on it. The joint work was interrupted a few times more, for instance by Haggard's journey to Iceland in the summer of 1888; furthermore, as it was the case with most occasional collaborations, both Lang and Haggard were engaged in other, independent projects during the composition of *The World's Desire*.

From a letter by Lang we learn that Haggard wanted to set the story in Egypt from the beginning, while he suggested that the protagonist should be Ulysses, and hence that he should first be introduced in his homeland, Ithaca, and only later travel to Egypt:

> I'd have begun with Odysseus in a plague-stricken Ithaca and have got on to Egypt. And I've had written in modern English. However, as it stands, I don't care quite for the way the Wanderer is introduced. He comes rather perfunctorily and abruptly on the scene to my feeling. It is a subject that wants such a lot of thinking out. It would be jolly if one had more time in this world of ours. Also, if the public had, for after "Cleopatra" they would not rise at Egyptological romance for a long time. I can't help regretting my veteran Odysseus – I don't think he would have been too "grey-eyed." If we really collaborated, as we proposed originally, I'd begin with him; bring him in your way to Egypt, introduce him to the old cove who'd tell him about Hatasu (as in yours) and then let things evolve […]. (Lang to Haggard, reported in Haggard, 1926, I, 281–82)

Ulysses was a figure with whom Lang, as a Greek scholar, was familiar:

> [h]aving nothing to do this afternoon I did a lot of Ulysses. I brought him home from the people who never saw salt in a boat of Dreams, and I made him find nobody alive in Ithaca, a pyre of ashes in the front garden and a charred bone with Penelope's bracelet on it! But the *bow* [Ulysses's magic bow that only he could bend] was at home. If you can make it alive (it's as dead as mutton), the "local colour" is all right. Then I'd work in your bit, where the Sidonians nobble him, and add local colour. (reported in Haggard, 1926, I, 282)

It also appears that it was Haggard who first conceived the idea of inserting the Exodus of the Jews into an already crowded narrative, with Lang expressing his concern about his collaborator's overwork: "[j]ust had your letter on the Jews. Do you think it worth while, if it won't run easily? You have so much on hand, and I am afraid you will tire out your invention. The idea of Odysseus and Helen is a good one, but don't thrash a willing and perhaps weary Pegasus" (Haggard, 1926, I, 280–81).

Another point of concern was the style. It seems that Haggard insisted on a mock ancient style, but Lang did not agree: "keep all the English modern, except in highly-wrought passages, incantations, etc. I dare say it would make a funny mixture" (Haggard, 1926, I, 282). Eventually Lang won the battle and they opted for his solution. However, they tried to evoke Homer's style by employing repeated epithets (for Ulysses: Ulysses, Laertes' son, or The Wanderer; for Helen: The Golden Helen or Argive Helen; for Meriamun: Meriamun the Queen, and so on) and by inserting poetic pieces within the narration. As for the form of publication, Lang was decidedly against serialization, as can be glimpsed from this letter from June 1889:

> I have been turning over "The World's Desire," and the more I turn the more I dislike the idea of serial publication. It is emphatically a book for educated people only, and would lower your vogue with newspaper readers if it were syndicated, to an extent beyond what the price the papers pay would make up for. I am about as sure as possible of this: it is a good deal my confounded *style*, which is more or less pretty, but infernally slow and trailing. (reported in Haggard, 1926, I, 283)

Nevertheless, *The World's Desire* ran serially in the *New Review* (nos 11–19) from April to December 1890, and was then published in one volume by Longmans (Charles Longman was a good friend of Haggard's). Rumours of the collaboration had built up high expectations: the partnership was broadly advertised, and its product expected with curiosity. "It is a remarkable conjunction, the issue of which will be watched with a wide and peculiar interest [...] We expect there will be a great rush for *The New Review* this month," the *Northampton Mercury* wrote (5 April 1890). The fact that Haggard and Lang had written together sufficed to raise interest: "[a]ny work emanating from the joint pens of the above named gentlemen necessarily commands the attention of all interested in literary matters" (*Northern Whig*, 29 November 1890, no. 25681, p. 6); "[the novel will] of course, be widely read, for both authors have a considerable *clientèle*, and their united admirers should make an almost incalculable gathering," *The Globe* pointed out (18 November 1890, no. 29787, p. 3). However, the bizarre alliance also brought about many doubts: the main perplexity was due to the fact that the two authors had very different styles and usually dealt with completely different material.

When it finally came out, *The World's Desire* was a commercial success. The title alludes to a passage in Tennyson's *In Memoriam*, where the poet, addressing the late Arthur Hallam, imagines a divinely gifted man who, "moving up from high to higher / Becomes on Fortune's crowning slope / The pillar of a people's hope, / The centre of a world's desire" (Tennyson, 2006a, stanza LXIV, lines 13–16). Tennyson too had famously written about Ulysses in his eponymous poem: there the Greek hero, long back from his adventures, cannot help feeling restless and, despite his old age, yearns to set out for another journey. In the final stanza of the dramatic monologue, he addresses his sailors and encourages them "to strive, to seek, to find, and not to yield" (Tennyson,

2006b, line 70). Haggard and Lang's indefatigable Ulysses was not much different.

The World's Desire adds another journey to Ulysses's wanderings. The book is a melting pot of an impressive number of historical, mythological, biblical, and supernatural elements, all mixed up together: characters from Heroic Greece, from the Egypt of the Ramessids, and events narrated in the Old Testament are all heaped up, so that the result is quite intricate. The co-authors wrote a preface in which they claimed that recent discoveries had "shown that there really was much intercourse between Heroic Greece, the Greece of the Achæans, and the Egypt of the Ramessids" (Haggard and Lang, 1894, 1). However, the way in which they structured the story was far from realistic. Coming back to Ithaca, Ulysses finds it empty and desolate: first a pestilence, then an earthquake, have destroyed everything and killed the population, including Penelope and Telemachus. Ulysses rambles in desperation around the island until he finds himself at the temple of Aphrodite. Here the goddess of love appears to him: she is irritated because Ulysses has never really loved any woman, and thus has never served her. She commands him to set out on another journey, this time on the quest for Helen of Troy: the most beautiful woman of the world, Aphrodite promises, shall be his. As the incarnation of Ideal Beauty, Helen represents the World's Desire. Then, the goddess makes Ulysses forget his sorrows and breathes love for Helen into his heart, posing only one condition for the accomplishment of his happiness: he must be faithful to Helen and have no woman while he searches for her. The hero thus leaves for a new adventure. While navigating, Ulysses is captured by Sidonian buccaneers and carried as a prisoner down the Nile, but he manages to slay the whole crew and becomes master of the ship. He lands at Tanis, where the sea is red with blood and the land is plagued with frogs and locusts; an additional plague afflicts the city: a new goddess, called the Hathor, has taken up residence in the temple, to which all men are mysteriously attracted, but as soon as they lay eyes on the beautiful divinity they drop dead, killed by invisible swords. Under a false identity, Ulysses is welcomed at Pharaoh's court. Here Meriamun, Pharaoh's wife (who is also his half-sister), instantly falls in love with him – which is the result of a previous prophecy. The queen is a sorceress: she has visions, communicates with the dead, uses the spirits at her pleasure, and can change her physical appearance. A sort of epic love triangle begins, as Meriamun wants Ulysses as her lover, while Ulysses longs only to find Helen. Meanwhile, Ulysses gains Pharaoh's trust by defending him during an uprising, thus becoming captain of a legion of the Egyptian army. After the death of his son (the death of the firstborn, another biblical plague), Pharaoh lets the Israelites go, and Meriamun curses Moses's people, condemning them never to see the land they are heading to. By this time, Meriamun has discovered her guest's real identity, as she has spied on Ulysses thanks to her magic tricks; on finding out the truth, she has fallen even more in love with him. Ulysses, too, has made a discovery: he has gone to the temple and has realized that the Hathor is actually Helen. The World's desire is portrayed as a tragic heroine, an immortal but unhappy daughter of the gods (it is not specified which ones). Ulysses and Helen confess to each other their mutual love, and he promises to take her away from the temple and elope together. Crazed with jealousy, Meriamun seeks revenge: on the night planned for the elopement she assumes Helen's shape and deceives Ulysses, who spends the night with her while Pharaoh is away chasing the Jews (it is the night of the parting of the Red Sea). Ulysses's vow to Aphrodite has thus been broken: he has slept with another woman. Consequently, the prophecy will remain unfulfilled. The goddess appears once more to Ulysses and makes a new prophecy: he will die in battle and shall never marry Helen. The following day, Meriamun poisons Pharaoh, blaming the Hathor for it, so that all the women of the reign proceed to attack Helen by setting fire to her temple; she is saved by Rei, a faithful priest who has become Ulysses's trusted confidant and helper. Rei tells Helen that Ulysses did not abandon her, but that he was deceived by the queen. At this point, the Achæans attack Egypt (the reason why is not clear) and Ulysses is sent to fight against them: this will be his last fight, and a whole chapter describing Ulysses's heroic deeds in battle follows, in which he also kills a giant. Helen follows him to the battlefield, and they reunite for a last kiss just before he is accidentally killed by Telegonus, the son he has had with Circe. Since Ulysses is wearing Paris's golden armour, which he took at the sack of Troy, Telegonus thinks he has the Trojan prince in front of him and strikes him to death. Ulysses dies in the arms of Helen and before the eyes of an inconsolable Telegonus, and is cremated with all the honours by the Greek. The final scene sees Meriamun throwing herself in desperation onto Ulysses's pyre, and Helen left to wander the earth for eternity.

The story, though engaging, is quite confusing. Moreover, it is all action: the characters are flat stereotypes that never evolve. Ulysses is the upright hero, never faltering, never doubting; Helen is the helpless, angelically beautiful heroine, always waiting for someone to save her,

FASHIONABLE COLLABORATIONS

Figure 8. *The World's Desire*, by Andrew Lang and Henry Rider Haggard (London: Longmans, Green & Co., 1894), p. 193. Source: Archive.org

'AND THEY WHISPERED EACH TO EACH,'

'THEN HE KNEW . . . THAT DEATH CAME UPON HIM FROM THE WATER.'

Figure 9. *The World's Desire*, by Andrew Lang and Henry Rider Haggard (London: Longmans, Green & Co., 1894), p. 312. Source: Archive.org

and totally without will; Meriamun, on the contrary, has quite a strong will, but she is presented as stubborn, lascivious, and uncontrollable – Haggard and Lang could not help portraying a wilful woman as dangerous. Meriamun craves power and demands to be Pharaoh's equal, traits that, according to Koestenbaum (1989, 159), could make her an embodiment of the independent New Woman that Lang and Haggard despised. So, the only two women depicted in the *The World's Desire* are either wicked or holy. In his homoerotic reading of Lang and Haggard's collaboration, Koestenbaum argues that the two friends' writing is to be understood as a return to pure romances, in terms of a revolt against the realistic Victorian fiction with its in-depth character analysis – novels which were either written by women or which focused on women's lives and marriage. From this perspective, we may venture to say that the stereotyped characters of *The World's Desire* are to be read as part of Lang and Haggard's shared agenda to counter realistic novels about and by women.

For all its commercial success, reviews were contrasting. Some were enthusiastic, some lukewarm, others utterly negative. As Haggard remembered in his autobiography, the novel "was violently attacked [...] All that I remember about [the reviews] is the effort of its assailants to discriminate between that part of the work which was written by Lang and that part which was written by myself – an effort, I may add, that invariably failed" (Haggard, 1926, II, 7). As a matter of fact, the main business of the periodical press was to discover and expose who had done what. Since both Haggard and Lang had established careers and were famous for specific areas of interest the two hands were thought to be easily distinguishable. Almost unanimously, the Egyptian setting, the adventure parts, the battles, and the magic were attributed to Haggard, who was fresh from the studies he had made for *Cleopatra*; the Greek parts, the mythological and biblical elements, the ethnology, and the poems (universally praised as graceful and musical) were ascribed to Lang. The flowery language with its archaic expressions was appreciated by some reviewers, while it was deemed tiresome and intolerable by others. Lang's style was generally said to have improved Haggard's usual exaggerations: "Mr. Lang's delicate style is an effective curb on long, sententious dissertations" (*Kerry Evening Post*, 4 June 1890, vol. 116, p. 3). Despite the two different contributions, the novel was universally judged to be beautifully united and flowing, as the *London Evening Standard* remarked:

[a] volume to which two such writers have obviously devoted serious, and even loving, care could not possibly be dull or crude. [...] The book is full of sorcery and enchantment, and it is just possible that the two authors, like some of the marvelous beings they portray, have had a transforming and assimilating effect on each other. (10 November 1890, no. 20699, p. 2)

However, the choice of subject divided the press. The decision to bring Ulysses once more back to life, along with the complicated maze of mythology and Egyptology, was considered by some the result of a formidable mixture of erudition (Lang's) and imagination (Haggard's), which could only have been attained through collaboration: "[p]erhaps neither Mr. Rider Haggard nor Mr. Andrew Lang would have ventured to do it alone" (*St. James's Gazette*, 2 December 1890, no. 3271, p. 6). "The authors have shown a large measure of courage" in the choosing of their characters, commented *The Globe*, and Lang "might be better occupied, many may think, than in the invention of romance; but the experiment was daring and not uninteresting" (18 November 1890, no. 29787, p. 3). The *Yorkshire Post and Leeds Intelligencer* (24 December 1890, no. 13569, p. 3) praised the original experiment: "[t]his addendum to an old story is wrought out with marvelous skill, and shows that the art of collaboration is by no means lost." The *London Daily News* (27 November 1890, no. 13930, p. 6) called Haggard and Lang the "two literary enchanters of today" who "summoned the phantom of Odysseus," so that "we have every reason to be grateful for their incantations." However, there were some violent attacks too. A particularly eloquent review, entitled "An Awful Warning" (*Pall Mall Gazette*, 13 November 1890, no. 8004), lamented the association of a man of culture with a writer of romances and boys' books. According to the *Pall Mall*, Lang was guilty of having let a passion for "Haggardism" take hold of him: it was one thing to read tawdry, gory novels as a guilty pleasure, quite another to write them. The review ironically traced the steps of the Scottish folklorist's "descent into the lowest depth of Haggardism":

[t]he spectacle of Mr. Andrew Lang's name on the title-page of such a book as *The World's Desire* should serve as an awful warning against the sin of paltering with one's literary conscience. [...] Attracted by inborn sympathy towards all that is primitive and spontaneous in literature, [Lang] steeped himself from his youth upwards in epic, ballad, and saga. Then dissatisfaction with [...] mythology led Mr. Lang to the study of folklore, and brought him into contact with modern as well as ancient savagery. When Mr.

Rider Haggard's earlier stories appeared, they naturally attracted Mr. Lang's attention. He found in them primitive manners, bloodshed, galore, and a certain grotesquely grandiose imagination which appealed to the schoolboy element in his character. He dwelt as little as possible on the weaknesses of the new romancer – the appalling triviality of his humour, for example, and the slovenly pretentiousness of his style. In other words, he paltered with his literary conscience by omitting to distinguish between a freakish personal predilection and a sober and serious critical judgement. [...] This whimsical taste, indulged at first in sheer wantonness, almost in bravado, has grown upon Mr. Lang until it has become a sort of monomania. And now we find Mr. Lang not only accepting but openly aiding and abetting a similar degradation of the great Ulysses. (*Pall Mall Gazette*, 13 November 1890, no. 8004, p. 3)

After that, the review – like several others – sought to tell the two hands apart:

[w]hat pleasure can Mr. Lang have found in transporting the hapless Odysseus from the great free air of Homeric myth and melody into the garish, gassy theatre of Mr Haggard's imagination? For it is pretty clear that Mr. Haggard's imagination has been mainly concerned in the bodying forth of *The World's Desire*. It resembles his former achievements too closely to leave any room for doubt. Helen and Meriamun are re-incarnations of two different aspects of "She-who-must-be-obeyed" [...]. We have the usual scenes of carnage (if possible gorier than ever) and the inevitable hocus pocus of incantation.

If Mr Haggard has not the chief share in all this, why then Mr Lang must have had chief share in *Cleopatra* and *She* – an alternative we shrink from considering. Mr Lang, we fancy, has contributed to the classical details, and possibly the general notion of jumbling up Ulysses and Moses and Aaron, and adding an eleventh affliction to the plagues of Egypt in the person of Helen of Troy. (p. 3)

The reviewer finally pondered that

[a] myth even if grotesque and repulsive, is interesting because it is a myth, a genuine document in the history of human mind. But when two literary gentlemen sit down in the year 1890 to let their imagination "bombinate in a vacuum," we have a right to demand the result shall be either beautiful in itself or very beautifully presented. *The World's Desire*, on the other hand, is as stodgy as it is sanguinary. (p. 3)

The only positive note concerned the style of *The World's Desire*, mainly ascribed to Lang's talent:

[i]n only one respect is this romance superior to Mr. Haggard's former production – it is notably better written. Mr. Lang's has succeeded in chastening his collaborator's "poetic prose", and almost entirely eliminating his philosophy and his humour. There are some passages of very pretty writing in the book, the echo of a Homeric turn of phrase being introduced now and then with happy effect. (p. 3)

The *London Evening Standard* commented that "the general result is *bizarre*, and almost touches the grotesque," but it conceded that the book was greatly entertaining and that "[t]he association of two writers of such dissimilar genius is justified by the result" (10 November 1890, no. 20699, p. 2). The *Kerry Evening Post* advanced an interesting culinary metaphor:

the gourmet who appreciates roast venison and currant jelly, the boumelier goose and apple sauce, or lamb and fragrant mint may perchance wonder what daring wight was first inspired to couple such apparently incongruous elements. Yet, once allied, there is no denying their quality. Quite as startling a literary juxtaposition is that of Mr. Rider Haggard and that of [...] Mr. Andrew Lang. Yet here, again, the result has justified the experiment. *The World's Desire*, now current in the *New Review*, says much for the success of that queer business known as literary partnership. [...] *The World's Desire* is a dreamy and fascinating romance [...]. (4 June 1890, vol. 116, p. 3)

Another criticism of *The World's Desire* was the alleged immorality of some of its pages, especially the direct reference to the night Meriamun spends with Ulysses. The figure of Helen, too, was said to inspire nothing but lust. Haggard was held as mainly responsible for this aspect:

the story [...] although powerfully told, [...] is a very unpleasant one, and [...] [Haggard] allows himself a license in some of his scenes which compels us to warn our readers that it is not a book which should be placed in the hands of the young. It is a pity that the talent and the erudition used in the composition of the work could not have been turned to more profitable purpose than the writing of a sensational and not too wholesome romance. (*Derby Mercury*, 19 November 1890, no. 9175, p. 6)

R. L. Stevenson seems to have enjoyed Haggard and Lang's novel, and sent them a letter of congratulations, together with a humorous poem, whose first three stanzas are worth quoting:

1.
Awdawcious Odyshes,
Your conduc' is vicious,
Your tale is suspicious

An' queer.
Ye ancient sea-roamer,
Ye dour auld beach-comber,
Frae Haggard to Homer
Ye veer.

2.
Sic veerin' and steerin'!
What port are ye neerin'
Aa frae Egypt to Erin
Ye gang?
Ye ancient auld blackguard,
Just see whaur ye're staggered
From Homer to Haggard
And Lang!

3.
In stunt and in strife
To gang seeking a wife –
At your time o' life
It was wrang.
An' see! Fresh afflictions
Into Haggard's descriptions
An' the plagues o' the Egyptians
Ye sprang!

(reported in Haggard, 1926, II, 8)

Stevenson had shown interest in a possible collaboration with Haggard some time before, but they never made anything of it:

> P.S. Further reflection on "K.S.M." [*King Solomon's Mines*] makes me think you are one who gets up steam slowly. In that case, when you have your book finished, go back and rewrite the beginning up to the mark.
> My case is the reverse: I always begin well, and often finish languidly or hurriedly.
> P.P.S. How about a deed of partnership?
> (Stevenson to Lang, reported in Haggard, 1926, I, 236–37)

After the publication of *The World's Desire* Haggard and Lang remained life-long friends. They continued to comment on each other's works, as their letters attest. They thought of collaborating again but never actually did so, probably because Lang had been "a bit discouraged about the 'W. Desire' because a lot of *ignorant* fools slated it" (Haggard to Lang, 28 December 1907, reported in Haggard, 1926,

II, 77). In 1907 they contemplated a new joint project in the same line as *The World's Desire*:

> [c]an you not think of something "big and beautiful," something that has an *idea* in it? Something for choice that has to do with old Greece (which you know) and with old Egypt (which I know)? Something with room in it for a few of your beautiful verses [...]. In short, a real *poetical* romance such as we might both be proud of. Now don't toss this aside, but think. You know all the old world legends: there must be some that would lend themselves to this general scheme. [...] Something grand and pure and simple, something to lift up! Now don't be discouraged, for though we are both antique, I know that we can do it, if only we can find the theme. (Haggard to Lang, 28 December 1907, reported in Haggard, 1926, II, 77)

Lang suggested "one of the old Greek legends that ended in the most horrible all-round tragedy" (Haggard 1926, II, 76), a theme Haggard rejected since, in his opinion, "a twentieth-century audience would require something a little more cheerful" (Haggard, 1926, II, 76). Some years later, in November 1911, Haggard tried to motivate Lang, by then increasingly melancholic, by proposing a new collaboration: "it occurred to me to try to cheer Lang up and take him out of himself a little by getting him to collaborate, or at any rate to think about collaboration, in another romance" (Haggard, 1926, II, 75). The suggestion was supported by Longmans, but Lang refused: "I don't think that I could do more. The W.D. [*World's Desire*] took in despite my ill-omened name; I brought you worse luck than you would have had alone" (Lang to Haggard, reported in Haggard, 1926, II, 75–76). During Lang's last years, despite the strong attachment that united them, the two friends saw little of each other, as they "lived totally different lives in totally different localities," and their letters became "scarce" (Haggard, 1926, II, 73). In his autobiography, Haggard narrated extensively his friend's slow decay and death, and deeply mourned his loss: "among men my best friend perhaps, and the one with whom I was most entirely in tune" (Haggard, 1926, II, 80).

"A lady who is impertinent to her Creator" and "a travelled American": Rhoda Broughton and Elizabeth Bisland[4]

The year following the publication of *The World's Desire* a sentimental novel by two women writers came out. *A Widower Indeed* was the

---

4 *Edinburgh Evening News*, 13 November 1884, p. 3; *Glasgow Evening News*, 2 May 1891, p. 2.

product of a collaboration between the queen of English "sensuous sensational excitement" *(The English Lake Visitor*, 3 November 1883, no. 337, p. 4), Rhoda Broughton, at that time a fifty-one-year-old author at the height of her career, and an "adventurous young lady journalist" (*Bristol Magpie*, 16 August 1890, no. 423, p. 7), the American Elizabeth Bisland, who had never written fiction before.

Broughton (1840–1920) had published her first novel, *Not Wisely But Too Well*, in 1867 in the *Dublin University Magazine*, which her uncle Sheridan LeFanu edited. LeFanu had introduced her to Bentley, who at first refused the novel as it was considered too transgressive, but accepted the next one, *Cometh Up As a Flower*, published it in the same year, and proceeded to issue most of her subsequent work. Her reputation for audacity, outspokenness, and caustic wit had at first led circulating libraries not to stock her novels; nevertheless, she became a firm favourite with readers. After living in various parts of the country, Broughton moved to London in 1890. The year before her collaboration with Bisland, she received her highest payment ever for a novel, *Alas!*, which proved, however, a commercial failure. Was it a chance that her next move was to try something new, like a collaboration? And was it a chance that the experiment occurred with a much younger, fresher partner?

While in 1891 Broughton had an established career as a novelist, the twenty-eight-year-old Bisland (1861–1929) had just attracted worldwide attention for a sensational seventy-six-day race around the world. Her journey was reported in a number of articles she wrote for the monthly New York magazine *Cosmopolitan* and which were later collected by Harper and Brothers in a book entitled *In Seven Stages: A Flying Trip Around the World*, issued in June 1891. The globe race had been an extraordinary event. In the late afternoon of 14 November 1889 Bisland had embarked on her journey at a few hours' notice to compete for the fastest trip around the world against another young woman journalist, Nellie Bly. Bly had left that same morning, aiming at setting the record: sixteen years earlier, Jules Verne had imagined that a trip around the world could be accomplished in eighty days; now Bly hoped to do it in seventy-five. The magazine she worked for, *The World* (whose publisher was Joseph Pulitzer), greatly advertised the enterprise, and on the morning of her departure a great crowd had gathered to see her embark upon a steamer bound to England. John B. Walker, editor of *Cosmopolitan*, smelled the potential publicity value of such a race: he immediately summoned Bisland, his literary editor, and asked her if she would go on the same journey, but travelling in the opposite direction.

If she wanted to have any chance of returning to New York before Bly, she had to set off that very day. Thus, at six o'clock Bisland was on a train from New York Central heading west. From San Francisco she took a steamer to Japan, then proceeded to Hong Kong, Singapore, Ceylon, the Suez Canal, Italy, France, England, and Queenstown, Ireland, where she finally embarked on a ship that took her back to the United States, arriving seventy-six days after her departure. Her voyage would have been the fastest ever recorded – if only Nellie Bly had not arrived four days before (*Shields Daily Gazette*, 1 January 1890, p. 3; *Pall Mall Gazette*, 27 January 1890, no. 7756, p. 4; *The Graphic*, 1 August 1891, no. 1131, p. 21).[5]

Both Bly and Bisland gained immense notoriety. However, Bisland did not enjoy fame. Genteel and elegant, she was born into a Louisiana plantation family ruined by the Civil War and its aftermath; although her education was mainly conducted at home by her mother and through what survived of her father's library, she was "highly literary, with refined tastes and wide-ranging interests" (Goodman, 2013, 42). She began her career by writing poems, like her mother, but she soon turned to journalism, in particular feature articles and reviews. At twenty she moved to New Orleans to pursue her passion for journalism and help support her family. After seven years, tired with what she considered the parochialism of the South, she moved to New York, where she

---

5 Nelly Bly was the pen name of Elizabeth Jane Cochran (1864–1922). Born in Pennsylvania, from the age of twenty she worked as a reporter. Bly became known for being the first female reporter to put herself, undercover, in dangerous situations to expose social problems: for instance, she pretended to be insane so that she might report first-hand on the mistreatment of the women patients in an asylum. Other women followed her example, and for some time she embodied a role model for young female journalists, called 'stunt girls.' It was Bly's idea to embark on a world race, and she had to convince her editor to let her try. After her return, she became one of the most famous women in the United States, with her book *Around the World in Seventy-Two Days* (1890) sold out within a month. Now too widely recognizable to go back doing undercover reportage, she got a contract for writing serial fiction, but left it unfulfilled. She disappeared from sight, only publishing occasional feature articles and interviews for *The World*. In 1894 she married the millionaire Robert Season and turned to the life of the New York wealthy wife. When her husband died in 1904 Bly took over the family business and seemed to do extremely well, but in 1914 she had to declare bankruptcy and flee the country because of legal charges against her. After World War I, when she lived in Austria, she returned to New York penniless, and worked for the *Evening Journal* until her death in 1922. For a biography of Bly see Goodman, 2013.

contributed to different magazines, such as *Harper's Bazar, Illustrated American, Puck, The World,* and *Cosmopolitan*. Members of New York's creative set gathered in the literary salon Bisland used to host in the apartment she shared with her sister. She became a self-supporting professional woman, who succeeded in carving out a successful career in the hypercompetitive, male-dominated world of big-city newspapers. When she took part in the race around the world she found herself popular almost overnight. Annoyed by life in the limelight, in the spring of 1890 she accepted the invitation of an English aristocrat she had befriended when staying in Colombo, and went to spend the upcoming London season with her. Through her hosts, Lady and Lord Broome, she was introduced to London's literary society, where she met, among others, Herbert Spencer, Rudyard Kipling (who apparently was impressed with her), and Rhoda Broughton (Goodman, 2013, 349). Later in the year, at the close of the London season, Bisland took lodgings in Oxford. One of her neighbours was Broughton. The two women became friends and set out to co-author a story featuring a young American woman dealing with Oxford's society.

As the title suggests, the protagonist of the novel is the "hapless widower" (*Pall Mall Gazette*, 15 February 1892, no. 8394, p. 3), Edward Lygon, bursar of an Oxford college, who has just lost his beloved wife Anne and lives alone with their two little children. He has lost all interest in life and is resigned to leading a melancholy existence in the memory of Anne. The fact that his in-laws live nearby does not help him move on with his life, as they all idolize the angelic dead woman. One day, Edward meets the new lodger at his neighbour's house (on Holywell Street, the same address where Bisland was living at the time), a lively woman from the South of the United States named Georgia Wrenn. Miss Wrenn has independent financial means and is travelling on her own. With her enthusiasm and optimism, she gradually inspires Edward to enjoy life again. However, on realizing that he is falling in love with her, guilt overcomes Edward; to make things worse, rumours begin to spread all over Oxford, and Edward's mother-in-law accuses him of making himself ridiculous by running after a foreign and frivolous woman and outraging the memory of his deceased wife. Confused and overwhelmed, Edward cuts all relations with Miss Wrenn, who expresses her indignation at what she calls "your English manners and customs" (Broughton and Bisland, 1891, 142). The unhappy widower runs away with his children to a country house, intending to live a secluded life, taking long walks and telling his children stories of their mother. But he goes from the frying pan to the fire, as he falls into the clutches of a mother and daughter who plan to entrap him: he is repeatedly thrown into the company of a distant cousin, the superficial Albertina Crichton, whose mother finds all kinds of excuse to leave Edward and Albertina alone on their walks. One day, Albertina has an accident and twists her ankle: the unsuspecting victim assists her in getting up in what could look like an embrace. At that moment, they run into Miss Wrenn, who is making an excursion. Being of a generous and forgiving disposition, she behaves as cordially as ever and helps Edward, who feels relieved at her appearance, and for a moment things look promising again. Nervous about Albertina's strange behaviour, Edward decides to return to Oxford. Yet later that night the girl, shocked by his decision to leave, sneaks into Edward's room in *déshabillé* and makes a hysterical scene. At first, Edward stands still in "dumb stupefaction" and "wild terror" (Broughton and Bisland, 1891, 198–99), before Albertina throws her arms about her cousin's neck and starts sobbing violently; he tries to disentangle himself, but he is forced to stretch out his arms to prevent her from falling. At this very moment, in what seems like a carefully planned move, Mrs Crichton and a servant burst in on them. Accused of having ruined the girl, Edward is forced to marry her. The novel ends quite abruptly and totally out of character, with Edward going "raving mad" on his wedding night and dying three days later: "at the end of the week, Anne – she must have heard him after all – makes room for him beside her!" (Broughton and Bisland, 1891, 254).

The most remarkable figure in the novel is doubtlessly Georgia Wrenn, who was probably modelled on Bisland. Her introduction to Edward by his sister-in-law as "Miss Wren, the American" (Broughton and Bisland, 1891, 56) immediately marks her as an outsider. Like Bisland, Georgia comes from a Southern state; resourceful, confident, and spontaneous, she refuses to share lodgings with her respectable connections and rents a little house only for herself, thus causing a scandal among the conformist Oxonian community. Her age is not specified, but she is described as a pretty woman in her twenties. Marriage is not the first of her interests, but she is not cold: on the contrary, she is compassionate and caring, and follows her natural inclinations. The novel foregrounds Georgia's astonishment at English rigid conventionalities and, by comparing them to the more direct and progressive American ways, it probably voiced Bisland's criticism of British parochialism – and most probably Broughton's as well, who had to face the ostracism of the Oxford community for the eleven years she resided there. Georgia's observations, at times amused, other times outright frustrated, express amazement at middle-class conventionality, especially its slavery to rumours and the dread of losing one's reputation, thus avoiding what could make one happy.

Significantly, all the British women in the novel are depicted in a negative light. The Oxford ladies are malignant scandalmongers, ready to be shocked at whatever violates their strict moral and social codes; Mrs Pennington Bruce, "a burly old woman with a voice like a bull, and a fine taste for believing the worst of her neighbours" (Broughton and Bisland, 1891, 121), leads the town's gossip; she is the first to spot Edward and Georgia's budding romance and loses no time in spreading the rumour, even personally announcing it to Edward's mother-in-law, Mrs Lambart, who, in turn, gives Edward the cold shoulder and mercilessly reproaches him. Even though she has always behaved like a mother to him, at the first sign of his finding happiness again – and with an unconventional woman – Mrs Lambart turns passive-aggressive and controlling: "'now that I am home again,' putting her hand eagerly on his shoulder as if in fear of his escaping her, 'you will not want her any longer; you will not want any strangers, any forward Yankee to poke her nose into your house'" (Broughton and Bisland, 1891, 135). Mrs Lambart's only concern is what people may think of Edward's conduct, thus disclosing her small-mindedness. As for Albertina and her mother, Mrs Crichton, they act like caricatures of Jane Austen's marriage-obsessed characters, as noted by Costantini (2022, 136). "Unscrupulous, deceitful and self-interested," Mrs Crichton is "a grotesque embodiment" of the attentive mother concerned with securing a proper husband for her naive daughter (Costantini, 2022, 137).[6] The idle Albertina is an exaggeration of the shy, fragile 'womanly woman,' an idealized and old-fashioned icon that Broughton and Bisland both struggled to counteract.

The American Georgia Wrenn thus stands in open contrast to all the other female figures, challenging dominant models of womanhood: her portrayal can be read as "Broughton and Bisland's attempt to conceptualise a fresh model of femininity," built as a combination of the New

---

6 Through a close analysis of *A Widower Indeed*'s main characters, Costantini (2022) illustrates how Broughton and Bisland deconstructed dominant gender roles and contributed to late Victorian debates on evolving models of femininity and masculinity. Costantini argues that the main achievement of Broughton and Bisland's collaboration was "to stage the dilemmas and relational conflicts of an age of crisis and transition" (142).

Woman with the American Girl (Costantini, 2022, 130). The latter was a literary figure that came to the forefront in 1890s British fiction, who not only personified British anxieties about the increasing power of the United States but also triggered reflection on "the changing nature and roles of women [...] shortly before the term 'New Woman' came into vogue" (Nicholson, 2019, 179). The woman question was something that always stirred Bisland's interest, before and after the collaboration: while still in her early twenties and living in New Orleans, she established the New Orleans Woman's Club, whose goals were equal salaries for women and assistance when a member was out of work or ill (Goodman, 2013, 55). In her collection of essays *The Secret Life: Being the Book of a Heretic* she wrote: "[t]he oldest of all empires is that of man; no royal house is as ancient as his" (Bisland, 1906, 189). According to her, female characters in books had basically been reduced to two main types, "the passionless goddess and the greedy child"; tucked in "between these extremes of virtues and vices on the heroic scale, an endless chain of rosy, smiling, comfortable young persons, with the morals of rabbits and the mentality of butterflies" (Bisland, 1910, 5). Her last collection of essays, *The Truth About Men and Other Matters*, appeared in 1927 and dealt once again, among other issues, with relations between the sexes: "[t]he record of the race, hitherto accepted as the truth about ourselves, has been the story of facts and conditions as the male saw them [...] No secret has been so well-kept as the secret of what women have thought about life" (Bisland, 1927, 1). It is likely that, with *A Widower Indeed*, she and Broughton were trying to create an innovative, empowering model of femininity. Throughout the narration, Miss Wren repeatedly violates codes of proper femininity. When Edward expresses his abject misery at the gossip concerning them, an incredulous Georgia bursts out:

> "And you *mind*? You care what a lot of old *chumps* say? You mind about an old cat like Mrs. Pennington Bruce, who probably does not know enough to come in when it rains? Why, you are perfectly silly," cries she, with as fighting a light flashing in her eyes as ever shone in those of her countrymen when they gripped each other's throats in that most murderous of all recorded wars of theirs. He would be deaf indeed if he failed to hear the withering contempt in her tone; a contempt that envelops himself no less than the objects of his reprobation. (Broughton and Bisland, 1891, 145)

Her independence of thought and use of strong words are combined with other displays of unladylike behaviour, as for instance when she eats chocolate bonbons out of a bag in public, a deviation from class and gender norms prescribing the nonappetitive lady. She also likes to give chocolate to Edward's children, thus alarming their father; by indulging the siblings' love for junk food, Georgia transgresses "norms of female nurturing with which Victorian women were taught to comply" (Costantini, 2022, 132). Another deviation from ladylike conduct is exemplified by Georgia's practice of calisthenics or "Swedish Slojd": by devoting herself to athletic pursuits aimed at building a vigorous body, she is characterized "as a sensational New Woman" who does not conform to Victorian myths of feminine delicacy and weakness (Costantini, 2022, 132).

In this respect she is the opposite of the frail Albertina, for whom the walks prescribed by her mother to entrap Edward are a painful struggle. When she falls into the stream, she has to be saved by Edward and then by Georgia, who, in contrast, crosses it with ease. Albertina's self-perception as a feeble person ("'my bones are so small, that I daresay my ankle is smashed,'" Broughton and Bisland, 1891, 182) is ridiculed throughout the narration, highlighting the absurdity of linking feebleness with refinement and sensitivity. Unlike popular representations of energetic but unfeminine New Women, Georgia remains "exceedingly pretty," not in a "fragile, hothouse style, but with a wholesome, vigorous and yet sufficiently slender comeliness" (Broughton and Bisland, 1891, 64). Moreover, Georgia's love for Edward's children and her affectionate disposition configure her as a peculiar New Woman, combining 'masculine' health, robust body, and self-confidence with 'feminine' traits. Thus, Georgia's unique combination of independence and domesticity make her a positive, fresh model of femininity, in opposition to both traditional gender roles and the threatening New Woman.

Unlike the typical American Girl plot of 1890s novels, in which the wealthy foreign woman sweeps in and upsets the established order by landing a British husband, Georgia fails to invade the British marriage market. The efforts of Mrs Crichton, Mrs Lambart, and the other Oxford conformists succeed in putting an end to her relationship with Edward. Notwithstanding the fact that she is the only positive character in the novel, Georgia is defeated at the end (even though future happiness remains possible for her offstage).

If Georgia Wrenn is a particular kind of New Woman, Edward is "a neurotic New Man" (Costantini, 2022, 127). His physical weakness, his sensitivity, and his emotional disposition make him an alternative to the flat, orthodox muscularity of Victorian masculine ideals. Yet, unlike the well-managed construction of Georgia's character, Edward remains an aborted version of a possible New Man. His intrinsic conformism, indecision, and helplessness, together with his mental instability, prevent him from embodying a viable alternative. To Georgia's provocation reported above ("'And you *mind*?'"), Edward snaps: "'Yes, I *do* care. I care so much that I would give everything I possess in the world – not' – with exceeding bitterness, – 'that I do now possess anything worth giving – to stop their poisonous tongues!'" (Broughton and Bisland, 1891, 146). Edward's answer exposes his victim-like attitude, always inclined to wallow in self-pity. Furthermore, his excessive attachment to his female in-laws, his concern about the gossip among the old ladies, and his lack of male friends underline a dependence on female approval, which is an ironic reversal of codes of female dependence upon men. Edward's incapacity to control his emotionality further prevents him from embodying a new gender model. He is kind and sympathetic, but he is frequently snappy and whiny. When at the end of the novel he falls prey to hysterics, he is associated with the "female malady" theorized by Showalter (1985) – an aspect he shares with his detested second wife, Albertina, whose melodramatic behaviour had been exactly what had condemned him to the marriage. The strength, both mental and physical, and the resourcefulness that the male protagonist lacks are instead gifted to Georgia. Edward dying "raving mad" represents another interesting reversal of the conventions of the Victorian novel, which typically see women as the ones ending up as lunatics.

After being released by three publishers in the same year (J. R. Osgood, McIlvaine & Co, Appleton, and Tauchnitz), *A Widower Indeed* had only one reprint in 1892, with no subsequent editions (except for a Dutch translation, published by G. J. Slothouwer: see Wood, 1993, 185). The novel earned mixed reviews; most agreed that neither author was at her best. The general feeling among critics was that Bisland's main contribution had been to provide character details about the American co-protagonist, along with the occasional bits of Southern dialect. The press saw Miss Wrenn as a charming and fresh character, "wholesome as a summer morning," although a little "too American" in her speech, which was perceived as exaggerated (*Pall Mall Gazette*, 15 February 1892, no. 8394, p. 3). Some called it an utterly tedious and disappointing book, others conceded that the plot was engaging, but the end was universally felt to be unnecessarily bleak and hasty. This is certainly one of the novel's main flaws: the fact that the rather pathetic protagonist is the architect of his own misfortunes does not prepare readers for his unexpected death as a madman. The *Pall Mall Gazette* described it as a "grim, pitiful tragicomedy," but appreciated "the delicate insight, the humour, the sympathy with which the situation of the hapless widower is depicted" (15 February 1892, no. 8394, p. 3). The problem with *A Widower Indeed* is that it somehow fails to emotionally engage the reader: Edward's grief is made obsessive and hard to relate to; his dead wife, Anne, features as an intrusive and rather annoying memory that prevents Edward from living his life; the characterization is often sketchy and parodic; the highly overdramatic passages are alternated with long, dull parts. Crucially, Georgia is cut out of the scene way too soon: the love story between her and Edward has potential, but is not given sufficient time to bloom, making it difficult to emotionally invest in it. What could have been a passionate and transgressive love story is cut short just as it is starting to ripen.

Unlike Georgia Wrenn's, Elizabeth Bisland's English stay ended with an engagement. She went back to America, where she got married, and her book *In Seven Stages: A Flying Trip Around the World* was published and sold well. Bisland and her husband settled first in Long Island, then in Washington, D. C., where she continued to work as a journalist and published essays on various topics, from gardening to the pleasures of literature to the rights of women. Her only fictional work after the collaboration with Broughton was an autobiographical novel, *A Candle of Understanding* (1903), which was highly regarded in her time. Bisland never wrote other novels.[7] When Helen Black compiled Broughton's biography for her *Notable Women Authors of the Day* (Black, 1893, 37–44), she did not mention that Broughton ever collaborated, and the episode, together with its outcome, was soon forgotten.

---

7 Bisland married the American attorney Charles Wetmore, who worked in a Wall Street law firm. They had met in New York before her race, and he came to visit her while she was staying in England. They got married in October 1891. In 1910 Wetmore was stricken with an unidentified illness (Bisland only said that it affected his nerves). In the face of an uncertain future, Wetmore put aside his job and he and Bisland travelled together for a year through Japan, China, Singapore, Ceylon, and India, revisiting many of the places she had first seen during her world race. In 1913 the couple moved to England, looking for rest amid what Bisland remembered as the peaceful English countryside. However, soon World War I broke out; Bisland volunteered in the local hospitals for a year before returning to the USA. In June 1919 Wetmore died, after months of suffering. Bisland spent her last years travelling alone in the places she loved the most, Japan and China, writing essays and travel accounts. She died of pneumonia in January 1929, at the age of 68.

A "literary crime," or, *The Fate of Fenella*[8]

The 1890s saw the peak of the clamour for collaboration: readers' appetite for curiosities of multiple authorship was higher than ever, but the decade also represents the beginning of the end for collaboration's popularity. The culmination of the trend can be seen in the appearance of a number of multiply-authored texts, and more precisely round robin novels. Among the crowd of such works, *The Fate of Fenella* took the trend to its extremes.

The novel was commissioned by *The Gentlewoman*, an illustrated weekly priced at sixpence, where it ran serially from December 1891 (the opening chapter was the special feature of the Christmas number) to April 1892. What made *The Fate of Fenella* stand out was its writers: twenty-four among the most famed of the moment. Listing the names as they appear on the title page of the novel, they were: Helen Mathers, Justin McCarthy, Mrs Trollope, Arthur Conan Doyle, May Crommelin, F. C. Philips, 'Rita,' Joseph Hatton, Mrs Lovett Cameron, Bram Stoker, Florence Marryat, Frank Danby, Mrs Edward Kennard, Richard Dowling, Mrs Hungerford, Arthur A'Beckett, Jean Middlemass, Clement Scott, Clo. Graves, H. W. Lucy, Adeline Sergeant, G. Manville Fenn, 'Tasma,' and F. Anstey. The co-authors, both men and women writing in alternated chapters, were all well known to the public, and at least three of them – Justin McCarthy, May Crommelin, and F. C. Philips – had already taken part in collaborations.[9]

The compositional method was peculiar as well, as each author wrote one chapter simply continuing the preceding one, then passed it on to the next author, without planning or communication. A similar scheme had been adopted the year before with *A 'Novel' Novel*, written by twenty women, all amateurs and readers of *The Gentlewoman*.[10] Following the

---

8 *London Evening Standard*, 6 June 1892, no. 21191, p. 2.

9 Justin McCarthy entertained a collaborative relationship with Rosa Campbell Praed from 1886 to 1890, writing *The Right Honourable*, *The Ladies' Gallery*, and *The Rival Princess*. May Crommelin worked with James Moray Brown on *Violet Vyvian* (1889). Francis Charles Philips experienced co-authorship with different writers. Between 1889 and 1891 he co-authored some novels with C. J. Wills (*Sybil Ross's Marriage*, *The Scudamores*, and *A Maiden Fair to See*) and, at the same time, three other novels with Percy Fendall (*A Daughter's Sacrifice*, *Margaret Byng*, and *My Face is My Fortune*). In 1908 and 1910 Philips and Fendall co-authored two other novels, *Disciples of Plato* and *A Honeymoon – and After*.

10 Lady Constance Howard, Miss Lane, Mrs Laughton, Mrs Sparshott, Miss

THE

FATE OF FENELLA.

BY

HELEN MATHERS.
JUSTIN N. MCCARTHY.
MRS. TROLLOPE.
A. CONAN DOYLE.
MAY CROMMELIN.
F. C. PHILLIPS.
"RITA."
JOSEPH HATTON.
MRS. LOVETT CAMERON.
BRAM STOKER.
FLORENCE MARRYAT.
FRANK DANBY.

MRS. EDWARD KENNARD.
RICHARD DOWLING.
MRS. HUNGERFORD.
ARTHUR A'BECKETT.
JEAN MIDDLEMASS.
CLEMENT SCOTT.
CLO. GRAVES.
H. W. LUCY.
ADELINE SERGEANT.
G. MANVILLE FENN.
"TASMA."
F. ANSTEY.

IN THREE VOLUMES.

VOL. I.

LONDON:

HUTCHINSON & CO.,

25, PATERNOSTER SQUARE, E.C.

1892.

[All rights reserved.]

Figure 10. Title page of *The Fate of Fenella* (London: Hutchinson & Co., 1892). Source: the British Library, General Reference Collection DRT Digital Store 012637.i.15

success of *A 'Novel' Novel*, the magazine decided to involve professional authors and take the experiment to a further level. The compositional method deeply affected the plot of *Fenella*: having just the space of one chapter to shine, the co-authors tried their best to impress readers; hence, an accumulation of increasingly shocking events was gradually built. Moreover, as there was collaboration but no consultation between the collaborators, some parts of the plot were abandoned, and some characters distorted as the narration went on. Each chapter ends with a cliff-hanger, and the plot is very dense, boasting an assassination, a hypnotic trance, an abduction and a following pursuit across the Atlantic, an evil Frenchwoman, prophetic dreams, a shipwreck, and a visionary fire.

The novel centres on a young woman, "slangy and lively" (*London Evening Standard*, 6 June 1892, p. 2), named Fenella Ffrench, who is separated from her husband and lives alone with their child, Ronny. She has a scandalous reputation: Fenella and her ex, Frank Onslow, broke up because of mutual jealousy over each other's very public flirtations. Her suitor now is Count de Murger, while Frank keeps a mistress, Madame de Vigny. The story begins when Fenella and Frank run into each other at a hotel in Harrogate, and both realize that they still love each other, but are too proud to admit it. One night, Frank goes to Fenella's room to slip a love letter under her door but overhears the German count talking with her. Overtaken by a sudden state of trance, or sleep-walking, Frank kills the count. When he comes back to himself he is in his own room, and it is early morning. He has no recollection of what he has done. Thinking of having lost Fenella to another man, he runs away to Paris, also abandoning Madame de Vigny. Meanwhile, the police arrive at the hotel and Fenella takes the blame on herself to protect Frank: she declares that the count tried to rape her and, to defend her honour, she killed him. She is tried for murder and released thanks to the help of the faithful Mr Jacynth, a barrister who is in love with her. After the trial, a wretched Fenella retires to a secluded life on Guernsey, in the Channel Islands, leaving the care of her child to Jacynth's sister. In the meantime, Frank's abandoned mistress finds the love letter Frank had

Ernestine Tate, Mrs G. B. Burgin, Miss Emma Wylie, Miss D. Bellerby, Miss Eva Roos, Miss Kathleen Watson, Mrs J. M. Bull, Mrs J. Alexander Kennedy, Miss Ethel Mackenzie, Mrs Vallance, Miss Minnie Laud, Miss Hilda Somers, The Countess of Munster, Miss Edith Ostlere, Mrs Lena M. Horsford, and Miss Daisy Moutray Read.

intended to give Fenella on the night of the murder: on discovering that he still loves his wife, she wants revenge; she accepts the marriage proposal of an American politician, then abducts Fenella and Frank's son and travels to New York with him and her new husband. Frank and Fenella meet again by chance in Guernsey, when he learns of the terrible trial she has endured. Fenella, too stressed by the memory of recent events, has a breakdown: from this point onwards, her role becomes an increasingly passive one. On learning of their child's abduction, Frank decides to cross the Atlantic. However, once there, Madame de Vigny manages to have him declared mad and shut up in a lunatic asylum – an interesting deviation from sensation novels conventions, which usually saw women locked up in madhouses. The situation is solved by Jacynth who, for Fenella's sake, followed Frank in the pursuit. He succeeds in having Frank's former mistress arrested for child abduction, thus playing the role of the hero. While they are all returning to Europe, however, a fire started by Madame de Vigny from her ship cell breaks out, causing a shipwreck, of which Jacynth, Ronny, Frank, and Madame de Vigny (who escapes) are the only survivors. Back in Guernsey, Madame de Vigny's ex-husband finds her and tries to kill her, but Frank mercifully saves her life; she is arrested again, this time for good. Fenella and Frank can finally reunite. But a final plot twist awaits the reader: moments after their reconciliation, Frank has a heart attack and dies. The novel closes with Fenella and Ronny walking out of the house – not even too shocked – accompanied by Jacynth, on whom she has been increasingly relying and with whom she feels she will be happy again.

Immediately after the serialization, *Fenella* was published in three volumes by Hutchinson & Co. in May 1892. The volume edition was carefully designed to emphasize the multiple authorship and the names of the authors, which are insistently repeated in many places, as they constituted the most important selling factor. The cover is probably the most interesting paratextual element: it bears the facsimiles of the signatures of the twenty-four authors and is clearly designed to make the potential buyer notice at just one glance the multiple collaboration. The names of the co-writers are also indicated in the table of contents at the beginning of each volume; moreover, at the beginning of every chapter, together with its title, the name of its author is mentioned.

Authors' names were also used to effectively advertise the novel. In the advertisement in the 28 November 1891 issue of *The Gentlewoman* the names of the co-authors are listed in bold capitals; each collaborator is described as "a well-known writer of fiction" and *Fenella* as the "most

Figure 11. Cover of *The Fate of Fenella* (London: Hutchinson & Co., 1892). Source: the British Library, General Reference Collection DRT Digital Store 012637.i.15

extraordinary novel of modern times" and "a literary curiosity." The original compositional method was also a part of the advertising strategy. The sentence at the bottom of the page, "orders will be executed with strict impartiality and in the order as received," fulfils an important marketing function, as it implies crowds of readers pushing and shoving to get the latest instalment by their favourite novelist. Interestingly, at this early stage not all the authors had been enrolled yet: no precise number of co-authors is specified in the blurb. Only twenty-one writers are listed as "authors already engaged." Of this list, the first eleven would actually write the first eleven chapters, while the other names are not listed in the order in which their chapters would appear; besides, five of the final writers are still missing and there is one novelist, F. C. Burnand, who would not write any chapter at all. This tells us that *Fenella* was produced as a work in progress while it was being serialized.

A preface by J. S. Wood, editor of *The Gentlewoman*, features in the volume edition. As most prefaces, this was a presentation and a recommendation of the novel it preceded. Remarkably, however, the recommendation drew exclusively on the double originality of its composition: no word was spent on the content, on a possible message, or on the reception when first published in instalments. Apparently, the multiple authorship and the experimental way in which it was carried out were thought to be enough to catch the interest of the potential reader: "[t]hat 24 well-known writers should each be able to affirm that 'I wrote a twenty-fourth part of that novel' is sufficiently striking even in these days of literary collaboration" (Mathers et al., 1892, I, v). The fact that it took twenty-four people to make a collaboration "sufficiently striking" speaks volumes for the popularity of the practice at that time, which Wood significantly called "these days of literary collaboration." The second original feature that Wood emphasized was the peculiar way in which the authors collaborated, or rather did not collaborate in the ordinary sense of the word: "[b]ut that each [author] should further be able to say that 'I did so without any collaboration whatever, without a word exchanged, or a reference made, to my twenty-three fellow-workers' will, I think, be regarded as somewhat startling" (Mathers et al., 1892, I, v). Wood justified the choice of not letting the co-authors talk by explaining that collaboration as it was generally intended brought along many arguments and, with such a crowd involved, it would have been madness to undertake it. He ironically declared that, if he was alive to write the preface, it was thanks to this caution: "had it been otherwise […] it must have produced a literary 'Frankenstein,' which would have fallen upon and pulverised me,[11] as soon as life was breathed into it, by twenty four persons discussing plot, plan, and characters from twenty-four points of view" (Mathers et al., 1892, I, v–vi). After this, the editor quoted Besant's rule that "there must be one dominant mind responsible for the production of the work of two or more collaborators," but he added that, given the particular modality in which *Fenella* had been developed, "it would be a little difficult to apply the theory in this case" (Mathers et al., 1892, I, vi). He challenged "the intelligent reader," however, to find out who had been the dominant mind in the composition of *Fenella* – which sounds like a veiled hint at himself. This hypothesis could make sense, as it was Wood who arranged and coordinated the entire project in "ten months of patient labour" spent in "matching off a dozen pairs of authors and authoresses" (Mathers et al., 1892, I, v).

Fenella proved a success with readers: one year after its first publication, a fourth edition was being issued (advertisement in the *St. James's Gazette*, 22 June 1893). But reviews tore the novel to pieces. The *London Evening Standard* (6 June 1892, no. 21191, p. 2) called the experiment "a grotesque idea" and declared that "*The Fate of Fenella* provokes our curiosity, but is emphatically not amusing." The reviewer wrote that the result might have been better had the co-authors preserved their individualities, and "each to contribute a chapter after his or her own manner"; on the contrary, they "carefully smoothed away their own characteristic styles in order to dovetail their manner as well as their matter with what has gone before, till the whole of the book is one commonplace level." The main problem with the book, according to the *Standard*, was that there was not "a grain of commonsense" in it: although the first chapters are brisk and entertaining, after Frank's hypnotic trance and Fenella's trial the story loses all compactness and coherence – which is rather true. Until chapter VII, "the story progresses fairly. We have the separated husband and wife, the distinguished barrister, the offending attaché, the foreign adventuress [....]" but then "[readers] feel ill-used. We are accustomed to having our credulity played upon by one author at a time: but to have four-and-twenty of them set upon us at once, all the same story, and doing their worst, is rather too much." From chapter IX, the story is declared hopeless, "so that when Mrs. Lovett Cameron begins

---

11 A review criticized this passage: "[w]hat can be the meaning of this? Frankenstein was a perfectly harmless and ingenious person. Can it be that the editor fancies that the name of Frankenstein's monster was also Frankenstein?" (*Belfast News-letter*, 18 May 1892, no. 23985, p. 7).

her chapter she has hardly a fair field." By chapter XI, when little Ronny gets abducted, "we have lost all curiosity in the story," and "in the middle of the second volume it falls to pieces, and everybody seems solely put to it to carry it on at all. [...] Mr. Richard Dowling [ch. XIV], Mrs. Hungerford [ch. XV], Arthur A'Beckett [ch. XVI], and Jean Middlemass [ch. XVII] all try, and all fail." In the third volume "Clement Scott, Clo Graves, H.W. Lucy, Adeline Sergeant, George Manville Fenn, and Tasma are as dull as may be [...]." F. Anstey, the writer of the last chapter, is bitterly attacked for ending the story in the most absurd way:

> [h]e is evidently merely poking fun at every one, and deals out poetical justice with a wicked gravity [...]. The naughty Madame de Vigny is carried off by detectives, the husband and wife (she does not in the least mind his having killed her man [the Count], and no one takes any notice of that little incident) fly into each other's arms in a long embrace, and the reader imagines that they are going to live happily ever after, and leave the virtuous lover out in the cold. But not a bit of it. Lord Francis suddenly throws his arms above his head, turns sharply round three times, falls against a wire flower-stand – and it is all over. This is quite a prize method of killing off a husband. Fenella felt too much for words. "Let me lead you away," says her lover, and she lets him. She looks up at him "with child-like, appealing eyes," and "she knows that happiness will return to her" [...]: she forgets all about her rapturous reconciliation of a few minutes before, and we are rather surprised that she does not sing the irrepressible refrain of a popular song as leaning over her lover's "strong right arm," she goes out to the goat chaise. (*London Evening Standard*, 6 June 1892, no. 21191, p. 2)

The final assessment of the *Standard* was utterly negative: "[i]f *The Fate of Fenella* is meant for a joke, it is [...] a dreary one enough. As a literary experiment it is a failure [...] and it is often heavy as well as foolish reading." The critic concluded that the twenty-four co-authors committed "four-and-twenty literary crimes. They ought to be tried, convicted, and sentenced to read each other's works for four-and-twenty months."

That *Fenella* was a literary crime was an opinion shared by many. *The Graphic* wrote:

> [f]our-and-twenty authors [...] have been found to insult their art by joining in the perpetration of *The Fate of Fenella*. [...] The idea of this literary crime, of which it is to be hoped that each of the four-and-twenty offenders is heartily penitent, was to see what would happen if a story, started by one writer, were successively continued, without co-operation, by a number of others. As a joke, or a game of forfeits, the experiment might pass, if taken in

the spirit of burlesque, and as an amusement for a single winter evening; but the authors of *The Fate of Fenella* have, through some incredible perversity, taken their task seriously. The practical result is the use of their names and autographs to advertise a proof that two dozen clever people may collectively be equivalent to a single imbecile. (9 July 1892, no. 1180, p. 23)

The *St. James's Gazette* remarked that, actually, it was not so much the compositional method that was amazing, as promoted in the Editor's note, but rather "to find that as many as two dozen well-known writers could lend themselves to such an ineptitude" (7 June 1892, no. 3739, p. 6). In a review entitled "The Fun of Fenella," the *Pall Mall Gazette* imagined that the collaboration that led to the assembling of *Fenella* would become an exemplar in Walter Besant's new Academy of Fiction, where "*The Fate of Fenella* might be proposed as a text-book in the art" (21 July 1892, no. 8528, p. 3). The *Belfast News-letter* (18 May 1892, no. 23985, p. 7) described the novel as a "patchwork" and compared it to a quilt made of many different fabrics all patched up together: "[o]ur American friends have a cover which they call a crazy quilt. The *Fate of Fenella* is a literary crazy quilt." The *Aberdeen Evening Express* defined the novel "an indigestible pie" (21 April 1892, no. 3908, p. 2).

A slightly more positive opinion was expressed by the *Dundee Courier* (8 October 1892, no. 12251, p. 6), which, on the publication of *Fenella*'s cheap edition, recommended the novel to "those who delight in curiosities of literature," if only for "the novelty of the work" and as "a criterion of what may be achieved in this direction." However, it admitted that the result "conveys the impression of being [...] a story without a soul," and that "the reader can hardly escape the conclusion that the opening chapter is undoubtedly the best." Similarly, *Freeman's Journal* wrote that the compositional method had "destroyed the artistic merit" and that "the only interest of the novel is the attempt which the lover of modern popular fiction may make to read into each chapter the peculiarities of the novelist to whom it is assigned" (3 June 1892, p. 2). On the whole, *Freeman's* concluded that

> we do not think the work, though it has its good points, justifies any repetition or imitation. At the best it is a *tour de force*, and in an age of startling novelties it will doubtless attract many readers, who will, at least, have a sufficiently diversified menu to suit their palate withal. (p.2)

The radical change in Fenella's personality was largely perceived, with justice, as the most incoherent feature of the novel. The *Pall Mall Gazette* (21 July 1892, no. 8528, p. 3) pointed out how the protagonist passes almost overnight from being a lively young lady ready to flirt with any man at hand, who carries cotton-wool in her purse to stuff coach-drivers' ears and who shamelessly winks at her ex-husband, to becoming the perfectly modest and quiet domestic angel, dressed with Quaker-like simplicity. At first, Fenella is presented as a powerful *femme fatale*; the novel opens with her description, in which her eyes are compared to those of a tiger: "[h]er hair, gloves, and shoes were tan-colour, and closely allied to tan, too, was the tawny, true tiger tint of her hazel eyes" (Mathers et al., 1892, I, 3). The choice of her surname, Ffrench, is not a chance; she pretends to be a widow and flirts with Jacynth without telling him that she has a husband; her reputation is on everyone's lips. As the novel progresses, however, she becomes increasingly sober and turns into the angel of the house; her role becomes more and more passive as Jacynth starts to act on her behalf. After the trial she falls ill of brain fever, too exhausted by the events, and she essentially waits at home while her husband and her suitor go around the world making or solving problems. By the penultimate chapter Fenella has been demoted to the role of the anxious mother; now that she has become "reasonable" (Mathers et al., 1892, III, 164), Jacynth likes her even better. He appreciates her incapacity to decide for herself:

> [c]ould she belong, [Jacynth] asked himself, to the order of women of whom Dumas, fils, speaks, when he says that in certain natures the instinct of maternity overcomes the instinct of wifehood, and that the woman ceases to be wife and mother, and becomes mother and wife, or possible mother only? [...] She was amazingly reasonable now, and might develop into a delightful companion for a man of sense. [...] Another point connected with the present state of affairs, which it was pleasant to be reminded of, was the way in which Fenella seemed to lean upon him. She would open the door [...] at all hours of the day to ask him to decide this or that question for her. (Mathers et al., 1892, III, 164)

From her initial fierce independence, living alone with her son away from her estranged husband, she becomes progressively more child-like and dependent upon the barrister's help: "Fenella allowed herself to be guided by him; she had got so much into the habit of depending entirely upon him lately that somehow it felt the natural thing to do" (Mathers et al., 1892, III, 226). The final image of the protagonist is that of a person with "childlike, appealing eyes" (Mathers et al., 1892, III, 229) who asks Jacynth what she is to do next. So, then, her tiger eyes have also changed. That *Fenella* appeared in *The Gentlewoman* suggests the readership it was aimed at: the magazine dealt with fashion, beauty, household matters, and gossip, and it was targeted at middle-class women. The taming of Fenella could thus be read as a message to its lady readers in an age when women were dangerously starting to emancipate themselves.

As the press observed, *The Fate of Fenella* and similar experiments were remarkable more for being freaks of literature than for an intrinsic artistic value. The year before *Fenella*'s publication, James Brander Matthews had theorized that multiple collaborations were "a woeful waste of effort" (Matthews, 1891, 4), "mere curiosities of literature," and that "[n]othing of real value is likely to be manufactured by a joint stock company of unlimited authorship" (Matthews, 1891, 4–5). His choice of words aptly highlighted the commercial quality of multiple partnerships. He went as far as to proclaim that double writing was "the only collaboration worthy of serious criticism" (Matthews, 1891, 5) and that "literary collaboration might be defined, fairly enough, as the union of two writers for the production of one book" (Matthews, 1891, 5). He had a point, especially when the multiple collaboration was carried out under the circumstances of *Fenella* – with his own country being not exempt from this appetite either. Even the showman P. T. Barnum rode the wave of enthusiasm for multiply-authored fiction and produced his own *Great Composite Novel*, entitled *His Fleeting Ideal. A Romance of Baffled Hypnotism*, written with eleven co-authors and serialized in the *Boston Globe* in 1890.[12] Coherently with what he had declared, Matthews turned down an invitation to participate in the multiple collaboration on *The Whole Family* (1907–08), commissioned and coordinated by the editor of *Harper's Bazar*, Elizabeth Jordan (who wrote a chapter herself) as part of her effort to generate publicity for the magazine. *The Whole Family* was co-authored by twelve writers (including Henry James), and, like *Fenella*, was a collaborative but not a cooperative novel; again like *Fenella*, each co-author wrote a chapter, but, differently from it, no instalment was accompanied by its author's name: readers were invited to guess who might be responsible for each chapter. Readers of *Harper's Bazar* eagerly embraced the challenge; the magazine published their letters, although neither confirming nor denying their suppositions. Only in the final instalment were the chapters attributed. As Ashton (2003, 147) notes, *The Whole Family* was even more remarkable because

---

12 John L. Sullivan, Bill Nye, Ella Wheeler Wilcox, Major Alfred C. Calhoun, Howe & Hummel, Inspector Byrnes, Pauline Hall, Miss Eastlake, W. H. Ballou, Nell Nelson, and Alan Dale.

Figure 12. Frontispiece of *The Fate of Fenella* (London: Hutchinson & Co., 1892). Source: the British Library, General Reference Collection DRT Digital Store 012637.i.15

it made its appearance at a point when the serial novel in America had almost disappeared, and its challenge was to be original and compelling enough to keep long-term interest; it was "truly a product of the end of the serial era."[13]

Interestingly, many of the last big collaborative efforts at the turn of the century were from the hands of groups of women exclusively. For instance, *The Affair at the Inn* (1904) was jointly written by the sisters Mary and Jane Findlater with their friends Kate Douglas Wiggin and Allan McAulay (pen name of Charlotte Stewart). The novel consists of a light-hearted story related through diary passages by the four main characters, each assigned to one of the four co-authors, with the division explicitly declared at the beginning. The collaboration was repeated in 1911 with *Robinetta*. The popularity of the female group novel was so widespread that *MacMillan's Magazine* (November 1901, pp. 70–80) issued an anonymous parodic response to it. "The Mystery of Collaboration (A Practical Experiment)" is a story that parodies a women's round robin group trying to co-author a novel, which goes disastrously wrong. A

---

13 See Ashton's analysis of *The Whole Family* (2003, 127–66).

serious crisis arises within the Minerva Literary Society – an exclusive club of seven young ladies "who had banded themselves together for the purpose of improving their minds on Thursday afternoons" united by "an ardent desire for the higher, indeed for the highest, culture" (70). They have had a terrible fight over the choice of readings and guests to invite. The Society's secretary is desperate to find a solution to bring the group back together. Thus, her brother (not without a certain malice) suggests that the ladies might co-author a novel and have it published, as "'[t]here's nothing like seeing yourself in print to put you in a good temper'" (72). The ladies all agree that they need "a wider scope for [their] energies" (73) and enthusiastically embark upon the project. They immediately agree on the cover design, but cannot quite decide what to write: "'But what do people write, when they want to write something, and don't know what?' said Miss Delabere. 'Novels, I suppose,' answered her friend" (72–73). So they set on a novel of romance and mystery, made up of seven parts, each to be written by one member of the Society: "'then all we have to do is to add the parts together and the novel will be ready'" (73). The ladies chose a title (*Aglione's Sweetheart, or The Weird of Deadly Grange*, to conciliate those who wanted to write of love and those who wished for a Gothic story), then roughly delineated the plot, to be developed single-handedly in chapters, one continuing the preceding one, without any communication or any word limit.

After four months of hard work, the ladies set up a meeting to read aloud their respective parts to their fellow members. The girl in charge of the first part starts reading, and it turns out that she has written the whole story by herself, so when the turn of the lady entrusted with the second part comes, the day is almost over. They agree to continue the meeting the next day, but the atmosphere is already one of "mutual suspicion" (77). During the following days, things go on as before: each girl has written a whole novel by herself. In the meantime, "all the members felt rather as if they were sitting upon a volcano, which might begin operations at any moment" (77). Each authoress reproaches the writer of the preceding turn for leaving her with no main events, for killing characters she needed, or for setting something into a different scenery than the one she had imagined:

> "I should like to know what she thought she was leaving for me! If Miss Trevor has made nonsense of her part, she has made mine ever worse, because when my turn came I had to marry lots of people for the third time. And what right she had to send the wicked uncle and aunt to penal servitude

when I wanted to use them again? It seems so silly to have to use people who have been killed once and afterwards sent to penal servitude, and it makes my last chapter, where they die, quite worthless." (79)

However, no one wants to alter or cut down her part, since they had taken so much trouble writing it. Violent discussions ensue, in which each proposes to censure the others. Notwithstanding the emotional disposition of the young women, no tears are shed: "the subject was too serious for weeping, and it may be that the consciousness that they were now authoresses in their own right sustained them in the hour of trial" (78). At the end, each publishes her own part as an independent novel. The Society is officially dissolved, and no one remains on speaking terms with the others.

The *MacMillan*'s satiric story is evidence that literary collaboration really caught the popular imagination, as the next chapter will further explore. But it also tells us that at the turn of the century it courted a certain disdain as a method of writing tainted with femininity and amateurism, destined to end in nothing but disaster.

CHAPTER FOUR

Literary Collaboration and the Late Victorian Imagination

So far, we have investigated the activity of some significant collaborators, analysed how they worked together, and explored their literary output. This chapter shifts the focus of the book from authors to readers: how did the late Victorian audience – one used to imagining the creative act as a solitary activity – react to the unprecedented expansion of literary collaboration?

As collaborative writing gained popularity, people paid more and more attention to it. The sharing of the textual space triggered a lively debate over the benefits and the limits of writing in double harness, as it was often called. Crucially, the idea of writing in partnership had become very popular and yet was very difficult to explain: the ways to collaborate were countless, the levels of actual cooperation varied, and the accounts of former agents in the practice ranged from stories of idyllic companionship to acrimonious literary divorces. In fact, collaboration eluded definite understanding. The more pervasive the phenomenon, the more people felt the need to discuss it in an attempt to dispel the mystery. This chapter addresses some crucial questions concerning the relationship between literary collaboration and the late Victorian public: how did the reader look at a shared creative act? Which were the most frequent questions people asked themselves about the collaborative process? Which aspects of joint authorship were the public most curious about, and which aspects did it stigmatize? In brief, how was literary collaboration represented by the late Victorian imagination, and how did the discourse change over the years, as the popularity of co-authorship increased, reached its peak, and eventually declined?

A way to answer these questions is to look at the periodical press of the time. In the last decades of the nineteenth century newspapers and magazines were so many and so pervasive that they played a prominent role in shaping the tastes and the lifestyle of the average Victorian. Periodicals both influenced and mirrored public opinion, being the natural home for discussion of the hot topics of the moment. By looking at articles on co-authored fiction, this chapter delves into the discourse about literary collaboration that developed in the British periodical press from the second half of the nineteenth century to about 1900.

Predictably, the highest number of articles on collaboration corresponds to a peak in the publication of co-authored novels: the 1890s were the years that saw the most intense discussion and a crucial moment in terms of critical interest was 1892, the year of Besant's "On Literary Collaboration." As for the papers that dealt with literary collaboration, *The Era* was a leading title during the 1880s and the 1890s. Originally a Sunday paper concerned with politics, after mid-century and various changes of editors it grew into a far more commercial success, and the theatre gradually became its main focus, so that *The Era* eventually became known as "The Great Theatrical Journal." In the last decades of the century it was regarded as perhaps the most important theatrical paper in London, a status symbol for those who carried it under their arm, with a lofty price of sixpence. A direct, cheaper competitor of *The Era* was *The Stage*, which also presented many articles on collaboration. It began publication as a monthly, priced at 3d, but by 1890 it had become a weekly and its price had dropped to 2d. It is not surprising that *The Era* and *The Stage* featured an impressive number of articles on collaboration: co-authorship had a long tradition in playwriting. Although they dealt primarily with drama, these papers prove to be valuable resources for our purposes: they usually start discussing a specific collaboration on a play and most of the times end up making general reflections on co-authorship as a literary practice.

The daily *London Evening Standard* published almost as many articles on collaboration as *The Era*, especially in the 1880s. Starting in 1827 as *The Standard*, by 1860 it had a morning and an evening edition, the latter eventually becoming the only edition. Generally conservative, it was known for its domestic and foreign news coverage, but also for its attention to the arts. In 1858 its price dropped from 5d to just one penny, thus becoming accessible to virtually everybody. The *Pall Mall Gazette*, the *St. James's Gazette*, the *Glasgow Herald*, *The Globe*, and the *Morning Post* also frequently discussed collaboration. Among these titles, only *The Globe* dealt primarily with art and literary topics. A London evening newspaper founded as a booksellers' trade journal originally supporting the Whigs, in 1866 it adopted a conservative stance and presented itself as a literary paper for London's educated classes. It became progressively cheaper, until, in 1870, it was finally priced at one penny. All the other journals dealing with co-authorship were popular penny dailies that reported general news and were aimed at a mass readership. The *Morning Post* and the *Glasgow Herald* were newspapers with a long tradition, as both had been established at the end of the eighteenth century and were respectively priced at six and seven pence; their prices steadily decreased over the course of the century, both turning into penny dailies by 1881. During the 1880s and 1890s the *Morning Post* maintained its blend of news from home and abroad, but also made space for fashionable society and advertisements; the *Glasgow Herald* started to allot more space to articles on literature and art from the late 1870s.

This quick overview testifies to the wide appeal of literary collaboration: what emerges is that the phenomenon was not at all confined to the sole attention of an elite of intellectuals or upper-class readers. On the contrary, the idea of collaboration entered the popular imagination and was mostly discussed by the regular, widely read newspapers. These periodicals are interesting for their news and advertising sections as well, which often reported curious real-life cases that bear witness to the pervasiveness of literary collaboration deep down into the layers of Victorian society.

The craze of the hour

Well into the nineteenth century literary collaboration was discussed in British newspapers almost exclusively in connection with the theatre. Collaboration had indeed a long tradition in stage-writing: Elizabethan dramatists collaborated largely and famously, and co-authorship remained a regular practice in playwriting over the centuries. "The providers of our daily dramatic diet have hardly produced one play a-piece single-handed," *The Graphic* observed, adding that joint authorship had given origin to "the greatest comic masterpieces of modern days" (13 September 1884, no. 772, p. 22).

Collaboration started to be associated with fiction mainly thanks to two Frenchmen, Emile Erckmann and Alexandre Chatrian. Erckmann and Chatrian met in 1847 when both were in their twenties; they became friends and spent the summer roaming in the Vosges. Their first novel was serialized in 1849, but fame came only ten years later with *L'Illustre Docteur Matheus* (their 1850 drama *L'Alsace en 1814* was a success but was banned after only two days). Praised by Émile Zola and Victor Hugo, they enjoyed international fame. The British press often compared them to Walter Scott, and their work was said to "have done for [Alsatia] what the Waverley novels did for Scotland" (*Aberdeen Free Press*, 22 August 1889, no. 6409, p. 4). When collaboration is mentioned in British newspapers during the 1860s and the 1870s it is frequently in connection with Erckmann and Chatrian, or with France in general. As a consequence, sarcastic or anti-French comments sometimes appeared: "[t]he art of welding two or more brains together [...] is supposed to be of essentially French growth – because, we have occasionally heard, it favours French indolence and superficiality. Collaboration is part of a vicious French literary system" (*The Graphic*, 29 January 1876, vol. 13, no. 322, p. 16).

The French novelists' writing partnership was considered to have set the example for British co-authors. From the early 1870s British co-authored fiction began to be discussed thanks to Besant and Rice. As seen in chapter 1, from 1872 to 1881 the works of Besant and Rice's literary firm appealed to readers and critics alike, and co-authorship in fiction writing started to seriously enter the public discourse. Besides, while the collaboration continued, neither of the two partners made any declaration as to how it worked, so that there was space enough for the press to speculate. Their well-constructed and amusing stories, with their smart dialogue, were often said to be suitable for the stage: thus, the link between collaboration and drama continued. Besant and Rice were compared to Erckmann and Chatrian, and were generally acknowledged as the English pioneers of collaboration in fiction writing: "our playwrights have frequently collaborated since the birth of the English drama; but Messers. Besant and Rice may be said to have set the fashion with English novelists" (*St. James's Gazette*, 12 July 1887, p. 3).

Owing to the success of Besant and Rice, around the mid-1870s co-authorship was usually represented by the periodical press as an original practice that could improve any work of fiction. Collaborating was still uncommon, and the press recommended it as a brilliant new device to produce better texts. In 1874 the *Morning Post* published an account of the collaboration between two fictional French writers with evocative names, the elderly M. Cocasse ('funny, quirky'), and the young M. Poupette, who, as suggested by his name, is manoeuvred like a puppet by his colleague into entering a literary partnership:

> [b]etween them there is little in common [...] but M. Cocasse has reached a time of life when ideas begin to fail him, and he is *constantly on the prowl after*

young and raising authors with whom he may strike up a collaboration – they furnish plots and he the dramatic ordinance of the same. [...] [M. Cocasse] looks like a pensioned gendarme in easy circumstances, and he rather startled rosy, yellow-haired M. Poupette when *he button-holed him at the Français and proposed that they should mount a "machine" together*. M. Poupette had never heard any work of literature described as "machine," nor had he ever met a man of letters so uncommonly shrewd in all the business details of authorship as M. Cocasse. [...] [M. Poupette] had sense enough to suspect that *he was wanting in the dramatic knack*, and that he well-knew that M. Cocasse possessed this knack to the full; on the other hand, M. Cocasse, glancing at M. Poupette's brow, [...] felt that *there must be a stock of ideas in this youth which would yield like a mine if worked judiciously*. So the two very soon came to an arrangement in the café of the Français, drinking beer. (*Morning Post*, 15 August 1874, no. 31864, p. 3; my emphases)

This sort of collaboration could prove useful for both parties: the older author would bring experience, technical skills, and diligence into the partnership, which would compensate for the younger partner's inclination to get distracted, despite the fresh ideas they would offer. Collaboration is represented here not as a spontaneous creative act but as an artificial activity undertaken in order to assemble a well-structured novel. This, however, was not presented in a negative light: quite the contrary, it was put forward as a model. In this period literary collaboration was simply seen as a good way to improve a text, from a two-is-better-than-one perspective. In 1878 a review in *The Graphic* wished that the author of *John Orlebar* had recurred to a helping hand (the novel came out anonymously, but the author was James Franklin Fuller):

> [a]fter reading a book like this, one cannot help regretting that the art of effective literary collaboration should, as far as novels go, seem a secret only possessed by Messers. Besant and Rice. Why should not a novelist in many ways so highly gifted as the author of *John Orlebar* have not been able to secure the aid of a colleague with just that fair turn for construction [...] ? (*The Graphic*, 16 March 1878, no. 433, p. 7)

The reviewer comments that the novel lacks action and a well-built plot: two shortcomings that a collaborator with a "turn for construction" could have easily remedied. Remarks of this kind were not unfrequent.

By the 1880s the press acknowledged that co-authorship in fiction writing had become a trend, and articles simply entitled "Collaboration" are easy to find. In 1882 the *Irish Times* observed that "literary partnership [...] is more in vogue than ever, and soon we may expect to find every other title-page inscribed with joint authors' names" (13 October 1882, no. 7959,

p. 5). In a letter to the editor of the *St. James's Gazette* in 1886, a reader complained that "[i]n your article on Collaboration sufficient stress is not perhaps laid on the extent to which literary collaboration is carried on at present" (7 September 1886, no. 1953, p. 4). This points to the fact that readers were aware of the amount of co-authored fiction available on the market, so much so that the writer of the letter felt the urge to underline the weight of the phenomenon.

In these years there were no particular worries about the diffusion of collaboration, and its popularity was presented in optimistic terms. The general idea seemed to be that collaboration was a good recipe for success: "[p]eople can collaborate either for business purposes or for pleasure, and the result is notoriety [...]. Literary collaboration in all its branches [...] has most frequently been attended with considerable success," commented the *Glasgow Evening News* (15 February 1888, no. 5665, p. 6). The article further reflected that, if two authors were successful separately, "[i]n collaboration they should make success doubly sure" (p. 6). The *Aberdeen Free Press* declared that co-authorship had "reached a point hitherto unknown in literature, especially in this country" (22 August 1889, no. 6409, p. 4) and the *Freeman's Journal* predicted that "[l]iterary collaboration is likely to become the craze of the hour" (3 June 1892, p. 2). In the same year, *Hearth and Home* classified collaboration as "one of the literary features of our age," and offered the following ironic but somewhat disquieting picture:

> at the present rate of progression there seems to be some prospects of its attaining alarming proportions in the future. The saying "Two heads are better than one" may develop eventually into "Four heads are better than two," and already there is in our midst a sort of literary centipede, each separate leg of which has been put into its place by a separate author. (*Hearth and Home*, 11 February 1892, no. 39, p. 1)

The increasing pervasiveness of collaboration is here recognized, but not only: the expansion of the practice is also seen as potentially "alarming." The co-authored text is depicted as somewhat monstrous, contaminated, a sort of Frankenstein's monster made up of different pieces of diverse origins, the result being unnatural and inharmonious, if not utterly unsettling: collaboration was beginning to acquire pejorative connotations. But why did late Victorians start to find co-authorship so troubling? One of the reasons could certainly be that, by the 1890s, it had become such a trend that it was often practised for business reasons only, thus producing much less blended texts that were generally of a markedly lower quality. But that would not explain its being "alarming." We shall look deeper into the question in the next sections.

Sociability, domestic bliss, and marriage

The sharing of the creative act was often associated with a harmonious comradeship of the collaborators. The early and most productive collaborations were grounded on a personal bond between the co-authors, who were friends or relatives, and the writing relationship was more or less interwoven with the emotional one. Besant recalled how he and Rice used to spend their days in each other's company, not only working but also having their meals together, playing cards, and going to the theatre; Somerville repeatedly voiced her nostalgic attachment to the days spent outdoors with Martin, riding, strolling, and talking their novels into existence; Lang and Haggard used to eat together at the Savile Club while working on *The World's Desire*. Apparently, the convivial side of collaboration was a prominent part of the whole experience. The periodical press promoted an image of collaborators as spending most of their time together in a pleasant and relaxed atmosphere, working and conversing over meals, walks, and various social activities. Conviviality and comradeship were thus seen as two key aspects of literary partnership. Co-authors were often represented as a unity, a cell, so much so that collaboration was sometimes labelled literary twinship.

Significantly, the *Morning Post* article mentioned above on the fictional alliance of Cocasse and Poupette was entitled "Seaside Collaboration," and described in great detail the co-authors' pleasurable residence in a resort in France (15 August 1874, no. 31864, p. 3). To better write together, the two left the chaos of the city and headed to the relaxing and secluded atmosphere of a small seaside town. They spent their journey talking and planning what to do once in the sole, delightful company of each other. However, the many diversions that waited for the two famous artists soon enough distracted them, as "no prince gets such a reception in a French hotel as an author of celebrity" (p. 3). In particular, the undesired attentions of two fashionable ladies took up all the time of the younger collaborator: "when ladies are good enough thus to lot out the hours of an artist or literary man, they leave him not five minutes for work, concluding, apparently, that he gets through his labours at night while other people sleep." But the vigilant Cocasse was "on the look-out," and saved his young friend, taking him back to their rooms, where they could finally talk, eat, smoke, and write.

Even if their alliance is aimed at producing a text, the emotional and convivial aspects are emphasized. Erckmann and Chatrian, too, used to live together "when they had any literary project on foot" (*Freeman's Journal*, 6 September 1890, p. 5). In the first edition of the *Dictionary of National Biography*, which started to appear in print in 1885, emphasis was given to the personal relationship between Beaumont and Fletcher: the *Dictionary* reports that, for most of their collaborative years, they lived together on the Bankside in Southwark, near the Globe, and were so united that they shared bed and clothes (Stephen, 1885, 55). The author of Beaumont's entry, A. B. Grosart, took care to underline that "the literary partnership, born of close intimacy, was not one of the sordid arrangements made between needy playwrights [...]; it arose at their own, not at any theatrical manager's prompting" (55).

The idea of collaboration as consisting of intimacy and isolation from society became the norm. The fact that it also involved entertainments of various sorts enjoyed by the literary friends between one writing session and another was also so common that in 1884 *The Graphic* denounced literary partnership in polemical terms, concluding that "[i]n all collaborations there is an inconceivable amount of cigarette-smoking, an extraordinary number of *café* appointments. It will be seen it is not an eminently moral institution" (13 September 1884, no. 772, p. 22). *The Graphic* gave voice to a part of the public opinion which perceived co-authorship as a less than decent occupation: if a writer engaged in a collaboration, it was implied that not much time would be devoted to working – much more time, in fact, would be spent in diversions and amusements. The act of co-authoring a novel, laden as it was with these negative connotations, thus became potentially harmful for one's reputation. *The Graphic* had already criticized collaboration as early as 1876, when it had connected it with France, indolence, and "eternal cups of coffee in the boulevards" (29 January 1876, vol. 13, no. 322, p. 16).

Co-authorship was often represented as a social activity rather than a serious artistic commitment. In the short story "Collaboration" (*The English Illustrated Magazine*, vol. 9, 1892, pp. 911–21), Henry James gave much emphasis to the social, and the somewhat immoral, aspects of collaboration. When the protagonist, the French poet Félix Vendemer, proposes the arrangement to his German friend Herman Heidenmauer, he says: "[w]e will dine together [...] at one of those characteristic places, and we will discuss [...] we'll go out and we'll walk together. We'll talk a great deal" (James, 1892, 918). Vendemer even gives up his engagement – although "he was really in love" (921) – to focus on the collaboration, also because his fiancée's mother opposes the venture.[14] The breaking of the engagement is the condition to form a new, more fulfilling connection, a "sacred engagement," as he ecstatically calls it (918). Then the two collaborators, looking for isolation, move to Genoa, "where sunshine is cheap and tobacco bad, where they live (the two together) for five francs a day, which is all they can muster between them" (921). Vendemer and Heidenmauer know that the public will consider their secluded collaboration an "unnatural alliance" (921) and an "unholy union" (921). The story ends with them being "very poor" (921) but happily engaged in their work.

In James's story, the idea of living together in poverty but in mutual sympathy is foregrounded. This was an aspect of collaboration often highlighted by the magazines too. In 1899 *Punch* parodied an advertisement which had appeared in the *Daily News*, which read: "[l]iterary collaboration or companionship. Author and Journalist, 39, would like to go shares in very cheap living with another." The poem in *Punch* was entitled "Grub Street Echoes" and went as follow:

I am growing sick and weary
Of the attic dull and dreary
Where in solitary state I wake and sleep,
And I want some fellow-sinner
Who will share my frugal dinner,
But the living must be very, very cheap.
Now the kind of man I've painted
In my mind, is one acquainted
With the shallows when the tide of Fortune's neap;
Who is not above tripe suppers,
Or a patch upon his uppers,
For the living must be very, very cheap.
One who scorns the oyster season,
When he has the feast of reason
And the flow of soul, whereof he drinketh deep –
It is advantageous, very

---

14 The fiancée's mother feels offended because Vendemer's collaborator is German, and her husband was killed by a German soldier. By associating with a compatriot of his father-in-law's murderer the protagonist is accused of dragging the family into shame, and is charged with monstrous perversity. Koestenbaum (1989, 143–44) argues that the mother-in-law's charges of immorality might be due to the shadow of homosexual ties rather than to xenophobic prejudices.

> To prefer bright soul to sherry
> Or to claret, when your living must be cheap.
> One who doesn't care a button
> If he has no beef nor mutton
> So his LAMB be there to bid him laugh or weep;
> Doesn't mind if egg's denied him
> If his BACON is beside him,
> Doesn't grumble though his living's very cheap.
> Doesn't think it really matters
> Though one's coat should be in tatters,
> And one's elbow through one's shirt-sleeves sometimes peep;
> With a friend like this to like one
> I believe 'twould seldom strike one
> That the living was so very, very cheap.
> (Punch, 15 November 1899, vol. 117, p. 237)

Significantly, the writer is looking for a "fellow-sinner," as if alluding to the view of collaboration as something indecent. Their dinners would be "frugal," their coats "in tatters," they would have patches upon their sleeves, but they would find consolation in literature and in each other's company.

Advertisements of people looking for a collaborator such as the one lampooned in *Punch* were not uncommon in those years. On the contrary, it is quite easy to find notices written by people who, allured by the popularity of the practice, ventured to advertise for a writing partner. Here are some examples taken from the "Situations Vacant and Wanted" and the literary sections of the *Daily News*:

> [w]ell-known Novelist-Dramatist requires a clever and bright Collaborator; preference given to one with private income, with spare time and fond of literary work. – Write Novelist, care of 54, New Oxford-street, W.C. (5 May 1894, no. 21790, p. 11)
>
> Bright young lady, with literary experience and connection, fluent writer, knowledge shorthand, to collaborate with author or dramatist: references exchanged. (18 July 1894, no. 21853, p. 9)
>
> Man of Eminence (Novelist, Dramatist) standing quite alone. Wishes to meet with a bright collaborator, lady or gentleman, of independent means and literary taste; advertiser (himself of independent means), a great traveler, linguist, and accomplished musician, could arrange for board and residence if a suitable, refined home is offered. – Write Confidence, Willing's, 152, Piccadilly. (2 May 1894, no. 21787, p. 10)

In the last advertisement, the aspiring collaborator proposes living together with his hypothetical partner, reinforcing the link between literary collaboration and domesticity. Even if sometimes characterized by (at least initial) poverty, the image of two co-authors living in domestic bliss was widespread. The ideal relationship between the literary partners was described as one of affection and mutual understanding. Very often such domestic harmony was represented in terms of marriage. An article in the *Glasgow Evening News* in 1888 was entitled "Stable Companions," and "companionship/stable companionship" were used as a regular synonyms for collaboration (15 February 1888, no. 5665, p. 6). Besant and Matthews linked collaboration to marriage, with the latter distinguishing between literary monogamists and polygamists (Matthews, 1891, 23). Besant made a distinction between "brief and fleeting partnerships, like amourettes of an hour" ("Lit. Coll.," 202) and long-lasting writing relationships. Both remarked that the recipe for a good collaboration was the same as the recipe for a happy marriage, and both warned that such a serious commitment was not to be taken lightly: Besant went to great lengths to discourage young writers from entering into a literary partnership with someone they did not know very well. If collaborators were compared to married partners, the act of writing was often equated with labour, with the co-authored text frequently represented as a child. The idea was already present in the 1860s, as can be seen from the prefaces to two collections of short stories, *A Bunch of Keys: Where They Were Found and What They Might Have Unlocked* (1865), and *Rates and Taxes and How They Were Collected* (1866), multiply-authored by six authors.[15] In the preface to the first collection, the collaborative book is said to be "the growth of a friendly communion, of pleasant chats of an evening, of fellowship of taste and feeling. It is a pet child – a hobby of ours in short, and a labour of love" (Hood et al., 1866, vi). In the preface to the following collection, the authors "submit the result of their united labours to the public" (Hood et al., 1866, vii).

Fights, scandals, and divorce

Collaboration was associated with marriage, but divorce stood lurking on the threshold. As co-authorship became a fashionable practice, more and more writers engaged in joint literary projects mainly for economic gain, and lacking the right attitude. In contrast to the serene image of two co-authors living in their domestic paradise, the idea of

---

[15] Thomas Hood, Thomas W. Robertson, Thomas Archer, William S. Gilbert, William J. Prowse, and Clement W. Scott.

collaboration as merely a business arrangement became progressively pervasive. Collaboration could be "a kind of intellectual joinery," *The Graphic* commented as early as 1876 (29 January, vol. 13, no. 322, p. 16). Some years later, it lamented the loss of "the old Arcadian collaboration of other days – the union of two sympathies, the marriage of two talents" to "the association of two cheque books," and reflected that "[p]urely commercial partnerships are rapidly succeeding to the literary friendships. [...] The collaborateurs of our days are nearly all men of business, and have little more than business relations one with another" (13 September 1884, no. 772, p. 22). The article called contemporary collaborators "manufacturers," ready to work with anybody capable of enhancing their reputation; such partnerships were defined as "monster machines" which produced "less glory but more hard cash" (p. 22). The association of collaboration with manufacturing is significant, as it implies the idea of co-authorship as basically consisting of a combination of skills: in this light, writing a literary text is like assembling an industrial product.

With such premises and almost no laws to regulate authorial rights, quarrels between literary partners broke out on a regular basis. After acknowledging that "[c]ollaboration in literature, in which the collaborators share the work, the pay, and the glory, was probably never so common in this country as at present," the *Edinburgh Evening Dispatch* stated that the public "would like to know the methods," but that "[a]ll is sure is that by and by the collaborators will quarrel, when each will insist that he is the real author" (27 November 1889, no. 1221, p. 2). The article remarked that

> [p]ossibly a few find collaboration an actual benefit, but the majority admit that it is a mistake. [...] The talk over plots is doubtless useful, but, after that, collaboration must be a nuisance. If they write alternate chapters the absurdity of the thing comes home to them at once, and they generally quarrel. No two writers want to work out an idea in precisely the same way, and so there is a danger of perpetual wrangling. (p. 2)

The *Aberdeen Journal* observed that

> [i]n England the principles of collaboration seem, morally speaking, so little understood that the columns of the *Era* are constantly filled with boasts, counter-boasts, accusations, and recriminations exchanged between gentlemen who, after proclaiming themselves joint authors of a particular piece, have afterwards fallen out as to which of the two did the best part of the work. (8 September 1886, no. 9851, p. 2)

The Era, but also *The Standard*, were well known for filling their pages with controversies over authorial rights between former collaborators. Petty yet lengthy disputes arose and escalated in the form of letters to the editor. Sometimes they were even taken to court. An example is the protracted lawsuit between a Mr Norton and a Mr Freeland reported by *The Era* in 1896. Apparently, Mr Norton purchased a short story from Mr Freeland, completed it, and then had it published as a co-authored work under their two names. Some time afterwards, the 'original' author, Mr Freeland, claimed total authorship over the work, disowning Mr Norton as a collaborator. To this, Mr Norton replied that he had regularly paid for the purchase, and could even produce a receipt, so that the ownership of the text was to be divided between the two of them. An extract from a letter by Mr Norton to the editor of *The Era* shows how these lawsuits drew heavily on the language of commerce:

> Mr. Freeland says that I did not purchase the story from him without restrictions, but that the transaction was in the form of a loan. Well. I *have his receipt for the sum I paid* him lying before me at the present moment, and I repeat that *the purchase was absolutely without restrictions*. I know nothing of any 'understanding' that Mr. Freeland could at any time have the copyright back by repayment of the amount received; and even if such an idea were mooted, three years have elapsed without his ever showing the slightest anxiety to resume authorship. (16 May 1896, no. 3008, p. 12; my emphases)

Mr Norton conceded that he had not collaborated to the writing of the original story but, since he had added one-fourth new matter, and had pruned and altered a portion of the remainder, he felt justified in associating his name with Mr Freeland as a joint author. He added: "I have no personal motives to serve in linking my name with his, as my name is sufficiently well-known in the literary world. It was simply in fairness to Mr. Freeland that I did so" (*The Era*, 16 May 1896, no. 3008, p. 12).

A notorious lawsuit was that between Erckmann and Chatrian in 1889. The divorce after forty years of collaboration was caused by an economic misunderstanding over the dramatization of one of their novels: each author claimed to have contributed more than the other to the writing of the book, and hence to be entitled to more profits when it was sold to be staged. The quarrel grew increasingly bitter (and public), and British newspapers reported the news with emotional participation. The *Aberdeen Free Press* dedicated a long article to it, commenting that "the friendship – the rarest type of friendship that exists – of forty years has been irrevocably broken, and in all probability their work is at an end [...] Some misunderstanding as to the profit has arisen, and the literary friends of nearly half a century have become sworn foes" (22 August 1889, no. 6409, p. 4). Comparing the collaborators to Siamese twins, the article wondered whether, "like the physical life of the twinship, the literary life of each twin has not ceased forever. [...] It is difficult to imagine that two minds so long linked together, and invariably linked together, can work apart" (p. 4). They could not, and Chatrian's death the following year put an end to hopes of a possible reconciliation:

> [t]he connection between Messers. Erckmann and Chatrian, whose differences have just been finally adjusted by the death of M. Chatrian, is an even more striking example of the difficulty of keeping a literary partnership intact. The two Alsatians had collaborated for forty years, when they suddenly discovered that they could not get on together. This tardy repugnance is to be seen sometimes between old married people [...]. In the Erckmann case one of the partners thought that he was doing all the work while the other spent most of his time sitting at the receipt of custom. So they quarreled and went their ways, and litigated. (*St James's Gazette*, 4 September 1890, p. 4)

The literary partners were compared to "old married people" who, after decades of intimacy, could no longer stand each other's company. Nine years later, Erckmann's death raised a new wave of reflections on the harsh end of the collaboration, but this time in less sentimental and more cynical terms: by the turn of the century, the atmosphere had definitely changed and opinions on collaboration were increasingly negative. The *St. James's Gazette* pondered:

> [i]n place of a literary firm one and indivisible, there were revealed to the world two squabbling Alsatians. [...] At least there would have been some compensation if litigation had led to any trustworthy revelation of the practice of literary collaboration and the shares of each author in the joint work. [...] Attempts have not been wanting to discriminate between the shares of Erckmann and Chatrian [...] [but] the litigation threw no light on the subject. Both partners did their best to justify the well-known views of Dumas and Mr. Lang, that in such cases one man does the work and the other takes half the profits; but they justified it on inconsistent ground, each claiming to be the man who did all the work. (18 March 1899, no. 5828, p. 12)

The case of Erckmann and Chatrian seemed to corroborate the opinion that had been circulating for some time: that literary partnership was the "most transitory of all forms of collaboration," and that collaborative relationships were all "bound in the long run to end in a quarrel"

(*The Globe*, 31 August 1889, no. 29409, p. 6). Noticing the unceasing interchange of literary partners that was going on in the literary scene, *The Globe* concluded that "the system works unsatisfactorily" (p. 6): if a harmonious collaboration was unlikely for two men, it was "hopeless for any two women to attempt it" (p. 6).

That dual authorship was doomed to end not only in a quarrel but in a very bitter one was an opinion supported by many examples. The news of the break-up of Gilbert and Sullivan in 1890 after twenty years of joint successes seemed further evidence that collaboration was "an ill-fated thing" (*St James's Gazette*, 4 September 1890, no. 3195, p. 4). The rift was due, as usual, to a business transaction,[16] and the lawsuit that followed led the two former partners to become enemies:

> [t]he partners, after getting on amicably for a number of years, and helping each other to make a great deal of money, almost invariably fall out at last. And when the quarrel comes it is commonly exceedingly bitter. Mr. Gilbert, having discovered heavy griefs against Mr. O'yly Carte as to the profits of the works with which he and Sir Arthur Sullivan have adorned the stage, is satisfied with nothing less than law, blood being now difficult to have. (*St James's Gazette*, 4 September 1890, no. 3195, p. 4)

In the 1890s articles on collaboration decidedly tended to focus on the inevitability of quarrels. Now, the formerly celebrated domestic bliss was presented as a phase preceding the unavoidable break-up:

> [n]ot infrequently collaboration leads to recrimination, and brotherly love is shown the door by egoistic spleen. (*Hearth and Home*, 11 February 1892, no. 39, p. 1.)
>
> Collaboration [...] is only successful when it is not collaboration. [...] Two friends live together and pass their evenings, side by side, in front of a common hearth, a cup of coffee beside them, a cigar between their teeth. [...]

---

16 The impresario D'Oyly Carte charged the cost for a new carpet for the Savoy theatre lobby to the partners; Gilbert objected, as he believed that this was a maintenance expense that Carte alone should pay; he was also convinced that Carte had been swindling them for some time. Sullivan supported Carte, as the impresario was building The Royal English Opera House to produce Sullivan's own attempt at serious opera, *Ivanhoe* (1891). Gilbert brought a suit (which he eventually won), and the two former collaborators resentfully stayed apart for some years. After the failure of The Royal English Opera House Carte tried to reunite them and, after many attempts, he succeeded. See Stedman, 1996; Trussler, 2000; Eden and Saremba, 2009; and Jacobs, 2020.

One composes and writes, the other commends or blames, corrects, gives ideas, throws new light on the subject. That is the ideal collaboration. [...] The only drawback to it is that the two friends usually quarrel about paternal rights. (*The Globe*, 4 May 1894, no. 30861, p. 1)

Literary partnerships, however successful, are not wont to be permanent. Even the famous Erckmann-Chatrian collaboration was dissolved. Had Mr. James Rice lived it is probable that the alliance of Besant and Rice would have ended in separate authorship. (*Aberdeen Press and Journal*, 16 August 1894, no. 12338, p. 5)

In short, there seemed to be no half measures when it came to literary collaboration: it was represented as leading either to ecstatic comradeship or to bloodshed.

Another curious aspect concerning the representation of collaboration in the periodical press was that it was often connected with swindling. In the last decade of the century co-authorship was so on trend that sometimes it was professed even when it was not true. Ashton (2003, 5) reports a certain Albert Terhune who, in the late 1890s, regularly made money by writing fake collaborative serial novels, signed "By The Beautiful Shopgirls" or "By The Beautiful Actresses." Cases of false collaborations and forgery crowded the pages of newspapers. In an article entitled "Literary Collaboration: Does It Pay?" the *Edinburgh Evening Dispatch* reported a lawsuit brought by a writer against a dead colleague, of whose novels he claimed to be the real author: "[t]he understanding between the two men, according to the claimant, was that Hedrich had the capacity to write the books, while Meissner had the name to sell them" (27 November 1889, no. 1221, p. 2). The article, however, was sceptical about the claim, as "[n]othing would have sold Hedrich's future works as well as a scandal such as that he has now raised" (p. 2). A similar episode occurred when a short novel, *The Lost Diamonds*, appeared in December 1891 under the joint names of Charles Ogilvie and Florence Marryat. The latter wrote an outraged letter to the *Athenaeum* to expose the forgery, claiming that her name had been used without her consent. Marryat maintained that she had only written "a scene in the story at Ogilvie's request, which he had expanded to make four chapters" (*Dundee Advertiser*, 11 January 1892, no. 9611, p. 8), and complained that the publication of her name in connection with the novel had caused her problems with some of her publishing contracts both in the United States and in England. However, the *Dundee Advertiser* suspected that it seemed "hardly credible that Florence Marryat would write anything of the kind merely as an amusement for herself, and without knowing it would be utilised. [...] Her letter, in this gossiping age, will serve to increase the demand for *Lost Diamonds*" (p. 8).

As the 1890s went on, collaboration was more and more represented as an undesirable arrangement, full of pitfalls and increasingly connected with deception. The *Blackburn Standard* (24 December 1898, no. 3279, p. 6) featured the account of a writer, Archibald Anstruther, reporting a strange case of collaboration that had happened to him. He narrated how, shortly after publishing a novel, he had received a letter from one Paul Desart, proposing a collaboration to turn the work into a play. "In a weak moment I consented," is the foreboding comment of the protagonist. Since they lived in different cities, the two co-authors never met in person and the work was carried out by letter. However, the mysterious co-author gradually took over the whole thing: "[o]nce having commenced, my collaborator calmly assumed the position of a dictator. I was to do this and do that, so ran his peremptory commands." For some time Anstruther put up with the whims of his literary tyrant, until a final disagreement over whether the hero of the story was to get married made him lose his patience. He sent a telegram to Desart with an ultimatum: "[y]ou must abide by my decision. Otherwise collaboration must cease. Decision irrevocable." Receiving no answer, he thought the matter was over, only to discover some time later that his collaborator had organized the staging of the play on his own. To the news that the work was to be staged the following night in Birmingham, Anstruther wondered: "[w]hat should I do? Get an injunction to stop the play, or tamely allow it to go on, and tacitly admit that I was defeated?" He decided to go and see the play, and afterwards confront Desart. Once at the theatre, the poster presented his collaborator's name first, and in capital letters too, while his own was printed in small letters. After seeing the play, Anstruther went looking for his deceitful partner, but could not find him anywhere; instead, the main actress, Isabel Lennox, told him that Paul Desart would be pleased to see him in his apartments the following day. In the end, a surprise awaited the protagonist, as Miss Lennox candidly confessed: "I am your collaborator. [...] Forgive me. I know the prejudice you men have towards women's work, and so I adopted this little innocent deception [...] When do you commence legal proceedings against me?" The legal proceedings Anstruther started were not those expected by Miss Lennox: he proposed to her, and the story has a happy ending – once again connecting literary collaboration with romance and marriage. The telling of the story draws on the lexicon of war (dictator, commands, ultimatum, defeated), in line with the rhetoric of the period, which equated collaboration with a battlefield.

Quarrels between co-authors and cases of unauthorized collaborations to adapt novels for the stage were innumerable. This triggered reflections on the thorny issue of copyright. *The Era* in particular would repetitively plead for measures to better regulate (co-)authors' rights:

> [w]e cannot find any good reason why literary and artistic copyright should not be as eternal as any other sort of property. If there is anything that may be said to "belong" to a man and to be bequeathable to his heirs and descendants for ever and ever, it is the product of his brains. The reason why property in land is permanent and that in plays and novels limited in duration is that the laws in times past have been made by landowners and not by authors and dramatists. (25 April 1896, p. 15)

Many were the petitions to decide upon a clear definition of co-authorship and, consequently, of authorship. In another article in *The Era*, a barrister advanced a solution:

> [i]f two persons undertake jointly to write [...] agreeing in the general outline and design, and sharing the labour of working it out, each would be contributing to the whole production, and they might be said to be joint authors of it. But to constitute joint authorship there must be a joint common design. Mere alterations, additions, or improvements by another person, whether with or without the sanction of the author, will not entitle him to be called joint author. (26 September 1896, p. 14)

Here the barrister put "a joint common design" as the necessary condition for a work to be considered collaborative. According to him, each writer, in order to be called a co-author, should contribute "to the whole production" and share the labour from the beginning to the end. But things were not that simple. Definitions of joint common design and shared labour were slippery. Where did the joint design begin? It could initially be the idea of one partner – the starting point must be by one only – and then the other would step in from a certain point onwards. In that case, had they not the right to be called a collaborator? In addition, co-authors could not always contribute in the exact same way or measure – and even if they tried, how was one to calculate if both shares had been equal? How was the contribution of each to be measured? Which criteria should be adopted? Did the writing part count more or less than the planning, or the painstaking process of revision? And if the shares were not equal, was the partner who supposedly contributed less not to have the right to sign their name on the title page? Maybe it could be specified that they were a partial or a minor author, and they shall reap lower profits, as in any business involving shares. When fights broke out between co-authors accusing each other of not having contributed enough, should a judge be called? But how were they to reconstruct the whole creative process? Collaboration posed infinite questions.

The barrister who wrote the article in *The Era* proposed that, at the end of every collaborative project, the co-authors should sign a contract in which they declared their shares, and agreed on the existence of a collaboration: "the written consent of all must be obtained, as one of them cannot bind the other or others" (26 September 1896, no. 3027, p. 14). What he did was to suggest treating co-authorship as a matter of contracts, as a business transaction like any other.

The popularity of collaboration gave origin to curious cases of gossip too: following the fashion of the moment, amateurs and people with literary ambitions from various backgrounds experimented with it in many ways; since collaborating implied spending much time in close contact with someone, ambiguous situations developed. A couple of examples are worth mentioning for the fun of it. In 1886 the *Sheffield Independent* (20 November, no. 10051, p. 2) reported a lawsuit known as "Adams v. Coleridge," where a father sued a young man accused of having "ruined his daughter," Miss Coleridge, with whom he was officially "engaged in literary work." However, the father suspected that something more was happening during their protracted writing sessions. The two young people claimed that "the only relations between [them] were those of literary collaboration" but the controversy was lengthy and acrimonious. Collaboration would be exploited as a suitable excuse for meeting people, for getting out of the home or for staying out late, as was the case in one "Erskine Suit," in which a husband wanted a divorce because of his wife's alleged adultery: apparently, the woman "absented herself from home, representing she was assisting a Miss Smith to write novels," when actually "she occupied apartments where she was visited by the co-respondent from whom the damages were now claimed" (*Hartlepool Northern Daily Mail*, 29 February 1892, no. 4285, p. 3).

These and many other scandals reported in the columns of newspapers contributed to further demean the way in which collaboration was perceived. Literary partnership came to be represented as a suspect practice, an easy excuse to cover ulterior motives, a snare that led to improper conduct. Surely, Besant's linking of collaboration with flirting and romance had not helped. Real-life cases did the rest. The result was that a connotation of frivolousness and impropriety, among all the other undesirable associations, remained attached to co-authorship.

How is it done? Unravelling the mystery

Since co-authorship broke established norms of composition based on the model of the solitary artist, in front of a collaborative text many people felt puzzled. Especially in the late 1880s, an impressive number of articles was devoted to the big question of 'how it is done,' as the following extracts will suffice to show:

> [w]hat the public is most curious to know about collaboration is, 'how it is done.' (*St. James's Gazette* 7 September 1886, no. 1953, p. 4)
>
> If there is any form of authorship which still puzzles the few persons who have written neither books nor plays, it is probably that joint form which goes by the name of collaboration. (*Aberdeen Journal*, 8 September 1886, no. 9851, p. 2)
>
> Literary collaboration is [...] one of the things that no fellow can understand. (*East Aberdeenshire Observer*, 21 June 1889, p. 1)
>
> No more curious problem has ever presented itself to the literary student than that of collaboration. Various theories have been put forward in regard to it: many and strange explanations of it have been given. But, in spite of all this, the 'art' has remained a 'mystery.' (*Pall Mall Gazette*, 19 October 1891, no. 8293, p. 3)

An idea that some mystery shrouded collaboration kept surfacing in the periodical press, as if a sort of secret, known only to the people involved, was hidden behind the collaborative work. Commenting on the partnership of Erckmann and Chatrian, the *Aberdeen Free Press* observed that "[t]he mysteries of collaboration have always been of intense interest, but in this case, as in most others, the secret has been *jealously guarded* by the authors." (22 August 1889, no. 6409, p. 4, my emphases)

The press would constantly endeavour to unravel what was seen as an impenetrable enigma: on this topic, the debate was lively and the points of view various and sometimes contrasting. A wealth of theories on the methods of collaboration were advanced. As *The Graphic* put it, "the systems differ as much as the fancies." (13 September 1884, no. 772, p. 22)

The most credited opinion was that collaboration rested on a division of tasks, typically an unequal one, with one partner doing most of the work and the other basically assisting. Besant and Rice's case remained the most popular model throughout the 1880s and the 1890s, and seems to have had a profound influence on public opinion. "Probably collaboration is most pleasant when one of the partners does most of the work, the other 'suggesting,' but not complaining when his suggestions are put aside," reflected the *Edinburgh Evening Dispatch* (27 November 1889, no. 1221, p. 2). Besant's view that two authors taking turns in writing was "grotesque" and "ineffective," since every character would talk "with two voices and two brains" ("Lit. Coll.," 205), was supported by the press. In the same year as Besant's "On Literary Collaboration," the *London Daily News* promoted his point of view and tried to dispel the aura of mystery that seemed to surround the practice of collaboration:

> [t]he subject is always interesting to the innumerable people who want to be authors. They think that there is some mystery in the matter, and that, had they the 'Open Sesame,' they could enter the cavern of treasure. There is really no mystery. If one dull man cannot write a successful book, it would be mysterious, indeed, if two dull men could do so. They cannot, there are no such happy results from the combination of two stupidities. But a dull man and a clever man may write a successful book – because the clever man writes it. (13 February 1892, no. 14319, p. 4)

The article contradicted Matthews's essay, which championed a model of co-authorship based on the equality of the partners: "[w]e venture so far to differ from Mr. Matthews as to say that the work is always done by one man [...] we have a theory that doing the actual writing is doing the work" (p. 4). So, he who does the writing is the real and only author, the sculptor who shapes the rock into a work of art, while the partner who does not write "is but the man who cuts the marble blocks out of the quarry" (p. 4). The sculptor can do without the assistant, but the assistant cannot do without the sculptor: "[t]he partner saves the great man some labour, which, if he chose, he could do better for himself." The work of the assistant, thus, may be useful, "but it leaves the one man dominant and indispensable." The *London Daily News* concluded that "[a] good-natured genius sometimes calls a man his 'collaborator,' when he is really only his companion" (p. 4).

The debate over 'who did what' in a collaboration prompted reflections on the question of authorship: what did it take to be defined an author? Could only those who actually put pen to paper be called so? According to Besant, the partner who did not write was to be considered an author just like the other one. But what did the periodical press think about it? On this point, it generally took its distance from Besant's position, and put strong emphasis on the connection between being an author and the act of writing: an author was someone who wrote a text, and no one else. At best, there could be a hierarchy of authors – a chief and one or more assistants – as in a theory advanced by the *London Daily News* (13 February 1892, no. 14319, p. 4). "Whether partnership really helps the master spirit much is a question which only himself can answer," commented the article, which went on: "[i]n Mr. Matthews's tales, it may be said that they probably would not be worse if he had written them alone." If both partners write, "the partnership is likely to be a failure":

> [t]he result might be diverting to the curious, but could scarcely be of much consistent value as a work of art. […] We might welcome cases of Miss Rhoda Broughton in the middle of the author of John Inglesant's disquisitions, but verily we should prefer Miss Broughton neat. All liquids will not blend, nor is currant jelly good with roast beef. Writers with marked styles and notions of their own had better not work together. The combination of two very distinct popularities may make one failure. (p. 4)

The culinary metaphor aptly expressed the awkwardness of two strong personalities juxtaposing and trying to mix. This view contrasted with the optimistic comparison suggested only two years earlier on the occasion of Lang and Haggard's collaboration by the *Kerry Evening Post*, which had enthusiastically noted that the mixing of two apparently incompatible ingredients could give origin to gourmet dishes. The article in the *London Daily News* instead ended with the following, utterly negative, conclusion:

> [t]he moral of the whole discussion seems to be that no two geniuses of a high order can work together: for this reason Mr. Matthew Arnold would never believe that Homer had partners. Therefore it is good for the second-rate literary player to get a partner of genius, but is it good for the partner, for the man who does the 'mere writing'? Except in plays, where co-operation is often necessary, […] and in translation, where two eyes are better than one, 'collaboration' seems a mere gift to the sleeping partner. (13 February 1892, no. 14319, p. 4)

The idea of the sleeping partner had been circulating for some time: "[p]robably all collaborators have their own way: and perhaps there is frequently a sleeping partner," the *St. James's Gazette* had pointed out in 1886 (7 September, no. 1953, p. 4). And again the *St. James's Gazette*, a few days after the article in the *London Daily News* of February 1892, arrived at a similar verdict:

[t]here is no mystery whatever about the art of collaboration, for the simple but sufficient reason that there is, in fact, no such thing as literary collaboration. Books may appear under the names of two authors, but it is invariably one of the two authors who does all the work. The other may make suggestions, talk things over, and so forth. [...] The real business in writing a book is the writing; that is always the work of one of the partners only. (*St. James's Gazette*, 20 February 1892, no. 3648, p. 12)

This opinion was shared by a great number of periodicals, and in those years the discourse on collaboration basically revolved around such a paradox: there was really no collaboration behind a collaborative text. *The Globe* ironically suggested that, when two writers decide to co-author a book, "one writes it while the other takes a trip to the African desert, returning just in time to draw half the profits" (4 May 1894, no. 30861, p. 1). The article also gave some advice to aspiring co-authors: "the intending collaborator had better look out for a partner who is fond of work; it is always easier to do the critical part of the job, and the cutting" (p. 1).

Most papers seemed to agree that, if a writer had talent, they had better not engage in any collaboration:

Mr Besant, writing alone, has produced better novels than the two wrote between them. This, of course, supports your theory that if a man has the divine afflatus, or even a touch of it, he does best by himself. (*St. James's Gazette*, 7 September 1886, no. 1953, p. 4)

A writer of high ability, or even of distinctive character, should avoid collaboration unless he is aiming, above all, at commercial success [...]. Who can fancy a writer of delicate taste, and accustomed to say things in his own way, taking a collaborator? [...] What collaborator would have dared to suggest to Victor Hugo that his interminable monologue on the portraits in Hernoni was a little long? What collaborator, again, could have touched the dialogue of *The School for Scandal* without really injuring it? Collaboration is for authors of the second rank and under. (*Aberdeen Journal*, 8 September 1886, no. 9851, p. 2)

It is not necessary here to make any estimate of the gain or loss incidental to collaboration. Of course it all depends on the collaborators, and even when these are of the best it is doubtful if the work will have the finest quality of genius. One cannot think of the *Divina Commedia*, or *Paradise Lost* as being the outcome of any joint effort, and though the case of Beaumont and Fletcher is a remarkable exception, it must, we think, remain an exception. (*Freeman's Journal*, 3 June 1892, vol. 126, p. 2)

Thus, from an efficient tool to improve any text, collaboration ultimately came to be seen as advantageous only for "authors of the second rank and under," the ones with little or no talent. If one had talent, collaboration was not only useless: it could be damaging. The fact that most periodicals mentioned the great classics of literature, saying that they could never have been the outcome of any joint effort, but that, on the contrary, the intervention of a collaborator would have ruined them, speaks volumes. Dante, Milton, or Hugo would only have been restrained by a partner standing in their way. The press supported Besant's and Matthews's opinion that "[n]o great poem has ever been written by two men together, nor any really great novel" (Matthews, 1891, 11), as co-authorship deprived the creative process of spontaneity and that occasional touch of excess that made a masterpiece.

Again probably influenced by Besant's and Matthews's writings, collaboration was generally believed to be very useful when satire and humour were concerned. This opinion was already present in earlier years, although much less widespread: "[a] piece of supreme literary excellence could scarcely be written in partnership. Human ingenuity can divide itself – not human genius" (*The Graphic*, 29 January 1876, vol. 13, no. 322, p. 16). *The Graphic* argued that collaboration's "legitimate sphere" was "amusing mediocrity," and that "the very highest walks of literature have remained free from collaboration," as it "cannot use the higher passions, nor deal in deep romantic philosophy." In his essay, Matthews stated that collaboration mostly "served the cause of periodical literature" (1891, 11). In novels to be published in weekly or monthly parts, a requirement of paramount importance was indeed a well-planned plot, capable of keeping the suspense up. In this respect, co-authorship was renowned for its successes. In a co-authored work of fiction "we are likely to find polish, finish, and perfection of mechanism" (Matthews, 1891, 11), almost as if it were a scientific construction: "to call the result of collaboration often over-labored, or to condemn it as cut and dried, would be to express with unduly brutal frankness the criticism it is best merely to suggest" (Matthews, 1891, 13). Still, his position is ambiguous, as it continually wavers between heavy criticism and renegotiation:

> [i]t has been objected that in books prepared in partnership even the writing is hard and arid, as though each writer were working on a foreign suggestion and lacking the freedom with which a man may treat his own invention. If a writer feels thus, the partnership is unprofitable and unnatural, and he had best get a divorce as soon as may be. (14–15)

The belief that collaboration could have no claims to high literary value continued to be held over the turn of the century. By the early 1920s, when co-authored novels were isolated cases and were mainly the final output of few long-lasting collaborative relationships, this notion was more widespread than ever. In 1922, *The Yorkshire Post* observed that "[n]owadays literary collaboration of the first order seems to be out of fashion in England" (20 May 1922, no. 23366, p. 10) and conveyed a very pessimistic view:

> [n]or, without pretending to exhaustive research in the matter would joint authorship seem to have been popular amongst the literary great of the nineteenth century. The Beloved Vagabond and his stepson, Lloyd Osbourne, made somewhat desultory joint effort in the direction of South Sea Island yarns. A more enduring success – as readers of *Ready-Money Mortiboy* will attest – fell to the united pens of Besant and Rice. (p. 10)

The article set out to list a long series of partnerships from Elizabethan drama onwards, only to reach the conclusion that

> [o]ne thing alone stands clear. That the greatest literary art has always been a product of the individual. [...] The ultimate expression of the great artist's soul demands solitary workmanship. No other hand than Shakespeare's could have finished Desdemona or Cordelia; no other touch than Hardy's could have moulded Tess. (p. 10)

A fading vogue

> It may be said that curiosity is the only useful vice, since without it there would be neither discovery nor invention; and curiosity it is which lends interest to many a book written in collaboration, the reader being less concerned about the merits of the work than he is with guessing at the respective shares of the associated authors. To many of us a novel by two writers is merely a puzzle, and we seek to solve the enigma of its double authorship, accepting it as a nut to crack even when the kernel is little likely to be more digestible than the shell. (Matthews, 1891, 1)

Matthews noticed that readers facing a co-authored text inevitably found themselves wondering "what was the part of each partner in the writing of the book?" (1891, 1). His observation could not have been more appropriate. As a matter of fact, the late Victorian press routinely tried to tell the different contributions apart: if one text belonged to two authors, critics sought to at least divide it into clearly ascribable parts. The content of articles on collaboration and reviews of co-authored novels suggests that the Victorian public was quite obsessed with trying to guess at the respective hands – so much so that, in 1894, *The Globe* suggested a solution "ensuring a fair share of praise":

> [t]here is, indeed, one safe way out of the wood, which, if literary rumour be accurate, has been taken by the authors of an impending novel. These two intend, it is said, to have the book printed in two different kinds of type, so that the reader shall know, however dull his literary palate, whether he is indulging in the sparkling Burgundy of Brown or the plain Swipes of Smith. (4 May 1894, no. 30861, p. 1)

To satisfy the urge to differentiate the individual parts, many co-authored novels of the 1890s and early 1900s adopted bizarre solutions. Some novels had prefaces with explicit declarations of the parts assigned; this was naturally easier for works made up of fictitious exchanges of letters, like *A Fellowe and His Wife* (1892) by Blanche W. Howard and William Sharp, whose preface stated that the letters by the female protagonist were Sharp's, while the ones by the male protagonist had been written by Howard.[17] Epistolary novels were classified as "the most convenient mode for the purposes of collaboration" (*Glasgow Evening Post*, 22 March 1892, p. 8). Another novel of this kind, *The Etchingham Letters* (1899) by Ella Fuller Maitland and Frederick Pollock,[18] was positively reviewed by *The Standard* as "an experiment in collaboration in what seems to be its most natural form – a novel in letters written by two persons of opposite sexes" (31 May 1899, no. 23377, p. 4).

Novels consisting of extracts from diaries of different characters were thought to be well suited to the collaborative mode too. An extreme case was *The Green Bay-Tree* (1894) by W. H. Wilkins and Herbert Vivian, which at the beginning of each of the three volumes had a Prefatory Note detailing the authorship for each chapter and even for each paragraph. The respective shares were more or less equally divided: Wilkins took care of twenty-one chapters, Vivian of seventeen, and three chapters were

---

17 William Sharp (1855–1905) was a Scottish writer who also published independently under the pen name Fiona Macleod. Blanche Willis Howard (1847–1898) was a best-selling American author who had settled in Germany and had become Baroness von Teuffel. *A Fellowe and His Wife* is a fictional exchange of letters between two aristocrats, Count Odo von Jaromar and his wife, Countess Ilse.

18 Ella Fuller Maitland (1857–1939), née Chester, was a novelist and a poet. She often used the pseudonym Bethia Hardacre. Sir Frederick Pollock (1845–1937) was an English jurist best known for his *History of English Law before the Time of Edward I*.

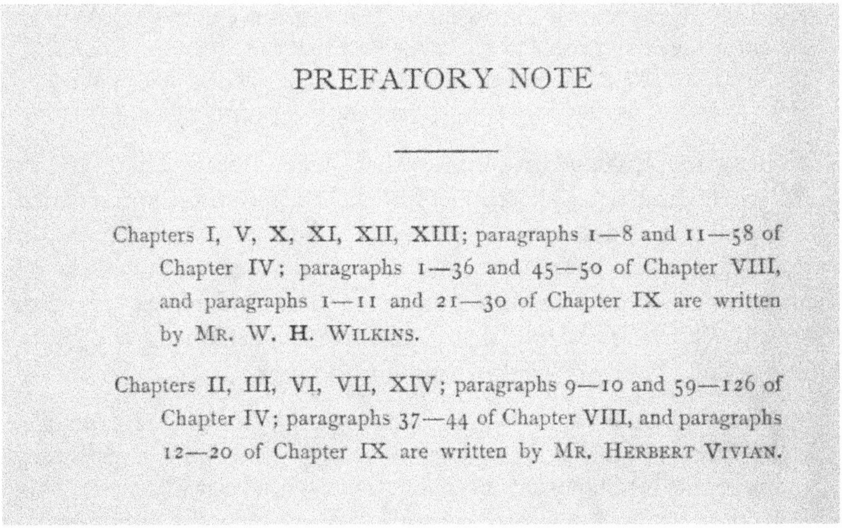

> PREFATORY NOTE
>
> Chapters I, V, X, XI, XII, XIII; paragraphs 1—8 and 11—58 of Chapter IV; paragraphs 1—36 and 45—50 of Chapter VIII, and paragraphs 1—11 and 21—30 of Chapter IX are written by Mr. W. H. Wilkins.
>
> Chapters II, III, VI, VII, XIV; paragraphs 9—10 and 59—126 of Chapter IV; paragraphs 37—44 of Chapter VIII, and paragraphs 12—20 of Chapter IX are written by Mr. Herbert Vivian.

Figure 13. Prefatory Note to *The Green Bay-Tree* by W. H. Wilkins and Herbert Vivian (London: Hutchinson & Co., 1894). Source: Archive.org

written by both. A blurb in *The Standard* announcing the forthcoming publication of the novel recited, as if to reassure readers: "[a]lthough written in collaboration, the authorship of each chapter is indicated" (8 May 1894, p. 9). This suggests a sort of annoyance about not knowing who wrote what. The press appreciated the solution adopted by these co-authors, and a review in the *Athenaeum* read:

> [t]his is an unusually successful case of collaboration, for, though the authors are at pains to indicate the chapters and paragraphs for which they are respectively responsible, the different parts are admirably welded together, so that it is difficult even with this knowledge to detect any differences of workmanship or division of interest. (9 June 1894, no. 3476, p. 737)

Later that same year, the third collaborative novel by R. L. Stevenson and Lloyd Osbourne, *The Ebb-Tide*, appeared in print. The press immediately set out to separate the two hands, although the two authors had given no hint about their compositional method:

> [t]his is, we understand, the last time that Mr. Stevenson and his stepson, Mr. Lloyd Osbourne, intend to write a story together, and though it is impossible to regret the resolution – for English readers, at any rate, have never taken kindly to literary partnerships of this sort – it attaches a special interest to *The*

Ebb-Tide. We have tried to parcel out their respective contributions to the present volume, and come to the conclusion that the earlier portion belongs chiefly to Mr. Lloyd Osbourne, and the second part wholly, or almost wholly, to Mr. Stevenson. (*The Standard*, 15 September 1894, no. 21904, p. 2)

The review in *The Standard* considered the second part of the novel the point where "the strength and genius of Mr. Stevenson are crowded" (p. 2), and proceeded to talk about the book as mainly Stevenson's output. The idea of the solitary genius pervaded the review, which largely focused on the famous man of letters only (also through the use of the possessive "his" instead of "their"), completely neglecting the contribution – nay, the existence – of young Osbourne:

> [t]he book is very short, one volume and large print, but Mr. Stevenson gives such vitality to his characters, and so clear an outlook upon the strange quarter of the world to which he takes us, that when we reach the end of the story, we come back to civilization with a start of surprise […] His method is as artistic and his style as masterly as ever. (p. 2)

As time passed and the vogue for collaboration declined, the disentangling of the co-authors' hands remained an ever-present feature of reviews and articles on co-authorship. As late as 1919, a letter to the *Aberdeen Daily Journal* thanked the editor for an article about collaboration recently published and for the "deft treatment of that interesting theme": "[t]he subject has for long had an attraction for me, chiefly because of the nice problem of disentangling the various 'hands' involved. […] There is an unfailing fascination […] in unraveling the detail of such 'syndicate writings'" (2 September 1919, no. 20178, p. 3). The need to know 'which is which' could be felt very sharply, and the *Academy* gave voice to all the frustration a reader could experience: "[t]o the critic or the student of literature such partnership is like enough to afford more irritation than pleasure. He feels impelled to disentangle the respective contributions of the pair, and can never be sure that he has made a just and accurate division" (9 October 1909, no. 1953, pp. 605–06).

Despite the public's preoccupation with the attribution of authorship, many co-authors professed that it was a pointless occupation. In the early 1880s, when the 'literary twins' Erckmann and Chatrian were still working together, *The Era* reported that

> [b]etween these two writers, in their work, there is always perfect unity, and it is an absolute truth that none of their productions can be said to belong more to one than the other. Similar sentiments, and the same work during fifteen years, combined with a love of the same country, Alsace, have

established between these two men a style of thought positively similar. Sometimes it is one who writes most, and the other who directs the work by furnishing the ideas, or plot. Often the roles change, but the result is continually the same. (1 Apr. 1882, no. 2271, p. 7)

Rosa Campbell Praed and Justin McCarthy declared in the preface of their first novel, *The Right Honourable* (1886), that "[e]very character, incident, scene, and page is joint work, and was thought out and written out in combination" (McCarthy and Campbell Praed, 1896, v). Neither of them ever withdrew these words, and in interviews over the years they stuck to their initial view of collaboration:

Mrs. Campbell Praed herself cannot tell her own share in the novels which she has written along with Mr. Justin McCarthy. "I write the bones of the chapters I think I can do most easily [...] and Mr. McCarthy does the same. Every sentence is joint work. I really don't know which is which, and now I wouldn't work in any other way." (*The Globe*, 4 May 1894, no. 30861, pp. 1–2)

George R. Sims, who wrote short stories, novels, and plays in collaboration,[19] explained in an interview of 1892:

[i]n the case of myself and my collaborators we literally live together till the play has been evolved, in which we have so intermingled that it would, and should, be difficult for one or other to point to his work. Two men come together bubbling over with ideas, and throw a plot together, as a sculptor takes a piece of clay. Then we reject and reject until we have paired it into a symmetrical shape, and then we set to work on the dialogue. Perhaps one man will write a whole scene. He will submit it to the other, who will ruthlessly revise it – and so we go on. (*The Era*, 27 August 1892, no. 2814, p. 9)

Matthews himself replied to the question he had asked at the beginning of his essay ("what was the part of each partner in the writing of the book?"), declaring the hopelessness of trying to distinguish the co-authors' hands. He wrote that the answer

can hardly ever be given; even the collaborators themselves are at a loss to specify their own contributions. When two men have worked together honestly and heartedly in the inventing, the developing, the constructing, the writing, and the revising of a book [...] it is often impossible for either partner to pick out his own share. (Matthews, 1891, 2)

---

19 Sims's most successful collaboration was with Henry Pettitt, with whom he co-authored several plays, starting with *In the Ranks* (1883). He also collaborated with Robert Buchanan.

However, this perspective on the issue was marginal and never succeeded in taking over public opinion, which remained fixed on attributing authorship.

In 1919, the *Aberdeen Weekly Journal* dedicated a very long article to literary collaborators, including Michael Field, a number of French authors, Mrs Campbell Praed and Justin McCarthy, and the ever-present Besant and Rice. After considering several kinds of co-authorship, it unceremoniously dismissed the practice, proclaiming that "[t]he Anglo-Saxon temperament, on the whole, is too shy and reticent to unbosom itself to a confidant with the unreserve for which collaboration calls" (12 September 1919, no. 8957, p. 2). Co-authorship was pronounced unfit for, and even incompatible with, the British national character. The press agreed upon the failure of collaborative writing, defining it as a transitory vogue that had served the cause of periodical literature, as Matthews had predicted.

Even without such farewell from the press, co-authored novels had already started to drift towards the margins of the literary market. Of all the production of the preceding fifty years, only a few works were still circulating. Soon enough they would sink into oblivion too, and almost nothing would remain to remind twentieth-century readers of late Victorian collaborators.

All in all, during the period we have considered, in the representations by the press the shared literary page could become either the site of a fruitful exchange or a field of bitter warfare. For some time, both sides of the coin coexisted: the debate illustrated in this chapter seems to point to a problematic understanding of authorship in the late Victorian imagination. On the one hand, the idyllic representations of collaborators working together for years in an atmosphere of productive sympathy effectively challenged the paradigm of the solitary author; on the other hand, the inevitable tensions implied in any collaborative relationship and the limits this practice presented seemed to confirm the need for solitude in order to create, thus reassessing and enhancing the myth of the solitary genius. The coexistence for a certain period of these oxymoronic positions exposes an ambiguity in the construction of the author. Ultimately, Romantic notions of the solitary man of letters were so deep-seated that the trend for co-authorship failed to uproot them; it even seems to have strengthened them, as if corroborating the necessity for the creative act to be carried out in solitude.

Moreover, even if the authors of a text were two, it was believed that there must be a *real* author, whom the reader had the challenging duty to detect. Some collaborators went to great lengths to explain that all their production was joint work; they endeavoured to convince the public that to dissect their contributions was impossible and pointless. However, their voices did not persuade readers, who kept figuring a co-authored text as not really so, in what I have called the paradox of collaboration. Such dismal view was conveyed by some co-authors themselves – and very influential ones too. Some talked about their collaborative outputs as mere entertainment and lacking serious artistic value, since the deeper things belonged to the lonely writer. The established idea of the creative single artist as opposed to the supposedly mechanic and/or playful collaborative practice was so pervasive that not only was it fixed within the public's representations but it also constantly lurked in co-authors' perceptions of themselves and their work. Indeed, the fact that popular writers who experienced collaboration held these opinions is significant, and their declarations had a huge impact on portrayals of co-authorship. Furthermore, the gloomy halo that surrounded commercial or fake partnerships swallowed up remarkable co-authored works. The reputation for frivolousness, indecency, and even immorality that the press built around literary collaboration over the years surely did not help to make it a practice worthy of attention. Fiction resulting from joint writing was not taken seriously and, though very popular and sometimes scoring perfectly respectable reviews, it did not stick. Victorian readers simply consumed and forgot it.

CHAPTER FIVE

Literary Collaboration and the Figure of the Author

We have seen how late Victorian readers perceived collaborative fiction as problematic and disturbing, as affording "more irritation than pleasure" (*The Academy*, 9 October 1909, p. 605). Co-authored texts were approached and evaluated according to the same paradigms employed for single-authored works, but, within collaborative writing, text and author turned into something very different from what the Victorians were accustomed to imagining.

This final chapter foregrounds the innovative potential connected to the figure of the author as understood by late nineteenth-century collaborators. By drawing on the experiences of Edith Somerville, Walter Besant, and James Brander Matthews, it unpacks the ways in which co-authorship challenged the rigid regime of the post-Romantic solitary genius. Metadiscoursive comments by other nineteenth- and early twentieth-century co-authors are considered as well. Although coming from different backgrounds, working under different conditions, and producing different outputs, these writers described their collaborative experiences in surprisingly similar terms: they all employed a rhetoric meant to highlight the unity of the co-authored work and the shifted position of the author with respect to the text. Reading their metadiscourses, a shared idea of authorship gradually takes shape: that of a diluted, deliberately weakened, and elusive hybrid author-figure that rejects the predominant role prescribed by the Romantic tradition and proclaims the necessity to remain concealed behind the text. In this light, one may wonder whether the late Victorian collaborative practice somewhat anticipated a certain independence of the text from the author. Without trying to go too far, I suggest that the late nineteenth-century collaborative practice might point to an early overcoming of the Romantic concept of authorship, strikingly akin to, and slightly anticipating, those twentieth-century literary and critical movements bent to systematically dismiss the importance of the author.

The making of the author

In order to better grasp the destabilizing force of late Victorian collaboration, let us first briefly track how the figure of the author acquired its privileged position. As it has been widely demonstrated, the author is a historically and culturally determined construction. Foucault's acclaimed essay "What Is an Author?" (1969) underlines the radical difference between the "modern" sense of the author and the medieval or pre-modern one, stressing that the "author-function" – as he calls it – "does not affect all discourses in the same way at all times and in all types of civilization" (Foucault, 1979, 153). The discourse unfolding in the late nineteenth-century periodical press, illustrated in the previous chapter, discloses a dominant understanding of authorship which identified the author with an inspired creative agent who produces works of art in isolation. This model, considered by the Victorians as the normal condition for the production of literary texts, in fact developed in the course of the seventeenth and especially the eighteenth centuries and found its consecration in the Romantic period. What the Victorians understood as the traditional author-figure was in fact the invention of the previous century.

The dawning of the author as a solitary genius and its increasingly central function during the eighteenth century were reflected in the lexicon, with the appearance of a whole set of new words all entering the English language in this period, related to or deriving from author, such as 'authorial,' 'authoring,' 'authorling,' 'authorly,' and 'authorship.' If language is the mirror of the society that generates it, then the appearance of these words is symptomatic of the emerging supremacy of the author. Once the single author was established, the first occurrence of the word 'collaborator' as connected with literature made its appearance: collaboration became a matter of consideration only within an ideology of authorship as singular. In other words, the idea of literary collaboration seemed to require its own terminology only when the conception of singular authorship emerged as the dominant ideology of composition.

Much early modern playwriting was collaborative in nature, as has been increasingly recognized.[1] It seems that virtually two-thirds of the plays written by professional dramatists saw the participation of more than one writer: from the celebrated case of Beaumont and Fletcher to now-forgotten plays,[2] the dramatic practice of Renaissance England was predominantly collaborative, often beginning with a manuscript which was then elaborated and improvised by actors in performance, and later revised and rearranged multiple times by book-holders, copyists, and other writers. Dramatic texts were not normally printed and, even when they were, they often came out without ascription of authorship; they were "pre-anonymous," to borrow Masten's terminology (1997, 13), in the sense that they appeared at a time when the attribution of texts to authors was not important. In point of fact, 'anonymous' acquired its modern sense of "bearing no author's name; of unknown or unavowed authorship" only in the late seventeenth century, as the *OED* attests. Earlier, it simply meant "nameless, having no name" or "of unknown name." After the seventeenth century, anonymity in the case of literary texts became acceptable only as a riddle to be solved. The emergence of the author is therefore "marked by the notice of its absence" (Masten, 1997, 12). In addition, the modern use of 'anonymous' emerges with the author as a singular entity: the authorlessness of Renaissance texts was often plural and collaborative.

In collaborative play-texts, the relationship between the author and the text seems to have been rather loose and blurred. In the absence of copyright laws, early modern playwrights had no claim or proprietary interest in their plays. Once they handed over their plays to a theatre company, they gave up ownership. Apart perhaps from Ben Jonson and a few others, most dramatic authors did not care to identify with or lay claim to their work.[3] As Clare (2012) underlines, despite the recent

---

1 See Bentley, 1986; Masten, 1997; Vickers, 2002a; 2002b; 2007; Knapp, 2005; Stern, 2009; and Clare, 2012.
2 John Fletcher (1579–1625) and Francis Beaumont (1584–1616) collaborated on plays from about 1607 until the latter's early death. Fletcher was engaged in other, even if less prolific, collaborations, especially after Beaumont's marriage, when he worked frequently with Philip Massinger. He also collaborated with William Rowley, Thomas Middleton, Ben Jonson, George Chapman, and William Shakespeare. Critics have long tried to sort out the different hands in the plays of Beaumont and Fletcher. See Knutson, 2004; and Birch, 2009, 378.
3 Jonson was one of the few authors to play an active role in the publishing of his plays. He oversaw the publication of his *Works* in 1616 and also the earlier publication of his quarto texts. He was not the first to publish an edition of his

growth of interest in Shakespeare's collaborators, most of the uncertain plays continue to be marketed under his name: over the centuries, the name of Shakespeare has reached a position of such pre-eminence that his status as an individual author seems impregnable; especially since the eighteenth century, the Bard started to be regarded as the embodiment of the Author – "the very anti-type of collaboration" (Masten, 1997, 10). However, the marketing of Shakespeare as an island "is a historical accretion at variance with the conditions prevailing in the theatre in his day" (Clare, 2012, 150).

The period around the late sixteenth and the early and mid-seventeenth century was a moment of transition, of in-between notions of collaborative fluidity, and of the emergence of presiding author-figures. The more frequent appearance of playwrights' names on quarto title pages and the publication of play-texts in folio format organized around authorial figures corresponds to developments in this direction. Masten (1997, 113–55) discusses the emergence of concerns about singular authorship, taking as an example the first Beaumont and Fletcher folio of 1647. Before it, forty-six editions of plays associated with the names Beaumont and Fletcher had appeared in quarto. Significantly, of these forty-six, all the editions that were published without attribution of authorship (eight in total) appeared before 1623, the date of the first Shakespeare folio; after that date, no edition of a play eventually included in the Beaumont and Fletcher canon was printed without ascribing authorship, whether to Fletcher or to Beaumont alone. Moreover, where earlier quartos had simply preceded playwrights' names with 'by,' 'written by,' or 'made by,' later quartos started to employ the word 'author.'

The emergence of the author, however, was not without its problems and contradictions. The 1647 Beaumont and Fletcher folio reads on its title-page *Comedies and Tragedies Written by Francis Beaumont and John Fletcher, Gentlemen* (with their names bracketed together), but the frontispiece presents a portrait of Fletcher alone, depicted as a classically sculpted bust out of a natural scene; he wears a toga and a crown of laurels, and is circled by Latin inscriptions denoting his position as a poet. The commendatory poems accompanying the edition are also unevenly distributed between the two authors. Humphrey Moseley, one of the folio's two publishers, wrote in the preface that he had had the intention to print only Fletcher's work, but that "since never parted

plays, but he "was the first to use the term 'works' in relation to the author and so asserting authorial possession" (Clare, 2012, 144).

while they lived, I conceived it not equitable to separate their ashes" (quoted in Masten, 1997, 123). This might explain the presence of only one portrait, and of the majority of the poems addressed to Fletcher. In addition, Moseley declared in the preface that he had received his copy of the texts from the acting company, which routinely altered the texts and circulated copies that bore these alterations; he added that some parts (mostly prologues and epilogues) were not written by Beaumont or Fletcher, but by others in the various revivals of the plays. From this perspective, it is clear that the term 'author' is working not in the sense of those who have written, and taken credit for, every word in the volume, but rather those who *authorize* it with their names, those who give it their primary authority. Beaumont and Fletcher are 'the authors' of the volume, but not entirely its writers. It may thus be said that the 1647 folio was not simply the product of a collaboration between Beaumont and Fletcher: it was the result of a larger teamwork. Here authorship does not necessarily imply single authorship: it does not exclude the notion of collaboration, and in its wider sense too.

The emerging emphasis on the individual author is usually linked by historians to print culture. From its introduction, print publication brought about new conceptions of authorship: first, the difference between having – and seeing – one's work and one's name in a fixed, permanent form, instead of writing something that most probably would be lost, or altered by copyists, or carried on and ultimately assigned to 'anon,' must have been striking; second, originality – the determining element in modern conceptions of authorship – had a totally different status before print was invented: without relatively accessible copies, no one could be sure that a new discovery was in fact new. Burrow (1982, 126) distinguishes between the "intermittent" culture of the manuscript age and the "continuous, incremental" culture of the age of print. In pre-print culture, invention was what in a different context Jacques Derrida calls "revelatory invention, the discovering and unveiling of what already is" as opposed to the production of something new, what he calls "creative invention, the production of what is not" (Derrida, 2002, 168, quoted in Bennett, 2005, 45). Also, by stabilizing the text and making it more controllable by the author, the introduction of print made new kinds of property right necessary, which ultimately led to an increase in prestige for authors. The new technology spurred originality and individuality perhaps as a reaction against its levelling impulse: the uniformity of the printed book triggered "a desire to express one's personality, one's self, to represent oneself as a unique individual," suggests Bennett (2005,

45). Finally, while oral and manuscript culture implied intertextuality, with one text building on another (manuscripts rarely contained only one text), the printed book gave the illusion of being separate from other texts, thus producing a strong effect of closure and stressing the individuality and separateness of the author (Ong, 1982, 133–34).

By the mid-seventeenth century print technology had become fully embedded within the culture of Western Europe. The Civil War had stimulated demand for printed material, and literacy rates rose steadily in the decades after the Restoration. By the 1690s, newspapers and periodicals had become a permanent part of the public and social sphere. The era of the literary mass market, though at its very beginnings, had begun. The commodification of literature significantly contributed to the invention of authorship.

The distinguishing characteristic of the modern author is proprietorship: what is generally considered the first real copyright law, the Statute of Anne (1709), affirmed the new understanding of the author not only as the originator but also as the rightful owner of a special kind of commodity, the literary text (Rose, 1993, 1–2). The driving force behind the Act was economic: copyright was first and foremost a device developed to protect the investments of those involved in printing and publishing. Significantly, the first laws towards a kind of copyright had been made to protect printers, not authors. In 1556, the Charter of the Stationers' Company had been granted, stating that no person should practise the art of printing unless they belonged to this corporation. The next key moment in the evolution of literary property was the Licensing Act of Charles II in 1662, but still no reference to authors was made. The Statute of Anne was the first law to take authors into consideration, even if they were put on the same level as publishers and booksellers: the copyright of a text could belong indistinctly to the author or to those who bought their copy (Feather, 1994, 4–5). And yet, notes Rose (1993, 49), an unintended consequence of the need to protect publishers' and booksellers' financial interests was the institutionalization of the author as a legal entity: for the first time, authors were legally recognized as possible owners of the text. The emphasis was extended from what the author *does* towards a sense of the author as *owning* a certain property.

As the eighteenth century witnessed a transformation in publishing practices, it started to become virtually possible to make a living by writing. But as authors were gradually emancipating from patrons, they became subject to the laws of the market: now, the author "ought to consider himself [...] as one who keeps a public ordinary, at which all persons are welcome for their money," Fielding remarked in the preface to *Tom Jones* (1749) (Fielding, 1962, 1). As a consequence, "[m]en who pay for what they eat will insist on gratifying their palates, however nice and whimsical these may prove" (Fielding, 1962, 1). The author, then, started to acquire a meaning close to the one we know today: that is, someone who makes money according to the commercial success of their literary work.

Copyright laws constituted the legal ground for the Romantic understanding of the author as originator and owner of the text, inseparable from it. It was at this point that the commercial paradox of Romantic authorship originated: at the moment when authorship became "financially and legally viable, an 'aesthetic ideology' of the transcendent and autonomous artistic work" came into play; in other words, "if a book has commercial value it is seen to lack aesthetic value" (Bennett, 2005, 52). The commercial system of publication was bound to contrast with the notion of the disinterested creative genius. The author should be uninterested in worldly matters like money: this doctrine, produced "just when the artist [was] becoming debased to a petty commodity producer," might be a sort of "spiritual compensation" for the humiliation that such an individual might feel at the prospect of writing for money (Eagleton, 1990, 53).

According to a tradition as old as Plato's *Ion*, the author was so because they were taken by a mysterious, divine-like inspiration, as in Socrates's statement that poets are "not the ones who speak those verses," but "god himself is the one who speaks, and he gives voice through them to us" (Plato, 2001, 42). This conception was taken up by Romantic poets. The idea that the author is both themselves and at the same time beyond themselves when writing was a commonplace in Romantic poetics. Blake intriguingly declared that he had written *Milton* (1803–08)

> from immediate Dictation, twelve or sometimes twenty or thirty lines at a time, without Premeditation, and even against my Will; the Time it has taken in writing was thus render'd Non-Existent, and an immense Poem Exists which seems to be the Labour of a long Life, all produc'd without Labour or Study. (letter to Thomas Butts, 25 April 1803, quoted in Saunders, 1964, 166)

Romantic authors insisted on immediacy and spontaneity, on the work of art as the direct manifestation of inspiration. In the much-celebrated passage from the 1800 Preface to the *Lyrical Ballads*, Wordsworth declared that "all good poetry is the spontaneous overflow of powerful feelings"

(Wordsworth, 2006b, 265). However, the declaration is complicated some pages later:

> I have said that Poetry is the spontaneous overflow of powerful feelings: it takes its origin from emotion recollected in tranquillity: the emotion is contemplated till by a species of reaction the tranquillity disappears, and an emotion kindred to that which was before that subject of contemplation, is gradually produced, and does itself actually exist in the mind. In this mood successful composition generally begins, and in a mood similar to this it is carried on. (Wordsworth, 2006b, 273)

So, the "spontaneous overflow" is not spontaneous after all. The emotion is "recollected" and "contemplated" rather than immediately acted upon or written about on the spot. Still, this emotion is "kindred" to the original and spontaneous one, and "actually exist[s] in the mind." The emotion thus produced is both a copy and the original. Coleridge claimed that "genius involves unconscious activity" (Coleridge, 1987, II, 222). In *A Defence of Poetry* (written in 1821 but published only in 1840), Percy Bysshe Shelley emphasized that poetry "acts in a divine and unapprehended manner, beyond and above consciousness," which is "not subject to the control of the active powers of the mind" and whose "birth and recurrence has no necessary connection with consciousness or will" (Shelley, 1986, 15, 42). In one of the most memorable passages of the essay, Shelley explained that

> the mind in creation is as a fading coal, which some invisible influence, like an inconstant wind, awakens to transitory brightness: this power arises from within, like the colour of a flower which fades and changes as it is developed, and the conscious portions of our natures are unprophetic either of its approach or its departure. [...] when composition begins, inspiration is already on the decline. (38)

He concluded that poets themselves are "perhaps the most sincerely astonished" at their work, "hierophants of an unapprehended inspiration," "the mirrors of the gigantic shadows which futurity casts upon the present," their words expressing "what they understand not" (44). Similarly, Hazlitt's "Whether Genius Is Conscious of Its Powers?" (1823) maintained that "what we have been able to perform is rather matter of wonder than of self-congratulations to us" (Hazlitt, 1889, 119). He argued that "those who have produced immortal works, have done so without knowing how or why," working under an "involuntary, silent impulse" (110–11), "the inspiration of the demon" (119), or as if taken by a "rapture" (111).

The image of the author emerging from such declarations is that of a sacred individual, a prophet. Shelley wrote that a poet "not only beholds intensely the present as it is, [...] but he beholds the future in the present, and his thoughts are the germs of the flower and the fruit of latest time. [...] A poet participates in the eternal, the infinite, and the one" (Shelley, 1986, 11). Thomas Gray's description of the poet in "The Bard" (1757) evoked an ancient practice of poetic narration, which takes us back to a tradition of oral epic narrative when the singer was respected as a seer:

> Rob'd in the sable garb of woe,
> With haggard eyes the poet stood;
> (Loose his beard, and hoary hair
> Stream'd, like a meteor, to the troubled air).
> And with a master's hand, and prophet's fire,
> Struck the deep sorrows of his lyre;
>
> (Gray, 1775, I, 2, lines 17–22)

This idea of the poet-prophet as fundamentally apart and isolated from society, central to the Romantic understanding of the author, also had its roots in ancient Greek culture, in which there was a tradition of mismatch between creative individuals – ahead of their times, alienated, and marginalized – and society – vulgar and conservative. The isolated author recurs in virtually all Romantic poets' self-constructions. Shelley famously identified "the Poet" with "a nightingale, who sits in darkness and sings to cheer its own solitude with sweet sounds" (Shelley, 1986, 15). Wordsworth's *Prelude* (1850) codified the creative process as ultimately a solitary one:

> Here must thou be, O Man!
> Power to thyself; *no Helper* hast thou here;
> Here keepest thou in singleness thy state:
> *No other* can divide with thee this work
> *No secondary hand* can intervene
> To Fashion this ability, 'tis thine,
> The prime and vital principle is thine
> In the recesses of thy nature, far
> From any reach of outward fellowship
> Else is not thine at all.
>
> (Wordsworth, 1959, 493, book 14, lines 209–18, my emphases)

In this passage, Wordsworth explicitly linked authoring with isolation: the author is and must be alone in the creative act, otherwise the creation "is not [theirs] at all." The inspiration, the "prime and vital principle," is to be found in one's deepest self. The insistent rhetoric of possession – five occurrences of "thy" or "thine" within ten lines – stresses the importance of authorial ownership over the text. The impossibility of having a co-author is remarked by the repetition of "no": "no Helper," "no other," "no secondary hand." Alone at the centre of his creation, the Romantic author "straddles the boundaries between man and God" (Ehnenn, 2008, 28).

A passage of *Tintern Abbey* (1798) reads:

> Therefore am I still
> A lover of the meadows and the woods
> And mountains; and of all that we behold
> From this green earth; of all the mighty world
> Of eye, and ear,—both what they half create,
> And what perceive; well pleased to recognise
> In nature and the language of the sense
> The anchor of my purest thoughts, the nurse,
> The guide, the guardian of my heart, and soul
> Of all my moral being.
>
> (Wordsworth, 2006a, 260, lines 102–11)

Wordsworth reconfigured eyes and ears as themselves creative, half-perceiving and half-creating the world around them: over the eighteenth century, to use M. H. Abrams's metaphor, the hegemonic model of literary creation had shifted from being that of a mirror held up to nature to one in which the author acts as a lamp emitting light.

Originality was another fundamental feature of the Romantic idea of authorship. The stress on individuality, uniqueness, and novelty central to this conception was also part of a more general development of the idea of the self: since the early modern period a new individualistic order, based on the prominence of the individual's personal experience, had started to emerge. This new emphasis was related to Protestantism's prioritizing of one's direct and personal relationship with God, but the individual was also the starting point for eighteenth-century liberalism; the principle that knowledge should be based on one's personal experience started to spread, with Locke's *Essay Concerning Human Understanding* (1690) marking a major shift in this respect. All these new discourses privileged the individual: the idea of originality thus underwent a transformation in value, allowing for a new growth of the author as autonomous and individualistic. From the classical idea of writing as mimetic, involving the reproduction of established models, the focus shifted towards originality and 'genius.' This idea was extensively articulated in Edward Young's *Conjectures on Original Composition* (1759), in which he classified authors according to two categories: originals and imitators. According to Young, the former are "great benefactors," as they "extend the republic of letters and add a new province to its dominion" (Young, 1918, 6–7). If imitators have to share their crown "with the chosen object of [their] imitation," "an Original enjoys an undivided applause." Young compared originals to plants that rise "spontaneously from the vital root of genius": a plant, he observed, "grows, it is not made"; conversely, imitators are "a sort of manufacture wrought up by those mechanics, art, and labour, out of pre-existent materials, not their own" (7). A few pages later, he equated genius with virtue and learning with riches: "[a]s riches are most wanted where there is least virtue; so learning where there is least genius" (14). Genius "inspires [...] and is itself inspired"; it is "from heaven," while learning is "from man"; genius is "knowledge innate, and quite our own," while learning is "borrowed knowledge" (17).

The importance of uniqueness and imagination was further stressed by Coleridge's *Biographia Literaria* (1817), which made a distinction between fancy and imagination (itself divided into primary imagination and secondary imagination, differing in degree). Fancy is "a mode of memory" that "must receive all its materials ready made from the law of association" (Coleridge, 1960, 167); it is mere mechanic and associative power, and is controlled by one's will. Imagination is "the living power and prime agent of all human perception" (167), the vital faculty that creates and explicitly imitates God: it is "a repetition in the finite mind of the eternal act of creation in the infinite I AM" (167).

The Romantic myth of the author as a solitary genius has led to an under-appreciation of the many collaborative relationships that connected Romantic writers. The discrepancy between later idealization and actual practice is glaring. Collaboration was "an indisputable fact of the Romantic period" (Hickey, 1996, 735), proven by authors' accounts of the genesis of their texts, personal journals, correspondence, publication history, and the testimony of contemporaries. Studies such as Stillinger's (1991) offer ample evidence of major Romantic writers' solid involvement in each other's production. The Romantic era was full of collaborative projects: just to name a few, one year before Wordsworth and Coleridge's

Lyrical Ballads, a poetic volume by Coleridge appeared in print with the addition of some sonnets by Charles Lamb and Charles Lloyd; in 1794, *The Fall of Robespierre* was published, a play to which Coleridge contributed the first act and Robert Southey the second and the third; Coleridge and Southey also collaborated on the satirical ballad "The Devil's Thoughts," published in the *Morning Post* in 1799. Recent studies have brought to light the crucial roles of Dorothy Wordsworth and Mary Lamb in their brothers' literary production. The collaboration between Mary and Charles Lamb is made particularly intriguing by their co-dependent, almost symbiotic, relationship: these two siblings' mutual influence was embedded in a life-long domestic and authorial partnership, the "double singleness" described by Lamb in "Mackery End" (Lamb, 1964, 223).[4] Percy Shelley was part of a wide network of literary comradeship, and shared an intense relationship of literary exchange with his wife Mary: his 'editing' of *Frankenstein* and his contribution of the 1818 Preface to the novel must be accounted for, along with his contribution to Mary's mythological dramas *Proserpine* and *Midas*.

The Romantic view of the author had important consequences for the relationship between author and text. In the first place, the text emerged as the direct manifestation of the author's self: "[w]hat is poetry? is so nearly the same question with, what is a poet? that the answer to the one is involved in the solution of the other. For it is a distinction resulting from the poetic genius itself [...]" (Coleridge, 1960, 173). Hence, due to its very nature, the Romantic text calls for the reader to look for its writer. The case of Byron immediately comes to mind, as his contemporaries insisted on identifying him with his characters, starting from *Childe Harold*. In the preface to the first two cantos (1812), Byron wrote that the hero was a fictitious character, "the child of imagination" (Byron, 2006, 617). However, in the manuscript version he had called his protagonist 'Childe Burun,' the early form of his family name. After the public's insistence on seeing Byron's own travels in those of his fictional hero, in the fourth and last canto (1818) Byron changed the narrator to a first-person voice. In the preface, he wrote that there would be "less of the pilgrim," and "little slightly, if at

---

4 Aaron (1991) offers an illuminating analysis of the Lambs' personal and writing partnership, although she focuses more on gender than collaboration. See also Hickey, 1996. Charles and Mary Lamb's most famous co-authored project was *Tales from Shakespeare* (1807), with Charles in charge of adapting the tragedies and Mary the comedies. Despite writing fourteen of the twenty stories of the collection, Mary's name did not appear on the title-page until the seventh edition of 1838.

all, separated from the author speaking in his own person." The fact was, he added, that he "had become weary of drawing a line which everyone seemed determined not to perceive" (Byron, 2006, 617). The work of art thus becomes explicitly autobiographic: the author as a biographical person is in the text; their personality and experiences are all poured into it; as a result, the author is extremely visible inside their work.

A widespread practice that contributed to strengthening the relationship between author and text consisted in public readings of one's works, whether in front of wide audiences or in small private circles. Through the act of reading aloud one's text, lending one's voice and one's body to the characters, the presence of the author-creator is made concrete. The literary creation is taken to a further level: through the use of their voice, facial expressions, and body language, authors give life to their characters. From an abstract, unknown, invisible creator – a quiet voice behind the written words – the author turns into a more complete creator, visible, audible, tangible, alive. Seeing authors reading their text generates in the public a sense of overlapping between reality and fiction: the public reading turns something that belonged to the world of the imagination, heard and seen only in one's mind, into something that is part of reality.

The Romantic cult of the author became even more intense in the course of the Victorian age, when a number of factors coalesced "to form the recognizable dynamics of modern celebrity, prominent amongst them being the spread of print and the visual media, urbanization and the creation of large, popular audiences, and the spread of commodity culture" (Plunkett, 2016, 540). Two markets converged to produce a new merchandising strategy, heavily influencing the production and consumption of literature: publishing and the fine arts. Intrinsic to this fusion of markets were some cultural trends on which editors and publishers, together with authors, capitalized: the Victorian emphasis on the 'art of seeing' (the passion for observation and for refining the skills of looking and seeing) and the increasing importance of portraiture (first engraved portraits, later photographs). Curtis (1995, 214) ascribes the portrait mania to the Victorian obsession for classifying all things, including the human face, itself a text to be read.[5] By mid-century, due to new and cheaper reproduction techniques, the market for fine

---

5 For a discussion of Victorian visual culture and the transformation of nineteenth-century models of vision, see Crary, 1990; Armstrong, 1999; Flint, 2008; and Pearl, 2010.

art engravings had shifted from an upper-class domain to the middle and lower classes. From a luxury item of wealth and power, the portrait acquired the status of a commodity in the mass market economy, with penny magazines offering rougher but accessible prints. Series and volumes appeared in print attempting to catalogue the famous people of the past and present through portrait biography. In this way, the face was democratized and commodified. Portrait imagery became a necessary promotional mechanism for products and figures in the public eye: just as faces of eminent doctors started to be used as stamps of authenticity and value on medicines, pictures of authors became ubiquitous.

A key figure in the portrait mania was Dickens.[6] During his life, he posed for over eighty photographs; in addition, pirated and counterfeit images of Dickens circulated widely. Considering that photography was invented in the 1820s, becoming more accessible towards mid-century, Dickens's can be counted among the first most photographed faces and "the first heavily promoted face of literature" (Curtis, 1995, 242). As we have seen, Dickens's portraits became the model for representing the middle-class writer. The face and the signature of the author became both a seal of authenticity and a trademark feature. In 1867 Dickens's face, photographed in an exclusive sitting by Jeremiah Gurney in New York, was employed to promote his reading tour in the United States:

> [s]ince the dust of the Pharaohs was sold as a nostrum and mummy became merchandise there has been nothing so precious and so wonderful in the market as the face of Charles Dickens. Hence it is natural there should be danger from counterfeit, and that the happy merchant who possesses a monopoly of the real article should take all pains to prevent deceptions. [...] Surely, Mr. Dickens's face is his own, and he has as good a right to make a cent a piece on his pictures. (*New York Herald*, quoted in Kappel, 1978, 170)

This passage shows how the concept of authorial identity had become more elaborate: to *know* the author we must *see* them. The public wanted to see the ultimate subject in the novel: the author themselves. The aspiration to gain some insights into their fictional world by observing their traits and expressions was not at all new, but was definitely taken to new levels.[7] Moreover, Victorian readers were not inclined to accept

---

6 On Dickens and the creation of celebrity culture see Plunkett, 2016.
7 The Victorians exaggerated a deep-rooted tendency. For instance, in the first folio publication of Shakespeare's plays there is a portrait of the Bard by Martin Droeshout; the page facing the portrait presents a warning by Ben Jonson: "Reader, look/ Not on his Picture, but his Book." In the first number of the

an invented world of fiction without the reassuring image of the real, nonfictional person responsible for its creation. The recognizable face of the author thus became the indispensable chaperon of abstract names and words; hence, the bond of the author with the text was further reinforced: the text intrinsically belonged to its originator, so much so that it physically bore their face and signature. The Romantic tendency to look for the writer in the text was thus sharpened by the market-driven conflation of text and image and the aggressive merchandising of the Victorian era.

Public readings became a staple of Victorian cultural life: readers could see and hear their favourite novelists reading their favourite scenes, and writers had the opportunity to engage with, and further profit from, their public. But this was not only an age of authors' faces and voices: it was an age of authors' names. Once established, the name of a writer was sufficient to make a book a bestseller, or at least to guarantee a certain standard of sales. Authors' names were given pride of place through various means in advertisements, blurbs, and in the paratexts of the books themselves.[8] In the latter half of the century, the author as a celebrity reached its highest point ever. Authors' names did not simply sell books: they were displayed to promote commodities of all types. They posed for, and lent their signature to, advertisements of the most varied goods, from cigarettes to the first industrial toothpastes; they were called on to speak their mind about the hot topics of the moment and became spokespersons for causes from women's rights to social, political, and religious issues. Walter Besant was even recruited from the grave as a whisky salesman: an advertisement appeared in 1906 in the gossip magazine *M.A.P.*, reading "Water Besant drew for us the character of a man who regretted that he couldn't sleep off hunger. He was an example

---

Spectator (1711), Addison reflected: "I have observed, that a Reader seldom peruses a Book with Pleasure 'till he knows whether the Writer of it be a black or a fair Man of a mild or cholerick Disposition, Married or a Bachelor, with other particulars of the like nature, that conduce very much to the right Understanding of an Author" (*The Spectator*, I, I, I).

8 In 1876 the Boston publishers Roberts Brothers reacted against (or perhaps exploited?) the 'trade in reputations' by publishing a series known as "The No Name Series": each book of the series was written by a famous novelist whose name was not revealed. The erasure of the name of the writer would force readers to rely less on reputations, trusting their judgement only. The absence of authorial names piqued the curiosity of the public, thus proving a useful marketing device, and the series lasted successfully until 1887 (Ashton, 2003, 170–71).

of those who seek results by wrong means. If you want benefit from a stimulant, select the right thing. It is the whisky known as Dewar's" (31 March 1906). Besant's name and that of the whisky were printed in bold letters, so that the association could be made at first sight.[9]

The conjunction between topography and literary celebrity inaugurated the era of literary tourism. The phenomenon had existed long before the late century, but it was then that it developed into a national culture: former homes of famous authors were converted into museums; railway companies advertised day trips to places of literary interest along their lines; the periodical press published readers' reports of visits to illustrious places, giving origin to virtual literary tourism (Boyce et al., 2013, 18–19). Hall Caine was an outstanding promoter of literary tourism, settling on the Isle of Man and associating his name with the place (Waller, 2008, 375). On the occasion of Tennyson's burial, in 1892, 10,000 people were refused admittance to Westminster Abbey. This markedly contrasted with the previous poet laureate's funeral: the service at Grasmere in 1850 for Wordsworth's death had been simple and unreported. In forty years, a cult of literary celebrity had arisen.

The late nineteenth century also witnessed an unprecedented proliferation of biographical material about authors. The 1897 edition of *Who's Who* in literature contained some 6000 biographies; the 1898 edition added another 1000, and the 1899 one another 1500 (Waller, 2008, 422). Interviews and (usually posthumous) publication of authors' correspondence became endemic. Finding that no method would prevent heirs from publishing their letters, in 1890 *Punch* advised authors that "perhaps the best plan will be, not to write [letters] at all" (*Punch*, 11 December 1890, p. 282). Magazines specialized in celebrity culture made their appearance, such as *Our Celebrities* and *The Bookman*, which directed assiduous attention to famed writers. The phenomenon grew so much that in 1890 the *Review of Reviews* remarked that "authors are more read about than read" (reported in Waller, 2008, 350). Literary gossip was an expanding branch of New Journalism, pioneered by Edmund Yates, who imported the style of the 'personal interview' from America. His journal, *The World*, owned its success largely to its personality focus, with features such as its "Celebrities at Home" series.[10] Autograph-hunting became a thing. In

---

9 For a discussion of advertisements and authors see Waller, 2008, 329–63.
10 On Yates and the more personalized discourse in New Journalism see Weiner, 1985, 259–74, and Plunkett, 2016, 553–55.

1890 *Punch* demanded a Society for the Protection of Celebrities and blamed *The World* for having started the trend. Naming a child after a favourite fictional character or novelist had been in vogue since the eighteenth century (when the Pamelas and Clarissas reached epidemic proportions), but in the Victorian period this was taken to new levels. In the great age of letter-writing, an author's postbag was another index of fame: confidences from readers asking for sympathy and advice flooded writers' mailboxes.[11]

The late Victorian author had become more visible, more hypertrophic, more inseparable from the text than ever, calling for attention as much as the text. The trend for literary collaboration emerged from this atmosphere. On the one hand, it exploited and strengthened the centrality of the author: popular writers would come together, sometimes paired by editors on the wave of the craze for authors' names, to produce highly marketable novels. The periodical press often associated collaboration with a clear-cut, mechanical division of tasks, in which each author would take care of their own part and then put it together with the other shares, each firmly the possession of its writer, thus giving origin to monstrous literary centipedes. In these cases, double authorship just meant doubling the author; co-authorship represented the extremization of mass-produced literature and a peak in the status of authors as marketable products themselves.

On the other hand, a part of the collaborative trend led to unforeseen ways of imagining the author. The understanding of co-authorship just described above did not fit with the kind of collaboration as intended by Somerville and Ross, James Brander Matthews, Besant and Rice (partly), and other late Victorian collaborators. The authorial figure emerging from their experiences was very different from both a craftsman and the Romantic inspired individual. Their collaborative relationships challenged pervasive notions of what an author was and should be; according to them, the truly collaborative author barely existed at all: through their experiences, they performed an embryonic dismantling of the authorial figure, a process that will be illustrated step by step in the next section.

---

[11] For prominent women writers, celebrity status was more ambivalent and complex. Plunkett (2016, 548–51) explores how the ideology of the separate spheres and sexual double standards made female celebrity problematic.

The dissolution of the author

Let us start from the word 'collaboration.' The collaborative writer, being someone who by definition 'works with' (lat. *cum*/*laborare* > *collaborat*) someone else, destabilizes the basic tenet of post-Romantic authorship: solitude. Collaboration implies being in close contact with someone else. Consequently, the collaborative author is not an individual isolated from society, living apart from humanity: they have significant relationships with other members of the society, their solitude is shared at least by another person, they are no longer a nightingale who sings to cheer its own solitude.

Therefore, the privileged relationship of the author with the text, the codified model of the literary work as the manifestation of the author's self, is undermined. The collaborator shares the creative moment, so that the possessive 'his/her' cannot apply. In the act of co-authorship, the "direct cause-and-effect scenario" staging "individual author + inspiration = original literary masterpiece" becomes somewhat less clear, Karell (2002, xxi) points out. Collaboration "calls attention to a possible weak link in this 'genial' conception of authorship per se": it emphasizes "the tenuousness of the idea of a legitimate relation between unitary author and unitary text" (Hickey, 1998, 306–07). The association of one author with one text is no longer valid, and the Romantic monotheistic system of the author as the one God at the centre of creation collapses.

When readers take up a book written in collaboration and look at its title page, they will find two or more names in the place reserved for the author: the control over the textual spaces and narrative responsibility must be distributed between the collaborators. Masten (1997, 19) points out that collaboration is "a dispersal of author/ity, rather than a mere doubling of it." This intuition, though just roughly outlined and referring to sixteenth- and seventeenth-century drama, holds true for nineteenth-century collaborative fiction as well. True co-authorship does not consist in the juxtaposition of individually created lots, hence in the doubling of the author. Quite the contrary: the sharing of textual spaces implied in collaboration gives origin to a double dispersion: in the first place, a dispersal of authority, as authorial power, ownership, and control over the text must be divided;[12] then, a dispersal of the author-

---

12 Interestingly, Hickey (1998, 306) argues that "the general anxiety about collaboration arises from the equivocal relation of collaboration to authority." Collaborators, she observes, beside "jointly producing texts, jointly produce authority." But

figure itself: in the collaborative process, a dilution of the author, rather than a strengthening, takes place. The author of a co-authored text is split into as many parts as the individuals who partook in its creation: the singular monolithic author is shattered, crushed, scattered around. As Koestenbaum observes, "double writing serves as a symptom to the monolithic author's decline" (1989, 8).

Such dilution is generally perceived as perplexing by a large portion of the reading public, and by some co-writers themselves. "A collaborative relationship that consciously disperses power and authority," remarks Karell (2002, 36), "appears not only unusual but psychologically unnatural," as if the co-authors were "breaking the laws of authorship." However, as composition theorist Anne Gere remarks, in writing couples or groups "trust and a sense of empowerment result from the giving and receiving of authority" (1978, 110). This is exactly what happened to many late Victorian collaborators. Studies of literary partnerships between women have demonstrated that the writing relationship was very frequently accompanied by a strong personal bond that provided validation, intellectual stimulation, and emotional support. This positive reciprocal exchange of authority was illustrated by Somerville in her autobiographical writings examined in chapter 2, as when she compared Martin and herself to "two dancers" who "yield to the same impulse, given by the same strain of music" ("Two," 186).

The co-authored text may thus be imagined as a space where authors must negotiate their differences.[13] No more closed up in themselves, the collaborative author must deal with someone else's self, must acknowledge

---

"whose authority? Each his own? Each the other's? Both together a collective authority? Collaboration leads to ambiguous relations of mutual construction and deconstruction of authority" (308). In this light, co-authorship acts as "a reminder that authority is not organic and inalienable," but "is constructed with reference to other people and forces, it is always partial, it is never fully controllable by any one party, and it is vulnerable to deconstruction" (307). Drawing a parallel between co-authorship and political upheavals (specifically the French Revolution), Hickey notes that as "in the political realm, the revolutionary refiguring of the patriarchal familial paradigm as a fraternity threatens the singular nature of political authority, so refiguring authorial paternity as fraternity jeopardizes the singular nature of writerly authority" (306). Similarly, Karell (2002, 31) maintains that collaboration is "an unmanageable dispersal of authorial control."

13 Stone and Thompson (2006, 24) argue that collaboration partakes of the same complex strategies of "negotiation, mediation, compromise, competition, retaliation, coordination, and obligation that operate in larger institutional structures and economies."

the Other. But acknowledging the Other often implies arguments: as we have seen, in the Victorian imagination literary collaboration was often associated with fights, so much so that, from a certain point onwards, the periodical press focused almost exclusively on this aspect. Even the collaborators who had productive and happy experiences did not try to tone down the practical difficulties of writing together. Somerville addressed "the question as how two people can write together, without battle, murder, and sudden death ensuing immediately" ("Two," 180); Matthews was more ambiguous and declared in his autobiography that "[i]t is a fact that the 'artistic temperament' is jealous and touchy [...] It may be that I am lacking in the 'artistic temperament,' since my varied associations only cemented the friendships which preceded them" (Matthews, 1917, 252).

Both Matthews and Somerville ascribed the good results of their collaborative writing to the "harmonious equality" (Matthews, 1891, 24) that the partners enjoyed. Such equality was necessarily the product of a certain degree of suppressed egos: to write with another, the self of the writer must undergo a weakening. The collaborators need to take a distance from themselves and open up to the other: "[e]ach must be ready to yield a point when need be. In all associations there must be concessions from one to the other" and "an ability to take as well as to give" (Matthews, 1891, 5, 23). In Somerville's and Matthews's partnerships we are in the presence of two consciousnesses that deliberately decided not to try to impose themselves, but to blend harmoniously: "[s]ometimes I may have thought that I did more than my share, sometimes I knew that I did less than I should, but always there was harmony, and never did either of us seek to assert a mastery" (Matthews, 1891, 27).

The deliberate suppression of one's ego was not experienced by Somerville and Ross, or by Matthews, as a loss – "the loss of half of himself" lamented instead by Besant (*Autobiography*, 188). Rather, they saw the shared creative act as an added pleasure, for instance when Martin asserted that writing with Somerville "double[d] the triumph and the enjoyment, having first halved the trouble and anxiety" (*IM*, 134), or when Matthews, in an astonishingly similar way, declared: "[i]f I may be allowed to offer myself as a witness, I shall testify to the advantage of a literary partnership, which halves the labor of the task and doubles the pleasure" (Matthews, 1891, 26). This ability to turn difference into a positive force during the process of negotiation is one of the most compelling aspects of such collaborations.

If these favourable conditions occur, two distinct authorial consciousnesses meet and, over the collaborative process, mix up, intertwine, and become more and more blended into each other. Gradually, a merging of the authors takes place, so that at the end of the process it is not possible to determine who is responsible for what, not even for the co-authors themselves:

> [e]ven the collaborators themselves are at a loss to specify their own contributions. When two men have worked together honestly and heartily in the inventing, the developing, the constructing, the writing and the revising of a book [...] it is often impossible for either partner to pick out his own share; certain things he may recognize as his own, and certain other things he may credit frankly to his ally; but the rest was the result of the collaboration itself, contributed by both parties together and not by either separately. (Matthews, 1891, 1–2)

Thus, while retaining their bodily borders, the co-authors metaphorically merge, giving origin to a new and independent author-figure. Borrowing Édouard Glissant's (1996) concept of cultural creolization, Medaglia (2014, 94) theorizes that collaboration "creolizes" the author, proposing a formula to represent the process: given a co-author X_1 and a co-author X_2, the result of the collaborative writing process shall not be X_{1-2} – a superficial juxtaposition of authorial individualities – but rather X_3, something new and independent from both X_1 and X_2 (Medaglia, 2014, 100–01). X_3 is the result of the merging of the co-authors, their consciousnesses, their social and cultural backgrounds, and their styles: X_3 is a hybrid entity. The authors who create a collaborative text, suggests Medaglia (2014, 96), cannot be circumscribed nor inserted into rigid categories: their major feature is precisely to fluctuate within the text, to have no fixed and pre-determined boundaries. The author-figure resulting from the collaborative project is no biographical person: they are depersonalized, because they do not correspond to an individual, a subjectivity, a self. Even though they have distinct traits, they remain abstract. Behind a co-authored text, then, there is no defined authorial self, but a creolized multiplicity of consciousnesses, which defies any untangling of the original contributors. In the collaborative practice, the hybrid triumphs. Therefore, contrarily to Ashton's claim that "[i]f we listen to collaborative texts [...] we hear individual voices" (2003, 12), I argue that we hear no distinct, singular voices, but rather a creole and fluid one.

It may be useful here to recover the metaphor employed by Somerville when she explained that her and Ross's styles were as different as blue and yellow, but that the final product was green. This new author, the colour green, appearing from the merging of Somerville and Ross, has its own recognizable characteristics; what is not recognizable are the individualities behind, the two hands involved. Likewise, Matthews wrote that, if the collaboration had been "a true marriage," any endeavour "to sift out the contribution of one collaborator from that of his fellow" would be as futile as trying to decide "whether the father or the mother is the real parent of a child" (Matthews, 1891, 9). As a baby bears the genes of both parents, but stands as an independent being with its own features, so does the collaborative X_3.

But how is this merging possible? How does it take place? Matthews and Somerville surprisingly offered the same answer. They both explained that they relied on a conversational method. Both co-authors accorded special significance to the act of talking, saying that the writing was secondary and was not nearly as important as the discussion that had preceded it. In a passage worth quoting once more, Somerville claimed that before any section of their joint work "found itself finally transferred into decorous MS.," it "would probably have suffered many things, but it would, at all events, have had the advantage of having been well aired" (*IM*, 133). Discussion was deemed fundamental by Besant too, so much so that he insisted on recognizing Rice as a full author even if he did not take part in the writing. Even if in Besant's model of collaboration there was no complete merging of the collaborators – at the end of the day, it was up to one partner to have "the final word" ("Lit. Coll.," 204) – a partial merging took place, at least during the phase of the discussion: Besant and Rice's novels are different from Besant's solo ones, and represent the product of the combination of the two. Besant claimed that it was "impossible [...] to lay hands upon any passage or page and to say 'this belongs to Rice – this is mine'" (*Autobiography*, 188, 189).

One of the consequences of the conversational method was the loss of the immediacy or the divine rapture so insisted upon by the Romantic poets. If the Romantic author declares that they write under ecstatic inspiration or immediate dictation, collaboration defies such belief, as obviously there may be no rapture, no sudden spontaneity, no immediacy when two individuals need to take their thoughts out, listen to the other, discuss, negotiate, and reach an agreement. Since every aspect of the co-authored text must be negotiated, the collaborative process takes longer – much longer – than solitary composition, as specified by Besant, Somerville, and Matthews. Shelley's declaration that "when composition begins, inspiration is already on the decline" (Shelley, 1986, 38) is thus further complicated by the process of collaboration: if inspiration is already fading when one begins to write in solitude, then collaboration would not stand a chance.

We have seen how, thanks to the conversational method, the authors become 'one,' making it impossible to tell the single hands apart. Furthermore, and crucially, both Matthews and Somerville insisted that there was no point in trying to do so. To the public's curiosity about who wrote what, the co-authors replied: what does it matter? These late Victorian collaborators considered the public's "supreme, almost invariable question, as to which of us held the pen – the inspired pen!" ("Two," 181) totally worthless, if not utterly irritating. Somerville confessed that "[t]he question as to which of us held the pen [...] was a point that never entered our minds to consider." Pestered by the media's unrelenting questions about the mechanics of her and Ross's collaboration, she voiced her exasperation in a letter to one of her brothers: "[i]t's the books that matter, not who held the wretched pen!" (quoted in Jamison, 2016, 46). Matthews insisted that if the joint work has been "a true chemical union and not a mere mechanical mixture, it matters little who holds the pen" (1891, 7). He resorted to the metaphor of the writing part as being merely "the clothing of a babe already alive and kicking" (7).

Somerville's and Matthews's final point seems to be one: the focus of the public's attention should be the text in its unity, not what is behind it – that is, not the authors. The writers of a collaborative work, being neither discernible nor perceptible, remain invisible, concealed behind the text. In a cultural atmosphere that paid increasing attention to authors' names, authors' biographies, authors' faces, authors' opinions, even authors' houses, the insistence of these collaborators on their own insignificance and invisibility was confusing. They discouraged readers from looking for them in the pages of their texts, because *they* were not in the text. Only the product in its final unity and independence, the colour green, the baby alive and kicking, X_3, should be visible. Only to it should readers devote their attention. The author-figure promoted by Matthews and Somerville is reduced to a scattered, blurred, and hybrid entity that simply "does not matter." The collaborative author fades away into an elusive presence that remains hidden behind the text: it turns into a ghost, which cannot – and should not, the co-authors exhorted – be seen or even looked for. And yet, as sometimes happens with phantoms, the ghost of the collaborative author kept haunting Victorian readers – who would see it as a puzzle to be solved, a mystery to be unravelled.

The experiences of the co-authors discussed above were by no means the only cases in which the dissolution of the Romantic author took place. I have taken them as case studies of a much larger phenomenon: similar references to the merging and fluidity of the collaborative authorial identity are present in comments by other nineteenth- and early twentieth-century co-authors. Katherine Bradley and Edith Cooper talked of their relationship in terms of a fusion of mind and body alike. Bradley took care of her niece from infancy, and later attended university with her; they shared a house that hosted gatherings of intellectuals and homosexual couples. They were associated with turn-of-the-century aesthetes, and the poetry they wrote together was regarded as Sapphic poetry: their texts are characterized by references to pagan celebrations, nature, and same-sex love. Like Violet Martin, Bradley and Cooper adopted male names for both their public and private identities, affectionately referring to themselves as 'Michael' and 'Field' or sometimes 'Michael' and 'Henry.' Comparing their domestic partnership to that of the Brownings, Bradley wrote that "these two poets, man and wife, wrote alone; each wrote, but did not bless or quicken one another with their work; we are closer married" (Field, 1933, 16). They described their joint works as a "perfect mosaic" (quoted in Sturgeon, 1922, 47) and, echoing Somerville's metaphor of the partnered dancing, Bradley declared that, during the creative moment, she and Cooper "cross[ed] and interlace[d] like a company of dancing summer flies. If one begins a character, his companion seizes and possesses it; if one conceives a scene or a situation, the other corrects, completes, and murderously cuts away" (Bradley to Havelock Ellis, May 1886; quoted in Sturgeon, 1922, 47). A passage from "A Girl," from the collection *Underneath the Bough* (1893), describes their joint writing process:

> [...] our souls so knit
> I leave a page half-writ –
> The work begun
> Will to heaven's conception done
> If she come to it. (Field, 1893, lines 10–14)

As Ehnenn (2008, 31) points out, "instead of divided writers battling over the 'last word,'" the poem documents "its own instance of creation as a seamless, almost effortless writing process." Like Somerville and Ross, Bradley and Cooper did not try to conceal conflict, but treated its inevitability light-heartedly. They highlighted the seamlessness of their joint texts and warned their readers, eager to uncover traces of the respective contributions, in religious terms: "as to our work, let no man think he can put asunder what God has joined" (quoted in Ehnenn, 2008, 31). Mary Sturgeon, their first biographer, observed that "it is not possible [...] to point to this line or that speech, and say 'It is the work of Michael' or 'It is the work of Henry.' You cannot do it, because the poets themselves could not have done it" (Sturgeon, 1922, 62–63). She adds that "one may search diligently, and search in vain, for any sign in the work both wrought that this is the creation of two minds and not of one" (Sturgeon, 1922, 62–63). In a letter to Vernon Lee, dated January 1890, Michael Field wrote: "[i]t cannot be too frequently repeated that belief in the unity of M.F. is absolutely necessary. [...] He is in literature one" (quoted in Ehnenn, 2008, 33).

Vernon Lee herself was one half of another late Victorian partnership, together with Clementina 'Kit' Anstruther-Thomson. They too played with metaphors of merging and boundlessness. Vernon Lee was the pseudonym of Violet Page (1856–1935), art critic, aestheticist, and essayist, who gained fame with *Studies in the Eighteenth Century in Italy* (1880). She shared a love and creative relationship with Kit Anstruther-Thomson (1857–1921) from 1887 to the latter's death. Their association resulted in many works on psychological aesthetics. Lee wrote of their partnership:

> [w]here do you end and I begin? Who can answer? We are not definite, distinct existences [...] we are forever meeting, crossing, encroaching [...] part of ourselves left behind in others, part of them becomes ourselves: a flux of thought, feeling, experience, aspiration complex, interchanging life which is the life eternal, not of the individual, but of the race. (quoted in Ehnenn, 2008, 172)

Images of unity and fluidity were also employed by a less celebrated but equally fascinating pair of collaborators, the Australian Marjorie Barnard (1897–1987) and Flora Eldershaw (1897–1956), who in the 1930s and the 1940s co-authored five novels, three historical studies, and a volume of literary criticism under the collective pseudonym 'M. Barnard Eldershaw.' Barnard and Eldershaw met during their first year at the University of Sydney and became life-long friends and collaborators. They are ranked among the leading Australian writers of the interwar period: their last novel, *Tomorrow and Tomorrow and Tomorrow* (1947), is regarded as one of Australia's major early science fiction works. It was censored for political reasons at the time and was not published in its entirety until Virago Press reissued it in 1983. During their time, they found a market for their fiction mostly in England, "where Australian literature, like Australia itself, was considered a curiosity" (London, 1999, 120). The two collaborators left few manuscripts and no journals; no account of the partnership written by the two of them together was ever found. The only description we have is Barnard's single-handed late-life essay "The Gentle Art of Collaboration" (1977), where she chronicled their partnership and briefly discussed their writing method. Crucially, she stressed the role of conversation, claiming that collaboration took place "in the discussion period" (Barnard, 1977, 126). She wrote that they negotiated every aspect until they came to an agreement and "talked about it to one another, discussed it at length, story, characters, background, treatment, in that order, getting the feel of it, coming to know it in depth, all this without putting pen to paper" (Barnard, 1977, 126). Over the conversation, their individualities merged: "[w]e worked it up together and our thoughts and ideas became inextricably blended into a whole. There was no mine and thine but ours. This not only excluded proprietary rights on either side but gave the book its unity" (Barnard, 1977, 126). Dever calls this process "unselfing" (1995, 70), which closely resembles the idea of giving up one's self in collaboration to successfully merge with the other. After examining the manuscripts of M. Barnard Eldershaw's first two novels, Dever comments:

> [t]he handwriting in both manuscripts alternates, and the balance between the two hands is fairly even. [...] There are instances where the handwriting changes in mid-sentence and where a different hand supplies either the opening or closing sentence of a given paragraph. No distinct pattern of division between the two hands emerges, and it appears that the division of labor was neither rigid nor mechanical. [...] The collaborative enterprise emerges, then, as an open-ended performance, the manuscript forming a ludic discourse. Here there is no revelation scene. (1995, 67)

Moreover, each manuscript presents a note written by Barnard (probably attached when they were donated to the public), where she warns that the alternation of their handwritings is not at all a solution to the question of 'who did what': "if anyone thought that this was a key to the collaboration they would be vastly mistaken" (quoted in Dever, 1995, 68). Dever observes that Barnard's use of metaphors of fluidity "conveys a sense of the inseparable or indivisible, a sense of something that dilutes or mixes to such a degree that the distinction between the one and the other becomes blurred: the mixed voices overflow the individual subject"

(69); "the two traverse the boundaries of discrete subjectivity to found a nonindividuated collective subject" (70).

Like Somerville and Ross or Michael Field, neither Barnard nor Eldershaw ever married. Their life-long exclusive friendship constituted an alternative to heterosexual marriage, viewed as incompatible with their aspirations. Even if they never lived together (Barnard living at home with her parents, Eldershaw being a live-in teacher at a boarding school), they maintained a flat in Sydney where they hosted literary meetings and worked together. Theirs is another case when the emotional bond provided a solid foundation for the literary efforts. Unlike their Victorian predecessors, however, Barnard and Eldershaw did not rely primarily on their writing to earn their income: the former was a librarian, the latter a schoolmistress. Only Barnard eventually gave up her job to become a full-time author. On this occasion, a crisis of the partnership could have arisen, as reported by Barnard herself, but did not, once again thanks to their profound friendship:

> [y]ou can imagine how easily she [Eldershaw] might envy me my greater leisure to wrestle with it [*The Glasshouse*] or be jealous of the time spent alone with our common property. But she isn't. The atmosphere between us is so clear that any speck would show up monstrously. I think collaboration (in creative work) is impossible, but now and then it happens. And an entirely satisfactory friendship that neither trails off at the edges into boredom nor gets clogged with emotion is another good thing in this rather dark world. (quoted in Dever, 1995, 70)

On another occasion, Barnard compared the partnership to "a bedroom secret" (quoted in Dever, 1995, 68), probably meaning "a privacy that cannot be violated" (London, 1999, 67).

The recurrence of discourses of ecstatic fluidity in women's collaborations may point to a gender peculiarity, an idea first advanced by Koestenbaum (1989) and developed by London (1999) and Ehnenn (2008). London argues that male collaborations inevitably falter because of the author's desire "to enjoy the reputation of his own good work" – to use Besant's words (*Autobiography*, 188) – while female collaborators usually do not betray such self-interest, such need of individual validation. Ehnenn (2008) too observes that, while men's collaborations are generally characterized by competition and hierarchy, women, perhaps because already excluded from the category of the solitary genius due to gender codes, tend to shape collaborative relationships around notions of equality. Such assumptions are largely true. However, Matthews's approach to collaboration seems to partially refute this binary opposition: conversational composition, harmonious union, and full equality are key features of his collaborative ethos. In his literary associations (always with male partners) no one sought to assert a mastery; the partnerships were the outcome of intimacy:

> [c]ollaboration has always been very attractive to me; and it has always been the result of the intimacy of friendship with its corresponding sympathy of interest. My collaborators were friends before we undertook a task in common; and they remained my friends in spite of the opportunities for dispute due to the partnership itself. (Matthews, 1917, 252)

In this respect, my reading differs from Koestenbaum's, who argues that in male writing couples each partner, more or less consciously, tries to dominate over the other, thus suggesting a model of male co-authorship as divided and engaged in a constant struggle for authorial control. Though offering illuminating starting points, critical readings so far have not included the wealth of different attitudes and practices that characterize literary collaboration: the dismantling of the solitary author within the collaborative practice is a complex and fascinating phenomenon which calls for further study – something I hope this work will stimulate.

Towards the death of the author

Some late Victorian collaborators aimed at an understanding of the author as invisible to the eyes of the reader, and at an idea of the text as a cohesive, autonomous unity, independent from the singular biographical personalities of the co-authors. Such notions present some common points with the Modernist attitude as to the relationship between text and author. Stephen Dedalus's declaration in the fifth chapter of Joyce's *A Portrait of the Artist As a Young Man* (1916) springs to mind: "[t]he personality of the artist finally refines itself out of existence, impersonalises itself [...] like the God of creation, remains within or behind or beyond or above his handiwork, invisible, refined out of existence, indifferent, pairing his fingernails" (Joyce, 2000, 180–81). Similar ideas are also present in *Tradition and Individual Talent* (1919), where T. S. Eliot attacked Romantic theories of authorship and illustrated his "Impersonal theory of poetry" about "the relation of the poem to his author" (Eliot, 1975, 40). "Honest criticism and sensitive appreciation," he argued, "is directed not upon the poet but upon the poetry" (40). Eliot insisted on the "depersonalization" and the "surrender" of the artist, maintaining that their progress "is a continual self-sacrifice, a continual extinction of personality" (40). An analogy with a chemical reaction is drawn:

> [w]hen the two gasses [oxygen and sulphur dioxide] are mixed in the presence of a filament of platinum, they form sulphurous acid. This combination takes place only if the platinum is present; nevertheless the newly formed acid contains no trace of platinum, and the platinum itself is apparently unaffected; [...] The mind of the poet is the shred of platinum. (40)

Eliot's theory could easily be applied to Victorian co-authorship: the work of art (sulphurous acid) stands as an independent unit, bearing no sign of the personalities of the individual co-authors (the platinum). Poetry, claimed Eliot, "is not the expression of personality, but an escape from personality" (40).

The idea of the fragmentation, the depersonalization, and the invisibility of the author in late Victorian collaborations appears all the more outstanding when we consider the historical and cultural context in which it developed, as seen in the first section of this chapter. Modernism arose in a totally different, rapidly changing atmosphere. In 1900, Freud's *Interpretation of Dreams* marked the shifting of the human mind from a positivistic unity into a shattered multiplicity; in the same year Nietzsche, who had declared God's death, died in an asylum; Einstein's theory of relativity and the models of the atom's structure by Rutherford and Bohr led to the revision of centuries-long ideas and the embracing of an understanding of knowledge as limited and partial. Trust in the human being, its internal coherence, unity, and reliability, was challenged. "In or about December, 1910, human character changed," famously wrote Virginia Woolf (1966, 320). It seems only natural that the arts reimagined human identity. Beside literature, artistic movements such as Expressionism and Cubism broke with tradition: one may think of "Les demoiselles d'Avignon" by Picasso (1907) or the Post-Impressionist exhibition in 1910 by Roger Fry at the Grafton Galleries in London, which introduced the English public to the works of Seurat, Van Gogh, Gauguin, and Cézanne, causing uproar and indignation. In this light, Modernism's position about the author is not surprising. Moreover, in considering the similarities between Modernist and late Victorian conceptions of authorship one must take into account the different kinds of public their production was aimed at: Modernism was targeted at an intellectual elite, while late nineteenth-century collaborations fitted into the market of popular literature, offering accessible texts to a large and varied audience.

We could therefore imagine late Victorian collaboration as a sort of intermediate step between the hypertrophy of the Romantic author and the cancellation of the authorial voice by Modernism.

A well-known text of New Criticism, "The Intentional Fallacy" by W. K. Wimsatt and Monroe C. Beardsley (1946), argues that the biographical background and the intention of the author are not only hard to reconstruct but, were they traceable, they would be irrelevant to understanding the meaning of the text, which has to speak for itself: "the design or intention of the author is neither available nor desirable" (Wimsatt and Beardsley, 1946, 468). According to Wimsatt and Beardsley, when reading a literary text one must not fall into the "intentional fallacy": that is, pay too much attention to the author's biographical and psychological information. In front of a text, they argue, only two alternatives are possible: the first is that the author has failed in realizing their intentions, and so the meaning of the work does not coincide with them; consequently, knowing their intentions will say nothing useful about the text; the second alternative is that the author has succeeded in realising their intentions, and so the meaning of the text coincides with them; but if the text expresses what the author wanted it to say, then the author's words will add nothing to what is already in the text. Wimsatt and Beardsley's conclusion is that the text alone is enough: the task of the critic, and of the general reader too, is to stick to it. Such exhortation sounds familiar: the resemblances with the metadiscourses of late Victorian co-authors are striking. In the case of a collaborative work, the very starting point is missing, that is the authors themselves – to be intended as the single biographical persons. As we have seen, the author resulting from collaboration is a slippery and elusive hybrid, being the product of the fusion of two different subjectivities, mixed up and intertwined in unpredictable and inexplicable ways.

The pointlessness of finding the ultimate explanation of the text in the author has been taken to its extreme by Roland Barthes's famous announcement of the "death of the author" (1967). In a key passage, Barthes exposes the tyrannical Romantic author:

> [t]he Author [...] is always conceived of as the past of his own book: book and author stand automatically on a single line divided into a *before* and an *after*. The Author is thought to *nourish* the book, which is to say that he exists before it, thinks, suffers, lives for it, is in the same relation of antecedence to his work as a father to his child. (1977, 145)

Barthes replaces the author in the traditional sense of the term with what he calls "the writer" or "scriptor," a subject in the grammatical sense, not a person in their biographical existence: "the modern scriptor is born simultaneously with the text; he is in no way equipped with a being preceding or exceeding the writing, is not the subject with the book as predicate; there is no other time than that of the enunciation and every text is eternally written *here* and *now*" (Barthes, 1977, 145). This interpretation may easily be applied to the author-figure surfacing from the collaborative process: the author is born when the phase of the discussion starts, and takes shape simultaneously with the advancing of the creative process, along with the text; when the collaboration comes to an end, and the text is finished, the author-figure ceases to exist, because it does not exist outside the text. It exists in the *here* and *now* of the creation of the text. Therefore, it is futile to look for an explanation of the text in the co-authors: they do not have it, because they are not 'the author' of the text.

The depersonalization of the collaborative author presents some similarities with Barthes's theory when he writes that "it is language which speaks, not the author: to write is to reach, through a preexisting impersonality – never to be confused with the castrating objectivity of the realistic novelist – that point where language alone acts, 'performs,' and not 'oneself.'" Significantly, and like the collaborative ethos, the performance has to be by the text, not by the authorial self. When the collaborative process begins, the co-authors enter their death.

Foucault's "What Is an Author?" (1969) argues that writing creates "a space into which the writing subject endlessly disappears" (Foucault, 1979, 142). Concerned above all with the idea of the "effacement of the writing subject's individual characteristics" (1979, 142), Foucault aims at analyzing literary texts by going beyond the conception of writing as the manifestation of a certain subjectivity, the expression of an individual who precedes, and is outside of, the text. Foucault's final, blunt statement, "[w]hat does it matter who is speaking?" strikingly echoes Somerville's "[i]t's the books that matter, not who held the wretched pen," and her various, impatient dismissals of questions about the authorship of her and Ross's books. Both Somerville and Foucault seem to yearn for a time in which the only response to the question "who is speaking?" would be a shrug, a "stirring of an indifference" (Foucault, 1979, 160).

To conclude, we may venture to say that the tendency towards impersonality established over the twentieth century from Modernist poetics to Post-structuralism might find, under some aspects, a partial anticipation in the collaborative practice of the second half of the nineteenth century. I am far from trying to imply that Modernist authors, Wimsatt and Beardsley, Barthes, or Foucault had the declarations of Victorian collaborators in mind – most probably, they were not even aware of their existence. Exploring the features of late nineteenth-century collaborative writing and its implications for the figure of the author led me to notice unexpected similarities with successive and radical theorizations of the death of the author. However, unlike Modernism, New Criticism, and Post-Structuralism, late Victorian collaborators never formulated a systematic theorizing of their positions and hardly saw themselves as radically transforming the nature of authorship. It is not clear whether they realized the full potential of their views – considering their reticence at discussing them, the answer is probably they did not. We only have desultory reflections, scattered among private correspondence, articles, essays, prefaces, and autobiographies. Such documents have never been collected and developed into a thorough, comprehensive aesthetics, and Victorian collaborators' ground-breaking experiences have long been forgotten. The present book has tried to fill this gap. Still, further study is needed to thoroughly unpack how literary collaboration relates to – and often challenges – past and present understandings of authorship.

Ultimately, so much more could have been done. In the case of the co-authors who also had success as solo novelists, like Besant, Broughton, or Haggard, it would have been interesting to analyse in more detail how their collaborative novels differed from their solo productions, or whether the process of collaboration figures in any way in their works: I have discussed collaboration in fiction writing, but what about collaboration *within* fiction? Did co-authorship become a theme explored within the novels, both in those written in collaboration and those written individually? This could be read as part of the debate about co-authorship, as a more indirect way of commenting on the discourses that circulated at the time. To engage with these questions would have been exciting, but it would have taken me too far away from the (already vast) main object of the project: to map late Victorian literary collaboration as a practice. It would have involved a more specific focus on the *product* rather than on the *process* of collaboration: the approach I have adopted in dealing with co-authored works centres on the workings of the collaborative process(es). This implied reading the novels foregrounding the collaborative ethics and the final unity of the product. But more in-depth readings are needed to illuminate the outputs of such a fascinating literary practice and their many facets. In addition, I have occasionally mentioned interesting nineteenth- and early twentieth-century partnerships, such as E. D. Gerard or the Findlater sisters, but I have not discussed them or any of their novels. They remain largely neglected, and would deserve more scholarly and readerly attention. As for the occasional collaborations of the 1890s, I have selected three relevant cases to represent the major trends, but that does not mean that the topic has been exhaustively investigated. So many collaborative adventures are still covered in dust. Without claiming to be exhaustive, I include an Appendix with a list of co-authored novels that appeared in print from the mid-nineteenth to the first decades of the twentieth century. These, and many others, are paths that remain open to exploration: Victorian collaborators and their texts have so much more left to say.

Appendix

A selection of co-authored novels, c. 1860–1920

Bennet, Arnold, and Eden Phillpotts.
— 1906. *The Sinews of War*. London: T. Werner Laurie.
— 1908. *The Statue*. London: Cassell.
Besant, Walter, and James Rice.
— 1872. *Ready-Money Mortiboy: A Matter-of-Fact Story*. London: Tinsley Brothers.
— 1873. *My Little Girl*. London: Tinsley Brothers.
— 1875. *With Harp and Crown*. London: Tinsley Brothers.
— 1876. *The Golden Butterfly*. London: Tinsley Brothers.
— 1876. *This Son of Vulcan*. London: Sampson Low & Co.
— 1878. *By Celia's Arbour: A Tale of Portsmouth Town*. London: Sampson Low & Co.
— 1878. *The Monks of Thelema*. London: Chatto & Windus.
— 1879. *The Chaplain of the Fleet*. London: Chatto & Windus.
— 1881. *The Seamy Side*. London: Chatto & Windus.
Broughton, Rhoda, and Elizabeth Bisland. 1891. *A Widower Indeed*. London: J. R. Osgood, McIlvaine & Co.
Cantwell, Fredericka Spangler, and Dora Eastwick Martyn. 1899. *The High Commission*. London: F. Tennyson Neely.
Castle, Agnes, and Egerton Castle.
— 1898. *The Pride of Jennico: Being a Memoir of Captain Basil Jennico*. London: Richard Bentley & Son.
— 1900. *The Bath Comedy: A Novel*. London: Macmillan & Co.
— 1901. *The Secret Orchard*. London: Macmillan & Co.
— 1903. *Incomparable Bellairs*. London: Archibald Constable & Co.
— 1903. *The Star Dreamer*. London: Archibald Constable & Co.
— 1905. *French Nan*. London: Smith, Elder & Co.
— 1905. *Rose of the World*. London: Smith, Elder & Co.

— 1906. *If Youth But Knew!* London: Macmillan & Co.
— 1907. *My Merry Rockhurst.* London: Smith, Elder & Co.
— 1909. *Wroth.* Leipzig: Tauchnitz.
— 1910. *Panter's Club.* London: T. Nelson & Sons.
— 1912. *The Grip of Life.* London: Smith, Elder & Co.
— 1912. *Love Guilds the Scene and Women Guide the Plot.* London: Smith, Elder & Co.
— 1913. *The Golden Barrier.* London: Methuen.
— 1915. *The Hope of the House.* London: Cassell & Co.
— 1916. *Count Raven.* London: Cassell & Co.
— 1916. *The Wind's Will.* London: Cassell & Co.
Conrad, Joseph, and Ford Madox Ford.
— 1901. *The Inheritors: An Extravagant Story.* London: William Heinemann.
— 1903. *Romance.* London: Smith, Elder & Co.
— 1909. *The Nature of a Crime.* London: Duckworth & Co.
Crommelin, May, and James Moray Brown. 1889. *Violet Vyvian M.F.H.* London: Hurst and Blackett.
Dickens, Charles, and Wilkie Collins. 1867. *No Thoroughfare. All the Year Round*, Extra Christmas Number (12 December): 1–48.
Dowson, Ernest, and Arthur Moore.
— 1893. *A Comedy of Masks.* London: William Heinemann.
— 1899. *Adrian Rome.* London: Methuen.
Findlater, Mary, and Jane Findlater.
— 1908. *Crossriggs.* London: Smith, Elder & Co.
— 1911. *Penny Moneypenny.* London: Smith, Elder & Co.
— 1923. *Beneath the Visiting Moon.* London: Hurst & Blackett.
Findlater, Mary, Jane Findlater, Kate Douglas Wiggin, and Allan McAulay [Charlotte Stewart].
— 1904. *The Affair at the Inn.* London: Gay and Bird.
— 1911. *Robinetta.* London: Gay and Hancock.
Freeman Bell, J. [Israel Zangwill and Louis Cowan]. 1889. *The Premier and the Painter.* London: Spencer Blackett.
Gerard, E. D. [Emily and Dorothea Gerard].
— 1880. *Reata; or What's in a Name.* Edinburgh: William Blackwood & Sons.
— 1882. *Beggar My Neighbour: A Novel.* Edinburgh: William Blackwood & Sons.
— 1885. *The Waters of Hercules.* Edinburgh: William Blackwood & Sons.
— 1891. *A Sensitive Plant.* London: Kegan Paul & Co.
Haggard, Henry Rider, and Andrew Lang. 1890. *The World's Desire.* London: Longmans, Green & Co.
Hichens, Robert S., and Wilson Barrett. 1899. *The Daughters of Babylon: A Novel.* London: John Macqueen.

Howard, Blanche Willis, and William Sharp. 1892. *A Fellowe and His Wife.* London: Osgood & McIlvaine.

Howard, Lady Constance, and Ada Fielder-King. 1891. *Master of Her Life: A Novel.* London: F. V. White & Co.

Howard, Lady Constance, Miss Lane, Mrs Laughton, Mrs Sparshott, Miss Ernestine Tate, Mrs G. B. Burgin, Miss Emma Wylie, Miss D. Bellerby, Miss Eva Roos, Miss Kathleen Watson, Mrs J. M. Bull, Mrs J. Alexander Kennedy, Miss Ethel Mackenzie, Mrs Vallance, Miss Minnie Laud, Miss Hilda Somers, The Countess of Munster, Miss Edith Ostlere, Mrs Lena M. Horsford, and Miss Daisy Moutray Read. 1892. *A 'Novel' Novel: A Strange Story. Twenty Chapters by Twenty Authors.* London: The Gentlewoman Library.

Hunter, Hay, and Walter Whyte. 1884. *My Ducats and My Daughter.* London: Kegan Paul.

Kipling, Rudyard, and Wolcott Balestier. 1892. *The Naulahka: A Story of West and East.* London: William Heinemann.

Lang, Andrew, and A. E. W. Mason. 1899. *Parson Kelly.* London: Longmans, Green & Co.

Lang, Andrew, and Walter H. Pollock.
— 1887. *He.* London: Longmans, Green & Co.
— 1887. *King Solomon's Wives.* London: Vizetelly & Co.

Maitland, Ella Fuller, and Sir Frederick Pollock. 1899. *The Etchingham Letters.* London: Smith, Elder & Co.

Marryat, Florence, and Charles Ogilvie. 1891. *The Lost Diamonds.* London: Ludgate Monthly.

Mathers, Helen, Justin McCarthy, Mrs Trollope, Arthur Conan Doyle, May Crommelin, F. C. Philips, 'Rita,' Joseph Hatton, Mrs Lovett Cameron, Bram Stoker, Florence Marryat, Frank Danby, Mrs Edward Kennard, Richard Dowling, Mrs Hungerford, Arthur A'Beckett, Jean Middlemass, Clement Scott, Clo. Graves, H. W. Lucy, Adeline Sergeant, G. Manville Fenn, 'Tasma,' and F. Anstey. 1892. *The Fate of Fenella.* London: Hutchinson & Co.

McCarthy, Justin, and Rosa Campbell Praed.
— 1886. *The Right Honourable: A Romance of Society and Politics.* London: Chatto & Windus.
— 1888. *The Ladies' Gallery.* London: Richard Bentley & Son.
— 1890. *The Rival Princess: A London Romance of To-day.* London: F. V. White & Co.

Meredith, Isabel [Helen and Olivia Rossetti]. 1903. *A Girl Among the Anarchists.* London: Duckworth & Co.

Murray, David Christie, and Henry Herman.
— 1887. *One Traveller Returns.* London: Chatto & Windus.
— 1889. *A Dangerous Catspaw.* London: Longmans, Green & Co.

— 1889. *Wild Darrie*. London: Longmans, Green & Co.
— 1890. *The Bishop's Bible*. London: Chatto & Windus.
— 1890. *He Fell Among Thieves*. London: Macmillan & Co.
— 1891. *Only a Shadow*. London: Griffith & Farran.
Oliphant, M. O. W., and Thomas Bailey Aldrich. 1888. *The Second Son*. London: Macmillan & Co.
Philips, Francis Charles, and Percy Fendall.
— 1890. *A Daughter's Sacrifice: A Novel*. London: F. V. White & Co.
— 1890. *Margaret Byng: A Novel*. London: F. V. White & Co.
— 1891. *My Face is My Fortune*. London: F. V. White & Co.
— 1908. *Disciples of Plato: A Novel*. London: Eveleigh Nash.
— 1910. *A Honeymoon – and After*. London: Eveleigh Nash.
Philips, Francis Charles, and Charles James Wills.
— 1889. *The Fatal Phyrne: Or, Love's Ordeal*. London: S. Sonnenschein.
— 1890. *The Scudamores: A Novel*. London: Gardner & Co.
— 1890. *Sybil Ross's Marriage: The Romance of an Inexperienced Girl*. London: F. V. White & Co.
— 1891. *A Maiden Fair to See*. London: Trischler & Co.
Pollock, Walter H., and Alexander J. Duffield. 1877. *Masston: A Story of These Modern Days*. London: Smith, Elder & Co.
Pollock, Walter H., and Guy C. Pollock. 1905. *Hay Fever*. London: Longmans, Green & Co.
Rolfe, Frederick, and C. H. C. Pirie Gordon.
— 1912. *The Weird of the Wanderer*. London: William Rider & Son.
— 1935. *Hubert's Arthur*. London: Cassell & Co.
Somerville, E. Œ. [Edith Œnone], and Martin Ross [Violet Martin].
— 1889. *An Irish Cousin*. London: Richard Bentley & Son.
— 1891. *Naboth's Vineyard*. London: Spencer Blackett.
— 1894. *The Real Charlotte*. London: Ward and Downey.
— 1898. *The Silver Fox*. London: Lawrence and Bullen.
— 1911. *Dan Russell the Fox: An Episode in the Life of Miss Rowan*. London: Methuen.
— 1919. *Mount Music*. London: Longmans, Green & Co.
— 1921. *An Enthusiast*. London: Longmans, Green & Co.
— 1925. *The Big House of Inver*. London: William Heinemann.
— 1928. *French Leave*. London: William Heinemann.
Stevenson, Robert Louis, and Lloyd Osbourne.
— 1889. *The Wrong Box*. London: Longmans, Green & Co.
— 1892. *The Wrecker*. London: Cassell & Co.
— 1894. *The Ebb-Tide*. London: William Heinemann.
Wilkins, W. H., and Herbert Vivian. 1894. *The Green Bay Tree*. London: Hutchinson & Co.

APPENDIX

Williamson, C.N [Charles Norris], and A.M. [Alice Muriel] Williamson.
— 1903. *The Lightning Conductor: The Strange Adventures of a Motor-Car.* New York: Henry Holt & Co.
— 1904. *The Princess Passes: A Romance of a Motor-Car.* London: Methuen.
— 1905. *My Friend the Chauffeur.* New York: McClure, Philips & Co.
— 1906. *Lady Betty Across the Water.* New York: McClure, Philips & Co.
— 1906. *Rosemary in Search of a Father.* New York: McClure, Philips & Co
— 1907. *The Car of Destiny.* New York: McClure Co.
— 1907. *The Powers and Maxine.* New York: Empire.
— 1907. *The Princess Virginia: A Romance of Royal Love.* New York: McClure, Philips & Co.
— 1908. *The Chauffeur and the Chaperon.* McClure Co.
— 1908. *Scarlett Runner.* London: Methuen.
— 1909. *Set in Silver.* New York: Doubleday, Page & Co.
— 1910. *Lord Loveland Discovers America.* New York: A.L. Burt.
— 1910. *The Motor Maid.* New York: Doubleday, Page & Co.
— 1911. *The Golden Silence.* New York: Doubleday, Page & Co.
— 1911. *The Vanity Box.* New York: Doubleday, Page & Co.
— 1912. *The Chaperon.* New York: A.L. Burt.
— 1912. *The Guests of Hercules.* New York: Doubleday, Page & Co.
— 1912. *The Heather Moon.* New York: Doubleday, Page & Co.
— 1913. *The Love Pirate.* London: Methuen.
— 1913. *The Port of Adventure.* New York: Doubleday, Page & Co.
— 1914. *A Soldier of the Legion.* New York: Doubleday, Page & Co.
— 1914. *It Happened in Egypt.* New York: Doubleday, Page & Co.
— 1916. *The Lightning Conductress.* London: Methuen.
— 1916. *The Shop Girl.* New York: Grosset & Dunlap.
— 1916. *Where the Path Breaks.* New York: Century.
— 1918. *Everyman's Land.* New York: A.L. Burt.
— 1919. *The Lion's Mouse.* New York: Doubleday, Page & Co.
— 1920. *The Second Latchkey.* New York: A.L. Burt.
— 1921. *The Great Pearl Secret.* New York: Doubleday, Page & Co.
— 1921. *Vision House.* New York: A.L. Burt.
— 1923. *The Night of the Wedding.* New York: Doran.
Zangwill, Israel, and Louis Cowan. 1899. *The Premier and the Painter: A Fantastic Romance.* London: William Heinemann.

Bibliography

Primary sources

Barnard, Marjorie. 1977. "The Gentle Art of Collaboration." *Ink* 2: 126–28.

Barnard Eldershaw, M. [1947] 1983. *Tomorrow and Tomorrow and Tomorrow*. London: Virago Modern Classics.

Beaumont, Francis, and John Fletcher. 1647. *Comedies and Tragedies*. London: Humphrey Robinson and Humphrey Moseley.

Besant, Walter. 1868. *Studies in Early French Poetry*. London and Cambridge: Macmillan & Co.

—. 1883. *All in a Garden Fair: The Simple Story of a Boy and Three Girls*. London: Chatto & Windus.

—. 1884. *The Art of Fiction*. London: Chatto & Windus.

—. 1887. Preface to *Ready-Money Mortiboy: A Matter-of-Fact Story*, by Walter Besant and James Rice, v–xii. London: Chatto & Windus.

—. 1888. *Herr Paulus: His Rise, His Greatness, and His Fall*. London: Chatto & Windus.

— 1890. *Armorel of Lyonesse: A Story of To-Day*. London: Chatto & Windus.

—. [1890] 1892a. "The Doll's House – and After." In *Verbena Camellia Stephanotis Etc.*, 317–38. London: Chatto & Windus.

—. 1892b. "The Demoniac." In *Verbena Camellia Stephanotis Etc.*, 157–317. London: Chatto & Windus.

—. 1892c. "On Literary Collaboration." *The New Review* 6.33: 200–09.

—. 1893. *The Society of Authors: A Record of Its Action from Its Foundation*. London: Incorporated Society of Authors.

—. 1895. *Beyond the Dreams of Avarice*. London: Chatto & Windus.

— [1882] 1896. *The Revolt of Men*. London and Glasgow: Collins' Clear-Type Press.

—. [1894] 1897. "Ready-Money Mortiboy." In *My First Book*, edited by Jerome K. Jerome, 2–14. London: Chatto & Windus.

—. 1899a. *The Pen and the Book*. London: Thomas Burleigh.

—. 1899b. *The Orange Girl*. London: Chatto & Windus.

—. 1899c. "One of Two Million in East London." *The Century Magazine* 12: 225–42.

—. 1900. *The Fourth Generation*. London: Chatto & Windus.

—. 1902. *Autobiography of Sir Walter Besant*. London: Hutchinson & Co.

—. [1882] 1997. *All Sorts and Conditions of Men*, edited by Helen Small. Oxford: Oxford University Press.

—. [1882] 2012. *All Sorts and Conditions of Men*, edited by Kevin A. Morrison. Brighton: Victorian Secrets.

—. [1886] 2015. *Children of Gibeon*, edited by Kevin A. Morrison. San Diego: Cognella.

Besant, Walter, and James Rice. 1872. *Ready-Money Mortiboy: A Matter-of-Fact Story*. London: Tinsley Brothers.

—. 1873. *My Little Girl*. London: Tinsely Brothers.

—. 1875. *With Harp and Crown*. London: Tinsely Brothers.

—. 1876a. *This Son of Vulcan*. London: Sampson Low & Co.

—. 1876b. "Titania's Farewell." In *The Case of Mr. Lucraft, and Other Tales*, vol. 2, 3–151. London: Sampson Low & Co.

—. [1876] 1877. *The Golden Butterfly*. New York: R. F. Fenno & Co.

—. 1878a. *By Celia's Arbour*. London: Sampson Low & Co.

—. 1878b. *The Monks of Thelema*. London: Chatto & Windus.

—. 1879. *The Chaplain of the Fleet*. London: Chatto & Windus.

—. [1872] 1887. *Ready-Money Mortiboy: A Matter-of-Fact Story*. London: Chatto & Windus.

Bisland, Elizabeth. 1891. *In Seven Stages. A Flying Trip Around the World*. New York: Harper and Brothers.

—. 1903. *A Candle of Understanding*. New York: Harper and Brothers.

—. 1906. *The Secret Life: Being the Book of a Heretic*. New York: John Lane.

—. 1910. *At the Sign of the Hobby Horse*. Boston: Houghton Mifflin.

—. 1927. *The Truth About Men and Other Matters*. New York: Avondale Press.

Black, Helen C. 1893. *Notable Women Authors of the Day: Biographical Sketches*. Glasgow: David Bryce & Son.

—. 1896. *Pen, Pencil, Baton, and Mask: Biographical Sketches*. London: Spottiswoode & Co.

Bly, Nellie. 1890. *Nellie Bly's Book: Around the World in Seventy-Two Days*. New York: Pictorial Weeklies.

Bowen, Elizabeth. 1950. *Collected Impressions*. London: Longmans, Green & Co.

Brontë, Charlotte. [1847] 2006. *Jane Eyre: An Autobiography*. London: Penguin Classics.

Broughton, Rhoda, and Elizabeth Bisland. 1891. *A Widower Indeed*. Leipzig: Tauchnitz.

BIBLIOGRAPHY

Byron, George Gordon. [1812–1818] 2006. *Childe Harold's Pilgrimage*. In *The Norton Anthology of English Literature*, edited by Jack Stillinger and Deidre S. Lynch, 8th edition, vol. 2, 617–35. New York and London: Norton and Company.

Coleridge, Samuel T. [1817] 1960. *Biographia Literaria*, edited by George Watson. London: J. M. Dent & Sons.

—. 1987. *Lectures 1808–1819 on Literature*, edited by R. A. Foakes. London: Routledge and Kegan Paul.

Devlin, Martina. 2022. *Edith*. Dublin: Lilliput Press.

Eliot, Thomas S. 1975. *Selected Prose*, edited by Frank Kermode. London: Faber and Faber.

Field, Michael. 1893. *Underneath the Bough*. London: Bell.

—. 1933. *Works and Days: From the Journal of Michael Field*, edited by T. & D. C. Sturge Moore. London: John Murray.

Fielding, Henry. [1749] 1962. *The History of Tom Jones*. London: J. M. Dent & Sons.

Gissing, George. [1891] 1985. *New Grub Street*. Harmondsworth: Penguin Classics.

Gray, Thomas. 1775. "The Bard." Chester: Poole, Barker & Co.

Haggard, Henry Rider. 1926. *The Days of My Life: An Autobiography by Sir H. Rider Haggard*. London: Longmans, Green & Co.

Haggard, Henry Rider, and Andrew Lang. [1890] 1894. *The World's Desire*. London: Longmans, Green & Co.

Hazlitt, William. [1823] 1889. "Whether Genius Is Conscious of Its Powers?" In *Essays of William Hazlitt*, edited by Frank Carr, 109–21. London: Walter Scott Ltd.

Hichens, Robert S. 1896. "The Collaborators." In *The Folly of Eustace and Other Stories*, 138–75. New York: Appleton.

—. [1894] 1992. *The Green Carnation*. London: Robin Clark.

Hood, Thomas, Thomas W. Robertson, Thomas Archer, William S. Gilbert, C. W. Scott, and T. Archer. 1865. *A Bunch of Keys: Where They Were Found and What They Might Have Unlocked. A Christmas Book*. London: Groombridge & Sons.

—. 1866. *Rates and Taxes and How They Were Collected*. London: Groombridge & Sons.

Howard, Blanche Willis, and William Sharp. 1892. *A Fellowe and His Wife*. London: Osgood & McIlvaine.

James, Henry. [1884] 1885. *The Art of Fiction*. Boston: Cupples, Upham & Co.

—. 1886. *The Bostonians*. London and New York: Macmillan & Co.

—. 1892. "Collaboration." *The English Illustrated Magazine* 9: 911–21.

Jerome, Jerome K., ed. [1894] 1897. *My First Book*. London: Chatto & Windus.

Joyce, James. [1916] 2000. *A Portrait of the Artist as a Young Man*, edited by Jeri Johnson. Oxford: Oxford University Press.

Kipling, Rudyard. [1937] 1987. *Something of Myself for My Friends Known and Unknown*, edited by Robert Hampson. London: Penguin Books.

Lamb, Charles. [1823] 1964. "Mackery End, in Hertfordshire." In *The Portable Charles Lamb: Letters and Essays*, edited by John Mason Brown, 223–29. New York: The Viking Press.

Le Fanu, Joseph Sheridan. [1864] 1899. *Uncle Silas*. London: Macmillan.

Maitland, Ella Fuller, and Sir Frederick Pollock. 1899. *The Etchingham Letters*. London: Smith. Elder & Co.

Marryat, Florence, and Charles Ogilvie. 1891. *The Lost Diamonds*. London: Ludgate Monthly.

Mathers, Helen, Justin McCarthy, Mrs Trollope, Arthur Conan Doyle, May Crommelin, F. C. Philips, 'Rita,' Joseph Hatton, Mrs Lovett Cameron, Bram Stoker, Florence Marryat, Frank Danby, Mrs Edward Kennard, Richard Dowling, Mrs Hungerford, Arthur A'Beckett, Jean Middlemass, Clement Scott, Clo. Graves, H. W. Lucy, Adeline Sergeant, G. Manville Fenn, 'Tasma,' and F. Anstey. 1892. *The Fate of Fenella*. London: Hutchinson & Co.

Matthews, James Brander. [1890] 1891. "The Art and Mystery of Collaboration." In *With My Friends: Tales Told in Partnership*, by James Brander Matthews, H. C. Bunner, Walter Herries Pollock, George H. Jessop, and F. Anstey, 1–29. New York: Longmans, Green & Co.

—. 1917. *These Many Years: Recollections of a New Yorker*. New York: C. Scribner's Sons.

McCarthy, Justin, and Mrs Campbell Praed. [1886] 1896. *The Right Honourable: A Romance of Society and Politics*. New York: D. Appleton & Co.

Plato. 2001. *Ion*. In *The Norton Anthology of Theory and Criticism*, edited by Vincent B. Leitch, 37–48. New York: Norton.

Roe, Owen, and Honor Urse. 1913. *By the Brown Bog*. London: Longmans, Green & Co.

Shelley, Percy B. [1840] 1986. *A Defence of Poetry*. Milano: Coliseum Editore.

Somerville, Edith Œ. 1930. *The States Through Irish Eyes*. Boston and New York: Houghton Mifflin & Co.

Somerville, Edith Œ., and Martin Ross. 1889. *An Irish Cousin*. London: Richard Bentley & Son.

—. 1891. *Naboth's Vineyard*. London: Spencer Blackett.

—. 1898. *The Silver Fox*. London: Lawrence and Bullen.

—. 1899. *Some Experiences of an Irish R.M.* London: Longmans, Green & Co.

—. [1889] 1903. *An Irish Cousin*. London: Longmans, Green & Co.

—. 1908. *Some Further Experiences of an Irish R.M.* London: Longmans, Green & Co.

—. [1889] 1910. *An Irish Cousin*. London: Longmans, Green & Co.
—. 1911. *Dan Russell the Fox: An Episode in the Life of Miss Rowan*. London: Methuen.
—. 1915. *In Mr. Knox's Country*. London: Longmans, Green & Co.
—. 1917. *Irish Memories*. London: Longmans, Green & Co.
—. 1919. *Mount Music*. London: Longmans, Green & Co.
—. 1921. *An Enthusiast*. London: Longmans, Green & Co.
—. 1925. *The Big House of Inver*. London: Heinemann.
—. 1946. *Happy Days! Essays of Sorts*. London: Longmans, Green & Co.
—. [1946] 1952. "Two of a Trade." In *Dr. E. Œ. Somerville: A Biography*, by Geraldine Cummins, 180–86. London: Andrew Dakers.
—. [1893] 1998. *Through Connemara in a Governess Cart*. London: Virago.
—. [1893] 2001. *In the Vine Country*. London: Vintage.
—. [1894] 2011. *The Real Charlotte*. London: Capuchin Classics.
Stevenson, Robert Louis. [1884] 2009. "A Humble Remonstrance." In *The Victorian Art of Fiction: Nineteenth-Century Essays on the Novel*, edited by Rohan A. Maitzen, 309–16. Peterborough: Broadview Press.
Stevenson, Robert Louis, and Lloyd Osbourne. 1894. *The Ebb-Tide*. London: William Heinemann.
Tennyson, Alfred. [1850] 2006a. "In Memoriam A.H.H." In *The Norton Anthology of English Literature*, edited by Jack Stillinger and Deidre S. Lynch, 8th edition, vol. 2, 1138–88. New York and London: Norton and Company.
—. [1842] 2006b. "Ulysses." In *The Norton Anthology of English Literature*, edited by Jack Stillinger and Deidre S. Lynch, 8th edition, vol. 2, 1123–25. New York and London: Norton and Company.
Trollope, Anthony. 1883. *An Autobiography*. Leipzig: Tauchnitz.
Wilkins, W.H., and Herbert Vivian. 1894. *The Green Bay Tree*. London: Hutchinson & Co.
Woolf, Virginia. [1923] 1966. "Mr Bennett and Mrs Brown." In *Collected Essays*, edited by Leonard Woolf, vol. 1, 319–37. London: The Hogarth Press.
Wordsworth, William. [1850] 1959. *The Prelude, or Growth of a Poet's Mind*. Oxford: Clarendon Press.
—. [1798] 2006a. "Tintern Abbey." In *The Norton Anthology of English Literature*, edited by Jack Stillinger and Deidre S. Lynch, 8th edition, vol. 2, 258–62. New York and London: Norton and Company.
—. [1800] 2006b. Preface to the *Lyrical Ballads*. In *The Norton Anthology of English Literature*, edited by Jack Stillinger and Deidre S. Lynch, 8th edition, vol. 2, 262–74. New York and London: Norton and Company.
Young, Edward. [1759] 1918. *Conjectures on Original Composition*, edited by Edith J. Morley. Manchester: Manchester University Press.

Secondary sources

Aaron, Jane. 1991. *A Double Singleness*. Oxford: Oxford University Press.
Alexander, Isabella. 2010. *Copyright Law and the Public Interest in the Nineteenth Century*. Oxford: Hart.
Armstrong, Nancy. 1999. *Fiction in the Age of Photography: The Legacy of British Realism*. Cambridge, MA: Harvard University Press.
Ashton, Susanna. 2003. *Collaborators in Literary America 1870–1920*. New York: Palgrave Macmillan.
Bachman, Maria K., and Don Richard Cox. 2019. "'I Have Altered Nothing': Walter Besant's Completion of Wilkie Collins's 'Blind Love'." In *Walter Besant: The Business of Literature and the Pleasures of Reform*, edited by Kevin A. Morrison, 55–72. Liverpool: Liverpool University Press.
Banerjee, Jacqueline. 2014. "'The Conduct of Life' in Walter Besant's 'The Ivory Gate' and 'The Alabaster Box'." *English Studies* 95.8: 890–906.
Barthes, Roland. 1977. "The Death of the Author." In *Image, Music, Text*, 142–48. Translated by S. Heath. London: Fontana.
Bennett, Andrew. 2005. *The Author*. Abingdon: Routledge.
Bentley, Gerald Eades. 1986. *The Professions of Dramatist and Player in Shakespeare's Time, 1590–1642*. Princeton, NJ: Princeton University Press.
Birch, Dinah, ed. 2009. *The Oxford Companion to English Literature*. Oxford: Oxford University Press.
Bivona, Dan, and Roger B. Henkle. 2006. *The Imagination of Class: Masculinity and the Victorian Urban Poor*. Columbus: Ohio State University Press.
Boege, Fred W. 1956a. "Sir Walter Besant: Novelist (Part One)." *Nineteenth-Century Fiction* 10.4: 249–80.
—. 1956b. "Sir Walter Besant: Novelist (Part Two)." *Nineteenth-Century Fiction* 11.1: 32–60.
Boucharenc, Myriam. 2000. "Plural Authorship in Automatic Writing." In *Subject Matters: Subject and Self in French Literature from Descartes to the Present*, edited by Paul Gifford and Johnnie Gratton, 100–14. Amsterdam: Rodopi.
Boyce, Charlotte, Páraic Finnerty, and Anne-Marie Millim. 2013. *Victorian Celebrity Culture and Tennyson's Circle*. Basingstoke and New York: Palgrave Macmillan.
Bunting, Kirsty. 2019. "Besant and Collaboration." In *Walter Besant: The Business of Literature and the Pleasures of Reform*, edited by Kevin A. Morrison, 19–38. Liverpool: Liverpool University Press.
Burrow, J. A. 1982. *Medieval Writers and Their Work: Middle English Literature and Its Background, 1100–1500*. Oxford: Oxford University Press.

BIBLIOGRAPHY

Cahalan, James M. 1988. *The Irish Novel: A Critical History*. Dublin: Gill and Macmillan.

—. 1999. *Double Visions: Women and Men in Modern and Contemporary Irish Fiction*. Syracuse, NY: Syracuse University Press.

Çelikkol, Ayse. 2019. "Workers as Artists: From Copyright to the Palace of Delight in Besant's Writings." In *Walter Besant: The Business of Literature and the Pleasures of Reform*, edited by Kevin A. Morrison, 131–47. Liverpool: Liverpool University Press.

Chadwick, Whitney, and Isabelle de Courtivron, eds. 1993. *Significant Others: Creativity and Intimate Partnership*. London: Thames and Hudson.

Chapman, Alison. 2015. *Networking the Nation: British and American Women's Poetry and Italy, 1840–1870*. Oxford: Oxford University Press.

Cheng, Vicky, and Heajoo Kim. 2019. "From Happy Individuals to Universal Sisterhood: Affective Reforms in 'All Sorts and Conditions of Men' and 'Children of Gibeon'." In *Walter Besant: The Business of Literature and the Pleasures of Reform*, edited by Kevin A. Morrison, 187–202. Liverpool: Liverpool University Press.

Clare, David. 2014. "Wilde, Shaw, and Somerville and Ross: Irish Revivalists, Irish Britons, or Both?" *Irish Studies Review* 22.1: 91–103.

Clare, Jane. 2012. "Shakespeare and Paradigms of Early Modern Authorship." *Journal of Early Modern Studies* 1.1: 137–53.

Colby, Robert A. 1990. "Harnessing Pegasus: Walter Besant, 'The Author,' and the Profession of Authorship." *Victorian Periodical Review* 23.3: 111–20.

—. 1994. "Authorship and the Book Trade." In *Victorian Periodicals and Victorian Society*, edited by J. Don Vann and Rosemary T. VanArsdel, 143–61. Toronto: University of Toronto Press.

Collis, Maurice. 1968. *Somerville and Ross: A Biography*. London: Faber and Faber.

Costantini, Mariaconcetta. 2022. "Transatlantic Romance and the Deconstruction of Gender Norms: Rhoda Broughton and Elizabeth Bisland's 'A Widower Indeed' (1891)." *Victorian Popular Fictions* 4.1: 126–44.

Cotta Ramusino, Elena. 2019. "The Dark Side of the Enlightenment: The Anglo-Irish (Ascendancy) and the Rise of Gothic." *Il Confronto Letterario* 71: 117–30.

Coustillas, Pierre, ed. 1978. *London and the Life of Literature in Late Victorian England: The Diary of George Gissing, Novelist*. Hassocks: Harvester Press.

Cowman, Roz. 1997. "Lost Time: The Smell and Taste of Castle T." In *Sex, Nation and Dissent in Irish Writing*, edited by Eibhear Walshe, 87–102. Cork: Cork University Press.

Crary, Jonathan. 1990. *Techniques of the Observer: On Vision and Modernity in the Nineteenth Century.* Cambridge, MA: MIT Press.
Cronin, John. 1968. "Dominant Themes in the Novels of Somerville and Ross." In *Somerville and Ross: A Symposium*, 8–18. Belfast: Institute of Irish Studies, Queen's University.
—. 1972. *Somerville and Ross.* Lewisburg, PA: Bucknell University Press.
Cummins, Geraldine. 1952. *Dr. E. Œ. Somerville: A Biography.* London: Andrew Dakers Ltd.
Curtis, Gerard. 1995. "Dickens in the Visual Market." In *Literature in the Marketplace: Nineteenth-Century British Publishing and Reading Practices*, edited by John O. Jordan and Robert L. Patten, 213–49. Cambridge: Cambridge University Press.
Deazley, Ronan. 2006. *Rethinking Copyright: History, Theory, Language.* London: Edgar Elgar.
Derrida, Jacques. 2002. *Without Alibi.* Translated by Peggy Kamuf. Stanford, CA: Stanford University Press.
Dever, Maryanne. 1995. "'No Mine and Thine but Ours': Finding 'M. Barnard Eldershaw.'" *Tulsa Studies in Women's Literature* 14.1: 65–75.
Diniejko, Andrzej. 2019. "Walter Besant: A Latter-Day Dickens?" In *Walter Besant: The Business of Literature and the Pleasures of Reform*, edited by Kevin A. Morrison, 225–42. Liverpool: Liverpool University Press.
Eagleton, Terry. 1990. *The Ideology of the Aesthetic.* Oxford: Basil Blackwell.
—. 1995. "Ascendancy and Hegemony." In *Heathcliff and the Great Hunger: Studies in Irish Culture.* London: Verso.
Ede, Lisa, and Andrea Lunsford. 1990. *Singular Texts/Plural Authors: Perspectives on Collaborative Writing.* Carbondale, IL: Southern Illinois University Press.
Eden, David, and Meinhard Saremba, eds. 2009. *The Cambridge Companion to Gilbert and Sullivan.* Cambridge: Cambridge University Press.
Ehnenn, Jill. 2008. *Women's Literary Collaboration, Queerness, and Late-Victorian Culture.* Aldershot: Ashgate.
Eliot, Simon. 1987. "'His Generation Read His Stories': Walter Besant, Chatto & Windus and 'All Sorts and Conditions of Men'." *Publishing History* 21: 25–67.
—. 1989. "Unequal Partnerships: Besant, Rice and Chatto, 1876–1882." *Publishing History* 26: 73–109.
—. 1999. "Author, Publisher and Literary Agent: Making Walter Besant's Novels Pay in the Provincial and International Markets of the 1890s." *Publishing History* 46: 35–65.
—. 2019. "Besant, Chatto, and Watt: An Income from Fiction in the 1890s." In *Walter Besant: The Business of Literature and the Pleasures of Reform*, edited by Kevin A. Morrison, 113–30. Liverpool: Liverpool University Press.

Faderman, Lilian. 1981. *Surpassing the Love of Men: Romantic Friendship and Love Between Women from the Renaissance to the Present*. London: The Women's Press Ltd.

Feather, John. 1994. *Publishing, Piracy, and Politics: An Historical Study of Copyright in Britain*. London: Mansell.

Flint, Kate. 2008. *The Victorians and the Visual Imagination*. Cambridge: Cambridge University Press.

—, ed. 2012. *The Cambridge History of Victorian Literature*. Cambridge: Cambridge University Press.

—. 2016. "Unspeakable Desires: We Other Victorians." In *The Oxford Handbook of Victorian Literary Culture*, edited by Juliet John, 193–210. Oxford: Oxford University Press.

Foster, R. F. 1993. "Protestant Magic: W.B. Yeats and the Spell of Irish History." In *Paddy & Mr. Punch: Connections in Irish and English History*, 212–32. London: Allen Lane.

Foucault, Michel. 1979. "What Is an Author?" In *Textual Strategies: Perspectives in Post-Structuralist Criticism*, edited by Josué V. Harari, 141–60. Ithaca, NY: Cornell University Press.

Frehner, Ruth. 1999. *The Colonizers' Daughters: Gender in the Anglo-Irish Big House Novel*. Tübingen: Francke.

Gabriele, Alberto. 2009. *Reading Popular Culture in Victorian Print: Belgravia and Sensationalism*. Basingstoke: Palgrave Macmillan.

—. 2019. "The Author Function in Walter Besant's Fiction: The Notion of Artistic Value in the Wake of Copyright Law and the Nationalist Restructuring of the Book Trade." In *Walter Besant: The Business of Literature and the Pleasures of Reform*, edited by Kevin A. Morrison, 90–112. Liverpool: Liverpool University Press.

Gannon, Christiane. 2014. "Walter Besant's Democratic Bildungsroman." *Narrative* 22.3: 372–94.

Genet, Jacqueline, ed. 1991. *The Big House in Ireland: Reality and Representation*. Dingle: Brandon.

Gere, Anne Ruggles. 1978. *Writing Groups: History, Theory, and Implications*. Carbondale: Southern Illinois University Press.

Ghosh, Tanushree. 2017. "'Witnessing Them Day after Day': Ethical Spectatorship and Liberal Reform in Walter Besant's 'Children of Gibeon'." In *Philanthropic Discourse in Anglo-American Literature, 1850–1920*, edited by Frank Q. Christianson and Leslie Thorne-Murphy, 162–89. Bloomington: Indiana University Press.

Gillies, Mary Ann. 2007. *The Professional Literary Agent in Britain, 1880–1920*. Toronto: University of Toronto Press.

—. 2019. "Walter Besant and Copyright Reform." In *Walter Besant: The Business of Literature and the Pleasures of Reform*, edited by Kevin A. Morrison, 75–89. Liverpool: Liverpool University Press.

Ginn, Geoffrey A. C. 2017. *Culture, Philanthropy and the Poor in Late-Victorian London*. London: Routledge.

—. 2019. "Altruism and 'The Monks of Thelema': Ideals and Realities." In *Walter Besant: The Business of Literature and the Pleasures of Reform*, edited by Kevin A. Morrison, 151–70. Liverpool: Liverpool University Press.

Glissant, Édouard. 1996. *Introduction à une Poétique du Divers*. Paris: Gallimard.

Goodman, Matthew. 2013. *Eighty Days: Nellie Bly and Elizabeth Bisland's History-Making Race Around the World*. New York: Ballantine Books.

Graves, C. L. 1913. "The Lighter Side of Irish Life." *Quarterly Review* 219.436: 26–47.

Green, Roger L. 1946. *Andrew Lang: A Critical Biography*. Leicester: Edmund Ward.

Greene, Nicole Pepinster. 2016. "Demystifying and Resituating the Somerville and Ross Writing Partnership, 1889–1915." *The Canadian Journal of Irish Studies* 39.2: 196–217.

Hadjiafxendi, Kyriaki, and Patricia Zakreski, eds. 2013. *Crafting the Woman Professional in the Long Nineteenth Century: Artistry and Industry in Britain*. Aldershot: Ashgate.

Hand, Derek. 2011. *A History of the Irish Novel*. Cambridge: Cambridge University Press.

Harrison, J. F. C. 2000. *Late Victorian Britain: 1875–1901*. New York: Routledge.

Heilmann, Ann, and Mark Llewellyn. 2016. "The Victorians, Sex, and Gender." In *The Oxford Handbook of Victorian Literary Culture*, edited by Juliet John, 161–77. Oxford: Oxford University Press.

Hickey, Alison. 1996. "Double Bonds: Charles Lamb's Romantic Collaborations." *English Language History* 63.3: 735–71.

—. 1998. "Coleridge, Southey, 'and Co.': Collaboration and Authority." *Studies in Romanticism* 37.3: 305–49.

Higgins, D. S. 1981. *Rider Haggard: A Biography*. New York: Stein and Day.

Jacobs, Arthur. 2020. *Arthur Sullivan: A Victorian Musician*. London: Routledge.

Jamison, Anne. 2016. *E. OE. Somerville & Martin Ross: Female Authorship and Literary Collaboration*. Cork: Cork University Press.

John, Juliet, ed. 2016. *The Oxford Handbook of Victorian Literary Culture*. Oxford: Oxford University Press.

Joyce, Simon. 1996. "Castles in the Air: The People's Palace, Cultural Reformism, and the East End Working Class." *Victorian Studies* 39.4: 513–38.

Kappel, Andrew J. 1978. "The Gurney Photograph Controversy." *Dickensian* 74.386: 167–72.

Karell, Linda K. 2002. *Writing Together/Writing Apart: Collaboration in Western American Literature*. Lincoln: Nebraska University Press.

Kark, Ruth, and Haim Goren. 2011. "Pioneering British Exploration and Scriptural Geography: The Syrian Society/The Palestine Association." *The Geographical Journal* 177.3: 264–74.

Kiberd, Declan. 1996. *Inventing Ireland: The Literature of the Modern Nation*. New York: Vintage.

—. 2001. *Irish Classics*. Cambridge, MA: Harvard University Press.

Kilfeather, Siobhán. 2006. "The Gothic Novel." In *The Cambridge Companion to the Irish Novel*, edited by John W. Foster, 78–96. Cambridge: Cambridge University Press.

Knapp, Jeffrey. 2005. "What Is a Co-Author?" *Representations* 89: 1–29.

Knutson, Roslyn L. 2004. "Working Playwrights, 1580–1642." In *The Cambridge History of British Theatre 1: Origins to 1660*, edited by Jane Milling and Peter Thomson, 341–63. Cambridge: Cambridge University Press.

Koestenbaum, Wayne. 1989. *Double Talk: The Erotics of Male Literary Collaboration*. New York: Routledge.

Kreilkamp, Vera. 1998. *The Anglo-Irish Novel and the Big House*. Syracuse, NY: Syracuse University Press.

—. 2006. "The Novel of the Big House." In *The Cambridge Companion to the Irish Novel*, edited by John Wilson Foster, 60–77. Cambridge: Cambridge University Press.

—. 2010. "The Novels of Somerville and Ross." In *A Companion to Irish Literature*, edited by Julia M. Wright, vol. 2, 50–65. Hoboken, NJ: Wiley-Blackwell.

—. 2020. "Recovery and the Ascendancy Novel 1880–1932." In *Irish Literature in Transition, 1880–1940*, edited by Marjorie Howes, 73–94. Cambridge: Cambridge University Press.

Laird, Holly. 2000. *Women Coauthors*. Urbana: University of Illinois Press.

Law, Graham, 2000. *Serializing Fiction in the Victorian Press*. Basingstoke: Palgrave Macmillan.

Lewis, Gifford. 1985. *Somerville and Ross: The World of the Irish R.M.* New York: Viking.

—, ed. 1989. *The Selected Letters of Somerville and Ross*. London: Faber & Faber.

—. 2004. "Somerville, Edith Anna Œnone (1858–1949), writer and artist." *Oxford Dictionary of National Bibliography* online.

—. 2005. *Edith Somerville: A Biography*. Dublin: Four Courts Press.

London, Bette. 1999. *Writing Double: Women's Literary Partnerships*. Ithaca, NY: Cornell University Press.

Lyons, F. S. L. 1970. "The Twilight of the Big House." *Ariel* 1.3: 110–22.

Marcus, Sharon. 2007. *Between Women: Friendship, Desire, and Marriage in Victorian England*. Princeton, NJ: Princeton University Press.

Masten, Jeffrey. 1997. *Textual Intercourse: Collaboration, Authorship, and Sexualities in Renaissance Drama*. Cambridge: Cambridge University Press.

Mattheisen, Paul F., Arthur C. Young, and Pierre Coustillas, eds. 1990–97. *The Collected Letters of George Gissing*, 9 vols. Athens: Ohio University Press.

McCann, Andrew. 2014. *Popular Literature, Authorship and the Occult in Late Victorian Britain*. Cambridge: Cambridge University Press.

McCormack, W. J. 1985. *Ascendancy and Tradition in Anglo-Irish Literary History from 1789 to 1939*. Oxford: Clarendon Press.

—. 1991. "Irish Gothic and After." In *The Field Day Anthology of Irish Writing*, edited by Seamus Deane, vol. 2, 832–45. Derry: Field Day.

McDonald, Peter. 1997. *British Literary Culture and Publishing Practice, 1880–1914*. Cambridge: Cambridge University Press.

Medaglia, Francesca. 2014. *La scrittura a quattro mani*. Lecce: Pensa MultiMedia Editore.

Moi, Toril. 1985. *Sexual/Textual Politics: Feminist Literary Theory*. London: Methuen.

Mooney, Shawn R. 1992. "Colliding Stars: Heterosexism in Biographical Representations of Somerville and Ross." *The Canadian Journal of Irish Studies* 18.1: 157–75.

Morrison, Kevin A., ed. 2019. *Walter Besant: The Business of Literature and the Pleasures of Reform*. Liverpool: Liverpool University Press.

Moynahan, Julian. 1995. *Anglo-Irish: The Literary Imagination in a Hyphenated Culture*. Princeton, NJ: Princeton University Press.

Murfin, Audrey. 2019. *Robert Louis Stevenson and the Art of Collaboration*. Edinburgh: Edinburgh University Press.

Neetens, Wim. 1990. "Problems of a 'Democratic Text': Walter Besant's Impossible Story." *Novel: A Forum on Fiction* 23.3: 247–64.

Newton, Esther. 1989. "The Mythic Mannish Lesbian: Radclyffe Hall and the New Woman." In *Hidden from History: Reclaiming the Gay and Lesbian Past*, edited by Martin Bauml Duberman, Martha Vicinus and George Chauncey, 281–93. New York: Penguin.

Nicholson, Bob. 2019. "The 'Most-Talked-of-Creature in the World': The 'American Girl' in Victorian Print Culture." In *Woman, Periodicals, and Print Culture in Britain, 1830s–1900s: The Victorian Period*, edited by Alexis Easley, Clare Gill and Beth Rodgers, 178–96. Edinburgh: Edinburgh University Press.

O'Connor, Maureen. 2010. *The Female and the Species: The Animal in Irish Women's Writing*. Oxford: Lang.
Ong, Walter. 1982. *Orality and Literacy: The Technologizing of the World*. London: Routledge.
Patten, Robert L. 2001. "From Sketches to Nickleby." In *The Cambridge Companion to Charles Dickens*, edited by John O. Jordan, 16–33. Cambridge: Cambridge University Press.
—. 2016. "The New Cultural Marketplace: Victorian Publishing and Reading Practices." In *The Oxford Handbook of Victorian Literary Culture*, edited by Juliet John, 481–506. Oxford: Oxford University Press.
Pearl, Sharrona. 2010. *About Faces: Physiognomy in Nineteenth-Century Britain*. Cambridge, MA: Harvard University Press.
Plunkett, John. 2016. "Celebrity Culture." In *The Oxford Handbook of Victorian Literary Culture*, edited by Juliet John, 539–58. Oxford: Oxford University Press.
Rauchbauer, Otto, ed. 1992. *Ancestral Voices: The Big House in Anglo-Irish Literature*. Dublin: Lilliput Press.
Reynolds, Lorna. 1983. "Irish Women in Legend, Life and Literature." In *Women in Irish Legend, Life and Literature*, edited by S. F. Gallagher, 11–25. Totowa, NJ: Barnes and Noble.
Robinson, Hilary. 1980. *Somerville and Ross: A Critical Appreciation*. Dublin: St. Martin's Press.
Rose, Mark. 1993. *Authors and Owners: The Invention of Copyright*. Cambridge, MA: Harvard University Press.
Sadleir, Michael. 1961. *Trollope: A Commentary*. Oxford: Oxford Paperbacks.
Saint-Amour, Paul K. 2003. *The Copyrights: Intellectual Property and the Literary Imagination*. Ithaca, NY: Cornell University Press.
Saunders, David. 1992. *Authorship and Copyright*. London: Routledge.
Saunders, John W. 1964. *The Profession of English Letters*. Toronto: University of Toronto Press.
Seville, Catherine. 1999. *Literary Copyright Reform in Early Victorian England*. Cambridge: Cambridge University Press.
Showalter, Elaine. 1985. *The Female Malady: Women, Madness, and English Culture 1830–1980*. New York: Pantheon Books.
Smalley, Donald, ed. 1969. *Anthony Trollope: The Critical Heritage*. London: Routledge and Kegan Paul.
Smith-Rosenberg, Carroll. 1985. *Disorderly Conduct: Visions of Gender in Victorian America*. New York: Oxford University Press.
Spilka, Mark. 1973. "Henry James and Walter Besant: 'The Art of Fiction' Controversy." *Novel: A Forum on Fiction* 6.2: 101–19.
Spoo, Robert. 2013. *Without Copyrights: Piracy, Publishing and the Public Domain*. Oxford: Oxford University Press.

Stedman, Jane W. 1996. *W.S. Gilbert: A Classic Victorian and His Theatre*. Oxford: Oxford University Press.

Stephen, Leslie, ed. 1885. *Dictionary of National Biography*, vol. 4. London: Smith, Elder, & Co.

Stern, Tiffany. 2009. *Documents of Performance in Early Modern England*. Cambridge: Cambridge University Press.

Stevens, Julie Anne. 2001. "The Staging of Protestant Ireland in Somerville and Ross's 'The Real Charlotte'." In *Critical Ireland: New Essays in Literature and Culture*, edited by Aaron Kelly and Alan Gillis, 188–94. Dublin: Four Courts Press.

—. 2017. *Two Irish Girls in Bohemia: The Drawings and Writings of E. Œ. Somerville and Martin Ross*. Cork: Somerville Press.

Stillinger, Jack. 1991. *Multiple Authorship and the Myth of the Solitary Genius*. Oxford: Oxford University Press.

Stone, Marjorie, and Judith Thompson. 2006. "Contexts and Heterotexts: A Theoretical and Historical Introduction." In *Literary Couples, Collaborators, and the Construction of Authorship*, 3–37. Madison: University of Wisconsin Press.

Storer, Richard. 2019. "'Another Like Me': The Literary Partnership of Walter Besant and James Rice." In *Walter Besant: The Business of Literature and the Pleasures of Reform*, edited by Kevin A. Morrison, 39–54. Liverpool: Liverpool University Press.

Sturgeon, Mary. 1922. *Michael Field*. New York: Macmillan.

Sutherland, John. 2009. *The Longman Companion to Victorian Fiction*. London: Routledge.

Swafford, Kevin. 2007. *Class in Late-Victorian Britain: The Narrative Concern with Social Hierarchy and Its Representation*. Youngstown, NY: Cambria Press.

—. 2019. "The Ethics of Perception and the Politics of Recognition: Walter Besant's 'All Sorts and Conditions of Men'." In *Walter Besant: The Business of Literature and the Pleasures of Reform*, edited by Kevin A. Morrison, 171–86. Liverpool: Liverpool University Press.

Trussler, Simon. 2000. *The Cambridge Illustrated History of British Theatre*. Cambridge: Cambridge University Press.

Ue, Tom. 2019. "Moral Perfectionism, Optatives, and the Inky Line in Besant's 'All in a Garden Fair' and Gissing's 'New Grub Street'." In *Walter Besant: The Business of Literature and the Pleasures of Reform*, edited by Kevin A. Morrison, 205–23. Liverpool: Liverpool University Press.

Vicinus, Martha. 2004. *Intimate Friends: Women Who Loved Women, 1778–1928*. Chicago, IL: University of Chicago Press.

Vickers, Brian. 2002a. *Shakespeare, Co-Author: A Historical Study of Five Collaborative Plays*. Oxford: Oxford University Press.

—. 2002b. *"Counterfeiting" Shakespeare: Evidence, Authorship, and John Ford's "Funerall Elegye"*. Cambridge: Cambridge University Press.
—. 2007. "Incomplete Shakespeare: Or, Denying Co-Authorship." *Shakespeare Quarterly* 58.3: 311–52.
Waller, Philip. 2008. *Writers, Readers, and Reputations: Literary Life in Britain 1870–1918*. Oxford: Oxford University Press.
Weekes, Anne O. 1990. *Irish Women Writers: An Uncharted Tradition*. Lexington: University Press of Kentucky.
Weiner, Deborah B. 1994. *Architecture and Social Reform in Late-Victorian London*. Manchester: Manchester University Press.
Weiner, Joel H. 1985. *Innovators and Preachers: The Role of the Editor in Victorian England*. Westport, CT: Greenwood Press.
Welch, Robert, ed. 1996. *The Oxford Companion to Irish Literature*. Oxford: Oxford University Press.
Wimsatt, W. K., and Monroe C. Beardsley. 1946. "The Intentional Fallacy." *The Sewanee Review* 54.3: 468–88.
Witcher, Heather Bozant. 2022. *Collaborative Writing in the Long Nineteenth Century: Sympathetic Partnerships and Artistic Creation*. Cambridge: Cambridge University Press.
Wood, Elizabeth. 1994. "Ghost Shockers: A Parable of Lesbian Life." *Australian Feminist Studies* 20: 9–23.
Wood, Marilyn. 1993. *Rhoda Broughton: Profile of a Novelist*. Stamford: Paul Watkins.
Woodmansee, Martha, and Peter Jaszi, eds. 1994. *The Construction of Authorship: Textual Appropriation in Law and Literature*. Durham, NC: Duke University Press.
York, Lorraine M. 2002. *Rethinking Women's Collaborative Writing*. Toronto: University of Toronto Press.
—. 2006. "Crowding the Garret: Women's Collaborative Writing and the Problematics of Space." In *Literary Couples, Collaborators, and the Construction of Authorship*, edited by Marjorie Stone and Judith Thompson, 288–308. Madison: University of Wisconsin Press.
Young, Arlene. 2019. *From Spinster to Career Woman: Middle-Class Women and Work in Victorian England*. Montreal: McGill Queen's University Press.

Index

A'Beckett, Arthur 186, 193
Addison, Joseph 247n7
Alcott, Louisa May 106n11
Alighieri, Dante 224
Anstey, F. (Thomas Anstey Guthrie) 60, 186, 193
Anstruther Thomson, Clementina 'Kit' 10, 257
Archer, Thomas 211n5
Arnold, Matthew 57, 89n55, 122
Ascendancy (Anglo-Irish identity) 96, 97, 99–103, 111, 120
Atlantic Union 56n32
Austen, Jane 181
Authors' Club 56n32, 82

Balestier, Wolcott 15n8
Banks, Elizabeth 70n44
Barnard Eldershaw, M. (Marjorie Barnard and Flora Eldershaw) 9n2, 257–59
Barnum, P. T. 196
Barrie, James M. 56, 56n32
Barthes, Roland 262–63, 264
Beardsley, Monroe C. 262, 264
Beaumont, Francis and John Fletcher 41n27, 208, 223, 235, 236–37
Bell, Florence 10
Bennett, Arnold 22
Besant, Walter
  as campaigner for authors' rights 28, 29n8, 53–59, 87, 89
  completion of Wilkie Collins's *Blind Love* 27n5
  on copyright law 57–58
  on critics 35, 68n41, 81
  early life 30–31
  fame and its decline 26–29, 84–93, 247–48
  on fiction writing 16–17, 29, 31–32, 76–84
  on the figure of the author 233, 249, 252, 254
  as French literature scholar 35, 89
  on George Gissing 82n51
  on hack writing 34–35
  on Henry Rider Haggard 162
  as a historian 28, 89
  on literary agents 52–53
  literary beginnings 31–35
  on money and literature (intellectual property) 27, 29, 53–55, 57
  as object of satire 71–73, 91–92, 194
  partnership with Edward Palmer 25n1
  partnership with W. H. Brodribb 25n1
  partnership with Walter H. Pollock 25n1, 161n1
  periodical publication (serialization) 36n21, 68n41
  philanthropy and social reform 27, 28, 29n8, 87, 89

slum life fiction 28n6, 89
solo works 85–87, 264
  All in a Garden Fair 31
  All Sorts and Conditions of Men 28n6, 29, 42n28, 54n30, 73, 89
  Armorel of Lyonesse 55n31
  The Art of Fiction 17, 28, 53, 54, 55, 76–80
  Autobiography of Sir Walter Besant 17, 26, 27, 29, 30, 31, 32, 33n15, 34, 35, 36, 39n25, 51, 52, 53, 54, 56, 58, 59, 62, 63, 68, 69, 71n45, 74, 75, 76, 81, 82, 86, 89, 90n56, 148, 252, 254
  Beyond the Dreams of Avarice 85
  Children of Gibeon 29, 89–90
  "The Demoniac" 85
  "The Doll's House – and After" 28, 91
  The Fourth Generation 85, 86
  Herr Paulus 55n31, 85
  My First Book 30, 36, 47–50, 61, 63n39, 155
  "One of Two Million in East London" 89
  "On Literary Collaboration" 17, 25–26, 27n5, 37, 51, 59–75, 146, 153, 192, 202, 221, 224, 254
  The Orange Girl 86–87
  The Pen and the Book 17, 31, 32, 52, 53, 54, 55, 56, 57, 81
  preface to 1887 edition of *Ready-Money Mortiboy* 32, 33, 36, 42, 51, 68, 75, 76
  The Revolt of Men 28, 37n21
  Studies in Early French Poetry 35
  A Survey of London 28, 89
  "Titania's Farewell" 35–36
on women and marriage 28, 65, 70–71, 90–91, 219
Besant, Walter, and James Rice 16–17, 23, 25–26, 30, 32–33, 35–42, 46–52, 58–59, 63–64, 68–69, 75–76, 86, 147, 148, 204, 207, 220–21, 223, 225, 230
works
  By Celia's Arbour 42
  The Case of Mr Lucraft, and Other Tales 36n20
  The Chaplain of the Fleet 46
  The Golden Butterfly 39–41, 69
  The Monks of Thelema 42
  My Little Girl 37
  Ready-Money Mortiboy 16, 33n15, 36–39, 42–46, 75n46
  This Son of Vulcan 39, 41–42
  With Harp and Crown 39, 52
Big House and its literary tradition 96, 99–101, 103, 114–15, 120, 124–25, 127, 130, 142
Bisland, Elizabeth 177, 178–79, 185
  collaboration with Rhoda Broughton *see* Broughton, Rhoda
  essays on women's rights 182
  race around the world 177–78
Blake, William 239
Bly, Nellie (Elizabeth Jane Cochran) 177–78
Bonheur, Rosa 110
Book of Kells 152
Boston marriage 109–10, 115
Bourget, Paul 77n47
Bowen, Elizabeth 101
Breuer, Josef 9
Brontë, Charlotte
  Jane Eyre 122–23, 124
Brontë siblings 9n2, 13, 106n11
Broughton, Rhoda 2, 177, 185, 222, 264
  collaboration with Elizabeth Bisland 18, 23, 177, 179, 180
  A Widower Indeed 18, 162, 176, 179–85

INDEX

Brown, Curtis 52n29
Brown, James Moray 186n9
Browning, Robert and Elizabeth Barrett 256–57
Buchanan, Robert 88, 229n19
Bunner, Henry C. 60
Burnand, F. C. 191
Bushe, Charles Kendal 96, 101, 111
Byron, George Gordon 244–45

Caine, Hall 248
Cambridge 31, 33, 39n25
Campbell Praed, Rosa 186n9, 229, 230
Carleton, William 125
Carlyle, Thomas 56n32
Castle, Agnes and Egerton 21
Castletownshend 101, 104, 107, 115, 152
Chapman, George 235n2
Chatrian, Alexandre 40n26, 67, 203–04, 208, 213–14, 220, 228
children's collaborations 106
Coghill, Egerton 105
Coghill, Ethel 104
Coghill, Nevill 156–57
Coleridge, Samuel T. 9, 240, 243, 244
collaboration and marriage 65–67, 70–73, 211, 218–19
collaboration and theatre 202, 203, 204
Collins, Wilkie 2, 15, 27, 52n29, 57, 74, 85, 135
  Blind Love see Besant, Walter
  collaboration with Charles Dickens 15n8
  No Thoroughfare 15n8
Columbia University 59
Conan Doyle, Arthur 2, 9, 19, 52n29, 56, 56n32, 186
Conrad, Joseph 2, 15
  partnership with Ford Madox Ford 9, 15n8

copyright law 57–58, 218–19, 235, 238–39
Corelli, Marie 110
Crampton, Nancy 96–98
Crawford, Jane 110
Crommelin, May 186
Cummins, Geraldine 13

Danby, Frank 186
De Goncourt, Edmund and Jules 65–66
Delany, Sarah and A. Elizabeth 9n3
De Morgan, John 163n3
Derrida, Jacques 237
Devlin, Martina 157–58
Dickens, Charles 2, 15, 16, 30, 39, 46, 48, 56n32, 74, 86, 87n54, 88, 133–34, 246
  collaboration with Wilkie Collins see Collins, Wilkie
Divina Commedia 223
Dorris, Michael 9n3
Dowden, Hester 13
Dowling, Richard 186, 193
Drapers' Company 90n56
Drishane 101, 104, 114, 120, 121n21, 128, 133, 142, 154
Duffield, Alexander J. 161n1
Dumas, Alexandre 214

early modern collaboration 234–37, 250
Edgeworth, Maria 96–98, 100, 124–25
  Castle Rackrent 99–100
Eliot, T. S. 9, 260–61
Ellis, Havelock 9
Erckmann, Emile 40n26, 67, 203–04, 208, 213–14, 220, 228
Erdrich, Louise 9n3

The Fate of Fenella 19, 162, 186–196
  authors' names 186, 189, 191

change in the protagonist's
personality 195–96
compositional method 186, 188, 191
marketing 189–91
plot 188–89
preface to volume edition 191–92
reviews 192–95
female friendship 107–11, 259
see also romantic female friendship
Fendall, Percy 186n9
Field, Michael (Katherine Bradley
and Edith Cooper) 9n2, 9n3, 10,
13, 110, 230, 256
Fielding, Henry 238–39
Finden, William 46
Findlater, Jane and Mary 9n2, 22,
197, 265
collaboration with Allan McAulay
and Kate Douglas Wiggin 197
Fletcher, John see Beaumont, Francis
and John Fletcher
Ford, Ford Madox 56n32
collaboration with Joseph Conrad
see Conrad, Joseph
Foucault, Michel 234, 263, 264
Frankenstein's monster 191, 192n11,
206
French, Alice (Octave Thanet) 110
French Revolution 251n12
Freud, Sigmund 9, 261
Fry, Robert 261
Fuller, James Franklin 205

Gerard, E. D. (Emily and Dorothea
Gerard) 9n2, 22, 146–47, 265
Gilbert, William S. 211n5, 215
Gissing, George 82
Gosse, Edmund 77n47
Gothic, the 120–24, 137–38
Graves, Clo. 186, 193
Gray, Thomas 241
Gregory, Lady Augusta 99, 104,
119

group (multiple) collaboration 20–21,
162, 186, 196, 197–99, 216
see also The Fate of Fenella
Guernsey 188
Gurney, Jeremiah 246

Haggard, Henry Rider 2, 22, 52n29,
56–57, 161n1, 162, 264
collaboration with Andrew Lang
9, 18, 162–64, 166, 171, 175–76,
207
The World's Desire 18, 162,
164–75, 176
The Days of My Life 163, 164, 165,
166, 171, 175, 176
Hardy, Thomas 27, 52n29, 56n32, 57,
77n47, 225
Harrogate 188
Hatton, Joseph 186
Hazlitt, William 240–41
Herbert, Emily 129n25
Hichens, Robert S. 1, 2, 23, 92
"The Collaborators" 1, 23
The Green Carnation 92
Hill Hearth, Amy 9n3
Holland, Mrs (Alice Macdonald
Fleming, née Kipling) 13, 106n11
Hood, Thomas 211n5
Howard, Blanche W. 226
Howells, William D. 76n47
Hugo, Victor 204, 223, 224
Hungerford, Mrs 186, 193

Ibsen, Henrik 28, 91
A Doll's House 28, 91
Irish Literary Revival 102–04, 137n27

James, Henry 2, 27, 77n47, 196
"The Art of Fiction" 76–80
The Bostonians 91–92
"Collaboration" 208–09
Jerome, Jerome K. 47, 56n32
Jessop, George 60

INDEX

Jonson, Ben 235, 246n7
Jordan, Elizabeth 196
Joyce, James 260
Juba, Jael B. (Lydia Fakundiny and Joyce Elbrecht) 9n3

Keats, John 9
Kennard, Mrs 186
Kipling, Rudyard 2, 15, 27, 31n11, 52n29, 57, 179
   collaboration with his sister Alice 'Trixie' 106n11
   collaboration with Wolcott Balestier 15n8

Lamb, Charles and Mary 244
Lang, Andrew 76, 77n47, 140, 141, 149–50, 152, 161n1, 163, 214
   collaboration with Henry Rider Haggard *see* Haggard, Henry Rider
Lee, Vernon (Violet Page) 10, 13, 77n47, 257
Le Fanu, Sheridan 120, 123, 177
Lever, Charles 125
Lloyd, Charles 244
Locke, John 242
Lovett Cameron, Mrs 186, 192
Lucy, H. W. 186, 193

Macleod, Fiona *see* Sharp, William
Maclise, Daniel 46, 48
madwomen 122–24
Maitland, Ella Fuller (née Chester) 226
Manville, G. Fenn 186, 193
Marcus, David 112n18
Marlatt, Daphne 9n3
Marryat, Florence 19, 186, 216
Martin, Robert 98, 117, 128, 141
Marx, Eleanor 91n58
Mason, A. E. W. 161n1
Massinger, Philip 235n2

Mathers, Helen 186
Matthews, James Brander
   "The Art and Mystery of Collaboration" 17, 51, 59–68, 73–75, 146, 149, 153, 196, 221 224, 225, 229, 230, 252, 253, 254, 255
   on the figure of the author 20, 60, 233, 249, 252–55, 259–60
Maturin, Charles 120
McAulay, Allan (Charlotte Stewart) 197
McCarthy, Justin 186, 229, 230
Meredith, George 56n32
Meredith, Isabel (Helen and Olivia Rossetti) 22
Micas, Nathalie 110
Middlemass, Jean 186, 193
Middleton, Thomas 235n2
Mill, John S. 9
Milton, John 224
Moore, George 125
Mórrígan 137n27
Morris, William 13
Moseley, Humphrey 236

New Journalism 87, 248
New Orleans Woman's Club 182
New Woman 109, 171, 181–83
Nietzsche, Friedrich 261

Ogilvie, Charles 216
Oliphant, Margaret 2, 52n29
Osbourne, Lloyd *see* Stevenson, Robert Louis
Oxford 179, 180, 181

Paradise Lost 223
Paris 105, 107, 108, 116, 134, 188
People's Palace (Palace of Delight) 27, 87, 89–90
periodical press
   Aberdeen Daily Journal 228

Aberdeen Evening Express 194
Aberdeen Free Press 204, 206, 213–14, 220
Aberdeen Journal 212, 220, 223
Aberdeen Press and Journal 215
Aberdeen Weekly Journal 230
Academy 87–88, 228, 233
American Queen 46
Athenaeum 38, 88, 126, 216, 227
Author 57
Badminton Magazine 140, 144, 151
Belfast News-Letter 46, 192n11, 194
Blackburn Standard 217
Blackwood's Magazine 129n24, 140
Bookman 51, 84–85, 87, 248
Boston Globe 196
Bristol Magpie 177
Cassell's Family Magazine 70n44
Century Magazine 76
Contemporary Review 57n34, 77n47
Cosmopolitan 177, 179
Daily News 209, 210
Derby Mercury 174
Dublin University Magazine 177
Dundee Advertiser 162n2, 216–17
Dundee Courier 194
East Aberdeenshire Observer 220
Edinburgh Evening Dispatch 212, 216, 221
Edinburgh Evening News 176n4
English Illustrated Magazine 91, 208–09
English Lake Visitor 177
Era 202, 212, 213, 218–19, 228–29
Evening Journal 178n5
Freeman's Journal 194, 206, 208, 223
Fun 90n57
Gentlewoman 186, 189, 191, 192, 195–96
Glasgow Evening News 176n4, 206, 211

Glasgow Evening Post 92, 93, 226
Glasgow Herald 202–03
Globe 166, 172, 202–03, 214–15, 215, 223, 226, 229
Graphic 42, 46, 105, 107, 156, 178, 193–94, 203, 204, 205, 208, 212, 220, 224
Greenock Telegraph and Clyde Shipping Gazette 71
Harper's Bazar 179, 196
Hartlepool Northern Daily Mail 219
Hearth and Home 71–73, 206, 215
Illustrated American 179
Illustrated London News 71, 76
Irish Times 106, 205
Irish Writing: The Magazine of Contemporary Irish Literature 112n18
Kerry Evening Post 171, 174, 222
Lady's Pictorial 99n4, 126, 135
London Daily News 46, 71, 172, 221, 222
London Evening Standard 45–46, 171–72, 174, 186n8, 188, 192–93, 202
London Society 41
Longman's Magazine 60, 76
MacMillan's Magazine 197–99
M.A.P. 247
Melbourne Argus 46
Morning Advertiser 66n40
Morning Post 126, 202–03, 204–05, 207, 244
Nation 85
National Observer 66n40, 92
New Review 77n47, 78n48, 91, 166, 174
New York Herald 246
Northampton Mercury 166
Northern Whig 46, 166
Once a Week 32–33, 36, 37, 48, 51
Our Celebrities 248
Outlook 85, 86–87

INDEX

Palace Journal 90n56
Pall Mall Gazette 76, 172–74, 178, 179, 184–85, 194, 195, 202, 220
Puck 179
Punch 92, 209–10, 248, 249
Review of Reviews 248
Saturday Review of Politics, Literature, Science and Art 88, 161n1
Scots Observer 92–93
Sheffield Independent 219
Shields Daily Gazette 178
Sketch 66
Spectator 40, 55, 119, 247n7
Stage 202
Standard 37, 73, 124, 213, 226, 227, 228
St James's Gazette 172, 192, 194, 202, 204, 206, 214, 215, 220, 222, 223
Sunderland Daily Echo 92
Times 33n16, 50, 141n28
Tinsley's Magazine 52
Toronto Globe 42, 46
Weekly Sun 134, 139
World (UK) 40, 56, 117–18, 119, 248, 249
World (USA) 177, 178n5, 179
Yorkshire Evening Post 71
Yorkshire Post 225
Yorkshire Post and Leeds Intelligencer 172
Pettitt, Henry 229n19
Philips, F. C. 22, 186
Picasso, Pablo 261
Pinker, James B. 52n29, 141, 142, 143, 144, 145, 146
Plato 239
Polidori, John 121
Pollock, Frederick 226
Pollock, Guy Cameron 161n1
Pollock, Walter H. 22, 60, 88, 161n1, 163

Poole, Hewitt 121n21
Port Louis 31
Pound, Ezra 9
Prowse, William J. 211n5
Pulitzer, Joseph 177

Queen Victoria 27, 90n56, 93, 163n3

Rabelais Club 56n32
Reade, Charles 57, 74
Redgrove, Peter 9n3
Restoration 238
Réunion, island 32
Rice, James
  as editor of *Once a Week* 32–33, 51
  life 33, 51, 75–76
  partnership with Walter Besant *see* Besant, Walter, and James Rice
  solo literary work 30, 33, 69n43
Rita (Eliza Margaret Jane Humphreys) 186
Robertson, Thomas W. 211n5
Robins, Elizabeth 10
Roe, Owen 145
Romantic authorship 4–5, 134, 230, 234, 239–45
romantic female friendship 106–111, 256–57
Roosevelt, Theodore 59
Ross, Martin (Violet Martin)
  before Edith Œ. Somerville 106
  collaboration with William Wills 106
  family 98–99, 100, 117, 128, 141
  health 128, 144, 145
  partnership with Edith Œ. Somerville *see* Somerville, Edith Œnone, and Martin Ross
Ross House 100, 101, 128, 133, 154
Rossetti family 106n11
Rossetti, Helen and Olivia 22
round robin novel 19, 21, 162, 186, 197–99

see also The Fate of Fenella
Rowley, William 235n2
Royal College, Mauritius 31, 34
Royal Institution, London 76
Royal St George's Society 56n32

Savile Club 56n32, 162, 207
The School for Scandal (Richard B. Sheridan) 223
Scott, Clement W. 186, 193, 211n5
Scott, Walter 204
Sergeant, Adeline 186, 193
Shakespeare, William 225, 235n2, 236, 246n7
Sharp, William 226
Shaw, George Bernard 91n58, 102
Shelley, Mary (née Wollstonecraft Godwin) 13, 244
Shelley, Percy B. 13, 240, 241, 244, 254
Shuttle, Penelope 9n3
Sims, George R. 229
Smith, Terence 112n18
Society for Psychical Research 149
Society for the Systematic and Scientific Exploration of Palestine 34
Society of Authors 3, 27, 28, 29, 56–58, 73, 87, 89, 141
Socrates 239
Somerville, Adelaide 116, 119, 139, 157
Somerville, Edith Œnone
  before Martin Ross 104–06
  on the figure of the author 20, 233, 249, 251–55, 263
  as painter and illustrator 105–06, 152
  post-Martin spiritualism 149, 157–58
Somerville, Edith Œnone, and Martin Ross 9n2, 9n3, 10, 16, 17, 95, 97, 104–20, 126–29, 132–34, 139–57, 158–59, 207, 230

collaborative method 107, 115, 116, 132–34, 147, 149–57, 158–59, 254
dealings with agents 141–44, 145, 146
family attitudes 112–13, 115–16, 118–19, 127, 152
friendship 107–11, 113–14, 117, 150, 157
letter writing 105, 115, 154–55
money matters (finances) 100, 127, 129, 142–44
plagiarism 142, 145
professionalism 18, 134, 141–43, 145, 147, 148, 149, 157
promotion and marketing 117–18, 134, 140–42
works
  The Big House of Inver 99, 103, 115, 123n23, 148, 154
  "Buddh Family Dictionary" 111
  Dan Russell the Fox 102–03, 133, 143, 144, 146
  An Enthusiast 99
  Happy Days! Essays of Sorts 128n24
  In the Vine Country 102n7
  An Irish Cousin 18, 99, 103, 106n10, 112–26, 133, 138, 143n31, 147, 151, 154
  Irish Memories 17, 97, 98, 100, 101, 104, 105, 106, 107, 112, 113, 114, 115, 116, 117, 118, 119, 125, 126, 127, 128, 129, 130n26, 132, 133, 134, 135, 139, 140, 144, 145, 146, 148, 151, 152, 153, 155, 156, 158, 252, 254
  Irish R.M. stories 103n8, 118, 133, 143–45, 146, 148
  from *Letters* (ed. by Gifford Lewis) 99n4, 100, 101, 104, 105, 108n14, 111, 115, 116, 117, 118, 119, 121n21, 124, 126, 127, 128, 130n25, 139, 140, 141, 142,

143, 144, 145, 147, 154, 155, 156, 157
Mount Music 99, 103
Naboth's Vineyard 126
The Real Charlotte 18, 99, 102, 103, 116, 128–40, 142, 143, 156
The Silver Fox 102, 114, 140–41, 142, 143, 154
Through Connemara in a Governess Cart 128n24
travel writing 128–29
"Two of a Trade" 18, 98n3, 112, 113, 148, 149, 153, 155, 159, 251, 252, 253–54, 255
Southey, Robert 244
Spencer, Herbert 179
Stein, Gertrude 9n3
Stevenson, Robert Louis 2, 15n9, 27, 76, 175
   collaboration with Lloyd Osbourne 9, 15n8, 225, 227–28
   "A Humble Remonstrance" 76, 80–81
   on *The World's Desire* by H. R. Haggard and A. Lang 174–75
Stoker, Bram 2, 19, 120, 128, 186
Stuart-Wortley, John Archibald 63n39
Sullivan, Arthur 215
Symonds, John A. 9

Tasma (Jessie Catherine Couvreur, née Huybers) 186, 193
Taylor, Harriet 9n3
Tennyson, Alfred 27, 56, 166–67, 248
Thackeray, William M. 39, 56n32, 88, 135
Toklas, Alice B. 9n3

Trinity College Dublin 149
Trollope, Anthony 83–84, 88
Trollope, Mrs 186
Twain, Mark 2, 81n49
Tyrone House 115, 154

United Universities Club 56n32
Urse, Honor 145

vampires 121
Verne, Jules 177
Vivian, Herbert 226–27
Vyver, Bertha 110

Walker, John B. 177
Warland, Betsy 9n3
Watt, Alexander P. 52, 141
Wells, H. G. 52n29, 56n32
The Whole Family 196–97
Wiggin, Kate Douglas 197
Wilde, Oscar 13, 56n32, 99, 102
Wilkins, W. H. 226–27
Will, C. J. 186n9
Wills, William G. 98–99, 106
Wimsatt, W. K. 262, 264
women's collaborations 21–22, 95, 146–47, 197–99, 215, 251, 256–59
Wood, J. S. 191–92
Woolf, Virginia 261
Wordsworth, Dorothy 244
Wordsworth, William 9, 239–40, 241–42, 244, 248

Yates, Edmund 118, 119, 248
Yeats, Georgie 13
Yeats, W. B. 52n29, 118
Yonge, Charlotte 57
Young, Edward 243

Zola, Émile 204

Printed in the USA
CPSIA information can be obtained
at www.ICGtesting.com
CBHW060854191124
17466CB00005BA/590